THE POLITICS OF ART

Stanford Studies *in* Middle Eastern *and* Islamic Societies *and* Cultures

THE POLITICS OF ART

Dissent and Cultural Diplomacy in Lebanon, Palestine, and Jordan

Hanan Toukan

STANFORD UNIVERSITY PRESS
Stanford, California

STANFORD UNIVERSITY PRESS
Stanford, California

Printed in the United States of America on acid-free, archival-quality paper

Library of Congress Cataloging-in-Publication Data

Names: Toukan, Hanan, author.

Title: The politics of art : dissent and cultural diplomacy in Lebanon, Palestine, and Jordan / Hanan Toukan.

Other titles: Stanford studies in Middle Eastern and Islamic societies and cultures.

Description: Stanford, California : Stanford University Press, 2021. | Series: Stanford studies in Middle Eastern and Islamic societies and cultures | Includes bibliographical references and index.

Identifiers: LCCN 2020044892 (print) | LCCN 2020044893 (ebook) | ISBN 9781503604346 (cloth) | ISBN 9781503627758 (paperback) | ISBN 9781503627765 (ebook)

Subjects: LCSH: Art—Political aspects—Lebanon. | Art—Political aspects—Palestine. | Art—Political aspects—Jordan. | Art—Political aspects—Middle East. | Art, Middle Eastern—Finance—International cooperation.

Classification: LCC N72.P6 T68 2021 (print) | LCC N72.P6 (ebook) | DDC 700.956—dc23

LC record available at https://lccn.loc.gov/2020044892

LC ebook record available at https://lccn.loc.gov/2020044893

Cover design: Kevin Barrett Kane

Cover image: Still image from "Motionless Weight." Ramzi Hazboun and Dia' Azzeh, 2009.

Typeset by Kevin Barrett Kane in 10.5/14.4 Brill

For Alaa and Randa

Contents

Preface and Acknowledgments

"The Revolution, when it comes, is not going to be funded by the Ford Foundation." My late friend, former work colleague, intellectual interlocutor, and "NGO partner in crime" Bassem Chit never tired of telling me this. Bassem was critiquing the nongovernmental organizations and the international development aid sustaining them, that is, the civil society and democratization programming focused on societies in "transition" to democracy. This critique began to emerge among activists and international development scholars from the mid-1990s onwards. Bassem, a revolutionary socialist activist and writer, worked with one of the myriad internationally funded social development NGOs in Lebanon, like many activists did at the time to pay his bills. Deep in his heart, though, he believed his was just a day job. A revolutionary through and through, he knew that radical change only ever comes from bottom-up demands, not by way of internationally brokered polite negotiation with the powerful. Bassem's infectious determination, energy, courage, and optimism that the revolution would come one day are undoubtedly remembered by those who knew him. When I told Bassem I wanted to focus my research on the inextricably intertwined fields of culture and international donor aid, as well as the politics of contemporary art, I did not receive the same response I had grown used to hearing: you are not a trained art historian, and the domain of politics and art are a lethal mix. Instead, he told me to read Gramsci on aesthetic criticism and political struggle, and then half-jokingly advised me to beware of Derrida.

Parts of the project I present here began some twelve years ago in Lebanon. Much of that work eventually made its way to the pages of this book. What I didn't know when I started my research all those years ago was that the ideas and contexts I grapple with here would eventually traverse numerous geographies beyond Lebanon's. The project would come to witness momentous historical events and shifting narratives about how we understand the relationship between resistance and culture. What I had no way of knowing then was that my research would become about a period in history referred to as the pre-2011 Arab world.

When Tunisian Muhammed Bouazizi burned himself alive in late December 2010, triggering copycat acts in Egypt and elsewhere by those communities' most downtrodden, the peoples of the region entered what would become a long, ongoing, and trying period of revolt. Most of us looked on at first in exhilarating adulation at the courage of the revolutionaries. But soon after, our admiration turned to horror at the vicious political events and counterrevolutions that unraveled—and that continue still. However, as is often true, these catastrophic events set in motion a call for hard questions. This productive element—if we may call it that—forces us to requestion what we thought we understood about the role of art in witnessing, recording, and archiving violence and change in our times.

Until 2011, academic teaching and speaking about critical theory, radical progressive politics, and their relationship to art and cultural practice were largely theoretical, confined to the booming number of cafés, art and cultural spaces, and other newly founded and often transnationally connected intellectual sites concerned with the role of art, film, literature, and theater in coming to terms with violent pasts. This conversation was led by a younger generation of artists, writers, and cultural workers standing amid the rubble of twentieth-century projects of liberation from colonialism and freedom for Palestine—with little, if any, chance to have impact on the ground. And, arguably to its own detriment, this conversation was unfolding against the backdrop of mostly Western cultural funding bodies and their local civil society partners operating within the rubrics of cultural diplomacy and international development aid. This meant that what was controversially perceived as "foreign-funded" cultural production and the discourses it produces were located at the heart of contentious debates that conflated Western-supported democracy programs with neoliberalism and imperialism. These tense debates emerged in most domains of Western-supported civil society NGOs throughout most of the region from roughly 1990 onwards. The events that started in December 2010 in Tunisia threw all these frameworks into disarray, at least in the early years. What emerged was an even younger, much larger, and more radical body of artists, activists and revolutionaries. This body was not only seemingly unbound by the diktats of international NGO civil society discourse, neoliberal capital, or authoritarian-propagated nationalism but also loudly and unambiguously opposed to each of them. Today, they continue to revolt for societal change from within by addressing social taboos like LGBTQ rights, corruption, racism, sexism and domestic violence, and migrant workers rights.

Bassem was right. When the revolution finally arrived in 2011, it wasn't the select few artists, curators, writers, intellectuals, or cultural NGO workers who were positioned comfortably in a global and neoliberal structure of culture and arts funding who made it happen, even if they did participate en masse and were probably the most well versant in the theoretical language of Western critical theory and radical critique that is so ubiquitous in global contemporary art. It was the invisible multitudes of workers, unionists, students, and peasants, as well as locally positioned and informed artists, poets, and writers, who had nothing left to lose who acted as catalysts for change. Today artists of all classes and calibers continue to act as witnesses and archivists in what is shaping up to be a periodic and sporadic decades' long revolutionary process. At the same time, the development aid institutions, the global culture industry, and regional dictatorial hegemonic politics, themes I cover in the following pages about the period between the late 1990s and the wave of uprisings that swept the region in the early 2010s, endure amid a colossal neoliberal and militarization project for the region whose modus operandi is disaster capitalism. This project is the backdrop against which the global art industry's relationship to art and artists from the Global South continues to play out with gusto.

Animating and sustaining my research from beginning to end has been this conundrum: how the complex structure of art unfolds into an effective cultural resistance to global neoliberal capitalism without losing its cosmopolitan and critical spirit. As I write these words, the Lebanese, the latest to take up the calls of the 2011–2012 revolutionaries, were subdued not by the violent response of the rotten regime they seek to overthrow but by a global pandemic compounded by financial collapse and mass hunger brought on by years of government incompetence. This setback is likely only temporary. But how the coronavirus pandemic interacts with and aggravates already existing crises is making visible the fiercely brutish, racist, and merciless nature of the state the world over. The pandemic will exacerbate governmental measures that threaten democratic and civil liberties: increased use of surveillance, restrictions on the freedom of movement and association, and the brutish expansion of executive powers. These issues have all been central to Arab revolutionaries' calls since 2011, indicating that the stretch of revolution will continue for years to come. The role of cultural production in this fight will be central.

I completed this book in 2020, a year that produced challenges and unsettling times. What helped carry this book to completion amid such turmoil was a commitment to understanding how economic and political systems encompass us, even when we're sure they haven't because we believe we dissent from them in our creative expressions of resistance. What I present here is only one analysis among many of a historical moment when neoliberal culture took hold in the art milieus of some of the smaller cities of the Arab Eastern Mediterranean. I do so in the hope that what it reveals about the different ways art and politics come together will contribute to the mammoth mission we have ahead of us to find a way out of the darkness.

I wish to say a final word here on my positionality and the gratitude I owe so many people who journeyed with me over the years in the making of this book. Before beginning my research, I spent a significant number of years living intermittently in Lebanon. Due to passport privileges that I must own at the onset, I was able to travel with relative ease from Lebanon to Jordan and Palestine, where I worked with NGOs in Amman and Ramallah. I spread my life across those cities I felt embodied not only my personal identity but also my family's history. This history encompasses the cosmopolitan lives of a late grandmother who grew up between Jerusalem and Damascus and went on to live in a long list of countries all over the world, and another between Amman, Salt, Birzeit, and Jerusalem. They also include grandfathers and great aunts and uncles who attended the American University of Beirut and carried, sometimes with anger in their hearts, the educational, cultural and political messages passed down to them by missionaries and intellectuals they encountered studying there at the turn of last century. This region of the Eastern Mediterranean known also in English by its colonial nomenclature as the Levant was central to the lives, loves, and passions of a multitude of Arabs witnessing the momentous changes that came with the dismantling of the Ottoman Empire and the European-imposed divisions that came soon after. The intertwinement of the geographical, political, and the personal in this region persists today.

Hence, what I present here about art, conceptions of resistance in cultural production, and the forces by which these intertwined dynamics are shaped is a political and cultural analysis that is also deeply personal. Not only have I been studying a part of the world that, like millions of others, I long to see free of imperial violence and foul domestic authoritarianism; I have also examined the politics that shape the productions of many artist and writer friends, as well as of acquaintances of different generations whom I deeply respect. And yet, I had to do this "objectively" and with as much critical distance as I could muster. Many of the words of this book were also written against the backdrop of numerous lives lost and countless bodies tortured and distorted on the path to freedom. It is with those lives in mind and the unspeakable tenacity they had to refuse subjugation at any cost that I often found myself thinking about how an effective resistance in the cultural realm might look like in our world today. Many who are familiar with the art scenes I describe will recognize some of the characters and organizations I engage with, even though most names are left unstated so that readers may focus instead on the text and what it reveals. I hope only that I have accomplished some of what I set out to do without doing injustice to any of the remarkable people, projects, works, and ideas I was compelled to leave out because of editorial regulations.

A number of brilliant minds and large hearts have supported, inspired, directed, and guided me at different points in my journey. I am forever grateful to these people and humbly acknowledge that I can never repay what they have so generously and graciously shared. I was lucky enough to have various chapters of this book read thoughtfully and commented on enthusiastically by these distinguished, inspiring first-class women scholars: Zeina Maasri, Nicola Pratt, Kirsten Scheid, Sherene Seikaly, Samah Selim, and Linda Tabar.

Of course, any and all errors or shortcomings in this book are mine alone. I would also like to thank Laleh Khalili, Suhail Malik, Corrina Mullen, Nandini Nayak, Rahul Rao, Julian Stallabrass, and Charles Tripp for closely engaging my writing in its early days and for following up with me intermittently in the years that followed. For inviting me to present my research, and for reading, commenting on, and challenging different iterations of the research I present here over the course of years and, sometimes even at the very end in the most unexpected of ways, I owe special thanks to the brilliant minds and support of Ariella Azoulay, Chiara de Cesari, Kay Dickenson, Beshara Doumani, Amal Eqeiq, Kareem Estefan, Ilana Feldman, Zeina Halabi, Dina Matar, Dina Ramadan, Ghalya Saadawi, Mayssoun Sukarieh, Foad Torshizi, Mandy Turner, Jessica Winegar, and Vazira Zamindar.

In Amman, Beirut, Berlin, London, Providence, and Ramallah, I am grateful for the support, inspiring conversation, and encouragement I received in diverse ways from various friends and intellectual interlocuters who shared relevant information and contacts and opened their files and archives for my viewing. By generously sharing their thoughts, lives, and work experiences, they indirectly shaped the content of this book and instilled the passion needed in me to complete it. I hope only that I have captured the essence of our remarkable conversations and, of course, accept full responsibility for any wrongful interpretations of their ideas. This list includes Maher Abi Samra, Ziad Abillama, Nidal Al-Achkar, Muhanna Al-Durra, Noura Al-Khasawneh, Mohammad Ali Attassi, Hani Alqam, Nabil Anani, Yazid Anani, Zeina Arrida, Marwa Arsanios, Rafat Asad, Raed Asfour, Roger Assaf, Mohammad-Ali Atassi, Sonja Meijer-Atassi, Michael Baers, Mirna Bamieh, Saleh Barakat, Abbas Beydoun, the late Kamal Boulatta, Tony Chakar, the late Bassem Chit, Faisal Darraj, Tania el Khoury, Samer Frangie, Hanane Haj-Ali, Raouf Haj-Yahya, Inas Halabi, Shuruq Harb, Samah Hijjawi, Areej Hijazi, Khaled Hourani, Samah Idriss, Saba Innab, Mohammad Jabali, Lamia Joreige, Bassem Kassem, Ola Khalidi, Yazan Khalili, Diala Khasawneh, Noura Khasawneh, Nidal Kheiry, Elias Khoury, Khalid Khreiss, Rola Kobeissy, Ghassan Maasri, Lina Majdalane, Ghassan Makarem, Suleiman Mansour, Samar Martha, Rabih Mroue, Nat Muller, May Muzzafar, Walid Raad, Hoda Rouhana, Walid Sadek, Khaled Saghiyeh, Rasha Salti, Tina Sherwell, Adania Shibli, Amer Shomai, Suha Shoman, Lockman Slim, Salim Tamari, Vera Tamari, Christine Tohme, Fawwaz Traboulsi, Hanan

Wakeem, Kaelen Wilson-Goldie, Paola Yaqub, Mustapha Yammout, Inas Yassin, Ala Younis, Tirdad Zolghadr, Himmat Zu'bi, and Sima Zureikat.

I also want to thank the blind reviewers of this book whose comments were clearly undertaken with an ethos of true camaraderie and generosity, which reminded me of the powerful potential that resides in constructive peer work. I especially want to thank Kate Wahl, Caroline McKusick, Susan Karani, and the whole editorial team at Stanford University Press. I feel honored to have had my project chosen by Kate for publication and for experiencing her immense patience, support, and astuteness in adapting to the project's metamorphosis along the years. Ryan Rosenberg's and Lisa Wehrle's genius copy-editing skills made the writing process all the more exciting. Thank you also to Ramzi Hazboun and Dia Al Azzeh for giving me permission to use an image of their work as a front cover for my book.

The fieldwork and the writing of this book were made possible by generous fellowships offered to me by several institutions along the way. I feel particularly indebted to the first postdoctoral fellowship in 2012–2013 granted to me by the Europe in the Middle East and Middle East in Europe (EUME) program at the Forum for Transregional Studies in Berlin led by Georges Khalil whose commitment to supporting a new generation of scholars working on the Middle East region has created an intellectual hub in Berlin for some of the most exciting research being produced today. The generous time off from teaching granted to me by the Alexander Von Humboldt Fellowship Award for Experienced Researchers, whom both Georges Khalil and Friedericke Pannewich supported me to obtain, along with the reduced teaching load that I enjoyed as a Visiting Assistant Professor of Middle East Studies at Brown University between 2016 and 2018, allowed me to finally complete my manuscript after putting it on pause for some time due to childcare commitments. Thanks are also due to Zentrum Moderner Orient, and in particular Ulrike Freitag; the Berlin Graduate School for Muslim Culture and Societies and the Center for Middle Eastern and African Politics at the Freie Universitate Berlin, where Bettina Gräf and Cilja Harders warmly received me and engaged my work; the American Center for Oriental Research in Amman; and the Kenyon Institute in Jerusalem for the financial support and research homes they provided me with over the years. My new faculty colleagues at Bard College Berlin and the students there, as well as those at Brown University and SOAS before that, have consistently inspired me to keep on going during the toughest days and despairing moments that naturally come with writing, especially during politically turbulent and violent times.

To my wondrous sisters, Alia and Oraib, I can't imagine traveling through life without you both. Your love and humor make the bumpier bits just a little bit softer and always a lot more entertaining.

And thank you too, Abed Azzam. The fatigue and exhilaration that came with completing this piece of work is as much yours as it is mine. For this, and for being a soundboard for political theory, a source of the silliest jokes, a well of love, and so much more, I am eternally grateful. For my Balkiso our "Bis," who first catapulted me head-on into the chaotic but magnificent terrain of motherhood, I am proudly in awe of you and honored to have been taught by you. Rayyan, you're the firecracker of my world and the heart in my heart. Thanks for keeping it real, you three.

Finally, Alaa and Randa, thank you both for being you, the "unit" that keeps my engines running. This book is dedicated to you, Alaa, for your indescribable courage and ceaseless inspiration. Despite the loss of your words and in spite of your silence, you still manage to teach me every day how to marvel at life and how to never stop asking questions in the process. It is also dedicated to you, Randa, for showing us all how to keep on walking, with love.

Note on Transliteration

Throughout this book I use a simplified version of the *International Journal of Middle East Studies* (IJMES) transliteration from Modern Standard Arabic guidelines. I use the diacritic ' for the glottal stop *hamza* and ' for the consonant *ayn*. I omit dots under certain letters, which in academic literature represent emphatic Arabic consonants. To facilitate readability, I use the most common English spelling names for personal or place names (example Shia, Hamra, al-Weibdeh). If several English spellings are common, I use the one that is closest to the *IJMES* guidelines. For example, the Arabic letter *qaf* is transliterated with q rather than c or k.

INTRODUCTION

IN 2013, THE RAND CORPORATION PRODUCED A REPORT ON THE dissenting arts and artists of the Arab region (Schwartz, Dassa Kaye, and Martini 2013). Written by a group of RAND's senior political scientists and security specialists, the report, titled *Artists and the Arab Uprisings*, was one among many others published in Europe and the US since 2001 that reflected on arts funding and its role in cultural diplomacy and the process of democratization in the Arab region. The RAND report called for further global investment to boost art's potential to facilitate democratization, especially in light of the proactive role artists played during the early, heady days of the Arab Spring revolutions of 2011–2012. Contending that arts funding was a tested method for winning the "hearts and minds" of enemies and critics of US policies in the region, the research, which was sponsored by the Smith Richardson Foundation and conducted within the International Security and Defense Policy Center of the RAND National Security Research Division (NSRD), was part and parcel of a body of work being produced by Rand at the time that explored cultural output in the Arab world that "promoted tolerance."[1]

The RAND report revealed that only a few years after the region's revolutionary process began in December 2010, the use of art in the promotion of democracy by Western governments and policy think tanks through the support of local civil society nongovernmental organizations (NGOs) had become mainstreamed. Yet RAND's interest in artists and artistic production reflected and reconfirmed the broader direction of many think tanks and NGOs that had been in line with the EU through the Euro-Mediterranean framework (EUROMED) and the US through the George Bush Jr. Middle East Partnership Initiative (MEPI), investing time and money to rethink the role of the arts as an engine for gradual regional reform, especially since 9/11.[2]

"Everyone," wrote one of the region's well-known art critics less than a year after the start of the Arab Spring uprisings, "seems to be jumping on the revolutionary bandwagon. From biennials . . . to art fairs . . . , the lip service paid to the spirit of change in the region has often been opportunistic and crass" (Wilson-Goldie 2011). Development policy planners and other champions of democracy aid had also jumped on the "funding revolution" bandwagon. They hoped to move beyond the rhetoric of countering violent extremism through development, reform, and democratization, as they had in the first decade of the millennium; and extend their support directly to those they deemed dissident artists who were equipped to fight the violent counterrevolutionary movements that had emerged from the revolutionary struggles of 2011–2012. Such logic gave credence to the idea circulating among policy communities in the US and Europe that the Arab revolutions happened in part because of democracy aid to civil society, especially projects targeting youth and technology that since the 1990s had poured into the region, in particular in Egypt.[3]

Hence, since the early rumblings of revolution in late 2010, the culture and arts domain in the Arab region has enjoyed renewed interest from US and EU governmental and nongovernmental funding bodies. Suddenly, as the *Independent* reported, "[It was] cool to be an Egyptian, totally awesome to be a Tunisian, Syrian, Libyan, Bahraini or Yemeni dissident and to be an artist from these places is, well, very heaven" (Alibhai-Brown 2011). In the first couple of years after the onset of the revolutions, institutional support for artistic production overtly related to the revolution came packaged as grants and renewed commitments on behalf of foreign policy arms of Western governments to fund social change through art. Yet this process had begun earlier as part of the battle for the "hearts and minds" of Arabs and Muslims, which became accentuated after the events of September 11, 2001, when international cultural funding organizations such as the Ford and Soros Foundations, the Dutch Prince Claus Fund for Culture and Development, as well as more traditional bilateral funding bodies such as Germany's Goethe Institute and Heinrich Boll Foundation, the British Council, Spain's Cervantes Institute, the French Cultural Centre, and even USAID became increasingly involved in funding projects designed to encourage Arabs of the post-1990 new world order to question the sociopolitical and cultural fabric of their societies. Regional umbrella grantee organizations formed in collaboration with international development organizations to invest in core organizational strengthening at the domestic level. These included, among others, the Arab Fund for Arts and Culture (AFAC), the Arab Theatre Fund, and Al-Mawred Al-Thaqafy. Smaller local organizations received funds directly from the larger regional umbrella organizations or the international donors themselves in that period included, among others, the International Academy of Art Palestine, the Khalil Sakakini Culture Center and the now defunct Art School Palestine in Ramallah and the Al Mahatta Gallery, Makan House and Al-Balad Theatre in Amman, Ashkal Alwan, Zico House, the Arab Image Foundation, Shams: The Cultural Cooperative Association for Youth in Theatre and Cinema, and Beirut D.C. in Beirut, and the Townhouse Gallery, Alexandria Contemporary Arts Forum, and others in Egypt.

Today, the collaboration of European, and to a lesser extent North American, arts institutions with counterparts in the Arab region is one of the central tenets of policies geared toward persuading potential migrants to remain in their home countries and rehabilitating and integrating those who have reached Europe. Hence efforts to promote stability, cooperation, and security across the region include funding exhibitions about refugees and displacement, artist travel grants, residency programs, museum exhibitions, capacity building workshops, and staff trainings at cultural organizations. This support represents a key feature of the transformations that have occurred in the arts terrain of various Arab capitals. These "independent" or "alternative" art spaces, as actors in this field call them, have seen exponential growth and include artist-run and -led projects, biennials, festivals, exhibitions, and other events understood to be self-organized structures operating adjacent to the official apparatuses of the state.[4] In recent years, local governments have increased their investment in building or upgrading new globally oriented, large-scale national museums, such as the Mahmoud Darwish and Yasser Arafat Museums in Ramallah, the Jordan Gallery of Fine Arts and the Jordan

Museum in Amman, the Sursock Museum and the National Museum of Beirut in Lebanon, and, of course, the renowned Gulf Museums sector such as Mathaf: Arab Museum of Modern Art and the Museum of Islamic Arts Doha, the Louvre in Abu Dhabi, and the planned Guggenheim Abu Dhabi. At the same time, the growth in the domain of contemporary art operating outside the framework of the state has inspired artworks and discourses that ask timely and urgent questions about the societies from which they emerge. In Beirut, Ramallah, Amman, Haifa, Cairo, and Alexandria, along with many other cities not covered in this book, this art scene is also a place where artists, intellectuals, and activists come together to organize, mobilize, produce, collaborate, exchange, exhibit, and disrupt outside of the mainstream institutions. In the last two decades, contemporary art has become an open space where varied artistic and social fields meet and intervene. For this reason, it is imperative that we study not only the aesthetics of this material production that composes our hyper-liberal economy but also what it signifies and encodes. Interestingly, these new sites of cultural production are part of a global movement redefining the nexus between culture and global markets.

The world's post-9/11 preoccupation with everything Middle Eastern, which was reinforced with the eruption of the Arab uprisings of 2011–2012, rendered the region a must-see in the busy travel itineraries of international curators scouring the globe for new ideas and talents. As a result, artists from the region have gained increasing access to Western art capitals, Western art critique, and audiences through their increasingly regular presence on the international biennial circuit. To a lesser extent, the presence of their artworks in museum collections has significantly contributed to the increased visibility of artists from the Global South. Artists and critics use these sites to compellingly argue through literature and curatorial statements that they are decolonizing the Western art world by contributing to the multiple modernities and global art histories that constitute it. Much of this has occurred under the guise of large, all-encompassing regional platforms where, as it has been argued before and as this book likewise suggests, identity politics and cultural representation have generally been the prevailing framework through which Western critics approach contemporary arts production from the region (Ramadan 2004). Despite the resilience of such paradigms, these larger developments have enabled the emergence of critical nodes in the articulation of an alternative set of conditions and possibilities for the production, consumption, and understanding of art in and from the region.

Coupled with a recent turn in the art world toward transforming art and curatorial practices into an educational or knowledge-based product and site of learning about alternative pedagogical methods, much of this reflection has occurred in a growing number of Arabic and English-language publications dedicated to the contemporary arts and culture of the region. Such art magazines, books, and alternative arts education programs in more recent years have encouraged a noticeably growing audience interested in critical discourses on art practices in the region.

These changes in the artistic and cultural production scenes have provoked intense debates within European and US policy circles on how to maintain cultural relations and abate extremism, particularly in times of increased securitization, rising right-wing nationalist movements, and global challenges of migration. Concurrently, a growing body of much-needed academic literature is being published, partly in reaction to the visible role that art played in the Arab Spring. This long overdue work, located in visual cultural studies, media studies, and Middle Eastern Studies, addresses the role of the visual in political processes and social transformation (e.g., Maasri 2009; Khatib 2012; Mehrez 2012; Abaza 2013; Tripp 2013; Downey 2014). Although this literature is more interested in the role of cultural production in countering the hegemonic state, it has begun the difficult task of theorizing the role of the aesthetics of resistance beyond the mere acknowledgment that visual cultural production is a site of dissent simply because it enables the galvanization of anti-establishment sentiment.

In this book about the cultural politics and political economy of contemporary art in the Arab Eastern Mediterranean, I explore another dimension of dissenting visual artistic practices. I primarily draw on one aspect of artistic and cultural interpretation: the political meaning and social function of transnationally connected and internationally funded nonprofit and nongovernmental art organizations (NPOs and NGOs), arts initiatives, and their associated art practices in and about Lebanon, Palestine, and Jordan. I focus primarily on the ways in which these dynamics were expressed and manifested in cultural discourse about contemporary art's role in counterhegemony and artists' articulations of dissent from the late 1990s through the initial outbreak of the Arab Uprisings of 2011–2012. This period laid the groundwork for the contemporary art scene and its relationship to the global neoliberal economy of culture and capital that prevails in the region today and is part of a longer dynamic of instrumentalizing art for political purposes in the region's historical relationship with Western hegemony.[5] Accordingly, in this book I analyze this dynamic interaction between art production and cultural diplomacy in relation to conceptions and practices of counterhegemony in the arts by the actors this interface between art and politics targets and the sites it interrupts: art practices and cultural discourse propelled by NPOs and NGOs that were primarily funded by what I conceive as neoliberal global culture funders. I use the latter term and conceptualization throughout the text because I believe it captures the global vision and the global aesthetics propagated by a specifically neoliberal form of capitalism as the supporting ideology of globalization, which so many cultural funders and practitioners adhere to in practice, even if never categorically expressed.

In this book, I do *not* include the financial market of art sales by collectors, buyers, and dealers or investments made by governments in the Gulf region to build up a momentous infrastructure, sites where art and neoliberal capitalism coalesce much more visibly. I do this to uncover how dissent is shaped and represented in those sites of production that seem most counterhegemonic precisely because they do not have their own art markets. Some of the most significant art transactions today are located outside the framework of commonly understood art markets. In the contexts of my research, it is cultural capital accumulation and circulation as it unfolded in the nonprofit sector, rather than financial profit per se, that drove the exchange and travel of objects, ideas, and people. By my use of "counterhegemonic," I draw explicitly on Antonio Gramsci's (1971) understanding of it as the site where organic intellectuals formulate ideas and construct, along with publics, critical counter-discourses to challenge hegemonic assumptions and beliefs about what cultural production can and should do in society. In this treatment I consciously move out of the hegemony/counterhegemony binary that dominates much of the literature on the region's art and resistance. Making claims to counterhegemony without simultaneously considering the particularities of the processes by which works come into being, circulate, and then get framed and discussed, even when they seem most resistant to power, obscures the different forms that dissent in cultural production take, the various reasons it takes those forms, and what role context plays in these transformations.

In the same vein, though writing on literary production, Terry Eagleton (1990) defines Marxist cultural criticism as more than a sociology of literature concerned with how novels get published and how they end up assimilating the working class (Eagleton 1990: 3).[6] Eagleton explains Marxist criticism's aim to explain cultural production more comprehensively. Thus, in addition to focusing on the political economy of works' formal styles and meanings, Marxist criticism grasps them as the product of their own historical circumstance that is equally central to their contextualization. Such criticism entails an analysis of how social and political forces influence society's aesthetical conceptualizations and how their meanings may transform with time. In the aftermath of 9/11, the inflection of the changing social and political dynamics in the works and processes I study in this book was exemplified in the way art and culture NGOs, and thereby the artists who received their support, were limited to a particular set of art practices and associated discourses linked to a specific neoliberal understanding of "counterhegemony." I read this understanding as being part of the larger social and moral philosophy of neoliberalism with its emphasis on entrepreneurship and individualism (D. Harvey 2005: 2). This translates into a professionalization of the art scenes whereby the centrality of art as a "product" being written about and exhibited in global platforms began to supersede the notion and practice of art embedded in an ongoing "process" that engages with a more localized, concrete, and rooted critical discourse, even if it is part of larger global capital flows.

The bigger question that concerns me is not about cultural hegemony under the guise of cultural diplomacy, even if it does relate to it. Nor is my question about how globalization, in its cultural sense, refers to Western hegemonic domination in the form of "cultural imperialism," "Americanization," or "McDonaldization"—a topic on which much ink has spilled (e.g., Featherstone 1995; Ritzer 1996; Schiller 1976). Instead, I flesh out how and by what processes the phenomenon of using art for the sake of social and political change contributes to shaping cultural actors' understanding of contemporary art's relationship to the political: in particular, its role and function in enacting and expressing counterhegemony to different forms of hegemony. I take a cue from the philosopher and critic Gabriel Rockhill, who writes that "there is no set recipe for the correct relationship between the social categories of art and politics; there is no panacea or ultimate equation" (Rockhill 2014: 182). Central to my conceptualization in this book is Rockhill's identification of a series of nodal points for possible encounters between art and politics; such points include cultural hegemony, collective identity, counterhistories, social experimentation, and political propositions, complicity, or critical intervention. I deal with my subject inspired by his viewpoint that "politicity" of artworks and their underlying possibilities "manifests itself in their inscription in the social field, and it cannot therefore be determined once and for all by ontological deduction" (182).

Of necessity, I limit myself to the dimension of the relationship between politics and art that aids me in reading how postmodernism's ironic tendency to universalize itself by multiplying the notion of "difference all over the world" (Eagleton 1996: 119) unfolded in the transnationally connected and internationally funded art scenes of the Arab Eastern Mediterranean cities I study. This propensity toward multiplying difference in the global art world of networked biennials and festivals has manifested in the transmutation of cultural difference into a "globally recognizable product, self-consciously preserving identifiable characteristics of cultural difference, for both global and local audiences" (Charlesworth 2013). Moreover, this phenomenon had the illusory effect of endorsing the modern colonial subject as a constitutive part of the democratic and inclusionary project of dismantling universalism that was initially pioneered by the liberal European zeitgeist. Yet does this intrusion into art, when it does occur through cultural hegemony, manifest without any critical interventions, counterpropositions, or unanticipated social experimentations from the communities it targets? If not, then with what aesthetical forms and processes and through what discursive language do the dialectics between hegemony and counterhegemony manifest as dissonant forms of dissent?

Cultural diplomacy is analyzed in this book not to reveal what it hides in its cultural hegemony but to better understand how people rationalize and work within its confines. This focus on rationalization allows me to purse my second aim, which is to demonstrate how and why the resistant dimension of contemporary art in the period I study became defined almost solely by its ability to represent what hegemonic politics appears to conceal. The following chapters reveal how tropes in artistic representations, which enjoyed global platforms and transnational circulation, hardly ever went a step further to consider how the local art world configures in global humanitarian discourses on development and democratization that indirectly perpetuate the very same concealment they critiqued.

As I discuss in the opening chapter, the narrative of *Ḥiwar* has accompanied me throughout the course of researching and writing this book. One of the region's most controversial avant-garde magazines from the 1960s, *Ḥiwar* was edited by the esteemed late poet Tawfik Sayigh and allegedly supported secretly by the CIA-funded US Congress for Cultural Freedom (CCF). "Do you know about the tragic story of Tawfik Sayigh and his journal?" "Your research reminds me of this related incident that occurred with one magazine in the 1960s . . ." "Western meddling in our cultural affairs never ceases—remember the story of *Hiwar*?" These are a sample of questions and remarks I received from my interlocutors upon introducing myself and my research topic. Sayigh's unknowing embrace of the CCF's mission inspired me to explore how ideas and interests around the political role of cultural production converge in the process of transnational movement and network formation sponsored by international cultural funding. The harsh criticism of Sayigh's journal by many actors in the arts and letters community drove me to examine the ways funding and transnational critique, and the discourses and representations they engender on a global level, still shape local experiences and sensibilities of making, seeing, and experiencing the counterhegemonic element of contemporary art in Beirut, Ramallah, and Amman.

TERMINOLOGIES AND FRAMEWORKS

It is useful to clarify some of the terminology and theoretical frameworks that appear throughout this book. In thinking about *Ḥiwar*'s tale of disappointment, hearsay, and intrigue, the question that nagged at me was what its story tells us about the exchange between global institutions of artistic and cultural support and processes of contemporary arts production in the Arab Eastern Mediterranean from the late 1990s to the present. I was especially interested in why interdisciplinary and media-based contemporary artwork was often regarded more contentiously than painting and sculpture. After all, for a long time modern art was considered one of colonialism's "cultural imports," though much writing has explained it as a liberationist, and therefore counterhegemonic, force (W. Ali 2001; Noorani 2007). To explain how artists navigated their way through a thorny politics of development funding by way of the civil society and democratization framework from the 1990s onwards, I am theoretically consumed with contemporary art's relationship to the political and the politics in which it is embedded. I locate the theories on which I base my analysis in the expansive literature devoted to the conceptualization of the meaning of the political as a constitutive element of politics that is being emptied of its critical role. In this sense, politics is now understood as "a dirty word, a term that has come to acquire a whole array of almost entirely negative associations" (Hay 2013: 153). Accordingly, I base my understanding of contemporary art's engagement with the political on Foucault's (1978) conceptualization of the workings of power; in *History of Sexuality, Foucault* frames the political as a form of critical discourse that is in a dependent relationship to the institutional apparatuses that constitute the domain of politics. This Foucaultian definition frames politics as a set of established institutions, where associated hegemonic discourses are exercised through a relation of forces that shape the discourses of society in any one era (Foucault 1978: 10–11). As such, art is itself a site of power and politics.

For both Hannah Arendt and Chantal Mouffe, "politics as evil" has dominated conceptualizations of the political. For Arendt (1998: 7–17), the political is represented as a site of "action," concerned with what people are doing, their praxis. For Mouffe (2005: 8–16), the political is a space of "antagonism," which constitutes human societies. It is how transnationally connected and internationally funded contemporary art features in these sites of antagonism and action that I query. In conceiving the relationship between aesthetics and politics, I do not aim to partake in the conceptual debate about whether the two are inherently separate or constitutive of each other to understand how art relates to the political. Instead, I subscribe to a frame of thinking that reads this relationship as always bound by the specific historical circumstances and concrete geographical locales in which it is embedded.

My reading of contemporary art's engagement with the political—specifically the ways its locally informed dimensions interact with its more global dimensions that often require travel, translation, framing, and representation—is based partly on Mouffe's articulation of the relationship between the "political" and "politics." By "politics," Mouffe refers to the ensemble of practices, discourses, and institutions that seek to establish a certain order and organize human coexistence in conditions that are always potentially conflictual and "constitutive of human societies" (Mouffe 2007b). The "political" for Mouffe is the dimension of antagonism that is inherent in human relations and that works to resist or reinforce hegemonic "politics" (Mouffe 2000: 15; Mouffe 2005: 9). She articulates it as a set of antagonisms that is essentially always in a bid for social power. Power is located not just in the state or in a political party, but in all hegemonic structures, including institutions that pride themselves on being anti-hegemonic such as the "independent" art scene at the heart of this book. Envisioning the "political" within Mouffe's framework means we see power, conflict, and antagonism as innate to the cultural politics of artistic production and its meaning.

Having said all that, I admit to being weary of falling back on a theory that sits too comfortably with an understanding of "the political" developed within a framework critiquing European liberalism in the early part of the twentieth century. Such a theory is perhaps best captured in Carl Schmitt's famous book *The Concept of the Political*, in which the friend/enemy distinction is thought to be central to the meaning of the political. Schmitt's notion of the political and his critique of liberalism do not deliberate over alternative conceptualizations of the political in postcolonial contexts that experienced and continue to endure colonial effects as the darker side of modernity. The friend/enemy binary in opposition to a state does not suffice to explicate the site of the political in contexts where legal boundaries overlap and the sovereign state is weak or nonexistent, because it does not initiate a mode of thinking from the "experiences of the colonial wound" (Mignolo 2011: 48). In its Western conception, the political locates civil society, the state, and interest groups (such as religious, tribal, and confessional identifications and affiliations) in the Middle East as essential building blocks of its society and, by extension, its cultural politics. Yet this emphasis explains away the problem of capitalism instead of tackling it head on (Hanieh 2013a). In this book, I am inspired by the approach of reading politics through the continued centrality of imperialism and the internationalization of class and capital. I see this approach as the means by which the relationship between the site of the political and art becomes most animated. It is therefore not the friend/enemy binary but the structural inequalities of the political economy of postcolonial societies that dictate how identities, class affiliations, and beliefs are constructed in the field of internationally supported and transnationally connected contemporary artistic production. These structural formations build an interdependent relationship with politics.

When I began the research for this book, I was partly inspired by an emerging body of scholarship that examines the relationship between US postwar ascendancy and cultural diplomacy during the early years of the Cold War and the unfolding decolonization in the Middle East. I was captivated by the idea of seemingly neutral global cultural funding organizations, such as the Ford and Rockefeller Foundations, intervening in the wider political field with a focus on culture. In supporting the arts, these organizations hoped to shape ideological beliefs and commitments.

In the very early 2000s, and particularly after 9/11, I was seeing and experiencing how vital this phenomenon had become to the West's relationship to the Arab world and in the Arab world's domain of cultural production in the larger field of the arts, including radio, television, theater, performance, the visual arts, music, and to a lesser extent literature. After the attacks of September 11, 2001, the US government launched a series of cultural diplomacy programs with the intention of winning "the hearts and minds" of especially Arab youth in the Middle East. The US invested in "efforts to improve cultural understanding," to increase foreigners' "voluntary allegiance to the American project" (Finn 2003, 20). In the same period, the EU's Barcelona Process was reinvigorated to deflect conflict by valorizing cultural commonalities and continued cultural cooperation in the domain of arts and heritage in the Mediterranean basin. At the same time, however, the EU Barcelona Process pursued firm policies on security, migration, and enlargement, which drew "a clear frontier in the middle of the Mediterranean" (Schäfer 2007, 333).

Cultural funding after 1990, and particularly after 9/11, was typically couched in the neutral terms and frameworks of international development and slow democratization processes operating within the larger rubric of cultural diplomacy and international relations rather than outright propagandistic cultural motives. Yet, regardless of the changes taking place in the field of international cultural funding and exchange, the logic of exchanging or influencing the everyday practices and value systems of a population through the support of cultural production remained at the heart of diplomacy between and across nations. In academia, a recent growth in literature dedicated to the practice and study of cultural diplomacy in the aftermath of the Cold War has stressed the positive dimensions of cultural and artistic exchanges in international relations, deeming them a softer, more liberal and progressive dimension of power with the potential to alleviate the harder blows of the global war on terror.[7] Assuming art can serve as a neutral platform of exchange, or undermine political dichotomies, or function as an indubitably resistant force in nondemocratic settings is not untypical considering the increasing calls for conferences, journal papers, workshops, and master's programs that approach artistic practice in cultural diplomacy from the angle of what it can do rather than what it actually does.

In its normative assumptions about the potential positive impact of cultural diplomacy, this body of academic work leaves out a reflection on the ways in which power relations may influence how we understand the role of culture as a means of anti-capitalist critique and how we understand its increasingly specialized form of meaning, that is, art as an identity marker (Eagleton 2000). Many critical literary and historical studies focus on how, during the height of its Cold War, the US government funded cultural diplomacy efforts through the CCF, supporting symphonies, performances, musical competitions, literary prizes, exhibitions, and festivals, in addition to scholars and writers.[8] Yet few of those studies have looked at how the US government's support for cultural production reshaped and refashioned the global landscape of literary and visual artistic production, altered the relationships between writers and their publics, and rendered those it supported more recognizable figures than others.[9]

The writing that has emerged concurrent with the growth in the contemporary art world of the region has tended to revolve around evaluating the individual practices of artists already enjoying major exposure in the West.[10] This literature has come in the form of beautiful coffee table books, exhibition catalogs, or glossy art journals and magazines, regional in scope, identitarian in focus, and celebratory in tone. Academic contributions, like Chad Elias's (2018) *Posthumous Images: Contemporary Art and Memory Politics in Post–Civil War Lebanon*, that rely mostly on artists' own narratives and generated material, and to a much lesser extent Bashir Makhoul and Gordon Hon's (2013) *The*

Origins of Palestinian Art, have distanced themselves from the preoccupation with identitarian and geographical readings in an attempt to bring individual practices to the forefront in their own aesthetical right. This tendency, most obvious in Elias's work, has come at the expense of locating art without historicizing Arab modernity or other issues pertaining to broader cultural production, such as art's relationship to vernacular culture or institutional politics. [11] Often articulated in terms of "hybrid" and "liminal" experiences resulting from war, diaspora, exile, and postcoloniality more generally, such art criticism largely relies on what artists say about their own work (e.g., Downey 2014 and 2016a); it has tended to interpret the art sphere in terms of the perpetually complex world of artists living or commenting on crisis zones. This form of analysis excludes commentary on what relations of domination imbued within art practices with transnational links and institutional support may be encoding and enacting.

Several key texts authored in the past few years by art historians and anthropologists of the Arab world have offered important new insights into what is still a relatively small but quickly growing and formidable scholarly field of study (Scheid 2005; Winegar 2006; Shabout 2007; Rogers 2008; Rahman 2015; Lenssen, Rogers, and Shabout 2018; Saadawi 2019; Lenssen 2020; Maasri 2020). These studies on modern Arab art mark a shift from conventional art histories, which framed artistic practice as always tied to nation and identity in the postcolonial state. Instead, they locate artworks, art writing, and artists in an intricate cultural history of multilayered contexts, intellectual debates, and events that defined the region's cultural production since the nineteenth century.

This book, besides being inspired by such works, departs from them through its particular focus on the question of the international political economy and cultural politics of the development of the contemporary art sphere in the region after 1990. Of direct relevance, methodologically as well as substantively, is Jessica Winegar's landmark 2006 study on the politics of art and culture in contemporary Egypt. As far as I know, *Creative Reckonings: The Politics of Art and Culture in Contemporary Egypt* was the first book to bring the study of art from the Arab world to social science classes within Middle East Studies in Western academic institutions. Winegar offers a fascinating ethnographic exploration of art in Egypt as resolutely positioned outside of traditional Eurocentric narratives of art history. She attempts a reading of cultural production in Egypt that favors a "non-teleological, non-universalist, non-totalizing way of understanding the relationship between the totalizing forces in the world and the fragmentary detailed and particular struggles against them" (Winegar 2006: 17). In doing so, Winegar shifts the focus to the potential avenues for agency that operate and are informed by how artistic production players in a changing Egypt reckon with global transformations that directly impact what they do and how they do it.

This book similarly reads crises of identity often understood to lie at the heart of the impasse between binaries of local/global, modern/traditional, and progressive/regressive as not emphatically predicated on historical developments but as institutionally constructed notions in their own right. Winegar, however, is not as consumed as I am here with epistemologically exploring art and artists' self-conception as counterhegemonic and the political economy by which ideas about dissent and resistance in the arts is shaped. Because of my international politics and cultural studies approach, I am compelled to extend the research field outside of the frameworks normally considered relevant to the study of art in Middle East Studies. In other words, and to borrow from Howard Becker (1982), I include in the "artworld" what I refer to throughout the book as the global cultural funding organizations and their local partners working under the wider umbrella of civil society and democratization. These groups bring a new dimension to the study of contemporary art in the region that concerns the place, power, and meaning of institutions of culture.

Finally, the attention I give to new organizational structures and forms of art—along with the generational tensions they trigger in conversations about globalization, dissent, cosmopolitanism, and authenticity—is in direct conversation with Winegar's now classic work and with three laboriously researched and recently published books on Palestine and Lebanon. Zeina Halabi's *The Unmaking of the Arab Intellectual: Prophecy, Exile and the Nation* (2017) uncovers the intricate ways in which the Arab intellectual's prophetic role in various publics has been received, probed, interrogated, and in effect "unmade" by a number of Arab novelists and cineastes since the early 1990s. Zeina Maasri's *Cosmopolitan Radicalism: Beirut in the Global Sixties* (2020) deals with the modes by which the generation of Arab modernists and the 1967 generation of committed artists and writers negotiated their transnational solidarities as a way of countering imperial hegemony during the global 1960s, thereby providing me with a rich account of a historical moment where artists had to confront some of the same questions as artists today. Finally, Najat Rahman's *In the Wake of the Poetic: Palestinian Artists After Darwish* (2015) has informed my readings of the political in works of art in the breakdown of a coherent agenda of Palestinian resistance to Israel's domination in the aftermath of the Oslo Accords, which were signed between Israel and the Palestinian Liberation Organization (PLO) in 1993, and in the post–Cold War Arab world more generally.

Within the framework of cultural diplomacy, contemporary art manifests in a variety of policies, strategies, and practices. In the early 2000s this manifestation mostly unfolded within organizations that go by the Arabic nomenclatures of *mu'assasat thaqafiyah* and/or *mashari' thaqafiyah*. These terms, which specifically reference the cultural work that these organizations and initiatives undertake, obscure the nongovernmental and nonprofit dimensions of their work and any implications this status may have. They also do not incorporate the internationally funded development and democratization initiatives they embroiled in the early 2000s that likewise shaped the art they aided in producing. These domestic but internationally funded organizations can possess a range of characteristics. They might be formally or informally structured, vertically or horizontally organized, nongovernmentally affiliated or funded, nonprofit, leaderless, privately endowed, artist-run collectives and art spaces, and even institutionalized and formalized organizations that offer grants and/or receive grants, such as Beirut's Ashkal Alwan or Zico House, for example, or Ramallah's Khalil Sakakini Cultural Center or the AM Qattan Foundation, and Amman's Darat Al Funun or the now defunct Makan House.[12] Defined by their fluid structures and "secularism," these partners self-consciously position their initiatives and the artists they work with as external to the state's formal structures.[13] Significantly, they are also almost always transnationally connected to any one or all of larger governmental and nongovernmental internationally located social and cultural development funding bodies, global art sites, and/or the cultural institutions and the cultural discourses that circulate within them. I call this complex network of support "global cultural funding" to emphasize the neoliberal and transnational dimensions of this network's vision and mission, to bolster the platforms of representations and the circulation of works that take an envisioned global audience, discourse, and aesthetics as its frames of reference.[14] Along these lines, I use the term "global art world" to refer to the forces, processes, and institutions in the world of contemporary art that cross borders without deriving their authority from the state (Sklair 2000: 2). I also use the term to demarcate a site that conceals through these dynamics the unrepresented counternarratives and debates that remain excluded from the story of contemporary art in the region because they belong to a category of cultural actors that has not directly benefited from global discourses on art and culture; hence, on some level these actors remain invisible in a process that claims to speak for them.

I hope that the attention I give to the systems of social relations between artists, arts organizations, funders, as well as cultural capital will play a part in shifting the focus of the literature on the cultural Cold War. Instead of centering the discourse on the now established historical fact that various artistic and literary movements such as abstract expressionism were wittingly or not deployed as weapons of the US government for ideological purposes, perhaps we can focus on the broader question of how post–Cold War transnational forces matter for local experiences in the Global South, and, in particular, how the mechanisms of international support for "local" artistic production manifests in discourse about contemporary art and its role in society today.

Typically, most Lebanese, Palestinian, and Jordanian public discussions and newspaper articles dealing with the issue of international funding for civil society NGOs tend to be framed simply within an "either with or against foreign (or western) funding" framework. Those accepting funds are usually portrayed as less nationalistic and more susceptible to the enticement offered by the West, and therefore as willing participants in an exercise of cultural imperialism. The question around which the issue revolves is more often than not whether there are any conditions offered with the money. The answer from recipients of such funds is always no. Most of what little debate exists in the press has been limited to presenting cultural actors' views of who accepts funding from Western organizations, who doesn't, and why (Habib 2011; Ben Jannat 2005). Or it has been replete with descriptions of a young and globally influenced contemporary art scene that is caught between a rock and a hard place vis-à-vis the lack of an adequate institutional infrastructure in either a public or private sphere willing to support artistic production on the one hand and financially able and willing foreign parties on the other.[15] As such, both journalists and local fund recipients remain caught in the throes of a defensive debate mired in accusations and assumptions about contemporary art's relationship to its funding sources. This does not include the nature of the cordial or antagonistic relationship between the funder and the local recipient, nor does it include whether the funder exerts indirect or direct conditionality on the content of production, or even whether its funds extend to Israel, as I was many times informed would lead the local recipient to boycott that particular funder. Rather, what seems to be missing, I sensed, was a much-needed conversation about how and why the unique internationally funded, nongovernmental trajectory toward nongovernmental and nonprofit "institutionalization" and "globalism" that the contemporary art scene underwent in Amman, Beirut, and Ramallah in the late 1990s and early 2000s has influenced perceptions of the role and function of art and the artist vis-à-vis society.

The fastidious reader might already be wondering where the art is in the work I present here. Let me say from the outset that this is not an art history or art criticism book. It is not about art as such. What I mean by this is that it does not focus on *how* the phenomenon of global cultural support for the field of the arts filters through the visual aesthetics and materials used within the artworks through an art historical lens, even if this analysis features in some chapters. Rather, I highlight the works discussed in chapter 3 onwards because I read their conceptual and theoretical, rather than aesthetical dimensions, as embodying from their inception to their realization, the very point I want to make about neoliberalism and the dematerialization of art into critical theories that reflect on rather than "do" resistance. Keeping in mind the Frankfurt theorists who pioneered the dialectical understanding of art's "double character" in relationship to hegemony, I am similarly invested in the idea that "every artwork is autonomous in so far as it asserts itself as an-end in-itself and pursues the logic of its own development without regard to the dominant logic of society; but every work is also a 'social fact' in that it is a cipher that manifests and confirms the reality of society, understood as the total nexus of social relations and processes" (Ray 2009: 80–81). I assume that for every artist the work is an autonomous critique of society. My struggle therefore is with the "social fact" of the works I address. To that end, I explore the site of international governmental and nongovernmental cultural funding organizations that have been significant players, though not the only ones, in a quickly mushrooming field of what is commonly termed "Middle Eastern" or "Arab" contemporary art—a phenomenon mutually supported by a growing body of local gallerists, domestic and regional art patrons, international arts investors, and more recently, governments.[16] Combined, these sites have played a role in constituting social relations and identities in the societies where they function.

As I already mentioned, in the course of exploring how the field of contemporary art took shape amid a post–Cold War global zeitgeist of NGOs, civil society, and democratization, I do not devote a great deal of time to discussing the role of the international arts market and galleries devoted to selling Middle Eastern art. I provide neither a retroactive look at nor close readings of contemporary artworks as they transpired since the end of the Cold War in 1990. In fact, I acknowledge that I have, often quite reluctantly, been compelled to remove from my analyses many of the artists, artworks, and art projects that I have sometimes found most compelling and that are indeed internationally recognized simply because my emphasis in the book is elsewhere than only the artwork. Using ethnographic methods that focus on interviewing and participant observation, I set out instead to understand the conceptions and perceptions of the role of art and its relationship to international cultural funding that is driving the people, organizations, and initiatives involved in processes of contemporary interdisciplinary artistic productions. Like Winegar (2006) writing on the cultural politics of art in Egypt, I found discourse to be a central pillar in the making of art in my three urban sites of research. Winegar's point that "of all the activities that went into art-making in Egypt, none was more prominent and widespread than discourse" (Winegar 2006: 10) was not only true in the context of my research but also in the often-heated conversations that erupted in studios, art shows, forums, workshops, gallery spaces, and above all cafés that I witnessed or was a part of. These encounters were of utmost importance in understanding how contemporary art, despite its assumed marginality also intervenes in that space on terms that cannot be understood within the bounds of traditional art history, but using a more comprehensive approach along the lines of a new sociology of art or new art history.[17]

This leads to my final point that my preference for focusing on art's modes of production, representation, and circulation rather than its "objects" does not stem from conceptual laziness but from a reasoned conviction that what is most interesting about contemporary art making in the region over the last 20 years or so is precisely that it unwittingly proposes novel ways of conceptualizing how art is made and understood. This reasoning is based on the deepest premise running through this book: that the meaning of an artwork is constructed in the course of its circulation and production as much as it is in its aesthetical form.[18] On that account, even if artistically formal concerns should remain a central node of analysis, they would still need to reference the overall context in which the art is being materially produced and consider both subjective and objective conditions and functions. The insistence on this—much in common with cultural studies—lies in the inference that such an approach offers a more robust conception of an artwork's agency in relation to structure, especially now that art has taken on a social and cultural life well outside of institutions.

What became known as the postwar scene in Lebanon, the post-Oslo generation of artists in Palestine, and the contemporary art generation (*jil al fann il mu'asir*) in Jordan generally engaged in works where the concept was the central aspect. In early 1990s Lebanon, and subsequently Jordan and Palestine, these art scenes began to counter existing social and political conditions, which the younger post-1990 generation saw as perpetuating a specific kind of art. This art was understood to be broadly associated with pan-Arabism, anti-colonialism and Marxism and socialism as a rallying cry, specifically in regard to the relationships between major Arab powers and Israel, and the Cold War confrontation between the Soviet Union and the US. The influence that this period had on the cultural world in the region's modern geopolitical history caused the post-1990 generation to aesthetically, conceptually, physically, and intellectually distance themselves from what they saw as collective struggles of liberation cloaked in nationalist rhetoric and anti-imperial discourse. Hence, the postwar contemporary art scene in Lebanon was not a movement heavily involved in aesthetical questions of beauty and representation. Rather, it sought to challenge the very discursive and institutional specialization of art itself. At the time, young artists demanded that the potential of the aesthetic be released from its traditional and social confinement to institutions of high modernist art and literature, and instead penetrate the public sphere, sometimes quite literally by intruding in public urban spaces, to form an art that "steps on the toes of politics and consumerism" and refuses to defend "art solely through art," as one well-known artist of the post–civil war generation in Lebanon put it to me in an interview.[19]

My understanding of "contemporary art" from and about some Eastern Mediterranean Arab cities builds on what Octavian Esanu describes as the sudden and unexpected emergence of that phrase in some parts of the world (Esanu 2012: 5). Similar to what Esanu suggests in regard to the Eastern European post-socialist states, contemporary art in the contexts of the Arab cities that I focus on has also been shaped by a specific set of conditions that have flourished under the latest phase of global capitalism—a phrase often termed neoliberalism but which may also be described as advanced capitalism, corporate capitalism, or free-market ideology. This set of conditions—infrastructure, corporations, capital, politics, work ethic, and imaginations—proved heavily invested in creating a global art world modeled on the principles of free trade and cultural exchange. It forged a temporality and form of commercialization that defined the transnationally connected contemporary art world more than any other universal and generalizable aesthetic of form or technique.[20] Hence, the art practices drawn on in this book almost always unite poetics and politics in a self-conscious effort to participate in a globally influenced, culturally diverse, and technologically advancing world. They sit resolutely between film, painting, literature, music, sound, and theater by borrowing techniques from each yet refusing to be defined by any. Hence, not only is the form of the art interdisciplinary, but so is its mode of exhibition and dissemination. Filmmakers and musicians exhibit in art venues, and artists exhibit outside of the white walls of gallery spaces, on the streets and in coffeehouses, on the World Wide Web, in informal art spaces, private venues in addition to prestigious biennials, museum shows, and art festivals. Finally, what I refer to as cultural actors intermittently throughout the book often also sit precariously between different professions. Some artists make art, but many others also curate, teach, write, and manage their own art spaces and art projects within the growing gig economy, reflecting the fragmented and insecure neoliberal market that rules.

BEIRUT, AMMAN, RAMALLAH

So, why Lebanon, why Jordan, why Palestine? Why am I writing a book about the contemporary art domains of three vastly different historical and political contexts with an emphasis on their relatively small and marginal capital cities? After all, many Lebanese would balk at the idea of having their cosmopolitan capital compared with Amman, the city often jokingly dubbed as the region's "most boring" city, or even Ramallah, the Palestinians' newly constructed de facto "capital." Despite being taken over by the hyper-capitalist and massively constructed art and culture scenes of the Arab Gulf, Beirut was, and for many still is, considered one of the pillars of Arab cultural life. On another level, Beirut's post-1990 cultural production scene operates within what some describe as the proto-institutional context of its failed state. Amman's art and culture scene, on the other hand, has historically been presided by its stable national institutions and bureaucracies, while Ramallah's contemporary art scene is located at the liminal nexus of the postcolonial and colonial, and therefore the noninstitutionalism of a colonized peoples and proto-institutionalism of a state supposedly in the making. The final three chapters of this book show how these differences define how the scenes respond to the neoliberal structural changes in the context of international development aid to civil society (Merz 2012).

As the old adage goes, "Cairo writes, Beirut publishes, and Baghdad reads." This saying evokes the literary culture that flourished in the region before it was attacked by successive governments that left little space for either individual expression or money for scholarly pursuit. Neither Ramallah, the sleepy town that until the 1990s had functioned as a suburb of Jerusalem, nor Amman, with its historical legacy of twenty-two years of martial law imposed after the Six-Day War in 1967 and lifted only in 1991, could compete with the seaside capital's traditional standing as one of the region's most dazzling hubs of commerce, culture, and politics for most of the late nineteenth and twentieth centuries, until the outbreak of the civil wars of 1975–1990. Yet despite its legendary role as a capital of modernist literary experimentation and hub for political activists of all hues, Beirut has refashioned itself as a resurgent postwar cultural and financial capital brimming with cafés, restaurants, shops, galleries, and world-class artists—"a somewhat surprising development given the continuing regional tensions and lack of institutional support" (Karabell 2018), as the typical Western mainstream media representation of Beirut's revival in the 2000s goes.

The early forces that shaped Beirut's contemporary art landscape are the same structures put in place in the 1990s, which also found their way to Ramallah and Amman. As a result, all three cities were able to consolidate their places as safe havens for internationally funded civil society and democratization projects, especially since the fall of Baghdad in April 2003.[21] Despite the severe political and economic challenges that define the relationship between people and their governing elites in each of these contexts, and regardless of the prevalent public sentiment critical of the West and especially the US's role in the region, these cities maintaine a semblance of stability captured in their openness to Western capital and financial investments, as well as World Bank restructuring requests. Especially in terms of size, these contexts appeared relaxed and manageable, for venture capitalists to navigate, aid workers to plan their projects in neighboring countries, and for expats to live, especially as the region around them crumbles under violent warfare.

Until the mid-1990s, international donors tended to support socioeconomic growth over cultural development projects. The foundations for this shifting political and cultural landscape in the parts of the region with which I am concerned were laid in the mid-1970s. During that period, Lebanon entered its long civil war, an official state of war continued between Jordan and Israel, and the Palestinian Occupied Territories writhed under continued Israeli occupation. Competition between the US and the Soviet Union, secular nationalist ideologies, and the balancing acts of nuclear threats governed global geopolitics in these years.[22] Specifically, the period of the 1970s was a turning point in that it marked the failure and decline of Arab nationalism, the turn toward partial privatization, and the growth of political Islam. The 1967 defeat shattered popular confidence in a pan-Arabist vision of liberation led by nationalist dictators. By the early 1990s, following the course of Egypt's *infitah*, a partial opening to private and foreign investment in the 1970s and 1980s, the struggles of the postcolonial period—firmly rooted in grand questions of liberation, modernization, and independence—began to make way for drastic neoliberal reforms and the breakdown of Arab unity that had already begun. With the fall of the Berlin Wall, Lebanon's "second republic" emerged from the blood and rubble of civil war. At the same time, the Hashemite regime in Jordan and the PLO signed their peace treaties with Israel, and thus, the chaotic period dissipated; a new era of global capital was consolidated. The simultaneous dwindling of Soviet influence in the region at the end of the Cold War, the onset of the first Gulf War, and the subsequent UN sanctions on Iraq came with lucrative perks of membership to the growing global economy of international development and humanitarian aid, real estate, banking, and the creative industries (Daher and Maffi 2014).

After expressing disillusionment with revolutionary nationalism, a part of Arab public discourse gravitated to political Islam, while another started to look at democracy and modernity—or rather, the lack of both—as Arab society's main problem. Often described in oppositional terms, these two worldviews nonetheless offered a range of propositions and alternatives for dealing with the region's problems that sometimes coalesced. These included one or a combination of socialist, liberal, Islamist, nationalist, and internationalist ideologies. In these years, civil society assistance in the form of international aid to local NGOs constituted the linchpin of "international MENA (Middle East and North Africa) democracy promotion efforts," which still today Lebanon, Jordan, and the Palestinian Territories benefit from.[23] This phenomenon initially focused on more traditional international developmental categories and working frameworks described by terms such as gender, micro-credit, conflict resolution, children's rights, human rights, good governance, and youth participation. These frameworks did not at first tend to the cultural production sphere as one of the antidotes to the problem of democracy in the region.

In the aftermath of 9/11, this cultural turn from purely economic development paradigms based on modernization theory toward attainment of human equality and freedom by way of top-down processes of democratization and human rights promotion became particularly acute. The attacks on the World Trade Center prompted the 2002 publication of the first series of Arab Human Development Reports, sponsored by the United Nations Development Program (UNDP). The report was the first comprehensive survey of the development status of the Arab world—its areas of concern ranged from education and health to knowledge production, freedom, women's rights, and security. It claimed that the region suffered from three major "deficits": knowledge, freedom/democracy, and women's empowerment (UNDP 2002). The politics surrounding this series of reports solidified and promoted a brand of thinking already prevalent among certain Western scholars, development agencies, and policymakers, along with their local partner civil society organizations in the region (Hawthorne 2004; Hamid 2010). If "secular Arab civil society" continues to pressure its authoritarian governments for meaningful reforms, this body of thought reasoned, then political transformations and a slow transition to democracy will reverberate across the region.[24] The first two volumes of the report were received ardently in the EU and the US, becoming the basis for the policy and practice of restructuring cultural and social fields within the framework of a renewed and more inclusive practice that emphasized cultural development as part of a culture and creative industry framework as opposed to "diplomacy," or the practice of conducting relations between nations. By the 1990s, the latter had become weighed down by its baggage of historical secrecy and its shadowy political role. Even some members of the Western governmental and nongovernmental cultural funding organizations that I interviewed during field research in the 2000s expressed a need to reshape the public perception of their work from diplomacy to cultural understanding.[25] For its part, the creative industry was shaped by the movement toward a postindustrial "knowledge economy" predicated on a rising class of horizontally networked global civil society actors, who emphasized and were invested in nurturing creativity and information as forces of entrepreneurship (Defillippi, Arthur, and Lindsay 2006). Globally, this cultural work has been defined by the immaterial labor and the precariousness of the working conditions that it perpetuates through the gig economy. In Amman, Ramallah, and Beirut, the freelance artists, bloggers, activists, translators, filmmakers, architects, and writers submitting journalistic and literary pieces to online magazines have embodied the local take on this global shift. Additionally, a network of writing and contemporary art residencies, guest lectureships, and curatorial gigs have ensured that precarious cultural work has contributed its fair share to the growing ubiquity of worldwide travel, a feature intrinsic to neoliberal globalization that was abruptly halted in the early months of 2020 due to the coronavirus pandemic.[26]

Subsequently, the international development industry's support for the arts grew in the mid-1990s into what has been deemed development's cultural turn in international development aid literature and policy circles, in reference to a shift away from positivist epistemology toward agent-centered approaches to understanding cultures and societies (Nederveen Pieterse 2010). In this light, individuals working in the domain of the arts, traditionally sidelined by mainstream international development aid, came to be seen by international donors working in policy as crucial partners for bringing about desired change centered around emancipated, democratic, economically liberal, and globally networked societies based on the rule of law. The camp of cultural producers primarily targeted was comprised largely of actors and local organizations loosely affiliated with the self-identified liberal progressive trend mentioned above.[27] This category, comprised of a hodgepodge of many of the children of former leftists, nationalists, and Arabists, was critical of a host of postcolonial Arab nationalist regimes and the politics that dominated Palestinian and Arab resistance discourse, especially after 1967.[28] At the same time, they were deeply inimical to the Islamist phenomenon that arose with the demise of the Arab left and the failures of the postcolonial nationalist regimes that came to blows in the Arab revolutionary process. This group of mostly Western-educated young professionals, comprised largely of members of the middle to upper classes, who self-identified as post-ideological and critical, and yet who partook in a global art industry constituted of uneven flows of cultural capital shaped by the neoliberal stage of capitalism is what I will call the post-1990 generation from here on. In recent years, global cultural funders have banked on the demographic cohort of the post-1990 generation as the progressive, intellectual, and creative face of hope for the region. In this book, I loosely distinguish this generation from what I will term the 1967 generation, that largely grew up during the "golden age" of pan-Arabism that shattered when Israel emerged victorious from the 1967 war.[29] This event, the defeat of 1967, profoundly impacted that generation of Arab intellectuals in general and visual artists in particular (K. Boullata 1970b:105) and shaped their worldviews. I return to the long-term impact of the rupture of 1967 throughout the pages of this book.

A new class of Arab artists, particularly from Lebanon and Palestine, and to a lesser extent Jordan, emerged against these changing political and economic landscapes and became noticeable in the late 1990s to the early 2000s. This group of artists and their supporting networks and organizations rose from the rubbles of conflict, occupation, official states of war with Israel, and twentieth-century projects of radical anti-authoritarianism, pan-Arab liberation, Baathism, and Nasserism to react to local histories in their works. In the case of Beirut and the tradition of the city's role as one of the leading cultural centers of the Arab world, its post–civil war generation of artists arguably led the way for Palestinian and Jordanian artists to join the ranks of a younger generation of Arab artists producing work that proposed new artistic language, form, and content. They did so first by subverting understandings of how the history of the twentieth-century wars in the region and the ideologies that drove them might be read and narrated by framing the artist as both witness and archivist, searching for traces of the past among fragments of memories from those still alive to share them; and second, by interrogating and challenging the traditional role of cultural institutions and the commercial gallery system in the creation of art by conceptual and physical intrusion onto public space; and finally, by probing prevalent and accepted understandings of hegemony and ideology in identity formation. Significantly, it was not necessarily that the formal emphasis was new but the more interdisciplinary exploration of intellectual and cultural development where theory, art engagement, and critical thinking coalesced in new ways and with a keener eye toward the global art sphere and its discourses, as opposed to more national concerns.

It is the post-1990 generation of cultural actors who have engaged more than any other group—either directly or indirectly, consciously or not—with the institutional manifestations of post–Cold War rhetoric on the role of cultural production and especially contemporary art in emancipation and societal development. These actors, who often possess the transnational links needed to accumulate cultural capital, include artists, curators, arts managers, art bloggers, art journalists, writers, and freelance art lecturers. These changes cannot be understood without reference to a larger body of poststructuralist literature related to the art of governance, which has been inspired by Michel Foucault's thinking around "governmentality" (Foucault et al. 1990) and the larger critique of neoliberalism that it is embedded in.[30] In this framework, neoliberalism is understood to be a set of global macroeconomic practices that construct new subject identities, mentalities, rationalities, spaces, and forms of knowledge production in the everyday micro-practices of societies that merge in the making of the political. Within the site of contemporary arts production, a new conception of art's relationship to the political has been articulated parallel to and, as I argue in the following pages, constitutive of neoliberal changes in the urban landscapes and sociopolitical contexts that have taken place over the past twenty years in the three settings I focus on. These neoliberal changes include above all the emergence of a body of young, educated, and liberal cultural entrepreneurs, curators, and investors in the arts who see the domain as a chance to reshape their cities' landscapes, legends, and futures without having to directly intervene in formal politics. This new political, so to speak, takes seriously the role of the publics, public space, emotions, and affective encounters, as well as the emphasis it places on the importance of the global circulation of ideas and praxis of cultural production inspired by local circumstances. It was arguably emblematized most brilliantly in the early days of the Arab uprisings of 2011, when the peoples of the Arab world entered what was to become a long and trying period of revolt. Even though the initial mass uprising that began in late December 2010 largely bypassed the Lebanese, Jordanian, and Palestinian contexts, it nonetheless ignited anew these subjective formations that were already in the process of unfolding vis-à-vis citizens' relationship to power and public space.[31]

Set apart from Damascus—the heart of *al-Sham* (Levant) to which these three cities also intrinsically belong—the narrow ruling elite from Amman, Beirut, and Ramallah have cooperated closely with the US and the EU on matters of regional security and economic ties, as well as the global war on terror (GWOT). Like Egypt, Jordan, a key ally in the GWOT, enjoys an extensive network of security assistance, military training and cooperation as well as intelligence sharing with the US, while the Palestinian National Authority (PNA) and the Lebanese military have similarly, although to a lesser extent in Lebanon's case, also benefited from US military aid and EU security cooperation in the form of military training, arms sales, army personnel equipment, and intelligence exchange (Jeffrey and Eisenstadt 2016).[32] Since the 1990s, these cities have also experienced a series of neoliberal reforms of their economic practices. Reformers believed that "citizen well-being" was best served through liberating entrepreneurial freedoms in an institutional framework that hinges on private property rights, which encourage heavy-handed urban gentrification, free trade, and free markets. The PNA's function in the Occupied Territories, the Hashemite regime's function in Jordan, and the Lebanese government under the policies of the late prime minister Rafiq al-Hariri have created and protected this institutional framework where the state and the business class are closely intertwined. The symptoms of this political shift are many. Political institutions and parties have retreated from any form of welfare provision. The seeming absence of any explicit decolonization agenda has led to both territorial and social fragmentation, rendering the Palestinian people even more vulnerable. The history of anti-colonial struggle with regard to Palestinian resistance to Israeli domination, the ideals of popular resistance and survival, the experiences of community organization, and the ethos of radical politics more generally have conceded for the sake of profit, free exchange, and open markets (Abourahme 2009). Urban lifestyles, emancipatory neoliberal discourses, claims to social sustainability, and sociospatial political dynamics, along with the changing roles of the US in both Lebanon and Jordan and the PNA in Palestine have cemented class disparities and consumerism by locking each into a growing service economy that has marginalized other previously thriving economic sectors.

Adam Hanieh (2011b) shows how the internationalization of Gulf capital throughout the economies of the Middle East has been a central feature of regional capitalist development over the last two decades. For instance, he argues that in regard to Palestinian class formation after Oslo, the internationalization of capital has gone hand in hand with the process of peace making, a development at the heart of the economic doctrine of neoliberalism. For Hanieh, Palestine's classes—and I would emphasize, too, its class of globally oriented artists and culture and arts organizations—cannot be understood solely through the prism of Palestine's subordinate position to Israel. Important Arab businesses and businesspeople based in the Gulf have played a critical role in restructuring society in ways that make it highly dependent on transnational capital.

Walking in Amman, Beirut, or Ramallah, one cannot help but be overcome by the noise, visual stimuli, and environmental pollution that comes with the construction boom of gated communities, malls, theme parks, and more recently, relatively large-scale museums and cultural centers that have replaced the old gritty streets, local specialty shops, and iconic turn-of-the-century and 1950–1960s modernist-style buildings in a violent process of gentrification. These cityscapes have come to both shape and express the particular vision of neoliberal economics, politics, and everyday life that is now the norm. Rami Daher explains that property is "the new consumer good *par excellence*" (Daher 2008: 22) and that real estate development is "the new religion in the Middle East" (22).[33] Daher elaborates on how cities, inspired and spurred on by developments in Gulf cities, and especially Dubai, compete for international investment, business, and tourism in marked contrast to the 1960s when cities like Cairo and Beirut represented cutting-edge modernism and urbanism. Remarking on this south-south form of urban identification from which the Palestinians—despite their inability to travel—are also partaking in, Lisa

Taraki and Rita Giacaman make the important point that the elites and the "new middle class" in the West Bank identify not just with Western urban spaces but also with the "hybrid trans-Arab urban culture" that has emerged in cities such as Amman and Beirut (Taraki and Giacaman 2006: 27).

Artists and artist spaces like large- and small-scale galleries, museums, archives, and performance centers have been central to these processes (Brones and Moghadam 2016: 239). Since the early 2000s in each of the cities, independent art spaces, partially funded by Western donor funding or local or regional art patrons, and most often registered as NGOs, have increasingly popped up in previously derelict parts of the city. Like in London, Paris, Mumbai, and Karachi, the cafés, art galleries, and restaurants followed suit (Daher 2007). More, the three cities are today humanitarian hubs. The scores of investors, international agencies, NGOs, and aid workers cycling through every few months to manage crises in Syria, Iraq, Yemen, or Gaza have also become part of the cultural fabric of these cities' global and cosmopolitan feel.

Finally, the cities of Amman, Beirut, and Ramallah also share a south-south history of exchange, travel, and movement not only on the level of business transactions and shared economic interests but also on a personal one where families, friends, and work colleagues transcend the rigid political borders that separate the cities from each other. The American University of Beirut (AUB) has proved over the course of the twentieth century to be fertile ground for the exchange of radical ideas about politics, culture, and the arts for students from all over the region (B. S. Anderson 2011). Older-generation Jordanian and Palestinian artists whom I interviewed spoke about Beirut and the "cosmopolitan Arab" experience of resistance they lived attending university there in the 1960s and 1970s. For them, the experience was formative for their careers and life stories. For one eminent Palestinian-Jordanian pioneer abstract painter, Muhanna Durra, for instance, "Beirut was a place many Arab artists but especially Jordanians and Palestinians of his generation flocked to because one could express oneself as Arab in the way one chose to do so, without the pre-determinants of what an Arab artist or writer should or should not adhere to in their work—stylistically speaking—because they were 'Arab.'"[34] For another renowned Palestinian artist, curator and educator Vera Tamari, it was where her radical ideas on the role of art in women's organizing and education in the Palestinian camps, which she attended to in Ramallah after her return from her studies in the 1970s, were consolidated.[35] For the post-1990 generation, this legend of Beirut and AUB, even as it reckons with ongoing and often violent neoliberal structural transformation, continues to enliven students' and activists' work even after they leave Beirut and return to their own cities to create cafés, art spaces, and reading and writing groups akin to what they experienced while living and studying there.

The direct exposure to the effects of Israeli domination in Palestine, and the indirect exposure in Lebanon and Jordan, is something the populations of each city continue to contend with. Israel's colonization of Palestine has always been central to public discourse in Amman, Beirut, and Ramallah in ways that go beyond the rhetoric of unity and solidarity that the state-owned media spew out. Since the establishment of the state of Israel, Jordan and Lebanon have had to contend with the effects of Palestinian displacement and expulsion by the Israeli army. Since 1948, the Palestinian story, and more so the Palestinians, especially those residing in the decades-old United Nations Relief Works Agency for Palestinian Refugees (UNRWA) refugee camps of Lebanon and Jordan, continue to trigger intense feelings among the populations in those countries. These range from sympathy and understanding to distrust and hostility. These sentiments manifest in different ways, not only on the level of everyday conversation and personal experiences of intermarriage and friendship, but also in public articulations, political statements, and legal statuses granted. Yet despite the obvious disparity between the conditions of sympathy and hostility that the discourse in various countries expresses toward the Palestinians, these attitudes are similar in that they tend to view the Palestinians (like the Syrians today) abstractly and Palestinian resistance as threating to national security and national cohesion. How the idea of Palestine and the imagination it historically inspired have played out in the discourse of public intellectuals, artists, and writers in the Levant is a common thread that intermittently ties the contemporary art scenes of Ramallah, Amman, and Beirut. This topic I occasionally return to in other sections of the book.

On a symbolic level, it was Ramallah and Amman that the late Palestinian poet Mahmoud Darwish, who has informed so many contemporary artists' works and writings (Rahman 2015), returned to after years of exile and the signing of the Oslo Peace Accords. An official invitation from the Jordanian government and its minister of culture led Darwish to agree to live between the two small and unassuming cities. It is known among his peers that Darwish said yes to the Amman invitation as a base to write, not because the city inspired his creativity but because it provided a retreat from the hustle and bustle of so-called state formation in post-Oslo Palestine's early years and relatively easy access to Ramallah following the signing of the treaty. Amman has been perhaps unfairly described as a corridor for Palestinian artists and writers unable to travel through Israel yet desiring to access the world. This belief is embedded in a complex and intermeshed history between Jordan and Palestine, a reality wonderfully tackled in the long-term art project *The River Has Two Banks* (2012–2017).[36] Yet the city has provided artists—especially those from Palestine (and later Syria and Iraq)—a safe haven through some of its most influential local art institutions, such as the Jordan National Gallery of Fine Arts since the 1980s, Darat Al Funun from the early 1990s, and later Makan House in the 2000s. And it was mostly to Beirut's most globally connected and well-known contemporary arts organization, Ashkal Alwan, that artists from Ramallah (who could obtain a visa to enter the city) and Amman flocked to in the 2000s. They still do so today to meet with international curators and to participate in the now internationally recognized and accredited courses and workshops through the informal arts education school, Homework Space Program, which was established in 2011. Ashkal Alwan not only provided a platform for discussion and arts training for artists unable to access the global arts market and a formal arts training in Western capitals, but also significantly invited members of the growing Palestinian contemporary art scene to participate in its series of *Home Works* events, a momentous biennial forum dedicated to "critical" and "contemporary" cultural practices in the region where international funders, curators, and critics embarked upon Beirut and wined, dined, and talked shop with a select group of artists from the region for a short period of time. This openness of the cities and their artists unto each other and the world, in addition to their proximity to each other and relative "stable" contexts, compared to war-torn countries like Iraq, Syria, and Yemen put them in the privileged position of being on the travel itineraries of European cultural managers and international curators scouring the globe for new art and new ideas.

CHAPTER OUTLINE

In a self-conscious effort to avoid the normative prescriptions often at the core of studies of cultural diplomacy and international relations, I take a descriptive approach rather than a prescriptive one. My approach does not look for a causal relationship as such but is invested in uncovering dynamics that were unfolding in various sites at the same time. It is also thematic rather than chronological, which allows for flexibility of movement between cities, experiences, ideas, and narratives. Each chapter tells a story in its own right, a story of a phenomenon experienced in multiple ways. I raise questions expressed to me during fieldwork through reiterating the arguments and frustrations of various subjects, some of whom were friends, others acquaintances, and many others who were strangers. The ethnography I carried out intermittently between 2008 and 2018 included semi-structured interviews, field notes, participant observation, focus groups, artworks, exhibition openings, event attendance, funder documents and publications, and archival newspaper and magazine research. The questions addressed by my interlocutors are highlighted here in a series of relayed conversations about the politics of contemporary art production among public intellectuals, writers, artists, curators, cultural NGO workers, local and international cultural managers, and representatives of international funding agencies. In these conversations, my interlocuters contend with some of the most pertinent questions—the practice, production, exhibition, reception, circulation, and sustainability of internationally funded contemporary art—that concern cultural practitioners in a rapidly changing context. While audiences are indeed central to these questions, I realized that to study them in any meaningful way would take this work in an entirely different direction from the one intended. Hence, when I occasionally venture out to the question of audience, I do so by attempting to unravel how it features in works of art and how artists conceptualize it in their work.

The book proceeds in two parts. Part 1 concerns the workings of power. Over the course of three chapters, it explores the structural and discursive transformations that have taken place since the 1990s in the sphere of internationally funded civil society NGOs working on contemporary arts production within the larger rubrics of cultural diplomacy. Chapter 1 sets the scene for what my exploration indicates about the way in which political meaning in cultural production is constructed. It begins by looking at how and why the issue of funding for Arab cultural production conducted under the umbrella of cultural diplomacy often highlights a constructed demarcation line between two conceptions of the role of contemporary art. In this binary, contemporary art is seen either as a critical voice in society, disrupting the political, or a space of cooptation and compromise, located on the margins of the political. By extension, this dichotomy frames art as positioned either within the framework of a postcolonial nationalism or as the effect of a Westernized liberalism, a theme that repeats throughout the book. I end chapter 1 by relaying the tale of a 1960s-era Arabic literary magazine and its abrupt discontinuation. This narrative foreshadows shifts in the public's understanding of the connections among visual artistic production, international cultural diplomacy, civil society, and Arab cultural politics in the past twenty years, another theme that I grapple with throughout the book. To understand the present-day tensions that revolve around contemporary art production in its various iterations, from inception to exhibition to circulation, I propose that we think back to the fears and liberating hopes that galvanized the region's post-1967 war atmosphere. Together, chapters 2 and 3 probe the myriad structural factors, both global and local, that shape that dichotomy and, by extension, what we understand of art's relationship to the political, as well as the sensibilities that constitute this understanding, beyond what it represents and how it is framed. Chapter 2 discusses the enabling factors that explicate how nonprofit and nongovernmental civil society organizations working in the arts evolved and accommodated themselves to the realities of the internationalization and local institutionalization of their domain through the changing politics and rationale of international funding. This sets the scene for the discussion in chapter 3 on how two generations, the 1967 and the post-1990 generations, view the role of contemporary art in counterhegemony.

Parts 1 and 2 of the book are intercepted by an intermezzo because the tone, scope, actors, and focus of the book shift from a macro-study of the structural dynamics that framed and supported the contemporary art scene to a micro-analysis of each city's take on these changes.

Part 2 starts with chapter 4, "Beirut," which explores how the progression of the neoliberalization of the contemporary art scene limited the understanding of counterhegemony in the transnationally connected art and culture milieu to a particular kind of aesthetical form and content of art. This art wasconsumed with positioning itself outside of nationalist art histories, intent as it was on showing the impossibility of ever truly representing history, trauma, or memory in post-civil war Beirut. Explored, too, is the local discussion on what happens to works of art upon travel through "colonial difference" (Delgado and

Romero 2000). Chapter 5, "Amman," shows how the "more desirable dimensions of economic liberalization" (Schwedler 2010: 548) became more accesible with neoliberal structural changes. These changes, I suggest, encouraged new spaces and forms of countercultural expression in the arts. In the final chapter, "Ramallah," I employ the *Picasso in Palestine* project (2011) as a micro-study of an emblematic work of contemporary art that brings together the major themes of concern to this book: cultural diplomacy and international aid, global contemporary art, dissenting practices, and the varied ways of understanding counterhegemony in cultural production.

Chapter 1

CULTURAL WARS AND THE POLITICS OF DIPLOMACY

> The Participation of Iraqi artists today in an exhibition organized by a foreign institution implies an acceptance of that institution's logic in preparing the exhibition. Participating in a foreign exhibition should not be rejected in and of itself; what should be rejected is any objective of an exhibition hosted by such an institution that is not positive, that aims at anything other than encouraging the artists and showcasing their talents. Most Iraqi artists also participated, for example, in an international exhibition held in India last year, and the Indian government has plans to organize an exhibition of exclusively Iraqi painters. But what does it mean when a colonial institution like the British Cultural Council hosts an exhibition for Iraqi artists?
>
> *Shakir Hassan Al Said, 1953*

"AL TAMWYL AL AJNABI"

Since Napoleon's invasion of Egypt at the end of the eighteenth century, Arab intellectuals have been embroiled in impassioned debates over the West's superiority versus the Arab "lag." From Amin Qasim's call for the "liberation" of women to Taha Hussein's situating of Egypt's civilizational trajectory within that of the West, and Abed al Rahman al Kawkabi's attack on despotism, the quest for modernity reverberated and found fertile ground in the debates around literature and poetry, and by extension the visual arts.[1] As Timothy Mitchell has argued, "Modern discourse occurs only by performing the distinction between the modern and the non-modern, the West and the non-West" (2000, 26). Such distinctions, I also suggest, buttress the foundation upon which the discourse of society's development from "backward and closed" to "open and free" has historically rested.

In 2007, the EU-funded, Mediterranean, culture-focused online journal *Babelmed* published an article translated from the Arabic by Lebanese critic, poet, and journalist Youssef Bazzi (2007a).[2] In the article, Bazzi recounts the story of *Hiwar*, a legendary literary Arabic journal from the 1960s, to launch an attack on contemporary local critics of global cultural funding for contemporary arts production. He derides them as adamantly and senselessly anti-Western—linking them to what he frames as the irrational and hyper-nationalist critics of the 1960s. In his words, the way the Arab public views its relationship to foreign funding for cultural production "is a relationship that can at best be described as 'dubious' and at worst as 'betrayal,' 'conspiracy' or working on behalf of the imperialist assault on the Arab nation or the 'Zionist-colonialist project.'" He goes on to complain "the list of charges runs through the full list of clichés that have comprised the Arab political dictionary for the last 60 years." Bazzi essentially attacks what he believes to be an oppressive element in the cultural practices and discourses produced by Arab nationalism that linger years after the beginning of its decline in 1970. He ends his piece by emphasizing the impressive growth of the Lebanese arts sector—and of contemporary visual arts, specifically—under the auspices of US and European patrons since the end of the Lebanese civil war in a plea to locals to shed any lingering ill-feeling toward international funders, thereby drawing on the West versus non-West and modern versus nonmodern binaries that Mitchell (2000) underlines about the modern discourse.

Al tamwyl al ajnabi (foreign funding) is the most bandied around term in the contemporary public discourse of cultural producers, funders, and activists in Palestine, Lebanon, and Jordan. The term refers to a set of questions posed and discussed largely by actors working in civil society organizations in the 1990s and the first decade of the 2000s. The discussion centers over the advantages and disadvantages of accepting funds from foreign, but especially Western, organizations, whether governmental or nongovernmental (Pratt 2006).

In fact, as a signifier in Arabic, the term *al tamwyl al ajnabi* is itself steeped in a deep imperial and neoliberal history, while the English translation of the term is neutral. As Nicola Pratt (2006) puts it, "the foreign funding debate is not about NGO financial matters, but rather about the identity of those who provide the funds (that is, organizations located in the 'West')" (114). Central to this debate is what is termed in Arabic discourse *ajindat gharbiyah* or *ajnabiyah* (Western or foreign agendas); that is, it is not how much money a funder gives a local recipient but what is understood to be done with the money, and specifically how much this power relationship affects production. These conditions prioritize the funder's interests over the recipient's.[3] In that sense, the foreign—or Western (the terms are often used interchangeably in public discussion)—cultural funding debate is not an empirical one based on objective facts about the impact of international funding on local NGOs. Instead it reflects the historical relationship between the Arab world and the West (Pratt 2006: 114). This relationship with the West is defined by a discourse that operates in the realm of ideas that have to do with representations and identities that are essentially the byproduct of 200 years of colonial encounters between the Arab world and the West. In the field of the arts, how this unequal relationship of power between funder and recipient materializes is hotly contested. What I mean is how recipients of funds, whether artists or local arts-supporting initiatives acting as "middlemen" with politically vested interests in the region, play a role in shaping the aesthetical and formal practices of cultural production. By extension, how do such initiatives end up influencing the way we understand the role of the artist as a critical voice for change in society?

Every Arab country inherited various forms of knowledge and technology from colonialism. When it was officially over, colonialism left behind a complex cultural and intellectual legacy that the Arab world is still trying to process (Abu-Rabi' 2004: 134). The region's persistent and historical grappling with multiple identities, memories, worldviews, and associated narratives—whether religious, secular, nationalist, socialist, liberal, globalist, or cosmopolitan—means that cultural production and representation, whether for a local or global audience, inevitably become domains of contestation. In turn, this contentious politics of cultural production links to the loftier encounter with any cultural practices understood to originate in the West, as was the case with modernist poetics, described at the beginning of this chapter (Salamé 1987: 52). Hence, Arab players alone do not attend to cultural production's contentious discourse. Reflecting larger regional and global geopolitical trends, international players make themselves felt via their funding, visions, and discourses, and like local players, they assert themselves, directly and indirectly, through an intricate confluence of sect, class, and geopolitics. The debate around the contextual nature of contemporary arts production, couched as it is in a longer historical debate concerned with the problem of modernist avant-garde poetics being perceived as too "Western" by some local actors, becomes the medium through which varying ideologies express themselves and challenge each other in response to experimental aesthetics. Foregrounded in these debates are two master narratives that were almost always pitted against each other during the interviews I conducted: the myth of "modern" abstract art (and, by extension, "postmodern" conceptual and overly theorized contemporary art) versus "authentic" and "domestic" social realist art committed to painting and sculpture as both form and content.[4] These narratives are predicated on a discursive framework that demarcates roughly two categories. The first is comprised of an older group of artists, writers, and intellectuals who came of age in the era of the 1967 Arab defeat against Israel or the *Naksa*, embodied in the term *al-muthaqaf* (the intellectual).[5] This category of cultural producers considers itself just as rooted in localized aesthetical practices informed by historicized understandings of art's role in attaining justice and freedom, as they are globally attuned to questions of aesthetics. The second group is, generally speaking, younger interdisciplinary artists born roughly between the 1960s and 1980s who tend to be more conceptually informed by the theories and practices afloat in more globally connected and professionally networked sites of art making. The latter category disparages in particular what it sees as rigid concepts in art, such as liberation and justice that have historically served the power politics of postcolonial nationalist regimes and their political rhetoric. In this framework, the binaries of authentic/modern, global/local, cosmopolitan/communal, and progressive/regressive inflame local discourses, sensibilities, and frames of thinking about the topic of international, but often especially Western, support for cultural production. This bifurcation, which was often underscored in my field interviews, conceals two sources of tension. First, how much "the modern must always have its other" (Deeb 2006: 13), and second, how much the construction of this other is inflected with capital, class, and power, whether we are talking about the so-called authentic-local or the cosmopolitan-global.[6] This inflection in turn is elided by the tendency I found for cultural actors—and this includes artists, curators, and representatives of cultural organizations—to focus on the identity rather than the politics of the funder when thinking about cultural production's relationship to its source of funding. This focus was often accentuated in conversations when the issue of the Arab Gulf art scene was raised, a topic to which I return in chapter 3. One well-known artist, writer, and cultural organizer succinctly summed up this prevalent perception: "Art and patronage is a dirty business, but at least the Gulf is Arab, unlike most of the other funders we have to work with."[7]

"In Beirut," notes Daniel Drennan, "the sponsors list of any given cultural event proudly lists the banks, foreign NGOs and other corporations that make such an *importation* and *implantation* of outside culture possible. No one seems to mind" (2010; emphasis added). This statement exemplifies the way in which art from the Global South is systematically located within the framework of a postcolonial nationalism, on the one hand, and as the effect of a Westernized liberalism, on the other. Accordingly, notions of "importation" and "implantation" abound in debates on cultural production and *al-asala* (authenticity) in the modern Arab world.[8] Yet such approaches are inherited from the dominant tradition/modernity debate mentioned above that too easily dismisses alternative interpretations of these tensions. Arguably modernity is not always a rude imposition or an "inauthentic appropriation,"[9] and cultural actors in contemporary Palestine, Lebanon, and Jordan are not passive postcolonial subjects.

As I try to show throughout the pages of this book, these actors are active agents involved in determining the contours of the debate by which cultural production is defined and represented. Hence, alternative interpretations to the constructed binary I observed in the field rely on a mode of critique that breaks out of the margins of established cultural regimes and proposes to rearticulate these binaries by grasping the situation as it is "lived." I am thinking here of Raymond Williams's (1977) understanding of hegemony as a "lived" process that requires continual renewal, recreation, and modification, rather than a static structure or system, allowing for a form of normative agency. Ellah Shohat's (1993) rationale, which emphasizes the need to account for the different ways in which the various "subjects" of empire actually encountered it, is helpful in thinking what this "lived" experience of hegemony entails. Shohat's claims are highly relevant because contemporary geopolitics in the Arab world continue to impact one's "encounter" with "Western" modernity based on class, gender, education, religion, sect, and confession—categories that testify to fragmented civil societies. The impact of this phenomenon in the contemporary art world is particularly acute. What I experienced in the three cities where I conducted fieldwork was an urban cultural elite who were very well aware of the structural constraints that bound them as subjects of the Global South. However, this elite simultaneously played a conscious role in asserting its own agency in relation to a cultural hegemony that is constantly in flux by way of a sober negotiation that involved either accepting, rejecting, or modifying what "encountering" the Global North entails.[10]

After 1990, the constructed binaries—historically drawn on to explicate the encounter with the darker side of Western modernity—arguably began to be expressed in a different tone, one less prone to the rigid categorizations of the pre-1990 years that the *Hiwar* experience that I mention above and return to at the end of this chapter highlights. Yet still somewhat dependent on cultural actors' transnational ties and how closely they relied on Western curatorial frameworks, the general public and many actors from within the cultural domain remained generally suspicious of the role of funding for social and cultural projects from Western sources. Yet this time, and especially after 9/11, the backdrop was what Barbara Harlow describes in *Resistance Literature* (2012) as the "drastic changes wrought—wreaked—in a catastrophically contested world order as the twentieth century turned into the twenty-first, relating a macro-narrative, perhaps, from colonialism, through decolonization, the polarized Cold War, a post-bi-polar world order, post-colonialism, globalization." The new tone reflected a more violent reality of a post-9/11 world but, at the same time, a more contingent postmodern world.[11]

In the coming chapters, I explore how these postmodern identities and approaches to the conundrum of *al-tamwyl al ajnabi* pitted not only generations of cultural producers against each other but also members of different socioeconomic classes, who affectively and intellectually experience cultural production in vastly different ways. But first, in this chapter, I call attention to the genealogical underpinnings to how funders and funding recipients frame their work in relative terms that obfuscate the work's more critically detrimental dimensions and neutralize the term "funding" as opposed to *tamwyl al ajnabi*. I argue, in a similar vein as Christine Sylvester (2009), that the political power of art is an instrument of international relations "where we least expect it." I suggest that blurring the role, purpose, and potential of cultural production in the nongovernmental sphere of civil society organizations working on arts and culture has affected the ways in which both global neoliberal cultural funders in the region and, more relevant for us here, the recipients of these funds see their roles as intermediaries in relation to the larger power dynamics of the first decade of the millennium.

Hence, despite both funders' and recipients' insistence on implementing normative frames of understanding to distinguish cultural diplomacy from cultural relations, the former cannot be viewed narrowly as a tool of foreign policy under the remit of public diplomacy alone, even though it is commonly defined as "the exchange of ideas, information, art and other aspects of culture among nations and their peoples to foster mutual understanding" (Cummings 2009). Instead, cultural diplomacy entails a multifaceted process of international cultural politics, realized through tools and practices of cultural policy as they manifest in various contexts. Within this framework, cultural diplomacy happens under a number of names. Its vast lexicon includes cultural relations, cultural cooperation, public diplomacy, public relations, cross-cultural exchange, and cultural development—all terms that encompass dimensions of culture as understood by Raymond Williams's (1961) articulation of its wide meaning, processes, and significations. Depending on the lexicon in vogue since the 1990s, it has also articulated itself as developmentally attuned, civil society and people-centered, and/or democratization in practice.[12] Although a neat genealogy could be constructed for each of these terms appropriated in the language of funders, and by extension the local fund recipients, I submit that in everyday life and on a practical level they form something of an ideological miscellany. Regardless of the particularities of its individual parts, cultural diplomacy has pushed an understanding of the arts as a motor of change in a society that badly needs to reform its culture and democratize its society. By extension, the blurring of the terms "cultural diplomacy" and "cultural relations" in scholarly literature and in policy practice is one of the most insidious ways that power works in cultural production: its invasiveness renders funders and fund recipients oblivious, unwittingly or not, to the fact that the funding of cultural production is always an instrument of power, even if it is intercepted by local actors—or, to borrow from Zeina Maasri (2020, 94), even when those participants are not mere "passive dupes."

DIPLOMACY OR RELATIONS?

In spring 2013, I met with the director of a leading and long-established European cultural funding institution in Amman. I noted to myself that the director's home, office, and favorite café were all located where we were sitting in Jabal al Weibdeh, one of Amman's oldest and, in recent years, most gentrified neighborhoods. In the midst of explaining that my research reflected an interest in the local manifestations of cultural diplomacy and how they intersect with and shape artistic practices and discourses, we were interrupted by an activist, artist, and mutual friend who wanted to say hello. We all chatted briefly about her latest work with a well-known local arts collective located in quickly gentrifying downtown Amman. Before walking off to rejoin her friends, she thanked the director profusely for all his financial support and proximity to the project during the time of its making. That interaction—the whole meeting, in fact—made clear that the director was on good terms with everyone in his vicinity, from the artists he informally greeted to the barista who served him his coffee, and even the local vegetable vendor and his children, whom he greeted informally on our way out. So, it was as though he read my mind when he said to me almost immediately after our mutual artist friend left that the term "cultural diplomacy" makes him uneasy. He went on to clarify his point, stating that he regards what he and his organization do in Amman and the region more broadly as *cultural relations* or, more precisely, mutual cultural exchange, rather than top-down diplomacy. He was interested in knowing why I chose the term "diplomacy" to describe his foundation's work. For him the word implied a distance from the people with whom his foundation worked, while "relations" alluded to a collective sense of ownership over a project. This was not the first time I had heard this in the field. In fact, it was one among a handful of times that a European or US funder adamantly insisted that he or she was invested in a two-way process of the exchange of culture rather than the top-down and rather archaic process of cultural diplomacy.

For these funders, cultural diplomacy harkened back to a place and time in the history of Cold War ideology that represented secrecy and espionage. They feel this comparison is a gross misrepresentation of what they do today. Perhaps I had gotten so used to meeting funders in their air-conditioned and finely decorated offices as opposed to local cafés where the interactions between the community and the funder are clearer. What the director said to me triggered my thinking about the difference between the two concepts: cultural exchange/relations (which in a way I observed him "doing" that day), and cultural diplomacy, and the way each interact with local cultural NGOs, activists, artists, and bloggers. Yet I also came to wonder whether the precise term used to define international funding for cultural production mattered so much if essentially what each of these terms describe is a relationship defined by local arts and culture NGOs, whether they be governmental, semi-governmental or nongovernmental, and the artists they support. As I mention in the above section, when the source of *Hiwar*'s funding was uncovered by the *New York Times* on the eve of the 1967 war, it triggered a genuine outcry that became instilled in the collective cultural memory. An understanding developed that the cultural encounter that brought the journal's editors and writers into the sphere of US government interests was directed and facilitated by the state for ideological purposes rather than organically produced in the direct interactions between writers and artists from different parts of the world. What did the designation of *al tamwyl al ajnabi* (foreign funding) convey about society's shifting perceptions of the relationship between funder and recipient within the context of the continuously growing number of foreign funded and transnationally networked arts projects? Precisely, whose interests are behind the obfuscation of the terms "cultural relations" and "cultural diplomacy," and why and for whom does it matter that the terms are obfuscated?

At the simplest level, cultural relations may be understood as interactions that "grow naturally and organically, without government intervention—the transactions of trade and tourism, student flows, communications, book circulation, migration, media access, intermarriage—millions of daily across-culture encounters," and cultural diplomacy as that which "take[s] place when formal diplomats, serving national governments, try to shape and channel this natural flow to advance national interests" (Arndt 2005: xviii). Yet in the post-9/11 era, definitions of public diplomacy, under which cultural diplomacy falls, have expressed a strong foreign policy orientation toward mutual understanding, which is reflected in terms such as "engagement," "relationship building," or "two-way communications." More, culture in the study of international relations has been defined as the "sharing and transmitting of consciousness within and across national boundaries" (Iriye 1991: 215). These terms emphasize horizontal, informal, and neutral exchange, insinuating good intention, rather than top-down formal diplomacy implemented solely to influencing politics. Viewed within this purview, cultural diplomacy has become a cornerstone of public diplomacy with an increased need to reconfigure soft power as a positive globalizing force (Kim 2017).[13] Hence, the new post-9/11 public diplomacy is being shaped in a context where nonstate actors such as NGOs have gained increasing access to domestic and international politics.[14] The optimistic view of these new multidirectional flows of ideas, finances, and projects is that they are leading to a situation whereby states are compelled to create dialogues with foreign publics where the boundaries between foreign and domestic are less and less defined (Melissen 2017).

Structurally reinforced by a global network that is understood to foster open spaces of dialogue across divides, these perceived changes in diplomacy's outlook and function unproblematically construe the global as a singular space through which continuous and unfettered links of people, ideas, capital, state and nonstate actors, institutions, and cities entwine in a series of projects, events, social interactions, and cultural exchanges. Yet this nongovernmental diplomacy that is understood to embody cultural relations as opposed to top-down cultural diplomacy, leaves unpacked the power dynamics that are being obfuscated in these normative approaches to international politics prevalent in academic and policy circles. And while the literature on cultural diplomacy indicates that the term's meaning varies according to context, a prevalent perception, especially among public diplomacy scholars, is that cultural diplomacy may be understood only within the larger rubric of public diplomacy and as a prime example of soft power—in other words, as a positive phenomenon.

However, these broad and commonly used normative definitions that depict cultural relations as distinct from and more effective as a soft power practice than cultural diplomacy are misleading. In practice, it is the norm to conflate "culture for the purpose of flourishing cultural assets, values and identities" and "culture as a means of foreign policy and diplomatic activities" (Kim 2017: 294). These essentialist definitions dilute the analytical and categorical, yet constantly evolving and interwoven, dynamics at play in Raymond Williams's three conceptions of culture and society, devised in 1961, and which I build upon throughout the following chapters: (i) culture as an "ideal"—a state or process of human perfection, in terms of certain absolute or universal values; (ii) culture as "documentary" that pertains to the body of intellectual and imaginative work, in which, in a detailed way, human thought and experience are variously recorded; and (iii) culture in the "social" sense that describes a particular way of life, which expresses certain meanings and values not only in art and learning but also in institutions and ordinary behavior (Williams 1961: 57–70).[15]

The former director of the Goethe Institute in Beirut explained the political role of cultural funding vis-à-vis Germany's and the EU's interests in democratizing the region in the following way:

> You cannot separate culture from democratization. In the 1960s and 1970s there was no social agenda in foreign cultural policy, it was more about entertaining people. But this is definitely finished today. Now we have strategic goals. We want to see open and democratic societies. Our focus is on the innovative and beyond the mainstream, not *dabkeh* [folkloric dance] for instance, and this creates irritation, especially amongst the more traditional in society. So culture contributes to pluralistic societies, something we are all working to achieve here. Yet, [this] is also quite a challenge.[16]

He then went on to speak of the way in which interaction with the local cultural elite was historically limited to a one-way exchange, whereby culture was transmitted from Europe to Lebanon and other countries in the region by way of exhibitions, shows, and events that brought European artists under a "purely cultural" mandate. According to the Goethe Institute in Beirut's former director, the Institute was "bringing culture in a more fluidly defined framework rather than supporting local culture through direct funding of institutions and organizations as is done today and which is perceived by the local population as carrying more of a political overtone."[17]

The director's comments line up with logic long established among Western civil society funders. This logic views the promotion of contemporary arts as part of a larger democratization framework among younger generations in Arab societies as having the potential to revise much of the old way of thinking. Reports like *The Challenges of Artistic Exchange in the Mediterranean: Made in the Mediterranean* , which read contemporary art as an "anti-fundamentalist vaccine," are not uncommon (Daccache 2006: 21). Before the Arab revolutionary process kicked off in late December 2010, interest in the arts as a mobilizer of revolutionary change from scholars, curators, and activists peaked. Young Arab artists were up against a growing Islamist conservatism because for many years, religious fundamentalism and autocratic Arab nationalist regimes had weakened the status of independent art in the public arena. Funders in this context aimed to correct this reality by bolstering "alternative" arts and encouraging Arab cultural NGOs. Their longer-term aim consisted of strengthening "the role of civil society in the promotion of human rights, political pluralism and democratic participation and representation" (Strategic Communications Division, EU 2016).

In spring 2008, I interviewed the then Culture and Arts Program Manager of the of the British Council in Beirut, which supports through direct program funding some of the most important contemporary arts organizations in Lebanon.[18] What did she mean, I asked, when she repeatedly mentioned that the Council wanted to see "change in society" and that "culture is a vehicle for change, like cultural diplomacy, but not the change in itself"? In a tone of deep frustration, she explained that Lebanese youth and Arab youth more generally, desperately wanted to openly discuss issues like gay rights and sexuality, issues deemed taboo by the larger population. Topics like these, she explained, were what the council aimed to tackle through the site of art. As a matter of fact, the assistant director was repeating what had already become common knowledge in policy circles by 2008. The attacks of September 11, 2001, impelled the EU and the US to place even greater emphasis on democratization (including human rights, the rule of law, and the free expression of ideas) in the Arab world as an antidote to Islamic fundamentalism. The 1995 Euro-Med Partnership initiative of the EU, for example, aimed to achieve security in the southern Mediterranean region with particular focus on political engagement with Arab regimes. It prioritized technical and financial support of civil society activism. The objective of the 2006 European Instrument for Democratization and Human Rights was to strengthen the role of civil society in the promotion of human rights, political pluralism and democratic participation and representation. By the same token, in 2002, the US established the Middle East Partnership Initiative with the promotion of civil society as one of its key objectives. Within these frameworks, culture, understood in a broad sense to include arts, heritages, value systems, traditions, beliefs, and identities, became a central feature in the relationship between governments, international donor agencies, and local NGOs.

Cultural diplomacy, which "can be practiced by either the public sector, private sector, or civil society," is malleable to being operationalized in various iterations.[19] Whether viewed within the scope of public relations, international exchange, or straight-out political/ideological ambitions, there is not much difference as to whether it is being utilized by a government, appropriated by an international donor agency, or applied by way of a local NGO as facilitator. As the arts project officer at the British Council in Amman put it to me after I asked her what term (cultural relations or diplomacy) best described the work the Council does:

> These terms and how people use them are not of much use to us in the real world of our work. What we care about is to help the local art and cultural scenes to grow by engaging in capacity-building based on their local needs, this is our intention and that is separate from what happens at the political level and that is why there is no relationship between what we do on the ground in Jordan and what is happening in the UK right now [against Muslim migrants].[20]

As mentioned, only in the past twenty years has "culture" become an ever-more significant dimension of international relations because of globalization and advancements in communication technologies that reconfigure the power dynamics between different social actors. This shift is most obvious to the extent that culture as both practice and product has seeped into the language, rationale, and rhetoric of local and international civil society organizations concerned with democratization programing in the region. The perception of the potential role of civil society as agent of democratization in the MENA region, which filtered into most development assistance agencies in the 1990s and the first decade of the millennium, is often understood to lie within the purview of international development policies, rather than public (or cultural) diplomacy. Yet at the same, the genealogical underpinning of the phenomenon of international funding for societal development through local NGOs emphasizes the same "universal" political and cultural values, needs, and aspirations that unproblematically drive the mission of cultural diplomacy.

During the late nineteenth century, the institutionalized use of culture in foreign relations emerged in Europe. Grandiose world expositions and fairs during the decades of post-1848 European nationalism were some of the earliest instances of the creation of a global public space where states could strategically instrumentalize culture and cultural representation for political ends; these large events were packaged as part of a panoramic "spectacle of modernity" that dominated representations of landscapes, industries, and especially the wealth of natural resources of societies colonized by Europe (Bloembergen 2006). Although international relations theorists tend to articulate culture's role in politics through descriptive frameworks that emphasize the functional and positive role of culture,[21] Timothy Mitchell has unraveled how culture factored into colonial practices by highlighting modern Europe's fondness for transforming the world into a representation through cultural exchange: the "exhibitionary complex" of cultural display (1989).[22] Through his discussion of nineteenth-century Parisian expositions, Mitchell shows how the preoccupation with organizing "the view" (of non-Western culture), as he puts it, is more than merely the content of a policy or a strategy of rule in cultural imperialism. By examining how the expositions objectified the cities and people they represented through miniature Cairene streets and buildings for their "Egyptian Exhibition"—in addition to his descriptions of the astonishing reactions to these models by Egyptian and other non-European visitors who encountered them when traveling—Mitchell shows that the preoccupation is in fact an intrinsic component of the cognitive methods of order and truth that constitute the very idea of Europe itself.[23]

In the same way that policymakers and scholars are preoccupied with the terms used to describe the cultural relationship between the West and its former colonies, Europe is obsessed with organizing the view for the sake of categorization and display of power—which concerns Europe's self-imaging vis-à-vis itself rather than the Arab region's interests. As I have already mentioned, *al tamwyl al ajnabi* is essentially a blanket term used in public discourse to describe a relationship of power that shapes cultural representation, cultural exchange, and cultural diplomacy between two unequal sides. The discussion of what cultural diplomacy constitutes and how it plays a role in global cultural relations is essentially a discussion centered in the North American and European hallways of power. From the British Institute, to the Goethe Foundation, the European Cultural Foundation, the Institute for Cultural Diplomacy, the Academy for Cultural Diplomacy, and even the American Advisory Committee on Public Diplomacy formed in the aftermath of 9/11, and to the growing body of scholarly literature dedicated to understanding its function and potential, the term is a construct that describes the Western liberal ethic and its historical relationship of cultural exchange with the rest of the world. That same phenomenon is labeled and framed as *tamwyl ajnabi*, where *ajnabi* (foreign) evidences "Western," rather than the more neutral and functionalist-sounding "cultural exchange" or "cultural diplomacy" taken up by Euro-American pundits, funders, and scholars.[24]

Globalization in the current epoch, in which Euro-American political and economic interests are exported to culturally dominate other areas of the world under an inclusive "world system," is not a new phenomenon.[25] Yet the form and process by which culture has conferred a function in imperial outreach has changed and continues to do so. After 1945, the competition between capitalism and socialism, along with the global entrenchment of modernization development discourse, promoted a gradual expansion of the concept of culture and how it factors in the relationship between nations. Initially restricted to high culture, the term gradually encompassed a more inclusive range of cultural expressions that included science and technology, the social sciences, and language learning (Paschalidis 2009). At the same time, in response to the increasing stigmatization of cultural propaganda for its association with the aggressive practices of the 1930s, the emphasis shifted to the more benign concepts of cultural diplomacy and cultural relations (283). As part of this turn, Western European countries redeveloped cultural diplomacy by internally creating governance structures—independent cultural institutions—to coordinate cultural relations programs and activities abroad more effectively by engaging various nonstate and private actors (Feigenbaum 2001: 17).

In the first decade of the global war on terror, despite the foundation of Cold War cultural diplomacy policy on which policymakers could draw to formulate an integrated strategy in the post-9/11 world, the Bush administration chose force as its primary tool of negotiation for shaping public perceptions.[26] Cultural diplomacy waned as the administration consolidated what was already developing in the years between the fall of the Berlin Wall and the 9/11 attacks. However, it did not drop out of the culture game altogether. In the years succeeding 1999, the State Department withdrew its support for some of its most popular programs like the Jazz Ambassadors Fund, American Houses, and the Embassy Libraries that allowed for the flow of ideas and artist exchanges between the US and other countries (Schneider 2004). Instead, funding went toward large-scale broadcasting projects like the Radio Sawa station and the Al Hurra television satellite programs that could more directly, and with greater impact, influence the negative public opinions of the US in Arab and Muslim countries.[27]

In contrast, at the end of the Cold War, the EU set about constructing its North-South cooperation aimed in particular at turning the Mediterranean Basin into an area of dialogue, exchange, and cooperation, with hopes of granting peace, stability, and prosperity (EU 1995). This move was fostered as part of an ongoing development toward regionalization taking place in international politics, which grew out of the collapse of the bipolar world system (Panebianco 2003: 2). It emphasized culture as one of the main pillars of exchange through the Barcelona Declaration, aimed at creating a zone of peace and prosperity based on a Mediterranean Free Trade Area by 2010.[28] The difference in the orientation and focus of the types of cultural diplomacy practices in this period highlighted how the perception and role of culture was a tool in international politics. "From the start, the US eschewed the culture-for-culture's-sake approach that often governs cultural diplomacy elsewhere" (C. Schneider 2004, 14). While the EU in general emphasized the longer-term, nonquantifiable nature of trust building through cultural diplomacy, the State Department, in line with its historical commitment to culture only as a vehicle for political gain, insisted that "winning the hearts and minds" of Muslims and Arabs could be achieved through a reduction in costs and a more targeted approach by broadcasting an effective means of conversion to US values.[29] Several studies of aid from EU countries have interpreted the cultural aid dispensed to the region through the prism of shared ideas, norms, and values (e.g., Schäfer 2007; Panebianco 2004; Dabbous-Sensenig 2002) This mindset of emphasizing the shared heritage of the Mediterranean Basin in cultural development policy has awarded Europe more legitimacy as an honest and less aggressive democracy broker in the region.[30]

With the arrival of the information age by the 1990s, diplomatic functions and systems were severely challenged, yet also consolidated by globalization. Traditionally, cultural diplomacy was almost always conducted through European or US cultural institutions located abroad, such as the British Council, the French Cultural Center, the German Goethe Institute, or AmidEast. The main programs of these cultural centers have often revolved around language training, archeological digs, and the coordination of artists' exchanges and exhibitions, after which artists would present on their work.[31] Such programs were traditionally seen as promoting lasting relationships between peoples of different cultures. After the 9/11 attacks, there was a paradigm shift in diplomatic activities in association with information and communications as well as in tandem with international development discourse focused on democratization and civil society practices, all of which defined the broader cultural relationship between the Arab world and the West from the 1990s onwards.

In this period, NGOs partnered with cultural institutes that until the 1990s had relegated their work to the field of knowledge transfer and cultural exchange. Before the 1990s, most activities and exhibitions were held in local art galleries, the Ministries of Tourism, cultural clubs like the Arab Cultural Club in Beirut and the Abdel Hamid Shoman library in Amman, and cultural centers of foreign missions like the Kennedy Center in Beirut, the American Embassy in Amman, the Soviet Cultural Centers, the British Council, and the French and Italian Cultural Centers.[32] In the new context, the democratization programs cultivated the creation of "post-ideological" productive subjects especially among the "youth" category that was constructed in the process.[33] By the early 2000s, due to the then new civil society and democratization frameworks (the zeitgeist of 1990s and early 2000s development aid), the institutionalized use of culture as a foreign policy tool and the onset of the global war on terror metamorphosed into an extensive machine of "smart power," meshing capitalist interests, cultural ideals, and identities that pushed forth US and European political and financial interests.[34]

According to Joseph Nye (2010), cultural diplomacy can be seen at times as propaganda, a notion that relates strongly to perception. What is regarded as cultural diplomacy by one actor may be seen as outright propaganda by another. Further, how a country's cultural diplomacy is perceived depends on legitimacy. Public opinion in the region knows all too well that for the West, the democratization of the Arab world has never been an end in itself. Active members of civil society are under no illusions about there being any "free lunches" when it comes to foreign aid for culture. They are acutely aware of precisely how they are used by Western governments for the purpose of securing Western economic and political interests, even if it is at the cost of regional stability. This cynicism and distrust in Western governments, however, is not necessarily a deterring factor in cultural exchange and cooperation between them and their Western funders (Zogby 2002).[35] In the domain of cultural nonprofits and NGOs, the upsurge of inflammatory conversations regarding any possible bearing geopolitical realities have on artists' visions and the form and content of their work both spurred and resulted from a renewed and more visible interest in funding theater, film, literature, and contemporary art, especially in and about the Arab world by Western governmental and nongovernmental donors. This renewed interest arose parallel to the violence of the ongoing wars in the region. Yet this interest in the arts of the region and the debates on culture, hegemony, and how the community of arts and letters features in them is not new and has persisted in a contentious form since at least the middle of last century.

CULTURAL MEMORY AND THE POLITICS OF FUNDING ART

On Sunday, January 3, 1971, forty-seven-year-old modernist poet, Tawfiq Sayigh, ascended to his apartment in an elevator, where, following a dinner party at a colleague's house in Berkeley, California, he suffered a stress-induced heart attack that is believed to have killed him immediately. His death was announced by the United Press International, which identified him as a "prominent Arabic poet and lecturer at the University of California and former editor of the controversial journal *Hiwar*" (I. Boullata 1973: 69).[36]

Relative to its time, *Hiwar* was no ordinary publication. Known for its global vision and experimental literary form, its visual content emphasized a strong desire for renewal and cosmopolitanism in a period when the loss of Palestine in 1948 had turned the Arab region inward.[37] The journal inspired some of the most prominent names in experimental modern Arabic literature to break from inherited and conventional modes of Arabic expression. Contributors were encouraged to invent a new vernacular, a narrative prose more reflective of the universal human condition.[38] Yet many questioned how *Hiwar* could compensate contributors so generously and produce a journal of such excellent quality and pleasing aesthetics while charging such a low price. In 1967, after only five years of publication, the cultural bimonthly ceased publication due to what is often described in Arabic as a *fadyhah*—a scandalous discovery.[39] It became known that its funding was linked to the US Central Intelligence Agency (CIA) through the Congress for Cultural Freedom (CCF). This is said to have rocked the literary world by challenging some of the biggest names in Arabic letters to rethink the meaning of independence, freedom, and commitment to anti-colonial and anti-imperial politics in literary and cultural production.

The CIA surreptitiously created the CCF following a June 1950 conference consisting of mostly European and US intellectuals in West Berlin. Tasked with stretching its influence over liberal, noncommunist yet leftist intellectuals and artists in various countries across the world, the CCF was designed as a secretive cultural front to fight against the Soviet Cominform by bankrolling cultural initiatives all over the world.[40] As the largest battlefield in the Cold War, Europe became the focal point of the CCF's work. Magazines such as *Encounter* in London—which was originally associated with the anti-Stalinist left—*Forum* in Vienna, *Der Monat* in Berlin, *Prevues* in Paris, and *Tempo Presente* in Rome were founded to promote the cause of autonomous cultural expression and democratic practice, the supposed hallmarks of American freedom.

The best-known narrative of Cold War cultural diplomacy efforts focuses on the CFF's initiatives in North America and Western Europe to erode communism's intellectual prestige. Its timeline pivots around the sponsorship of the abstract expressionism visual arts movement and the Iowa Writers' Workshop.[41] The organization also played a secret role in commissioning a Russian-language edition of Boris Pasternak's *Dr. Zhivago* for publication in Europe at a time when it was banned in the Soviet Union. By the 1960s, abstract expressionism was bound up with ideals of freedom and the individual right to expression (Stonor Saunders 2013),[42] while the works coming out of the Iowa Writers Workshop valued "sensations, not doctrines; experiences, not dogmas; memories, not philosophies" (Bennett 2015), and journals like *Encounter* emphasized the free-thinking spirit and liberal values of the West (Harding 2017). The US, it appeared, was intent on winning the cultural Cold War by constructing a clear delineation between "good" (the West/democracy) and "evil" (the Soviet bloc/communism). The covert publication of the Russian translation of *Dr. Zhivago* defied Soviet censorship and landed it in the hands of citizens all over the Eastern Bloc.

The story of US foreign policy and how it penetrated the field of cultural production during the Cold War has been told and retold. Its defenders maintain the CCF as a genuinely pluralist effort to undermine totalitarianism, while critics abhor the CCF's use of soft power as a cover-up for weapons transfer, military coups and interventions, counterinsurgency efforts, and embargoes—the real stuff of empire. What is lost in this ongoing historiographical debate and Western academic literature's dominant focus on the cultural Cold War in Europe is the way that local artists and writers in cultural centers outside of Europe, like Tawfik Sayigh, were also entangled, unwittingly or not.[43] These initiatives and other similar attempts, notably by the UK, targeted regions like the Arab world, which gravitated toward the intellectual and cultural life of the Soviet Union because of its rhetorical defense of Arabs against Western—and, more specifically, Israeli—imperial aggressions and colonial designs. Examples of such defense include the Sinai war, after which French and British influence began to wane, paving the way for the Soviet Union. Later, during the 1967 war, the Soviet Union severed ties with Israel and helped the Arab states rearm, an action that was felt again in the 1973 war when it became known that the US was airlifting ammunition and supplies to Israel.

In the Arab world, as in Europe, the aim was to shape, define, regulate, administer, and co-opt writers and artists whose dissenting practices threatened to undermine the episteme on which the Cold War was based—a seemingly relentless conflict between "totalitarianism" and the "free world" (Rubin 2012: 13). As such, the CCF sought to co-opt the literary Arab avant-garde, with its experimental modernist edge and critical anti-imperial stance, through the creation of *Ḥiwar*. The journal's writers were granted both material compensation and supposed cultural freedom, which the Congress exalted as an antidote to the communist "cultural offensive" (Oshinsky 1989). While the CCF's goal of winning over the public by way of artists and literati was arguably never accomplished (at least not in the Arab context); if anything, it showed just how difficult actualizing imperialist objectives in the cultural field can be (Maasri 2020). But the intervention did make a lasting impression. In April 1966, the *New York Times* published a front-page article entitled "Electronic Prying Grows: the CIA Is Spying from 100 Miles Up," the third in a five-part series that exposed the CIA's covert cultural funding mission. But even before this reveal, rumors began to spread in Arab capitals that *Ḥiwar* was an instrument of Western imperialism. The fact that the magazine was decidedly global in outlook and insisted on dialogue between cultures at a time when Western imperialism continued unabated probably did not help matters.[44]

Already in November 1965, two years before the demise of *Hiwar*, famed Egyptian novelist Yusuf Idriss publicly refused a CCF prize of 10,000 Lebanese Lira based on these suspicions (I. Boullata 1973). Nonetheless, the *Times'* confirmation that the rumors were true quickly spread to Beirut and Cairo, forming the basis of an unrelenting campaign against Sayigh, his magazine, and literary modernism in general. In these cultural centers, where resistant nationalist and anti-colonial sentiments already dominated political and cultural discourse, the magazine became a symbol of Western conspiracy to subdue Arab culture and society in the face of imperial designs. On a micro-level, in the coffeehouses, cultural clubs, and newspapers, the role that the literati might have played, knowingly or not, in propagating these imperial intentions was being anxiously interrogated.[45]

The attacks on the magazine and the structure that supported it, led mostly by intellectuals who identified as anti-imperial nationalists and communists, included everything from calls to boycott the journal, demands for resignations of key editors, and appeals to Arab governments to liquidate the offices that were suspected of having links to the CCF in the region.[46] These pressures, compounded by Sayigh's inability to find alternative local sources of funding after severing ties with the CCF, brought about the demise of *Hiwar* on the eve of seismic shifts in the region's cultural and political landscapes by the catastrophic 1967 Arab defeat by Israel (Shurayḥ 2011; Holt 2013). The fact that the scandal was still seething in 1967, the same year as the collective Arab disbelief and humiliation that followed the swift, crushing defeat of Egypt, Syria, and Jordan at the hands of Israel in six days is not a mere detail.[47] The war, which enabled Israel to seize Egypt's Sinai Peninsula, the Syrian Golan Heights, and the West Bank and Gaza, eventually became the death knell for the idea of Arab nationalism embodied in Egypt's then president, Gamal Abdel Nasser. The defeat was a defining moment, one that would vitally shape the 1967 generation: the thinkers, writers, artists, and ordinary citizens who would devote their work and thoughts to a critical examination of their role in the region's future. The thick ideological tones and postcolonial nationalist rhetoric of the pre-1967 cultural consciousness, which had emphasized Palestinian liberation and Arab unity, were about to change into a more militant, radical, and indeed disenchanted generation of politically committed artists and intellectuals.[48] To this day, *Hiwar*'s tumultuous years, what some of Sayigh's friends describe as an unrelenting and unjustified campaign leveled against its editor, remain planted in the subconscious of many Arab cultural producers concerned with questions of empire, globalism, modernity, international funding, and cultural production.

Hiwar's example demonstrates the extent to which relations between cultural production, imperial hegemonic politics, and the site of the political in local contexts can be fraught. Even when artists or writers have well-defined intentions about the political meaning or potential interpretations of their work and its making, critics, audiences, readers, and viewers can interpret its function in radically diverse ways. Additionally, politicians, diplomats, governmental agencies, and civil society organizations may project their own ideas, interests, and fears onto what the function of the works should be, manipulating public perception. Whether it be modern or contemporary art, literature, theater, or cinema, it seems that everyone has a stake in interpreting cultural production, sometimes, perhaps unfairly, rendering art a mere vehicle for "meaning" waiting to be decoded. Sayigh's published notes on the period during which he was setting up *Hiwar* in 1962 attest to this (Shurayh 2011). He writes of his intentions in editing *Hiwar* and his choice of work to translate as a form of cross-cultural dialogue about modernity and aesthetical experimentation. Such accounts differ markedly from the way in which his story has been remembered: one of traitorous politics and imperial connections.

As *Hiwar*'s legacy demonstrates, part of the way these debates over interpretation play out is through competing historiographies. With that in mind, what warranted Bazzi's return to *Hiwar* in his article that I describe above so many years later as a defining moment in the region's cultural history? Why did Bazzi single out *Hiwar* as opposed to other instances of politically motivated collaboration in the cultural field to argue in favor of international cultural funding to encourage civil society development? After all, the CIA had secretly funded visual artists from the Arab region several years before the launch of *Hiwar*, primarily in the form of supporting their travel to the US in an effort to expose the American public to the Middle East and bring both of them closer together.[49] Yet visual artists who are known to have benefited from these programs remained, to the best of my knowledge, more or less unscathed in their local contexts.[50] *Hiwar* differed because it showed the CIA's strategic interests and direct extension of its ideologies into the local public, literati circles, and communities. Zeina G. Halabi (2017) describes the archetypal Arab intellectual, *al muthaqaf*—specifically the writer and the poet, as opposed to the visual artist—as a historically "prophetic nationalist" figure. When this persona was infiltrated by outside forces, it threw into disarray the project of modernization and its literary manifestations.

According to literary scholar Elizabeth Holt, it was a blunt realization that "all along 'freedom' had provided strategic cover as *Hiwar*'s authors unknowingly did the Congress's work for reasons they had believed to be their own" (2013: 100). It is arguably this apprehension that made such a profound impact on generations to come. In other words, it was made shockingly clear to artists, writers, and intellectuals that their commitment to art and politics could be rendered vulnerable in the face of larger political forces. These forces were understood to have the power to manipulate the potential of creative work as an avant-garde force of change when literature in its form *al adab al multazim* (committed literature) was a central trope in cultural discourse.[51] *Hiwar*'s story unfolded and circulated in the heart of the region itself; it was passionately discussed in the coffeehouses, cultural centers, and gallery spaces frequented by the then local literati circles of cultural capitals like Beirut, Cairo, and Baghdad (and, by extension, smaller and less culturally significant cities such as Amman). Its context has kept Sayigh's specter present in discourse around international support for cultural production today and, as I mention in the introduction, has limited the conversation in both the media and among cultural actors to a simple "either with or against *al tamweel al ajnabi* (foreign funding)" framework. In this view, "with" funding signifies a willingness to cooperate with an imperialist, specifically "Western" agenda that disguises itself as cultural exchange, while "against" indicates a supposed anti-imperial nationalism and therefore an unwillingness to compromise with Euro-American hegemonic power.

By returning to the pinnacle of literary political relevance in recent cultural history, Bazzi purposefully reminds his readers and *Babelmed*'s European funders of the damaging inheritance of the CCF's Arabic literary activities that formed, to quote Holt, "the long shadow of suspicion cast upon the possibility of avant-garde poetics and literature in Arabic" (Landeau 2015). Bazzi believes this damage continues to have far-reaching implications for local recipients of Western cultural funding who are today trying to build up an infrastructure for a globally relevant contemporary art scene. Bazzi also sheds light on the very question that animates the local conversation on the efficacy of art, its political function, and its relationship to society. In his short piece, republished in English, Bazzi draws a blunt line between what he sees as the progressive, liberal cultural scene intimately linked to international funding and the more local and avowedly radical, anti-Western camp of Arab nationalists that was, in his analysis, preventing the scene from reaching its full potential. In the article, and likewise with regard to many of those I interviewed throughout Beirut, Ramallah, and Amman, the issue of cultural funding from Western institutions and the sentiments it provokes signifies an invisible demarcation constructed between the two different conceptions of the function of contemporary art: either as a critical voice in society or a space of cooptation and compromise. By extension, this dichotomy frames art as located either within the framework of a postcolonial nationalism or as the effect of a Westernized liberalism. The following comments made by the director of Beirut's most globally well-known, internationally funded, and transnationally connected contemporary arts organization exemplifies this constructed dichotomy and its real implications:

> Our work reflects our politics. Do you really think we have political autonomy? Who rules [Lebanon]? The West, Iran and Syria. So what is this bullshit about financial autonomy in the arts? Why would the Ministry of Culture have any money at all for us in this set-up? Does the Ministry of Finance even have money? Why in the issue of funding for culture [do] people suddenly want autonomy and Arab nationalism? We work with what we have. Half of the country is sidelined with Iran and Syria and the other with the West. What autonomy? Give me a *watan* (a homeland) and then come talk to me about autonomy . . . when that is the case, then I will resort to local funding[.][52]

I highlight these remarks because they allude to the difficult position of cultural actors vis-à-vis funding sources in the region and how they rationalize their orientations within these confines. Accordingly, they explain the choices they make as well-known, major recipients of global cultural funding, and how this decision is located between two "evil" hegemonies of which they choose the lesser one as their own form of resistance. This logic underlines the tendency for liberal discourses to treat power structures as neutral agents, disinterested entities that can be inserted into a situation for a specific purpose and limited timeframe. I elaborate on this tendency in the following chapter. For now, let me just say that the impulse to posit a stark antagonism between a supposedly backward "local" in relation to a progressive and multicultural "global" was not prevalent among all international funding recipients working in the domain of culture.

How cultural actors negotiated their positionalities vis-à-vis the powers that be often depended on the extent to which they already felt at ease in circuits of global capital and culture. The more affluent, well-connected, well-educated citizens with foreign language proficiency and the ability to travel outside the region were more prone to seeing the global art world as comprised of continuous and unfettered links of people—artists, curators, critics, institutions, and cities—that entwine in a series of events and social interactions that are consensually negotiated between two equal entities (Tao Wu 2009). The contentious politics that intermeshes the influences of elitist, colonial, socialist, nationalist, and internationalist histories of cosmopolitanism and alternative modernities is elided in either "with or against" frameworks. What goes amiss in this morass is something akin to what Andrew Rubin (2012: 10) has described in regard to literary formations as the "modes and means" through which dominant forms of knowledge and understanding are expressed. In other words, such mutually exclusive theorization is bound to mystify more than it explains.

In 2004, images of naked and hooded brown male bodies—piled on top of each other in a pyramid shape, surrounded by US soldiers in uniform, who smiled, holding two thumbs up in the infamous Abu Ghraib prison—began to trickle into the Arab media. Whatever disdain the publics in Jordan, Palestine, and Lebanon had for US-Arab relations was further compounded. The launch of the global war on terror with the illegal invasions of Iraq and Afghanistan followed by exposure of the humiliation and abuse at Abu Ghraib and then torture in Guantanamo, the first decade of the millennium saw an increase in the legitimacy of the EU and its support of civil society projects. With the exception of the UK, the EU was seen as a marginal player in the US-led military aggression in the region. In any domain of civil society, "working with the Americans" was deemed inappropriate and distasteful; when done, it was often done quietly. In contrast, the EU's support to civil society was deemed not only increasingly acceptable but necessary for the survival of what the many cultural actors I interviewed perceived and framed as a "secular" civil society in the face of a growing Islamism. This was especially the case in Palestine and in Lebanon where the relationship with the US was particularly strained due to what the US saw as the unchecked presence of Hamas and Hezbollah. In Jordan, however, the regime-organized civil society played doublespeak in regard to its critical stance toward the US's support of Israel and the war in Iraq, while still maintaining a special relationship with the US for stability and, some argue, regime survival (Yom and Gause 2012).

In the following chapter, I reveal how the professionalization of the field of cultural production through aid to nonprofit and nongovernmental initiatives working on contemporary art unfolded. I show in particular how the professionalization of the field constituted the backdrop against which debates on the role of the artist as an effective critic and art as a counterhegemonic force that "accepts its supporting institution's logic," as Al-Shakir insinuates in the opening epigraph of this chapter, raged in the first decade of the millennium.

Chapter 2

"AN ARTIST WHO CANNOT SPEAK ENGLISH IS NO ARTIST"

AS I INDICATE IN THE PREVIOUS CHAPTER, WHEN I FIRST encountered *Hiwar* I took the accepted narrative about it and its reactions to exemplify what Halim Barakat describes as a real and constant struggle in Arab culture (1993: 197). Imbued in this tension are a range of reactions, one of which is embodied in journalist Yussif Bazzi's frustration with *Hiwar*'s enduring impact on local perceptions of international cultural funding, and what he regards as the more regressive elements of the Arab region's cultural life. For Barakat, the struggle of culture in the Arab world has always been defined by creativity versus conformity, modernity versus tradition. In this dichotomy, "the authentic was related to the past while the modern was related to the relationship with Western cultures" (Khoury 1990: 1). By extension, the authentic conferred local bearing while the modern was associated with the cosmopolitan global, thereby tethering the latter with (Western) power and the former with communitarian and nationalist sentiment. These two currents, Barakat explains, manifest themselves in much of Arab life, from the religious to the political, the ideological to the cultural, and especially within literary and artistic aspects of Arab culture. In every period of Arab history, "there has been a modernist trend that rejected prevailing traditions and static values. This creative trend aspired to change the world and to create a new mode of thinking as well as new forms of literary expression" (Barakat 1993: 197).

Crucially, as I progressed in my fieldwork, I learned that how these currents were being revisited and when they were called on were symptomatic of the very categories Barakat delineates. In reality, these binaries were far more nuanced sites of tension between generations, classes, worldviews, and personal and collective memories and interests, battling out their own conceptions of what being modern entailed than was represented in public discourse. That is, while they may be felt as anxiety revolving around the existential questions of collective identity and the modern nation-state, especially in their postcolonial iterations, and represented as two ideologically opposed streams of thought, what these binaries embodied more than anything was the often contentious and always constructed claims brought forward during troubled moments in a society's history. In this chapter, I shed light on the role of nonprofit and nongovernmental arts and culture organizations and initiatives, the mechanisms they employ, and the politics in which they are embedded that correspond to and also reinforce these societal anxieties over authenticity. I look at how, despite their nonprofit ethic and self-professed universal empowerment agendas, culture and arts initiatives are intermeshed with hegemonic global cultural and financial capital in ways that make it harder to assert either their independence or their roles as counterhegemonic.

Very early on in my fieldwork, in 2008, I telephoned one of the most well-known and established theater directors and actors in Beirut to explain the nature of my research and to request an interview. In those days of my field research, I was still articulating my questions in the very broad terms of the new phenomenon of international funding for local arts production. The immediate reaction I received from him was one of indignation. He said that he would not be able to give me what I was looking for, as the issue of *tamwyl* (funding) was in reality a non-issue. When I asked what this meant, he explained that his work is undertaken independent of the pervasive phenomenon of global culture funding of interest to me. It is a side issue, he explained, one that has no resonance in either the work his organization undertakes or the debates that circulate among his colleagues and friends about the theater's productions. He curtly suggested I look elsewhere and provided me a list of other well-known nongovernmental cultural organizations that are supposedly on funders' favorite lists. He argued that the works coming out of these other organizations were more "tied" to funding because they explicitly work with contemporary artists. However, the list consisted of organizations not unlike his, as they were also set up in the 1990s, but they were—in contrast—headed and directed by actors of Lebanon's post–civil war generation who were more plugged in to transnational networks of production. The director's reasoning was a clear example of how when the "contemporary" in contemporary art was used by actors in the field, it often referred to a global network and discourse rather than a specific form of art. After engaging with him in conversation for a bit longer, I managed to arrange an interview.

Our two-hour-long conversation the following week at his theater was rich with information, both historical and current, regarding the changing dynamics of the connections between ideology, funding, and cultural production that Lebanon has witnessed since its heyday as a cultural capital of the Arab world in the 1950s and 1960s. While many individuals I spoke with quite openly engaged me in conversation about an infrastructure built in large part on the vested political interest of donor countries in seeing Lebanon, Jordan, and Palestine thrive culturally, others remained cautious about assigning any potential meaning to the phenomenon. In either case, the reactions were more often than not initially defensive.

On being asked to reflect on the role of funders, cultural organizations and even those artists associated with them would reply with the standard "there are never any conditions tied to funding." They thereby affirmed their independence and essentially their authenticity. For them, that was the end of the discussion. When I was not able to elaborate on my research interests quickly enough, often the immediate assumption made was that my question concerned the kind of aesthetic readjustments that were supposedly being made with the acceptance of international funds. This implied touching on a sensitive issue related to that "vicious dichotomy" formulated in the wake of the Arab Nahda between the second half of the nineteenth century and the beginning of the twentieth century that I describe at the opening of this chapter, where the authentic was related to the past and the modern to imported Western values. The director of one of Lebanon's most well-known culture and arts nonprofits, which has enjoyed the support of a vast array of US and European funders, and which uses art and film to tackle the memory of Lebanon's wars through documentation and archival research, reflected in a newspaper piece on this sort of constructed framework very well:

> Who respects Muslims more, the British or the Lebanese? Who respects Sri Lankans more, the Americans or the Lebanese? [. . .] America respects culture more than the Ba'athist regime in Damascus or the Egyptian regime[.] Saudi Arabia nor Egypt or others have any values to contribute to the market. For thoughts to be produced, freedom is needed and freedom produces richness. In reality we are appendages to the West. So we are dependent on Western culture and on Western richness. (Slim 2007; my translation)

What interested me more than such bifurcated and ahistorical structures of thought, however, was uncovering what went amiss when members of the post-1990 generation of artists and cultural organizations discussed their relationship to global art funders, wedged as they were in the throes of these inflammatory discussions. What I was probing instead, I often found myself explaining, was what the emphasis on the relationship between authenticity and the modern concealed about the workings of power and the neoliberal structuration of contemporary art in the field of cultural production. What I wanted to know was whether a counterhegemonic resistance with a non-Western cosmopolitan ethos from the Global South was imaginable in the domain of contemporary art. And if it was, in what form could it articulate itself within the Euro-American-led civil society, NGO, and democratization zeitgeist of the late 1990s and early 2000s?

Before answering this question, I needed to uncover what this zeitgeist of civil society in the region during the late 1990s and early 2000s entailed. As was the case with *Hiwar*, at stake in accusations of inauthenticity and the discussions they provoke is, first, the prevalent perception that Western institutional funding for the arts has always had and continues to have the potential to tame dissident artistic practice, by bringing it to the center; and second, the perception that a clear demarcation exists between local and global forms of cultural expression. Yet, unlike in the *Hiwar* story, beneficiaries of funding today have not necessarily had the quality of their production publicly slandered for being traitorous to a bigger collective nationalist or anti-imperial cause, even if they have had to defend themselves from a scrutinizing media and local audience from time to time, as well as bear the brunt of censorship from government officials.

Despite some harsh criticism from local audiences for being inauthentic, an issue I address intermittently, contemporary artists in general have had the option, especially in more recent years, of being passive to local criticism should they choose to be. They have been able to do this by turning their gaze outwards precisely because they found outside of their borders by the early 2000s a very interested collection of mostly Western arts funding institutions, audiences, critics, and curators that came with the multicultural turn that took place in the years following the end of the Cold War in Europe. This period that took off in the 1990s embraced artists and writers from "margins" unbeknownst to the cultural metropolis like New York, London, Paris, and Berlin.[1] More important, as the following chapter examines in more detail than the mere mention I make here, it was in this period of neoliberal structural transformations that a new understanding of the artist's role—as more introspective and aesthetically focused than ideologically and collectively driven—began to take shape.[2]

PROJECTS NOT POLITICS

One rainy day in Beirut in early 2005, I received a call from a friend who wondered whether I would be interested in meeting with the editor of a newly formed and financially struggling but well-respected Beirut-based, pan-regional arts and culture magazine published in Arabic. The editor, a well-recognized if also very controversial intellectual, journalist, and cultural critic in Lebanon and the region, was interested in speaking with me about the possibility of raising funds from international donor organizations and governmental bodies to sustain his quickly growing journal. His journal, which often showcased the works of experimental and well-known artists, writers, and intellectuals, had a wide readership in the cultural milieus of North Africa and the Levant, but, as he explained, it could not sustain itself through sales only. He needed funding from international organizations and I, or someone with my qualifications working with international donor and local development projects and knowing their "inner workings," as he put it, could help him obtain it by writing proposals that would convince funders that the magazine was in line with their interests and vision for cultural development in Lebanon and the region at large.

That day, the editor and I exchanged sometimes funny but also cynical notes about dealing with the different forms of development aid supporting the myriad nongovernmental and nonprofit initiatives in the contexts in which we had experience. Prime among these, it turned out, was the support funders who were increasingly interested in providing for cultural organizations focused on art projects aimed at social reform. The editor shared his experience in the field of literary and artistic production, which reinforced what I had heard in interviews that I carried out with funders: that funding organizations know very well that artists seldom, if ever, directly impact policy; but the hope is that they will condition the atmosphere and rhetoric in which political and ideological trends are conducted. This rhetoric (which artists sometimes mocked in private) emphasized gradual and top-down controlled social, political, cultural, and economic reforms contrary to what the protesters demanded in the early days of the revolutionary process—since the self-immolation of Mohamed Bouazizi in Tunisia late 2010—and that continues to unfold today in different iterations throughout the region. The rhetoric that funders hoped artists will indirectly influence how politics is conducted matched with the kind of democracy aid that came from Western countries in the name of civil society development; while it was labeled democracy aid, it was not aimed at promoting democracy. NGOs that received Western assistance knew to avoid anything that could be construed as directly supporting regime change instead of reform (Hamid 2011).

Significantly, the first two volumes of the UN Development Program's *Arab Human Development Report*, which embodied the zeitgeist of the rhetoric of gradual reform in the early 2000s, were received ardently in Western capitals and relevant development institutions (UNDP 2002, 2003). The report won the prestigious Dutch Prince Claus Award in 2003, recognizing UNDP as a significantly generous and influential funder of contemporary art in the region at the time; and in 2004 the G8 endorsed the US administration's vision for a "Greater Middle East" in accordance with the recommendations set out by the document. The dire state of development in the Arab world, it asserted, lay at the root of terrorism in the Middle East, which the G8 acknowledged as detrimental to the Middle East's own national interests (Bayat 2005: 1228).[3]

Rather than merely subsuming ideological/political critique under the doctrine of an abstract formalist aestheticism, Antonio Gramsci insists that the form itself is always the product of a specific sociohistorical context, that is, the political of that moment (San Juan 2003). Likewise, for funders confronting the cultural roots of terrorism and other social ills by engaging with "contemporary" artistic practices, "contemporary" took on a very specific meaning.

It pertained not to the works' aesthetic qualities as viewed in their own particular trajectory, context, and art history but to their perceived significance as necessary counterhegemonic elements in the effort to attain a new society embracing neoliberal versions of democracy, freedom, and reform.[4] "What the Arab world needs today is a new language and new media to create a new image, to question Arab identity. Show this in the West and they will understand there is more to the contemporary Arab than camels and sand" (Chenal 2008: 60). These words by Moroccan artist Abdellatif Benfaidoul, quoted in a document published by the European Cultural Foundation to reflect on its fifteen years of funding cultural cooperation between Europe and the Southern Mediterranean countries, demonstrate how the logic of employing art for the betterment of society was articulated as a joint project between funders and artists that aims to create *together* a new identity for the region.

As such, it was largely the appearance of archival, video, and performance aesthetics that complemented the global art world's preoccupation with engaging conceptual approaches and refuting meta-narratives that coincided with funders' increased presence in the cultural domains. Most projects and festivals that received funding engaged with conceptual and immaterial approaches to art, emphasizing the idea rather than the aesthetical form as would be the case with painting and sculpture for instance. Despite this focus, there continued to be those who believed and worked in the realm of painting and sculpture as contemporary cultural practices and not merely as a form of postmodern parody.[5] Yet funders worked to actively exclude some of these works for the meanings and affiliations they ascribed to them, be it their appeal to popular culture or their links to a more provincial Arab identity. The regional director of a global grant-making network aimed at justice, democratic governance, and human rights that has invested generously in contemporary art in the region, put it quite brusquely to me in 2008 when he stated that in the Middle East "there is a distortion of culture. It is one based either on Umm Kalthoum or Haifa Wehbe habibi habibi stuff. There are no contemporary cultural practices occurring. We have a culture here everyone says. But what is it actually? Cultural practice is nothing here, it's like a loaded gun. Yet the lack of it is the basis of all problems here."[6]

Not uncommon among critics and curators were claims that works produced by a younger generation of artists from the late 1990s and especially in the early 2000s were affecting the way in which people conducted themselves in the city and constructed their identities or that non-Western visual arts—in contrast to film and literature—could not contribute to understanding the complexities of our contemporary world.[7] Assumptions like these highlight the dubious understandings of the time that contemporary art possessed transformative capacities, and that it could not use "traditional" media if it was to be critical. Along these lines, for global art world critics and curators more specifically, Arab "contemporary" art presumed a curatorial understanding closely linked to the global art world's. "Contemporary" for funders, and for curators and critics alike, became synonymous with terms connoting certain politically subversive qualities vis-à-vis their own Middle Eastern contexts. Some of the terms repeatedly used in the early 2000s, and still today in art journals, newspapers, donor documents, and exhibition catalogs to describe such works and the processes in which they were embedded include "clanestine," "radical," "subversive," "countercultural," "alternative," "political," "freethinking," and "critical."[8] Such terminology recalls Peter Burger's definition of avant-garde as "a break with the tradition and a subsequent change in the representational system" (1984: 62). This understanding relies heavily on notions of artistic avant-gardism as revolutionary: that is, as a set of practices thought to be disruptive of the conventions of the bourgeois social order, which is not necessarily always the case, as I show in the following chapters.

Returning to the journal editor who was hoping to solicit funds from donors, he went on to explain to me that grant applicants had to submit clean-cut proposals that depict the organization as representative of the younger generation of Arabs, whom the funders believed to be the vanguard of change in the region. We must show, he continued, our intent on transformation ourselves, whether or not we agree on the route that will take us there or even on what kind of change we would like to see. Funders did not need to know the latter. The editor's account exemplified the critique that was quickly emerging among civil society members on the possible detrimental effects of aid and the subsequent "NGO-ization" of civil society.[9] It also triggered a series of questions that a decade later made their way into this book. If we are merely ticking boxes for funders and then doing only what we want with the money, does that count as subverting the supposedly "hidden" agendas of the politics of international aid? Further, could the culture sphere really be "the final bastion" in the battle for Arab reform, as one communication and cultural programing manager at a cultural organization in Amman crudely explained to me about her European funders' interests some years later?[10] Was there really such a thing as an "imposed funding agenda"? And if there was, did it really matter whether we agreed on the need to transform the way politics works and how society thinks, as many of those around me and those I interviewed for my research some years later argued?[11] Finally, in what ways did the production of culture and the effects of aid mirror larger changes in the domain of activism, which increasingly was becoming professionally compartmentalized into "art and culture," "human rights," "environment," "gender," "good governance," "youth," "democratization," "rule of law," and so on?

An Iraqi artist and critic of the 1967 generation living in Amman who witnessed and remembers the drama around the exposure of *Hiwar*'s source of funding explained to me that while she ran an arts organization in dire need of funding—its mission was dedicated to preserving the works of her late husband, a much-loved Iraqi painter—she would still rather "starve" than have to submit a proposal to the British or French to save her organization because she refuses to be a "pawn in the west's war on Arab culture." Notably, I heard multiple variations of this theme from mostly members of the 1967 but also some from the post-1990 generation. Implicit in her musings is an underlying assumption that cultural production has been stripped of its political efficacy and, specifically, that an entire generation of visual artists lauded globally for its post-ideological and supposedly subversive form is at the same time criticized locally for proposing seemingly normalized and elitist discourses on the role of art in social change. Civil society's negotiation with hegemonic support structures is addressed in the below comment made by one of Lebanon's foremost cultural managers, in charge of what is today the country's oldest and most transnationally networked and recognized local contemporary arts organization formed in the early 1990s:

> I don't condemn anyone who accepts foreign funding because we do not have a structure that will protect us otherwise. Why are we always dealing with art and art structures like they should be any different from other fields? Tell me why? It's a structure like any other that is tied to the city, its problems and the structure we live in; it's tied to everything around it. So why do we always deal with it like local funding is a serious option?[12]

In many ways, these words resonated with my anxious questioning about what contemporary art can and cannot do in a fast-changing neoliberal context.

They conveyed the denigration of the idea of resistant artistic production—at least in its most conventional form—which so many members of the 1967 generation seemed to also critique. By asking why we should deal with art and art structures differently than other fields, the director confirms the view that art's self-perceived role as exceptional, and counterhegemonic, avant-gardist, and critical has been compromised in the face of the larger social and moral philosophy of neoliberalism with its emphasis on entrepreneurship, professionalism, and individualism in all sectors of the economy and society (Harvey 2005).

At the same time, this apathy does acknowledge the role of Western policies in the region. Most interviewees, whether in Lebanon, Jordan, or Palestine, expressed being under no illusions about there being any "free lunches" when it comes to foreign aid for culture. They understood that the cultural aid that trickled their way embodied power relations in international politics. In spite of that understanding, however, almost all the artists and supporting organizations that I interviewed, in Beirut especially, agreed that the realpolitik of cultural aid affected neither the content nor the aesthetical form of the artworks they produced.[13] Interestingly, this view demonstrates an overall recognition, acceptance, willingness, and perceived need to sidestep the effects of realpolitik in the world to "get on." If we accept that power works by "creating truth and subjects and sites of apparent autonomy," as Timothy Mitchell (1990: 555) puts it, then we can understand that cultural actors are not passive postcolonial subjects. Instead, they are active agents involved in determining the contours of the debate by which cultural production will be defined and represented, through "sites of apparent autonomy."

Reminiscing in a tone of deep frustration, one of Lebanon's most celebrated theater directors, playwrights, and actors of the 1967 generation described to me the changing landscape of cultural production that he witnessed over the course of almost half a century:

> In the Beirut of the 50s, 60s, and 70s, there was a conglomerate of artists made up mostly of an Arab bourgeoisie comprised of cultured people and intellectuals often on the run from places such as Jordan and Egypt. This created a cultural, political, and commercial center for Lebanon in the arts. The local Arabists were major supporters of the arts and culture then. At the time, there really was never any major difficulty in finding support for your work, and by support I do not necessarily mean financial support, but rather an audience of

> engaged people theaters relied on to fill up their halls and keep their galleries alive—not only in terms of buying work but also, and more importantly, in terms of generating discourse around what was produced. The private sector, which was largely educated, had a personal interest in seeing Beirut develop as a cultural center. . . . The upper classes wanted to see it that way. The change we see today is a root one which began with the Civil War. It used to be that the parties encouraged by the intellectuals and artists conglomerating around them took on the role of cultural financiers. The PLO for instance was a major source of cultural support for political reasons. They would buy books, film, painting, music, and magazines; they would fill up theaters, music halls, and exhibition galleries. In the place of parties, today you have foreign funded NGOs. It's very different today. Then, there was an overarching culture which facilitated production and consumption. Culture was prevalent: it was not a "project"—a project funded by an international organization. Culture then was everywhere and everything.[14]

The "project" that the theater director and actor refers to is both metaphorical and real. It describes a manufacture of dissent that NGOs have been accused of partaking in by organizing projects at the expense of a radical politics geared toward radical change.[15] In the arts, this issue of the nonprofit and nongovernmental NGO shaping a compliant generation of contemporary artists expressing dissent consensually was raised in almost every single interview I conducted with active members of the cultural milieu of Beirut, Amman, and Ramallah, whether they agreed with it or not. What was being critiqued in these observations, which Assaf succinctly describes above, is the overall process of top-down organization that has enabled art's project-based focus and promotion of transnational circulation, which is then packaged as contemporary art and compartmentalized in contemporary art discourse. Frequently presented in English, this discourse is often unable to penetrate the publics to which it purportedly speaks.[16]

Chatting about my research over coffee with famed Palestinian artists Suleiman Mansour and Nabil Anani in Mansour's studio in Ramallah one summer morning in 2018, one issue that came up was the professionalization of resistance in cultural production. Both artists talked about how the Palestinian struggle as a form of resistance featured in some of their most distinguished paintings, such as Mansour's 1973 *Jamal al Mahamel* (Camel of Burdens) (fig. 1).

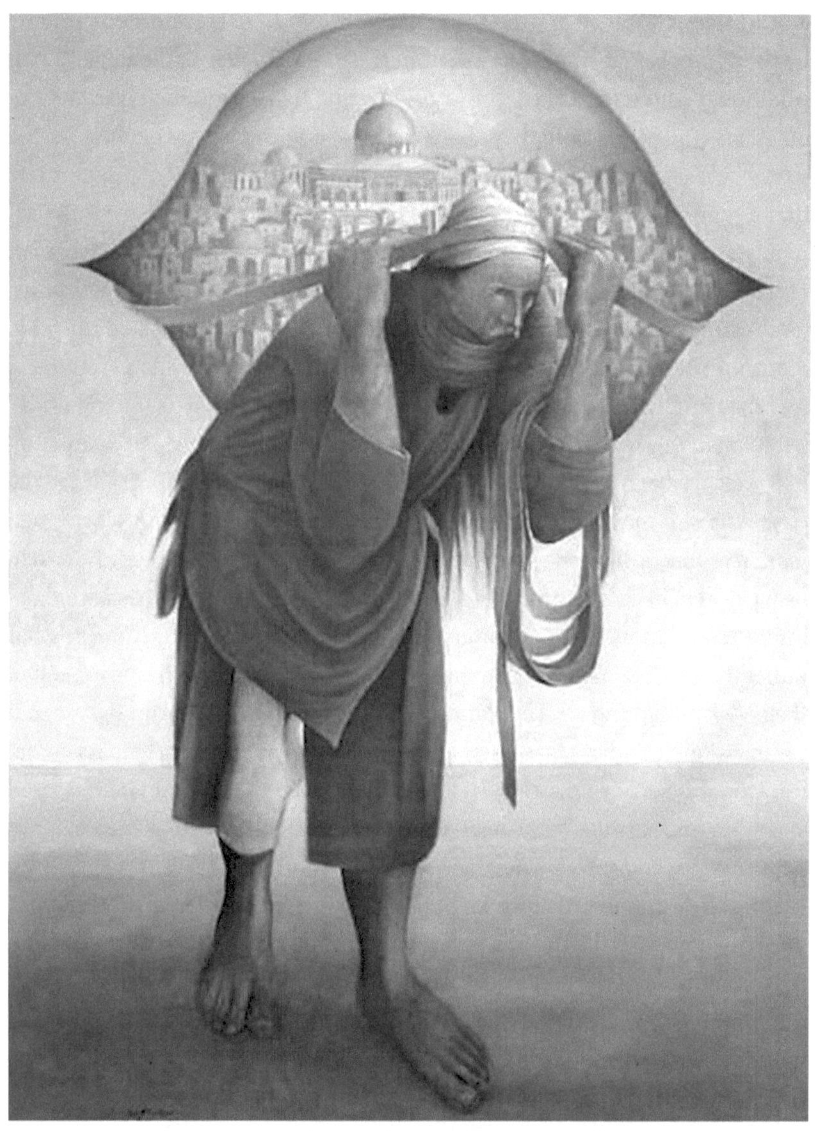

FIGURE 1. Suleiman Mansour. *Jamal al Mahamel*. 1973. Private collection.

Palestinian resistance and *sumud* (steadfastness) were represented not only by the symbols and tropes they used in their works, such as the depiction of traditional embroidery, the land, Jerusalem, the figure of the refugee, and the olive tree (fig. 1). Nor were they about the aesthetic and formal qualities of the work.[17] The resistant dimension of their work, they explained, lay just as much in the production process in which it was embedded as it did in what the art represented. This process held fundamental collective resistance as a form of protest against Israel, a phenomenon that, according to many Palestinians, was destroyed by the effects of the Oslo peace process. Through laughter-filled morning, the two artists described in detail the haphazard and unsystematic way they produced art before "the NGOs arrived." Their most well-known contribution in this regard was during the first Intifadah against Israeli occupation (1987–1993) when Mansour, Anani, and other artists like Vera Tamari formed the New Vision art movement in response to the 1987 popular call to boycott Israeli market products. Instead of buying Israeli art supplies, the collective resorted to using local materials like mud and henna in their work. But the artists were not interested in discussing that famous chapter in their career that morning but rather the unsystematic and haphazard process that defined the movement of their work until the 1990s. They humorously spoke to me of lost paintings, unpaid commissions, unattended workshop and exhibition invites from embassies and festivals abroad, to works and artists randomly being held up and interrogated at borders and customs in the region and the world whenever they tried to move paintings, or themselves, from one location to another. [18]

Most Palestinian artists undoubtedly still suffer from a denial of freedom of movement imposed by the Israeli Occupation and compounded by the exploitative conditions of the precarious neoliberal art market. But what is markedly different today and what I believe Anani and Mansour were commenting on that day is the sheer volume of supporting liberal-minded institutions and individuals that although not able to ameliorate the bureaucratic hurdles of border passages are nonetheless providing the structural framework for a professionalization of the field of art production, global circulation and representation.. They are accomplishing this not only through exhibitions but also through publications, artist residencies, and the funding of international travel. For older artists like Anani and Mansour, the structure of support is not the problem, as many aspects of it are pivotal in getting Palestinian art the exposure it needs and artists the means to survive in a precarious context. Rather, the problem lies in the depoliticizing effect that the facilitation of the art scene has had on many young middle-class artists because it demands they become part of a professionalized career structure shaped by global market forces that dictate the aesthetical form and content of work as well as the means the artists use to promote their work and connect to their audiences. As Mansour reflected to me that early summer morning in 2018:

> I am glad that I didn't have the chance to exhibit at the MOMA when I was starting out because had I known that I might have that possibility as a young artist I might not have cared to develop my own style, I would have always in the back of my head seen MOMA as the ultimate achievement of my career.

To explain, the regional reformulations that came with the Oslo Accords were the initial and primary factor for the new standing of the NGO under the civil society umbrella as the vanguard of revolutionary change. The Oslo agreement signaled the willingness of representatives of the Palestinian resistance—and, after them, of a majority of Arab states—to cease armed resistance against Israel in favor of diplomatic efforts and to sideline important segments of nationalist, leftist, and pan-Arab intelligentsia. Even though they were not entirely alone, the Islamists found themselves occupying the legacy of the first generation of Palestine's "secular" nationalists. In Palestine, as well as in Lebanon and Jordan, and with the support of both religious and secular segments of the population, the Islamists spearheaded criticism against the perceived capitulations of the Oslo peace agreement and, even more, a rejection of normalizing relations with Israel (Burgat 2003: 26). This politics of peace and the anti-normalization mobilization that it provoked was especially evident in Jordan, where the public mounted pressure through political campaigns pressuring the regime into withdrawing from the Jordan-Israel Wadi Araba Peace Treaty signed on October 1994. The Islamic Resistance Movement (Hamas) partly succeeded the PLO, and in Lebanon, Hezbollah placed itself on the front lines of armed struggle, first against the continued Israeli occupation of the southern part of the country and then after the liberation of the South and the withdrawal of the occupying Israeli Army in 2000, as Israel continued to be a regional force to reckon with. In this context, internationally funded, non-faith-based Arab NGOs took on particularly pivotal roles as mediators and facilitators between funders, themselves, and faith-based civil society organizations (Yom 2005: 18–19).

Since the early 1990s, civil society assistance in the form of aid to NGOs has constituted the linchpin of what is known as "international MENA (Middle East and North Africa) democracy promotion efforts." The United Nations Development Program (UNDP) emphasizes civil society as a necessary force in advocating human development and fostering transparent political governance (UNDP 2003: 31); the World Bank and European Commission offer a wide array of international aid to promote civil society, often circumventing governments and transferring funds directly to designated local partners; and US foundations like the Ford Foundation and the National Endowment for Democracy run numerous grant competitions for Arab NGOs, providing them with funds to attend transnational conferences, training workshops, and exchange programs. Much of the programming initially focused on the domains of gender, micro-credit programs, conflict resolution, children's rights, and later good governance and youth participation. Traditionally, these categories were associated with international development programming, before expanding into the field of cultural production. Perceived as simultaneously critical of the state and committed to society's development, they were understood to simultaneously endorse development and democracy.[19]

At the same time, the crescendo of neoliberal values concomitant to the transformations described above has prompted many to question the depoliticizing effects of the "NGO-ization" of society and the professionalization of activism as a clear manifestation of social change as constituted in the new global order.[20] In the Arab Eastern Mediterranean region, there is ample evidence from the cases of Palestine and Egypt (and increasingly Lebanon and Jordan) to illustrate that under the impact of donors' criteria and priorities, grassroots initiatives evolved into professional and often elite organizations, redesigning their projects to complement the new international development agenda. In many cases, they shifted from grassroots programming to professionalized advocacy (Hammami 1995).[21] Arturo Escobar was the first to describe this process as the "professionalization" of development, where it became possible "to remove all problems from the political and cultural realms and to recast them in terms of the apparently more neutral realm of science" (2011: 45). "Professionalization" defined funders' priorities in the early 2000s. Its constantly changing categories, yet concrete manifestations, are highlighted in the below statement by the director of one arts and culture organization in Beirut:

> First, they told us that they wanted us to "network" and we began to work around this idea, forging partnerships with others in the region and elsewhere, hopping on flights to France and Egypt to learn how to run our own organizations back home. Then they changed their mind and decided what we needed was "capacity building," then there was the frenzy of "institutionalization" which we attended to by setting up nominal boards and announcing positions etc., and now, finally we have arrived at art "spaces" or "informal" art schools. If you have not yet noticed, [they are] the hottest thing in town right now.[22]

The director of the NGO explained that these constantly changing demands pushed the organization to implement what are essentially wide thematic areas regarded as essential by the funder. Instead of empowering the local actors, as international development discourses often claim, the organization must rely on a set of global standards that might not fulfill its vision or domestic needs as it gets caught up in the day-to-day bureaucracy of running a donor-funded organization. The manager of one of Amman's most novel and experimental theater performance spaces described funders' priorities as more utilitarian than the needs of local actors, which tended to concern aesthetics and their relationship to the community and neighborhood in which they were located, rather than the benefits that the process might have for the functioning of the organization: "'transparency,' 'sustainability,' 'accountability,' 'gender equality,' you kind of lose 'the art' right there, and I am not sure if that is intentional or not, if you see what I mean."[23]

In relation to the ways in which "professionalization" in cultural organizations in Lebanon and the wider region manifested, a curator and writer who worked closely with nongovernmental and nonprofit organizations associated with the postwar contemporary art scene in Beirut, shared what she observed about the field in the years between the late 1990s and the early 2000s:

> I believe these cultural organizations have evolved into profoundly professionalized ones. Writing a grant proposal has become very professionalized. The

> impact of funding has taught us to write grants; it used to be the purview of academia. We learned how to write grants. This means that you can now explain your project in four sentences. This means determining the mission statement of your organization. This is all very necessary in a process of selection.[24]

The curator and writer's apt observations about what she saw unfolding highlight what many cultural actors view as the benefits that the transnationalization of arts production brings. Relevantly, Partha Chatterjee's notion of "political society" (2004: 137) highlights the space within which the majority of the populations of the Global South actually negotiate their agency, and thereby emphasize their differences from the "professionalized" civil society referred to here—a space, he argues, that is historically occupied by elites in postcolonial settings. Reinforcing Chatterjee's claims, one cultural actor who opened one of the first artist-run gallery art spaces in Ramallah—with funding from the Ford Foundation's Triangle Arts Trust—explained, "I needed to write my proposal in English so I had to get a proposal writer to write my ideas for me because my English is not so good. I then had a friend who edited what I never wrote anyway . . . ! It worked for me. But I keep thinking, how many other projects and people and ideas are [funders] marginalizing?"[25]

What is articulated here, and what was reiterated to me by artists in both Beirut and Amman, is an awareness of the kind of social mobilization proposed by funders that arguably operates within a framework of exclusionary politics and demands basic proficiency in the English language and a cultural capital that would enable upward mobility in an international context. This results in what the older-generation cultural critics I spoke with criticized as "*tafreez al nukhab*" or a (re)allocation of elites, whereby new cultural elites with transnational capital replace the old guard of cultural patrons, the state, and its attendant ministries.[26]

In 2005, I attended a round-table discussion in Beirut between some of the most prominent "alternative" cultural organizations in the region, along with their international funders.[27] These included representatives from the Ford Foundation, the Heinrich Boll Foundation, and the Prince Claus Fund—organizations that had by that point already become prominent players in the field. Interestingly, the heated debate that ensued after each presentation was mired within the boundaries that normally define discussions concerning the politics of externally funded cultural and arts projects in the region that I have discussed above. Consequently, topics discussed in the two-hour panel touched on the frustrating challenges of dealing with a local population suspicious of foreign funding and how this makes for an uncomfortable environment in which the foreign funding body and the recipient organization attempt to function effectively. Also discussed was the way local cultural organizations sometimes felt compelled to work within the broad guidelines set out by the funder, even when these guidelines coincided with the organizations' own visions and ambitions. Most interesting, perhaps, was the way in which representatives of the funding organizations expressed limitations as to what they can or cannot support due to the larger European or US bureaucratic networks and institutions to which they report. Here, mention was made of a contentious Ford Foundation memo, published in part as a consequence of 9/11, that asked its local regional partners to denounce acts of terrorism and association with any groups the US State Department designated as terrorists.[28] Even the regional coordinator did not personally agree to issuing such a memo. The Ford representative on the panel argued that aligning with the memo could be considered a subversive act cloaked in the language of bureaucratic procedure. The point he was trying to make was to get on, do the work, and produce culture, rather than remain caught up in conversation that pits cultural production and its external supporters as foreign infiltrators, that is, as inauthentic.

Interestingly, none of the issues raised at the event tackled the question of how the infrastructure built under the new international development and democratization paradigm actually related to either the type of production emerging or broader cultural practices in society. One audience member known for his leftist politics and tireless political activism did ask about links between emerging production and funding. The reply by the panel members quickly debunked any association made, as there were emphatically no conditions regarding either the form or content of the production. The speakers were not wrong; there really never were any direct conditions that came with the provision of cultural funding to a specific aesthetical form of art. Rather the implicit conditions, when they did come, and they always did, could be seen in the type of local art partner chosen by funders and the broad parameters for topics of choice, such as "gender," "sexuality," and "multiculturalism," which may then indirectly shape the content of art. Class politics in Ramallah, Amman, and Beirut meant that the liberal secular bourgeoisie who predominantly make up the transnationally connected contemporary arts and culture scene focused on in this book do not generally interact with Islamic civil society and its social movements outside of formal politics. Excluding an entire segment of the population through international funding stipulations indicates that boundaries are already set out that are not intended to be crossed. Part of what makes these conditions on the "type" of "partner" preferred problematic is that most of the artists who graduated from the local to the international were already situated within transnational networks, which in some sense indicated their belonging or affiliation to a certain group or class of society: the secular, more affluent, well-connected, well-educated citizens with English language proficiency and the ability to travel outside the region. Whatever the generally perceived class affiliation may connote here, inherent is its inescapable assumption of a certain level of cultural and social capital. In bifurcated societies where class largely determines culture and access to information, such attributes initially placed some artists and their supporting organizations/initiatives in a position to gain from the global art market's new focus on Lebanon's contemporary artistic production. Against this background, it is understandable how proficiency in English—what has been studied as neoliberalism's preferred language (Holborow 2015)—and the enabling of international travel for artists to attend workshops, establish residencies, and exhibit their works internationally can be seen to constitute the very foundation of the changes taking place.

The series of interviews I carried out with funders and local NGOs all made clear just how intrinsic travel and exchange are for their programs.[29] Travel is relevant here both in the metaphorical and real senses of border crossings, dislocations, and exilic experiences. The travel of ideas however, like the travel of the actors who carry them, is never unfettered. Members of the contemporary art world might regard themselves as active agents in a truly "global" art industry and art discourse, perceptions that are based in large part on dynamics that have, since the end of the Cold War, permitted artists from formerly peripheral areas to appear center stage in events executed in major Western art capitals. Yet scholars like Chin Tao Wu (2009) have argued that globalization theorists like Arjun Appadurai (1996), who give credence to such perceptions, have unproblematically construed the global as a neutral or truly open space. Keeping in mind James Clifford's proposition (1997) that travel is where modern culture reveals itself in the most nuanced ways, I propose rethinking cultural practices in contemporary art within a framework that appreciates the absolute necessity of travel and exchange without overemphasising travel's indubitably emancipatory potential. When I return to this point in part 2, it becomes clearer that transnational flows of travel and exhibition, while necessary and fruitful, have not been able to overcome the structural challenges of a global art world defined by the global inequalities that shape it.

The difficulties that nonprofit and nongovernmental arts organizations in the region face conglomerate around various structural challenges that global cultural funding has not been able to tackle. Arguably, such funding has exacerbated the rift between a rooted local politics and a conceptual global universal politics. The shrinking of the traditional middle class, which has incorporated within it the traditional consumers of culture in much of the Arab Eastern Mediterranean, is an important factor to consider (Laïdi-Hanieh 2008). Compounded by the prevalence of illiteracy, this shrinkage has been more generally affected by eroding national educational systems, which have historically provided inadequate education in the arts, and more recently in understandings of current practices of cultural and artistic productions.[30] Such educational deficiencies have led to a situation whereby local audiences and potential clients of cultural NGOs may feel intimidated and sometimes even hostile to contemporary—as opposed to more traditional—understandings of what cultural production is supposed to look, feel, or sound like.[31]

As a result, and as expressed during various interviews, contemporary artists may feel more attuned to their global audiences than the local ones, which they perceive as being too bound up with ideological discourses to understand art for the sake of art. Relatively small audiences attend events that funders and the promotional organizations consider "high culture," and the minuteness of this elite occurs not just in Lebanon but also in other countries of the region. This audience is primarily comprised of expatriates and bilingual or trilingual Western-educated persons from middle- to upper-income brackets. However, as I was reminded by several artists I interviewed, contemporary art events in the capitals of Europe such as Paris, London, Berlin, or Amsterdam also do not represent their societies. Statements such as "contemporary art is not for everyone," "culture is essentially a 'trickle-down effect,'" and "contemporary art has a privileged standing" were made intermittently by the people I interviewed, including prominent international cultural supporters, artists, and representatives of contemporary arts organizations in receipt of international funds. They essentially used these justifications to explain the challenges they face in bridging the gap between themselves and local audiences. Such statements contradict the official discourse of some of the most important funders of cultural production. The Ford Foundation (2008), for instance, claimed to "create new opportunities for cultural and artistic expression, *especially among the poor and marginalized*" (my emphasis).

ON "ALTERNATIVE" ART AND THE MARKET

In 2007 and 2008, global auction houses Sotheby's and Christie's began to discover Arab contemporary art. As Mary Anne DeVlieg notes in a 2008 article, "Not only Swiss banks, art auction houses, wealthy art collectors and galleries have discovered a new market, but governments too." But after next describing a contemporary traveling art exhibition, *Arab Artists in Italy and the Mediterranean*, DeVlieg asks: "How is it that Egypt, a country which physically punishes homosexuality as illegal is proud to host a contemporary art exhibition?" She hints that "political chic" might explain the phenomenon.

Undoubtedly DeVlieg had good reason to suspect such a cause, especially given her position at the time, secretary general of the International Network for Contemporary Performing Arts (now IETM). Notably, the *Arab Artists* exhibit used the more traditional mediums of painting and sculpture to demonstrate how Italian artists have historically influenced those from the Arab Mediterranean. The show also overtly tied to European and, specifically, Italian diplomatic efforts in the region—often perceived as independent and non-ideological by their partners and therefore easily dismissed as pawns in the hands of politicians in both Italy and the Arab Mediterranean countries on which it focuses.

The "discovery" of high-end Arab contemporary art during this period, however, largely ignored the simultaneously emerging but less-marketable type, which DeVlieg (2008) wrote "interrogates rather than celebrates." Her article draws a clear boundary between the old (high-end art) and the new (interrogative art), thus establishing what type of art and which processes deserve support.

The specific art that DeVlieg (2008) believes is worth supporting does not "so easily reach the Google heights proposed by young experimental, interdisciplinary artists, artists for whom the prefix 're' is central: re-locating, repositioning, re-configuring, reflecting, re-presenting." Hence, the description of this "other" simultaneously unfolding art phenomenon, which experiments with postmodern literally and visual techniques of "re" doing, summarizes the complex, recent dynamic of interested foreign funders. These funders increasingly invest in what they deem "alternative" contemporary cultural production in the Arab region. The prevalent understanding among policymakers and global cultural funders that nonmarketable contemporary art operates necessarily to engage its "audiences" is not palpable. In her analysis, DeVlieg (2008) dichotomizes the two art worlds by romanticizing one at the expense of another. In her appeal to the EU to continue supporting this booming infrastructure, which indeed it has, DeVlieg essentializes what this so-called alternative art production.

The following statement by a Beirut-based art critic and journalist was a typical representation in the first decade of millennium of the phenomenon under discussion. It shows, too, how a discourse of an alternative and independent art scene was constructed and perpetuated by different cultural players in the field, not only the funders:

> Beirut is home to one of the most active and dynamic contemporary art scenes in the region. The engine of that scene is a self-organising group of artists' collectives and independent non-profit associations that have, over the past decade, constructed an *alternative* infrastructure for the making and exhibiting, as well as the documenting and archiving, of contemporary art practices. . . . The contemporary art scene in Beirut has taken shape at a time when similarly *independent, alternative* scenes have emerged in cities such as Cairo, Alexandria, Istanbul and Amman. (Wilson-Goldie 2009b; my emphasis)

Implicit in this kind of essentialism is the understanding that supposedly independent processes of production and the counterhegemonic works they give rise to could potentially represent subversiveness and dissidence in the face of established orders regionally and internationally. Such understanding discounts the possibility of producing and promoting artwork for reasons other than explicit reflexivity and discourse that disrupts established norms within already alternative spaces. The questions of "subversive to whom" and "countercultural to what" abound when contextualized locally, as illustrated in chapters 3, 4, and 5, through my conversations and exchanges with artists, critics, observers, and intellectuals within Lebanon. Finally, referring to such initiatives as "independent" prompts the question of "independent from whom?" and thereby diffuses the implications associated with their history as being part of larger political developments in the region since the aftermath of the Cold War, after 9/11, and then in 2005 when funders showed even more intense interest in Lebanon. The latter gives rise to issues concerning the possibility of funders in the region actually supporting "art" with the stated mandate of social engineering rather than considering the intricacies involved in the evolving role of art simply for art's sake in smaller cities operating on the margins of the global art world.

The burgeoning market for Arab art, particularly epitomized in the Emirates' growing role as cultural center for the Arab world, alongside Qatar, has, if anything, blurred the boundary between art that is made solely to sell and art produced to engage in a broader critical discourse on society, politics, and its own role with respect to each—in other words, what DeVleig refers to as "alternative." First, contemporary artists based in culturally thriving cities such as Beirut, Cairo, Damascus, and Tehran increasingly rely on cities such as Abu-Dhabi, Dubai, Sharjah, and Doha as a commercial window to the international art scene, even though how they describe this experience ranges from outright excitement to overt contempt to embarrassed reluctance to succumb to the Emirates' and the Gulf's role in replacing the old cultural capitals of Beirut, Baghdad, and Cairo. Yet even the most cynically minded artists recognize the wider range of international exposure these emerging cities give them compared to the days when they had to seek grants and exhibition invites from the US and Europe.

DeVlieg indicates that the less-marketable scene is not party to the "political chic" that explains the ability of certain governments, including some with records of human rights abuses, to hold contemporary art shows. One such art show is the Sharjah Biennial, a noncommercial initiative committed to exhibiting artwork without regard for market value and with an emphasis on art as process and critical discourse. There, contemporary "other" artists exhibit, collaborate, and win awards in settings where fundamental human rights violations occur. Worth mentioning here is the 10th Sharjah Biennial, *Plot for a Biennial*, that opened in the midst of the regional turmoil of the 2011 Arab uprisings. During this period, the UAE was involved in fulfilling a request made to the Gulf Cooperation Council by Bahrain's Sunni rulers to send in troops to participate in the crackdown on the majority Shia population's protest against their government's repressive regime.[32] In so doing, the UAE made clear its zero tolerance position toward the forces of progressive change sweeping across the region. Hence, when the Emirates sent in troops to aid the Bahraini government in violently quelling protesters, most participants in the Biennial looked on and felt powerless to act. During the official opening, artist Ibrahim Quraishi (not an exhibiting artist) attempted to protest, along with a handful of others. On the day of the opening, this small group stood on the red carpet distributing the names of those killed in Bahrain while the UAE's ruler entered the main building. Security forces clamped down on the protesting artists within minutes and hauled them off to a five-hour interrogation by the Sharjah internal security services. But most participants, despite their expressed horror, went on with business as usual, as they discussed works, networked, and accepted awards over celebratory gala dinners from Sheikh Sultan Bin Mohammed Al Qasimi, member of the UAE Supreme Council and ruler of Sharjah. For many of the artists, drawing up petitions, declaring walkouts, and refusing awards seemingly had no place in the space in which they were invited as guests of the sheikh.[33]

Interestingly, what ultimately triggered a reaction from some members of the global art world was not the protest and the subsequent silencing of it but the April 6 decision by the ruler of Sharjah, Sultan Bin Mohammad Al Qasimi, to summarily dismiss Jack Persekian, the then Palestinian director of the Sharjah Art Foundation and art director of the Sharjah Biennial, over what he deemed an offensive work by Algerian artist Mohammad Benfodil (Simpson 2011a, 2011b). Benfodil's work, *Maportaliche/It Has No Importance*, consisted of an installation of mannequins in football uniforms emblazoned with Arabic phrases that were deemed blasphemous (fig. 2). In the piece, two teams of mannequins sat in a public space in Sharjah's heritage area. The first team wore white shirts imprinted with the artist's own literary texts. Included in the prints was a monologue from Benfodil's play *Les Borgnes*, which takes place in a mental institution and recounts a young woman's experience of kidnap and

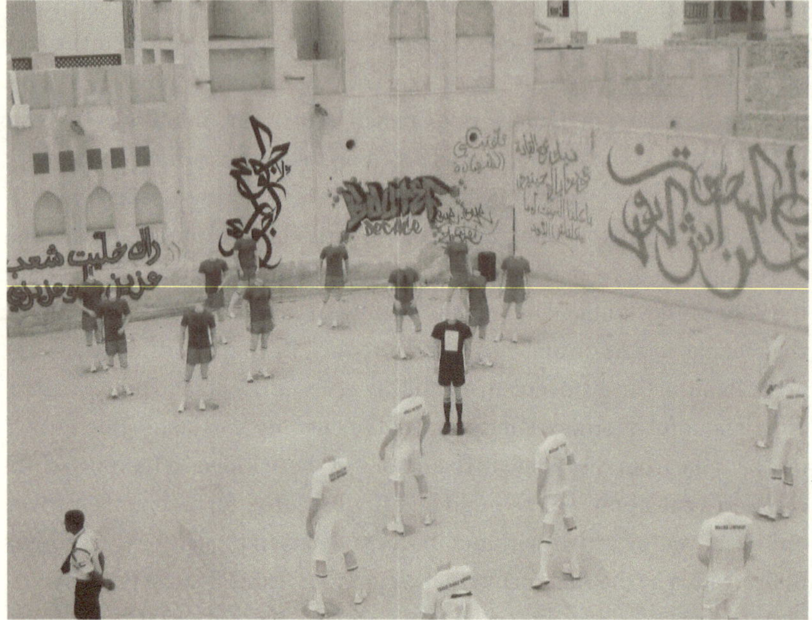

FIGURE 2. Mohammad Benfodil. *Maportaliche/It Has No Importance*. 2011. Mixed-media installation. Courtesy of the artist.

rape during the Algerian civil war of the 1990s. The second team wore green and red gear—the Algerian flag's colors—with texts borrowed from Algerian pop culture: jokes, recipes, proverbs, and folk songs. In the sound part of the installation, the artist used recent recordings of protests that took place in Algeria as part of the Arab uprisings, which had begun that winter (Paynter 2011). According to Benfodil, it was the sound part of the installation, which gives the effect of an actual revolt taking place in Sharjah, and the graffiti of slogans referencing the protests that took place in Tunisia and Egypt that mostly contributed to the decision to censor his work.[34]

The move to dismiss Persekian inevitably led to heated discussions and reflections from within the global art world about censorship in the UAE. Persekian told the UAE paper the *National*: "It was very foolish of me, I had not looked at it [the piece] carefully because I couldn't. There were so many works" (Simpson 2011a). In defense of Persekian, members of the Biennial curatorial team distributed a petition, an act that some mocked but others critically reflected on, especially considering his undefiant and apologetic statement in the *National*.[35] Those who reflected in conversation with me or later in writing considered the denigration of the very act of resistance and its place in a longer genealogy of coopting artists and intellectuals by Arab regimes.[36] Others engaged with the incident from the purview of institutional critique in art, asking that the art community deal with the Emirates like any other Western government that employs human rights abuses while patronizing art that is critical and progressive (Saadawi 2011), while others still read the incident through the lens of the cultural politics of exhibiting art during revolutionary times in authoritarian settings (Tripp 2013). This author contributed a piece to the brewing debate by interrogating the larger political dynamics underlying the Biennial's self-positioning as an alternative venue for art practice in the region (H. Toukan 2011).

In the eyes of cynics, the Sharjah Biennial falls far short of its marketing assertions that it is an open space for critical dialogue where regional cultural practices are put on the global art map. In their view, it remains an autocratic regime's diplomatic attempt to market a humane face to the world. By focusing on national identity, societal development, and international understanding in ways that serve its geopolitical interests, the Biennial's intentions differ from those of global culture funders only in its identitarian focus. In recent years, Gulf states, but especially the Emirate of Sharjah in the UAE, have been credited with taking the initiative to de-Westernize and decolonize Arab representations by delinking them from their original source: Western museums and their historic relationship to the nation state in the time of empire (Mirgani 2017; Mignolo 2013b: 11–12; Dabashi 2017). Likewise, with the development of its programming and self-positioning as an alternative platform for art and knowledge production, the Sharjah Biennial has gradually taken the lead in promoting the idea that modernism everywhere was part of the same tangled knot, which unraveled in different ways and provoked different forms of engagement simultaneously around the world. Through its March Meeting organized by the Sharjah Art Foundation, which began in 2008, the Sharjah Biennial has also proactively engaged the nonprofit and nongovernmental sectors, in not only the UAE but also the region and internationally. Most arts NGOs, artist collectives, art spaces, and more established institutions diligently attend the annual meeting for a chance to network and speak about new ideas and developments in the region and outside of it. For example, Palestinian artist Khaled Hourani's 2011 *Picasso in Palestine* project, which I delve into in chapter 6, was first publicly introduced and discussed at the 2010 Sharjah March Meeting.

Hence, for the less cynical, including a large cross-section of artists in the region today with the accessibility and social mobility needed to engage with a significant sample of the global art world's institutions, curators, and critics, the city of Sharjah provides the platform, space, and money needed to forge a new progressive space for artists, supported in these efforts by groups such as the Sharjah Art Foundation and, more recently, the Barjeel Arts Foundation, an independent foundation established by businessman and political commentator Sultan Sooud Al-Qassemi to preserve and exhibit his personal art collection. Together, these initiatives are seen as creating a site for engaging with the most pressing social and political concerns of the day by pushing forth the role of "the intellectual, the critic and the avant-garde," in Persekian's words about Sharjah specifically (Davidson 2011).[37] This has rendered Sharjah to become the focal point and marker of success for many young artists understood by those writing about them to be producing critical, urgent, and timely work. My task in this chapter is to go beyond the assumption that contemporary art is counterhegemonic because it is an "other" form of art that has developed contra the state, collective nationalist rhetoric, and oppressive religious dogma. I ask, then, what the significance is of the movers and shakers of the status quo in the region showcasing work and debating its critical relevance in the UAE?

To my thinking, what gets elided in the optimistic view of the rise of the Gulf as the cultural center of the region is the provenance of capital for art development there, to what end it is being developed (Shannon 2012), and the abuse of migrant labor it is known to involve.[38] For some of the Gulf states, the museum boom serves as a support for a constructed national narrative while aiding the political instruments of the state (Al Ragam 2014: 665). This investment in a national heritage defined by these countries' Gulf and Arab identity, Muslim heritage, and regional strength (especially in the case of the larger states of the UAE and Saudi Arabia) has inflected the thinking of cultural actors in the region around questions of identity and representation.

As Partha Chatterjee (1993) and the Subaltern Studies Group more broadly have recognized, delineating the boundaries between nationalism as a political movement and nationalism as a cultural construct helps us to see how a modern project that is nevertheless not Western can be fashioned out of such competing claims. As a political movement, nationalism confronts imperialism directly. As a cultural construct, it prompts the postcolonial to carve out an autonomous space where subjectivities may be formed. The entire Gulf art scene, despite its diversity, is regarded by many members of the Arab world's cultural milieu as local and regional. In interviews, this identity was posited in contradistinction to the "foreignness" of global cultural funding that comes from mostly Western aid agencies, Western governments and international NGOs; often I was reminded that the Gulf is, for all its flaws, at least Arab. Hence contemporary artists criticized for their "inauthenticity" can find in the Gulf a shelter from such accusations. This emphasis on the identity of the arts funder shifts the framework in which cultural actors are viewed from one of capital and class to one of identity politics. This quintessential postmodern manifestation conceals the workings of power under neoliberalism.

The changing role of Gulf countries such as the Emirates, Qatar, and even Saudi Arabia as art centers, markets, and supporters of experimental practices on an international platform reflects and culminates the politically motivated space that has been developing in between the new markets, on the one hand, and the civil society formula as the conduit for international cultural diplomacy and soft power, on the other. Owing in part to their openness to trade and commerce in the arts, Dubai and other Gulf cities were regarded by funders in the first decade of the millennium as part of the solution to the region's "dismal" record on human rights and democracy (Roberto Cimetta Fund and Fondation René Seydoux 2006). They are places where "the sun rises," alluding to their unrestrained liberal economies, aggressive approaches on societal development, and self-appointed positions as centers for arts of the Arab world (Roberto Cimetta Fund and Fondation René Seydoux 2006). In such a context, advancing (under the civil society project) the establishment of cultural nonprofits and NGOs and their associated artists to enable the emergence of a specific kind of avant-garde and "other" scene becomes a regional enterprise. If seen through the role of globally funded local cultural mediators focusing on communication, arts education, and artistic training, the opportunity to exhibit and sell artwork in Dubai (and elsewhere) inextricably ties one project to another. Specifically, it ties the nonprofit and nongovernmental scene to the global financial and cultural markets.

Sangeeta Kamat (2004) argues that nongovernmental and nonprofit civil society organizations do not always play the innocent, altruistic role that nonstate actors are often perceived to; rather, they aim to rework democracy in ways that coalesce with global capitalist interests, prime among them a "new citizen culture" that advances an active and dynamic civil society in which all citizens are encouraged to seize the opportunities of the global economy. This perceived innocence that Kamat alludes to relates to a theoretical body of work that emphasizes civil society's space as a nongovernmental, noneconomic base for democratic social interaction and social resistance, as opposed to Gramscian understandings of it as being part of capitalist expansion (Zubaida 2010). Kamat's point elucidates the links between the various nodes at play in the rise of contemporary art as well as other forms of cultural production in the last ten years. These nodes are comprised of an interplay between a simultaneous growth of newly formed cultural nonprofits and NGOs working under the larger umbrella of internationally funded civil society and democratization efforts, the philosophy of cultural diplomacy, and the rush to the Emirates' art market, including the bandwagon of "alternative" spaces and production in other Arab countries, which international curators, critics, and arts journalists have jumped on.[39]

Do developments in the visual arts scene, then, result from a teleological vision of a progression of events, beginning with civil society and ending with the global market? Or have they progressed more haphazardly, opening the way for the visual arts to enter into the global circuit of both the art market and global art discourse? The progression on all fronts probably occurred concurrently and in two-way traffic. Regional artists engaged the global aesthetics and discourses while globally oriented neoliberal funding institutions and curators scoured the region in search of art to present abroad and to bring to their home contexts. The various processes are thus inseparable. In 2002, Lebanese artist Akram Zaatari claimed that for the Beirut postwar art scene, "demand does not dictate production" (Wright 2002: 15). Yet it is not because of the lack of an existing local contemporary art market in Amman, Beirut, and Ramallah that the cultural logic of global capitalism would necessarily bypass them. In his comment, Zaatari discounts the developments I describe here, which had implications for the ways in which, by 2002, his work, as well as some of his contemporaries', was modulated on exhibition outside of Lebanon.

In the neoliberal world, the practices, institutions, and role of contemporary art have been accommodated to the requirements of state and corporate power (Stallabras 2004: chap. 2). But in Ramallah, Beirut, and Amman, neither the established institutions nor the market or conventions of contemporary art have mainstreamed what Stallabras posits as art's core function: "propagandist of neoliberal value" (72). Interestingly, the art world's neoliberal turn could be detected first in those cities from the way in which it tied itself to international funding for cultural production in the nonprofit sector and embedded itself within a process of producing and international exhibiting that valorizes culture within the larger remit of "cultural policy"—a professionalized form of art where, some have argued, politics becomes the art of display (Leslie 2006), in the same way that artists Anani and Mansour expressed in the conversation described in a preceding section.

If the economic and political expressions of neoliberalism worldwide manifest along intensifying inequalities in response to deregulation and privatization in a multicultural world, then its cultural expression must be the twofold phenomena of unrestrained consumerism paralleled with postmodern rationale and expressionism. On another, more "regional" level, it can be argued that the Emirates' growing role as the region's cultural center, where "other" art scenes from Lebanon, Jordan, Palestine, and elsewhere converge, embodies this neoliberal system of values. It is precisely the logic that undergirds these values and the structural foundation that binds civil society, the art market, and the "alterative" art scene that is concealed in the fixation on authenticity versus the modern that opened this chapter. In the following chapter, and in keeping the background I describe here in mind, I look at how two generations have been grappling with the fundamental changes in the role and function of art in society.

Chapter 3

THE DISSONANCE OF DISSENT

Art and Artists after 1990

IN 2010, A FRIEND OF THE ARTIST MARWA ARSANIOS GAVE HER A pile of his father's collection of back issues of the 1950s' and 1960s' state-owned Egyptian cultural magazine *Al-Hilal*. The magazine was founded in 1892 by Jurji Zaydan, the well-known Nahda-era writer and intellectual. Printed in Egypt, the journal was long Nasserist in outlook and pan-Arab in scope. The content of the issues that Arsanios received advocated a secularism aimed at both incorporating Islamic elements of society and promoting socialist ideals. Included were industrialization, social housing, utopian urbanization, and an Arab feminism, which emphasized the role women, peasants, and workers might play in the attainment of each ideal. For Arsanios, this was an opportune moment to reread the region's history through one influential magazine's changing aesthetical form and intellectual output, especially in regard to the role of women (fig. 3).[1] Supporting her view was a body of work steeped in the rereading of the region's modern history, especially its experiments with postcolonial modernization in the twentieth century through its cultural memorabilia and its public's reading rituals.

She decided that same year to invite well-known public intellectuals and writers from the 1967 generation of intellectuals and writers known for their leftist past to reread the magazines alongside her and her generational cohort of writers, artists, filmmakers, and other interested members of the public.[2]

Arsanios's invitation list included controversial journalist and critic Hazem Saghieh, the well-known liberal Shia cleric Hani Fahes, the scholar and writer Dalal Al-Bizri, and the writer and journalist Hassan Daoud, all of whom were once avid readers of the magazine.[3] The invitees were asked to rethink the content of the magazine articles they chose to reflect on.[4] This series of intergenerational, open discussions, titled *al-Hilal: On Reading*, occurred in the space that Arsanios and a former collaborator (and her cousin), the writer Mirene Arsanios, had acquired for the research art collective, 98weeks.[5] For the artist, the series started a conversation between two generations on the visual and textual role of aesthetics in shaping a nation's identity and politics. In retrospect, it attempted to grapple with some of the region's biggest challenges on what turned out to be the eve of the Arab revolutions of 2011–2012 and the momentous events that soon followed.

The project emphasized the practice of scrutinizing reading, writing, and publishing, and their relationships to the public in the region's modern history of postcolonial nation building and anti-colonialism. In a sense, so much of *al-Hilal*'s content seemed to be sardonically commenting on the long-gone promises of regional liberation, unification, and independence that came with the heady days of Arabism's finest revolutionary moment in the 1950s and 1960s. According to Arsanios, the conversations, what she called collective

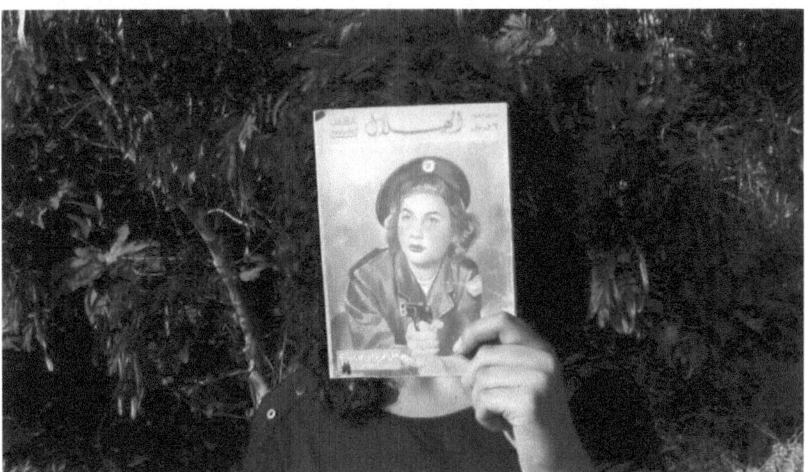

FIGURE 3. Marwa Arsanios. *Have You Ever Killed a Bear? Or Becoming Jamila, 2013–2014. 2014.* Video, color, sound; 28 min. Courtesy of the artist.

reading exercises, were often tense and peppered with fierce debates, defensiveness, and misunderstandings between the two generations on how to read that time period. In conversation with her some years later in Berlin, she reflected openly with me about the project. As the conversations progressed, she shared, other realizations set in. Above all, there was the very real and visceral disappointment that the 1967 generation felt in the postcolonial nation-state project as visualized in *Al-Hilal* and the subsequent loss of all of Palestine in the wake of the *Naksa* (the day of the setback), which marked the loss of the rest of historical Palestine to Israel in the Six Day War of 1967. They interpreted the developments after the shock of 1967 as countering their own political and personal journeys of collective liberation from colonialism, which they had worked so hard to attain. The extent of this disenchantment countered Arsanios's initial hope that a more nuanced and in particular feminist reading of political resistance in the region's recent history —one that considers the diverse subjectivities, identities, representations, and cultural creativity—might help to articulate a new understanding of emancipation in the contemporary moment. She imagined this nuanced joint rereading of history would be an opportunity to reorient the past so that a conversation between generations about the nature of resistance and revolutionary change might evolve. She hoped not for a reconciliation of political values but a coming-together in their joint oppositional attitudes to the neoliberal and authoritarian state. Alas, Arsanios conceded that her project would not bring the conversation—or conclusions—that she had hoped for. Something unimaginable at the start of her project had arisen. The Arab uprisings that had exploded at the end of year put in stark reality the changed nature of resistance in the region (Chalcraft 2016) and, in a sense, imposed on the 1967 generation this transformed reality: different methods of civil resistance, leadership roles, and aims of popular movements.[6]

Listening to Arsanios speak about the initial stage of these works, inspired by the *Al-Hilal* conversations, reconfirmed how much the 1967 generation—as a whole and as embodied in the Arabic term *al-muthaqaf* (the intellectual), shaped by their historic criticism of the postcolonial Arab nationalist and authoritarian state and their ideal of Marxism and socialism—haunted contemporary debates on what it meant to be counterhegemonic in cultural production at the time of my fieldwork.[7] Their haunting, I observed, continued mostly because they still considered their own revolutionary conscience the yardstick by which to measure their younger counterparts' achievements in the global art circuits.

Explicating the mood after 1967, Palestinian art historian Kamal Boullata acknowledged in 1970 that Palestinian and Arab artists underwent a radical change in how they perceived their societal role as artists and their artworks. The "galleries of Beirut," he wrote, speaking of the period of the late 1960s, "are becoming a body without a soul for the soul was set free in the streets and the camps. . . . If art is the indispensable means of 'merging of the individual with the whole,' then art produced by Palestinians, especially after June 1967, is a first step toward this Union" (1970b: 105).

One interviewee commented on this collective revolutionary mindset about art and its radical potential: "[The 1967 generation] got stuck in the 1960s. They can't come out of it. They did something great then, but they are stuck in it and they have not been able to progress. They are kind of living off of the [revolutionary] legend they created, and they still think that the revolution must start from the same place."[8] When I spoke with her, she directed an internationally funded, influential art house cinema in Beirut, which is now defunct. She was also part of the disillusioned post-1990 generation, which I describe in more detail in the following chapter.

I wondered at the time the director uttered those words what the terms "revolution" and "place" were referencing exactly. Did these terms refer to the Palestinian revolution of anti-colonial resistance against Israel, which dominated the rhetoric and sentiments of the post-1967 critique of the colonial and nominally anti-imperial Arab nationalist regimes and publics, and which saw armed struggle as the central means of fighting back and art as a tool in that endeavor?[9] Or was it a metaphysical revolution that concerns a specific cause as much as it does a collective desire to resist power in all its forms, universally? Or tellingly, was the revolution she referred to an informally organized and subversive one? Was it instead explicit and confrontational, similar to what occurred on the streets between December 2010 and 2013 and again, in 2019 to 2020, in Lebanon, Iraq, and Sudan? The director's apropos statement that "the revolution" cannot start from the same "place" took on precisely *that* political. In other words, and in relation to what I discuss in the introduction about the political and its relationship to politics, her words reflected on how institutions, actions, conflicts, and discourses define how resistance and dissent in the arts will look in any particular era.

The post-1990 generation's perception of the spirit that the theater director conveyed as outmoded and increasingly irrelevant in its reliance on the grand narratives of resistance and revolution was bluntly stated or wheedled into almost every conversation I had when the concept of dissent, arts funding, and art production came up, whether in Amman, Beirut, or Ramallah. It was committed political art influenced by *iltizam* or the legacy it left in the wake of its collapse in 1967—with, in the words of Lebanese journalist and poet Youssef Bazzi in the usual depiction of this generation, "its leftist revolutionary tone" and "immense amount of anger, despair and the call for revolution . . . made in a singing and somewhat naïve tone" (2010: 4)—that was in the process of being deconstructed and then reconstructed though a self-understood nonideological process of making art that prevailed in the three cities of focus from the 1990s onwards.

Yet, as I argue in this chapter, the dichotomy represented and often relayed by the generational "camps," post-1967 and post-1990, occludes the fact that both defined counterhegemonic cultural production in terms of its modernity, cosmopolitanism, and avant-gardism, even if they did so in divergent ways. In this chapter, I grapple with how to make sense of the ongoing commitment of artists in the region to speak truth to power under very changed circumstances and with aesthetically and conceptually altered means of doing so. These changed circumstances are the professionalization and NGO-ization of the art production scenes under the larger umbrella of democratization and civil society funding that is described in the previous two chapters. This chapter focuses on how artworks and the local discourses around their meanings and roles are discursively constructed. In line with Janet Wolff's conception of ideology as always being transmitted in aesthetics under two particular circumstances—the "conditions of production of works of art" and the "existing aesthetic conventions" (Wolff 1981: 61)—I relay these debates on the role of art and its relationship to the political. I am interested in the wider public and the institutional infrastructure to which it belongs, within the contours of the postmodern interdisciplinary artist expressing critique visually and the committed modernist intellectual armed with the legendary power of language in Arab culture.

I focus on two central sites of meaning inspired by and in conversation with Zeina G. Halabi's (2017) uncovering of the intricate ways in which, as she terms it, the Arab intellectual's "prophetic" role in its various publics has been received, probed, and in effect unmade by a number of Arab novelists and cineastes since the early 1990s. I am interested in the ways in which this unmaking has been shaped and enunciated as a form of counterhegemony. These sites are the relationship between visual and textual forms of cultural production, and the concomitant (re)presentation of the committed Arab intellectual as addressed in various works of art undertaken by the post-1990 generation of cultural producers. I ended the preceding chapter by uncovering how nonprofit and nongovernmental sites of art making inextricably tie to the global economy of cultural production. I do not claim the artists with whom I engage in this chapter have benefited from direct donor funding operating within this framework, but I do suggest that they are part of a locus of resistance in cultural production that has been shaped by the very neoliberal forces that it critiques through its dissenting practices. Of course, some production, like *Al-Hilal*, happens without any donor funding, but these sorts of projects don't tend to last—a phenomenon in itself telling of the dynamics of international funding toward arts production that often stipulate a concrete final product that can be exhibited, rather than a process, such as conversations. At the same time, other groups or artists have grown from exhibiting their works at the local sites of their inception with support from global cultural organizations, with the eventual aim of exhibition and circulation in global platforms, like biennales and museums. These examples of "growth" remain part of a discursive structure of cultural production abetted by efforts in cultural diplomacy where expressions of identity and their representations as markers of a democratic and tolerant society are encouraged over "impassioned revolt," as Terry Eagleton has described it when calling for the practice of culture as critique (Eagleton 2016: 10). Ideals of equating identity expression with tolerance have become the norm in the era of postmodern expression and neoliberal economics. Unraveling how and why the post-1990 generation possesses the impulse to requestion, remake, and rearticulate assumptions about the previous generation's self-conceptions and ideals about dissent in cultural production places both generations in a continuous and longer history of war, revolution, colonialism, and resistance in the region. By the same token, unraveling how the older generation views the introspection of artists gives us insight into a larger debate on identity making and framing within the context of global platforms and their reception back home, which I turn to in more detail in the second section of the book.

STARTING THE REVOLUTION FROM SOMEWHERE ELSE

In Palestinian artist Yazan Khalili's 2013 photographic installation *Scouting for Locations: Film Title: Traces of a Scream* (figs. 4 and 5), a search takes place for a fictional film crew that has disappeared in Sharjah while scouting locations for a film based on an adaptation of Ghassan Kanafani's novel *Men in the Sun* (*Rijal fi-l-shams*, 1963). All that is found of the crew are film location photos and the sound of a scream that witnesses heard coming from an empty, dimly lit alley. The project sets out to find the missing crew by reconstructing their journey and encounters. The artwork itself is made up of a series of photographs as well as text recounting the story of the scream, its possible meanings, and myriad detonations. In the artist's words:

> The scream is examined as proof, but no one is certain whose scream it was; the crew's or that of the witness of their disappearance. These photographs were found in an email sent to their producer without any details. We organise them on a wall in a timeline chronicling their movement in the city, looking for clues we find that many witnessed their disappearance but no one remembers them, everyone remembers the scream that night but no one recollects its author. The project is scouting for a public space in the public space through the possibility of a scream. Whose voice is heard? who is there to witness [it]? was that scream the result of fear or was it a demand for visibility? can one be invisible in the public space? or is it even a public space if the public is invisible? perhaps that scream is the demand for visibility? but isn't demand for visibility in the public space a demand for political existence! Someone said that the crew are still roaming in the city, scouting for public spaces, that is why they will not be found, as soon as they enter the public space, they are devoured by invisibility. The inaudible scream that lingers in those photographs perhaps brings into question their political existence. (Khalili 2013)

The images depict a desolate, dry landscape with vacant lots, deserted restaurants, and seemingly empty high-rises, sparsely dotted with Asian workers appearing only as props against an otherwise bleak backdrop of a city

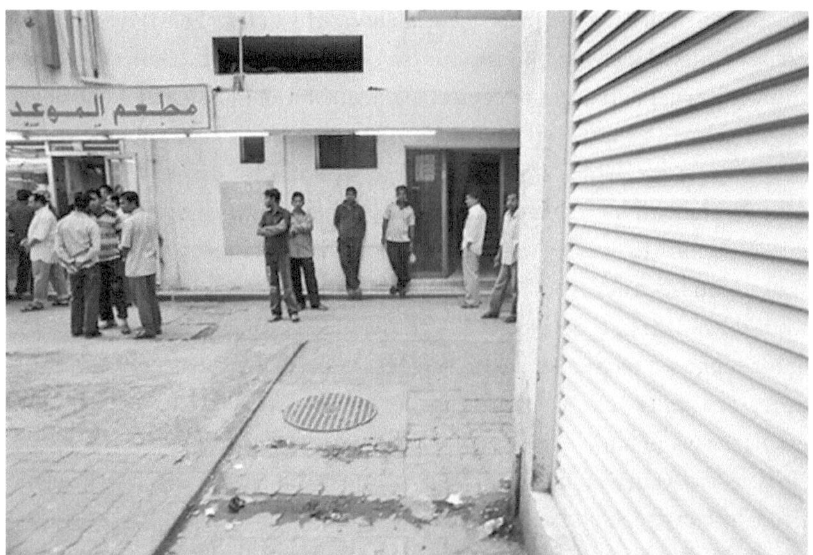

FIGURE 4. Yazan Khalili. *Scouting for Locations—Film Title: Traces of a Scream.* 2013. Color photographs and text. Courtesy of the artist.

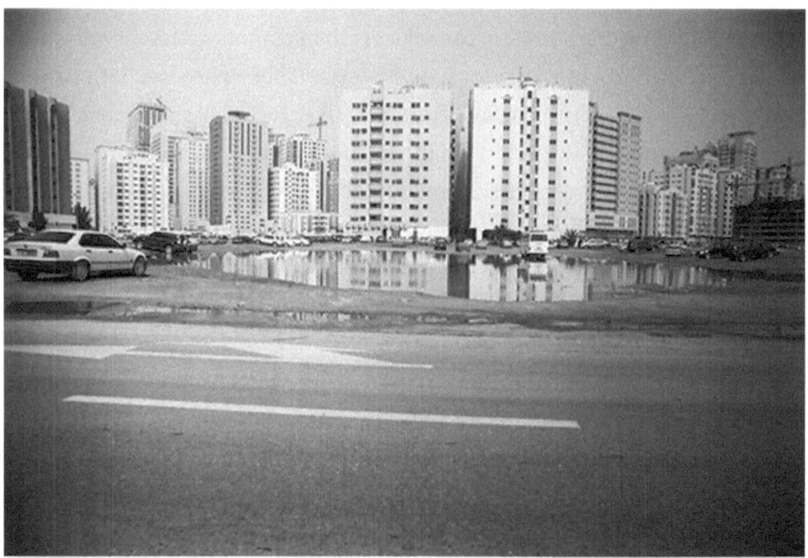

FIGURE 5. Yazan Khalili. *Scouting for Locations—Film Title: Traces of a Scream.* 2013. Color photographs and text. Courtesy of the artist.

devoid of a soul. Poignant in form and elaborate in nuanced narratives of what are seemingly lonely and precarious lives of laborers in the Gulf, the images show the cruel dynamics of capital and transnational migrant labor flows. Inspired by the characters in Kanafani's book, Khalili forms hollow spaces devoid of voices, which ironically recall with painful urgency protagonist Abu Al-Khaizaran's repeated cries—*Why didn't you knock on the sides of the tank?*—upon discovering the death of three Palestinian men he attempted to smuggle in his truck from Basra to Kuwait (Kanafani 1999: 74). In the novel, Abu Al-Khaizaran is delayed at the border when officials take time to laugh at his supposed relationship with a dancer in Basra instead of completing his necessary paperwork. Upon his release, Abu Al-Khaizaran rushes back and opens the water tank to let the men out, already suspecting what he will find. He decides to bury each body in his own grave when he arrives. However, too tired, he leaves the bodies by the garbage dump. In the morning, the bodies are discovered by municipal employees and are buried under official auspices (Kanafani 1999: 73). Abu Al-Khaizaran returns once again after abandoning the bodies to take their money and belongings.

Al-Khalili, whose work was first commissioned by the Sharjah Art Foundation for its 2013 Biennial, is not alone in his endeavor to reach back into modern Arabic literary history to make art in and about today's Arab world. Arabic literary texts in visual art have historically been used as both subject and object of artwork in an array of forms, such as recorded speech, sculpture, and performance.[10] I single out Khalili's *Scouting for Locations* here because the story that it tells of the precarious condition of laborers in the Gulf today and the formal aesthetics it uses to tell that story, in addition to the structural process of production in which the work is embedded (its commission by the Sharjah Art Foundation), frames the changing conceptions of art's relationship to the political that I explore in this book.

To further explain, for Khalili, resurrecting Abu Al-Khaizaran's pained wails is an ode to the Palestinian people in a changing world, specifically, a globalized world, where the principal issues of the age-old Palestinian struggle are now also the central tenets of larger transnational struggles. These struggles are related to migration and labor flows, the movement of refugees and their human rights, the securitization of states, and the legalities of illegitimately constructed borders and walls. They include and reach beyond the scope of an anti-colonial nationalism and the narration of a people struggling against the routine Israeli tactics of constructing an undisputed history, territoriality, and identity in Palestine that have tended to dominate the representation of the struggle in the twentieth century. Hence in *Scouting for Locations* in 2013 and in its art book form also published by the Sharjah Art Foundation in 2017, Kanafani's commitment to the Palestinian struggle is not abandoned, only contextualized and historicized within some of the twenty-first century's most gripping global challenges so that Palestine becomes a metaphor for the larger condition of the world. Here the notion of a public space—or lack thereof—and the "invisible" voices and bodies at play within it are both a testament to and a statement on the dire situation of South Asian workers in the Gulf today, as well as a reminder of the Palestinian voice devoured in dominant diplomatic discourse.

Thus, the border-crossing Palestinian smuggled across vast Arab territory and through the bureaucracies of border posts in search of a decent life is also, ironically, the low-paid South Asian migrant worker in the United Arab Emirates of today that has built Sharjah, among other emirates, the much-loved city among the global art elite for its Biennial, perceived creative edge, and openness toward formal experimentation in art.[11] The precarious life of the neoliberal subject is at once packaged, framed, and represented in an art context that exists because of the benevolence of an authoritarian regime with family members deeply and personally invested in cultural diplomacy to realize one aspect of its visionary plan of making of itself an "Athens of the Arab World" (Al Qassemi 2017b) at the same time as it is venerated and reviled for its flagship of the neoliberal agenda.[12] For the well-known artist and director general of the Jordan National Gallery, the role of the Emirates today in attracting artists is simply a sign of the times. As he despaired to me in a conversation at the National Gallery in Amman one morning in summer 2017,

> Every young artist from Jordan, Palestine, Lebanon, Egypt, Tunis, and the other [Arab] countries feels the need to be acknowledged by the Emirates art market, to exhibit in the forum [Global Art Forum], and be invited to Sharjah [Sharjah Biennial]. That the artist needs the money is self-understood, the problem is that art is now standing in for capital, art with a problematic relationship to its society but which has economic value has become the proof of our cultural heritage and political sensibilities.[13]

In her 2010 short video *Blessed Blessed Oblivion* (fig. 6), Jumana Manna focuses on young male thug culture in Jerusalem to embody that very shift in representation and narrative that Khalili's work proposes and the director general laments. Manna's twenty-minute piece was inspired by US underground experimental filmmaker Kenneth Agner's short films *Scorpio Rising* (1963) and *Kustom Kar Kommandos* (1965), both lyrical explorations of boys, cars, and violent eroticism. As in her larger body of work consumed with power dynamics, in *Blessed Blessed Oblivion* the body and place in Palestine's history gazes voyeuristically into East Jerusalem's underworld of marginalized male Palestinian youths. Hungry sexual appetites, raunchy jokes, and crude workings of imagination permeate the piece. But there is an underlying tension too. "When Martyr Abd Al Rahim Mahmoud wrote, this poem, he wrote for people to believe in it. Not for being put in a film, which isn't convinced by its words," says the main protagonist toward the end of the film. By juxtaposing the youth's seemingly hedonistic and depoliticized lives against the intermittent recitation of Abdel Rahim Mahmoud's well-known poem *"Al-shahid"* ("The Martyr," 1936), Manna insinuates that humor, recklessness, and lack of discipline may constitute forms of political intervention. But instead of lamenting Jerusalem and its role as the symbolic national center

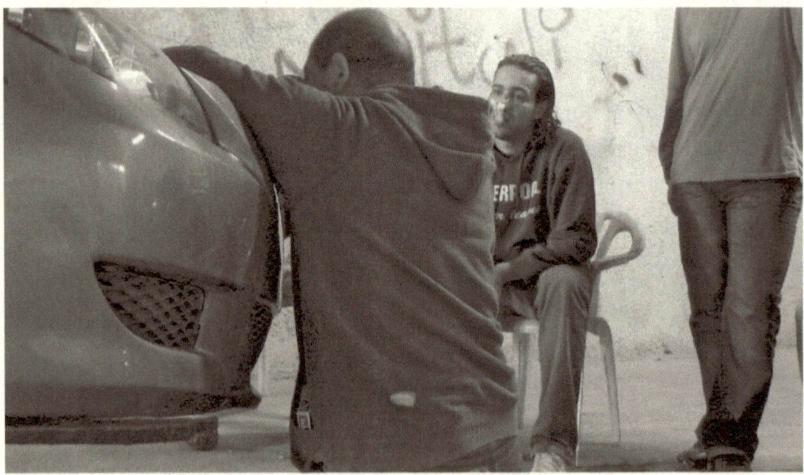

FIGURE 6. Jumana Manna. *Blessed Blessed Oblivion*. 2010. 21 min. HD video, screen shot. Courtesy of the artist.

as most artists tended to do before 1967, Manna seems to mock Jerusalem as an elusive "national hallucination" (Makhoul and Hon 2013: 113).[14] More, by referencing the notion of political commitment existent among poets in the 1930s and playing with the different forms their work may take today by emphasizing an everyday form of resistance (Scott 1985), Manna reminds viewers that counterhegemony in colonial and "postcolonial" post-Oslo Palestine is not only linked but also lived, renewed, recreated, and modified unremittingly. But in this process, Manna also stretches resistance to the point that it might sit uneasily with those who understand resisting colonial violence as a fundamentally collective and confrontational act against the violence of capitalism and class, as opposed to merely a reflective act embedded in an everyday resistance.

Khalili and Manna, both artists of the post-Oslo generation of middle-class, well-traveled, educated, and transnationally located Palestinians conversant in global art theory and practice, denote a class of cultural producers that views the framework of international cultural funding as an ipso facto part of any artistic career. Like others of their cohort in Ramallah, Amman, and Beirut, they operate as part of the global cultural funding framework made necessary by economic survival in a neoliberal climate of de-valorized labor. In this precarious climate, many artists form a global "precariat" of a contingent freelance labor force, often compelled to juggle multiple jobs and work either for free or for abhorrently low, nonunionized wages because capitalism does not value what they produce or, especially, what ideas underlie their work (Siegelbaum 2013: 48).

In this way, the assumed universal humanism of global cultural funding for local arts production and social change is consolidated as part of a global arts conversation that interrogates, often theoretically and conceptually, issues of memory making, the violence of civil wars, global immigration, urban gentrification, terrorism, wars, and the cruelty of neoliberal capitalism. These issues connect to the opening up of the "artworld to *artworlds*" (my emphasis) by their penchant for localized inflections in art (Belting, Buddensieg, and Weibel 2013). I propose that this preoccupation with how cultural differences define the experiences of these fundamentally universal issues leaves unchallenged the rise of the global art elite, its tastes, and the predilections it encourages as a form of cultural capital, which I discuss in the previous chapter and which I am taking up here once again. This impels us to question how contemporary art may critique the local manifestations of global neoliberalism, yet synchronously be part of its very cultural and social constitution.

A VISUAL CHALLENGE TO A TEXTUAL WORLD

Historically, Western representations of Arab culture privileged the spoken and written word as the highest form of intellectual practice. By extension, visual representations of thought, concepts, and sentiments have suffered a legitimate deficit in the academic milieu and have been considered "non-Islamic" (Gruber 2019). Hence, scholarship in Middle Eastern Studies generally has largely neglected artistic and aesthetic practices as socially, politically, and culturally formative sites worthy of examination. By the same token, however, the modern and contemporary visual arts spheres in the region have been incapable of penetrating popular imagination or competing with the dominant position that literature has in Arab high culture or that music occupies in Arab popular culture (Laïdi-Hanieh 2008; K. Boullata 2015).[15] This categorization has occurred despite the visual arts' and individual artists' centrality in informing many of the debates around modernity and tradition at various points in history and in vastly differing ways. The ways young visual artists in the region today have figured their relationship to the larger cultural sphere is most discernible in the ways in which they speak back to and rework the interpretations of literary legends in their multimedia-based works. Yet, since the turn of the millennium, the Middle Eastern visual arts terrain has witnessed major transformations that have allowed for its increased visibility, arguably posing a challenge to literature as the dominant form of culture representing the region, at least on the global level.

Tension between the two mediums is part of the global development of visual culture both as subject matter and lived experience, which has contested the hegemony of the word over the image. As visual theorist Nicholas Mirzoeff compellingly argues: "the visual disrupts and challenges any attempt to define culture in purely linguistic terms" (Mirzoeff 1999: 5). He further posits that the visual is to postmodernism what literature was to modernism. Beginning in the late nineteenth century and extending throughout most of the twentieth century, colonial power, modern technology, discursive modernist praxis, and a modern reorganization of society in the Middle East fostered the formation of the postcolonial nation-state primarily through channels of urbanization and print cultures (most notably magazines, newspapers, journals, and novels). Today, fragile states, corrupt regimes, and structural violence imbricated in imperial wars and ongoing colonialism have resulted in mass exile, disrupted lives in the diaspora, and frequent migrations across national and transnational borders. These distortions have nurtured a generation of dislocated selves who no longer claim to speak for a nation or community in the face of an empire but rather—through the production of culture—as political subjectivities with a transnational frame of reference. As an amalgamation of vision, thought, text, image, and phenomenological experience, the field as a whole, especially when viewed within the context of the new media revolution, creates politicized subject positions. This production of political subjectivity occurs, in turn, through a framework "in which the viewer exists in and contributes to a society marked by practices of looking" and interacting with the many "visual industries that cater to an ever-expanding public" (Gruber and Haugbolle 2013: xxiii). The new media revolution has affected all forms of communication—whether image- or text-based—including the information acquisition, manipulation, storage, and dissemination, allowing for a novel eclecticism in the employment of texts in connection to images (Manovich 2001: 5). Consequently, visual literacy and the impact of visual forms of thinking and working today arguably play a more crucial role in how society shifts and progresses than they ever have. This growth of the visual production field as a channel of protest, dissent, and political voice came to prominence in the myriad forms of production emerging as part of the Arab revolutionary process that began in Tunis in December 2010. Political cartoons, hip-hop, rap, street graffiti, public art performances, installations, video and Internet art, experimental poetry, and literature inundated the cultural production of the Arab revolutionary process, largely by their transmission through a global scopic field. In turn, the growing academic concern with the visual cultural production of the region both testifies to the expanding modes of representing its histories, subjectivities, and forms of resistance to power and acknowledges the visual field as a crucial site of study into the societies, politics, and cultures of the region.

I suggest that the tensions between the visual and the textual was further complicated in the first decade of the millennium, specifically in the case of the contemporary visual arts field, by its proximity to "suspect" sources of funding, the "*tamwyl ajnabi*" that I mention in chapter 1. As I have already discussed in chapters 1 and 2, these funds for contemporary art came mostly in the form of international development organizations or bilateral aid projects directed at cultural production. The tension is equally compounded by the "persistence of a constructed oppositional binary between 'traditional Islamic' arts and 'new' arts. This binary is based on a perceived historical discontinuity between the two" (Amirsadeghi, Mikdadi, and Shabout 2009: 8). Moreover, the "boundaries between what is and what is not visual art are increasingly blurred as to become barely discernible" (Makhoul 2013: 24), which intensifies this already complicated relationship. Video art, for instance, arguably the most critical, widely used, and circulated of the new art forms, sits resolutely between film, painting, literature, and theater, borrowing from but also critiquing each by refusing to be limited to any discipline.

Concurrent with these trends, when giants of modern Arabic literature and poetry such as Samih Al Qassem, Emile Habibi, Mah-moud Darwish, Ghassan Kanafani, and Hannah Minah are referenced in contemporary art circles, they are not so much disavowed as lamented in conceptual, formal, and aesthetic terms. Although greatly admired and often nostalgically addressed, these figures are also equally bemoaned and interrogated through different art forms for embodying a failed aesthetics of resistance. Artists today return to them to understand their critical role in the life, death, and afterlife of a botched modernist project of liberation, where the centrality of writing was an unquestionable tool in the collective experience of subjugation and hence resistance and commitment to change.

Visual artist Oraib Toukan proposes the text as an artistic strategy in an effort to mend the binarized division between text and image. In a powerful essay, written in English and titled "We, the Intellectuals" (2014), Toukan intervenes in the world of intellectual ideas through an online English language arts and culture platform. In her piece, Toukan muses on the notion of commitment to a cause; its historically paradoxical relationship to ideology, institutionalism, intellectualism; and its dominant role in the region's processes of liberation and nation building. In the artist's words:

> Painter Ismail Shammout was a member of the Palestine Liberation Organization (PLO) before he became Palestinian Director of Arts and National Culture in 1965; the novelist and poster artist Ghassan Kanafani was a spokesperson

and a writer for the Marxist Leninist movement of the Popular Front for the Liberation of Palestine in 1967 until he was assassinated by the Mossad; cartoonist Naji Al-Ali joined the Arab Nationalist Movement (and was barred a few times too many for lack of party discipline) before he too got assassinated, and so on. Kanafani once summed it up by saying: "My political position springs from my being a novelist. In so far as I am concerned, politics and the novel are an indivisible case and I can categorically state that I became politically committed because I am a novelist, not the opposite."[16]

Toukan underscores the phenomenon of commitment to a cause that manifests itself within the framework of top-down institutionalized politics of state formation. She interrogates the historic relevance of dissenting intellectual voices and their relationship to the audiences and institutions in which they were embedded, both in the anti-colonial struggle and the subsequent nation-building project. To drive her point home, the artist then zooms forward in time to hone in on one image that, for her, shows how artists "performed" resistance in the Gulf art world in reaction to the UAE's support of the regime in Bahrain during the height of the Arab uprisings in 2011 that I describe in the previous chapter. Toukan articulates her feelings about seeing media coverage of the public action undertaken by a tiny group of artists protesting the Emirati role in the quelling of the 2011 pro-democracy protests occurring in next-door Bahrain at the same time as the Sharjah Biennial that they were participating in was taking place:

> Looking at an image of this public action in *The Guardian* a week later, I was bewildered as to why I could only see a parody of protest—a re-enactment even of a strike scene from Jean-Luc Godard's 1972 film *Tout Va Bien*. The awkwardness of the picture distracted me from the urgency of the issue at hand—especially for those of us who did participate in the marathon programmes of that Gulf art week, with ambivalence and directionless despair at the contradictions and our possible implicitness within them. Was it the framing of a mere six protestors that stood there? That cropped arm facing the protestors with a cigarette, taking in the spectacle? That "look and feel" of internationalism? (O. Toukan 2014)

Like Toukan, Palestinian artists Ramzi Hazboun and Dia Al Azzeh also grapple with changing forms of dissent and protest and the role of art and artists in each. In *Motionless Weight* (2009), a blue free-flowing bag that held "The Butterfly's Burden" in Arabic by Mahmoud Darwish, is discarded at the start of the four-minute video (fig. 7). So begins a short journey that takes the viewer through the bustling streets and run-down alleyways of post-Oslo Ramallah. Commencing the journey with the bag flowing across a book kiosk, we are given a glimpse into the types of "high" and "low" translated and Arabic popular literature on sale in a typical Ramallah street book kiosk. The journey finishes at the memorial site and tomb of Palestine's "Poet of Resistance," Mahmoud Darwish. Along the way the bag lingers against the backdrop of eerie instrumental music in front of a now obsolete mural of Darwish gazing at the scores of people going about their daily business without so much as a backward glance at the mural before them. As if prodding the camera to follow it, the bag then gives us a glimpse of the city's consumerist culture by finally arriving at the city's municipal garbage dump, located very near, perhaps too near to the PNA-built Al-Birweh Park/Mahmoud Darwish tomb near which in 2014 a museum dedicated to the poet was opened.

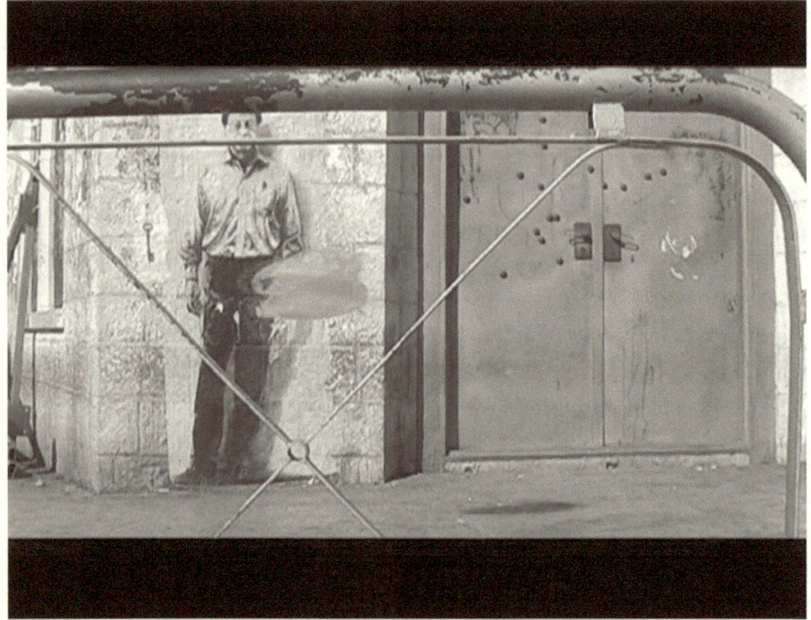

FIGURE 7. Ramzi Hazboun. *Motionless Weight*. 2009. 5 min. HD video, screen shot. Courtesy of the artist.

Through the specter of Darwish presiding over crumbling walls, alleyways, and disinterested people, the poet's musings on the tension between presence and absence in his prose poem "Absent Presence" (2006) pointedly alludes to the failures of the Oslo peace process, the delusions of supposed statehood, and the PNA's rhetoric of resistance. Pairing the image of Darwish's grand memorial and his specter in the mural with the city's garbage dump, al-Azzeh and Hazboun, like Toukan, are concerned with how resistant voices from the past feature as counterhegemonic elements in our contemporary world. Al-Azzeh, however, juxtaposes these questions against the PNA's imperatives of profit, free exchange, open markets, and consumer subjectivity in neoliberal times, issues that place Palestine in a global context and transnational frame. Toukan, on the other hand, is concerned specifically with the artist's relationship to the institution—specifically what the Frankfurt theorists pioneered as the dialectical understanding of art's "double character" in relationship to hegemony (Adorno 1991:116).

Works like these are in line with what is known in the global art world as critical art practice. This type of practice fosters what it insists it is doing: making interdisciplinary art that intervenes in the political as opposed to making political art. Critical art practices and practitioners seek to transform the world through activist, socially engaged, and intellectual approaches that engage with political theories and concepts.[17] Building on a genealogy of critical art practices as a form of counterhegemony that informed artists especially from 1968 onwards, critical art endeavors to give a voice to the marginal and oppressed, author radical manifestos to address social inequalities, excavate archives and archival processes to rewrite histories and prevent forgetfulness, and to more generally intervene in social, political, intellectual, and economic norms and flows. What is understood as a critical practice in the twenty-first century may draw from multiple formal and technical traditions, even within the confines of a single work: "What critical practices share is a fundamental aspiration: to present questions and challenges about the way the world is[.] Thus, critical practices are always in a basic sense politicized" (Wang 2003: 69).

The 1967 generation of Arab artists, writers, and intellectuals, arguably similar in sentiment to the revolutionaries of 1968 Europe, likewise demanded a new form of critical expression that called for abandoning galleries to advance a more revolutionary art.[18] Interestingly, however, this generation did not inspire the post-1990 cohort's interest in interdisciplinary work that sought to intervene in public spaces and engage global and local audiences by excavating archives, trauma, and collective memory in Lebanon, upturn the tropes of resistance circulated in twentieth-century Palestine, and enunciate a new desire to engage the impacts of neoliberalism on society and the centrality of Palestine to Jordan's fate as a nation. Rather, it was the changes envisioned in new approaches to art history and criticism through political philosophy that have engaged the writings of Arthur Danto, Jacques Derrida, Gilles Deleuze, L, Hal, Michel Foucault, and Jacques Lacan in addition to those of Chantal Mouffe and Jacques Rancière, among others, who have encouraged new ways for post-1990 artists, critics, and curators in the globally attuned art world to articulate their practice and how it relates to a more global (and less nationalist) politics.[19]

As I have been arguing, one of the main challenges for artists who self-identify as critical today is the question of their relationship to the audiences, processes, and structures shaping their work. Contextualizing artists' formal and conceptual questioning of the boundaries of art's reception by institutions, audiences, communities, and constituencies, in addition to interrogating the latter's interactions with the political, public, and artistic fields, are central to understanding what has been termed the "artist as public intellectual." This descriptive term is employed in global art theory discourses in relation to the role artists play in society as organic intellectuals in the Gramscian sense (Becker 2002: 13–14). No longer relegated to the gallery space, museum, or artist studio, the description of the "artist as public intellectual" denotes an art that has taken on a social, political, technological, and cultural life well outside those nodes of production and exhibition that traditionally accounted for it. The artist, or more specifically the representation of the artist, is therefore no longer "the artist on the fringe," the "bohemian," the "socially irresponsible," the "fraudulent," and the "esoteric" (Becker 2002: 11). Rather the artist, or at least those globally networked and transnationally located artists of concern to this book, see themselves as taking on the role of critiquing and thereby effectively engaging audiences and each other through accessible visual experimentations and performances in public and private spaces that tenaciously insist on representing society back to itself.

Inspired by Deleuze and Guattari's (1987) aforementioned concept of assemblage, this category of critique refers to the assemblages that link actors and resources from the art circuit to projects, events, and processes that extend outside the art institution and into the social and political worlds, exactly in the way the *Picasso in Palestine* project that I delve into in chapter 6 does. This category bestows on the artist many other roles besides that of the intellectual as disrupter of the status quo who unearths the forgotten and makes connections between seemingly disconnected phenomena (Said 1996: 22). The artist as "writer," "orchestrator," "poet," "archivist," "ethnographer," and "director" are among the roles produced by the contemporary conditions of labor that have pluralized the economy of art and thereby the role of the artist (Burns, Lundh, and McDowell 2018: 9–10). Ironically, these new roles bestowed in the neoliberal global economy have widened to include even "cultural diplomat" (e.g., Channick 2005). But this last role is not framed as it was in the strategies of the US Information Agency on cultural diplomacy as far back as the 1950s.[20] Rather, it is framed in the unproblematic way cultural diplomacy today is defined: cultural relations that shift from a focus on cultural events to development projects, from bilateral to multilateral funding, from the presentation of international products to the transnational and cooperative process of art making, and "from telling to listening, from self promotion to values promotion and, at the end, the general shift, from selling an image to communicating it through image cultural values and attitudes" (Jora 2013: 43).

On the notion of critical art as counterhegemonic practice, artist and theorist Hito Steyerl (2010) maintains that "even though political art manages to represent so-called local situations from all over the globe, and routinely packages injustice and destitution, the conditions of its own production and display remain pretty much unexplored." It has also been argued that in the era of neoliberal globalization, corporate and state powers have transformed the institutions and conventions of contemporary art to adapt art's social functions to the needs of the new world system (Stallabras 2004: 34–36). This includes, above all, a process of production and exhibition that valorizes culture within the larger remit of "cultural policy"—a professionalized form of art where politics becomes the art of display (Leslie 2006). As I have shown, the past decade has witnessed a flourishing of what have been constructed and then termed "independent" or "alternative" art spaces, as well as artist-run and artist-led projects, biennials, festivals, exhibitions, and other self-organized events operating adjacent to official state apparatuses. This phenomenon in

Amman, Ramallah, and Beirut was coupled with a turn toward cultural diplomacy as well as "civil society and democratization" programming on behalf of international donor organizations working in the field of development in the region, first in the 1990s, then with full force after the events of 9/11, and again with the onset of the revolutionary process in 2011.

These conditions of production have prompted prominent critics from the 1967 generation such as Faisal Darraj, the Syrian intellectual who resides in Amman, to ask, "How is it possible to incorporate this 'artistic globalization,' which Arab artists are living, into the dominant socio-cultural fabric of their home countries?" (2013: 91). In conversation with me on this point, Darraj inquired how the global art world structures that rely on the precarious labor of artists and writers, publishing in mostly English-language online journals dedicated to the art of the region, can reach a wider public and truly engage it when these artists' point of conceptual departure and readership speak a different language and possibly even frame of thinking about what constitutes the global and the local. When I raised the issue that most artists consider the public to be "a partner rather than a spectator" (Mikdadi 2009: 28), he responded that the global neoliberal art market dictates who the consumers and therefore the public of the artists will be. Despite criticisms that the post-1990 generation has withdrawn from localized experiences and debates, another claim is that what distinguishes twenty-first-century artistic practices from those of previous generations is their openness to public participation and their use of public spaces as sites of production and exhibition, even in highly securitized cities such as Amman and Ramallah (Mikdadi 2008).

To begin thinking through the question Darraj raised about incorporating artistic globalization into the local cultural fabric, I return briefly to that moment of mid-twentieth-century modernity to unravel how and why modernism in the Arabic literary field was and continues to be associated with counterhegemony and what implications it has for contemporary art making today. Specifically, why is it that as the nonprofit and nongovernmental art scene grows in visibility, its relationship to its audiences remains ambiguous (Darraj 2013: 55)?[21] This moment pinpoints the overturning of the traditional order and its values by those who lived it and gives us a glimpse into the logic that underpins the thinking of those who denunciate contemporary art as irrelevant to the larger site of the political.

COUNTERHEGEMONY AND THE PROJECT OF MODERNITY

During a 2009 post-roundtable discussion at the Beirut Art Center (BAC), one audience member, a journalist and cultural critic, pitted the prewar and postwar generation of artists against each other. He claimed that the former generation tended to produce works without "exportation" in mind or, more precisely, without the consideration of a foreign audience and funders.[22] The comment referred directly to Lebanon's so-called "post–civil war" generation of artists and their concomitant support structures—most notably, Ashkal Alwan and the Ford Foundation. Occasional accusations held that these artists were indifferent to the local contexts that inspired them, instead showing interest only in forming transnational networks to exhibit and enable critique of their works. Explicably, the comment provoked an outcry from various members of the audience, especially those working as artists within said generation. The tense discussion that ensued revolved around how the marked increase in attention from the international art market affected the content of artistic work in Lebanon.

The cofounder and director of the BAC, who is also an internationally recognized artist of the "postwar" generation, defensively explained that "serious" artists "[dig] inside of themselves" with a bona fide intention to produce works without regard for a fickle international market that happens to be showing interest in Lebanon. Another artist of the same generation, also loosely tied to the postwar artists, protested that the reason artists of the prewar generation worked without regard to the international market was simply because no possibilities existed outside their local context. The artist elaborated:

> [The 1967 artists] would never have dreamt of being in an international book on contemporary art by the age of 30. . . . [Artist] Abdel Hamid Baalbaki, let's say, might have not been able to become recognized outside before, and outside maybe they would not have wanted to know about him the way they do want to know about us now—from the 1990s onwards that is. Today, we finally have a chance for outsiders to recognize us. Now it's that they want to know. Before, artists could have made a hundred paintings, but no one would have included [them] in the history of art at the international level.

The artist's comments are a powerful statement on what is considered to be the marker of success in the contemporary art of the region: recognition and approval has to come from *barra*, "outside," or beyond her native Lebanon's borders and beyond the region itself.[23] The comment also reminds of the lack of knowledge regarding the region's cultural history, a form of amnesia that continues to prevail in the circuits of production and discourse in which contemporary artists flowed. I was reminded of this blind spot several times by members of the 1967 generation whom I interviewed.[24] The assumption implicit in the artist's words is that today exists an unprecedented opportunity to cross the boundary from the "marginal" place her predecessors occupied to the "center"—a historically novel phenomenon, in her view. The artist correctly paints a picture of the global art scenario as it unfolded with the neoliberal capital dynamics that penetrated the art world and aided its transformation into "art worlds" of multiple hybrid sites (Belting, Buddensieg, and Weibel 2013). This depiction of the artist was especially true in her description of an international market showing increased interest in "local" cultures and artists. At the same, she insinuates that possessing a global sensibility is a phenomenon related to her generation alone, discounting the equally captivated if less capitalistic sense artists of the 1967 generation identified with the global. More, in her comment, the young artist omits the possibility that the 1967 generation of artists might had been involved in a different project all together.

Instead of contextualizing the two generations' distinct relationships to the global art world within a framework of unique on-off opportunities and desires, I suggest we read the responses of each generation to the global encounter as imbricated in two differently expressed yet related imaginations and normative ideals relating to modernity. Accordingly, I propose that the 1967 generation understood "modernity" to be a "counterhegemonic project" led by a group of avant-garde intellectuals for collective social change and cultural reform, a value in itself; an instigator of social transformation and not its result, such as the poet Abbas Beydoun personally lived and described (2003: 27–30) and Yaseen Noorani (2007) theoretically conceptualized.

For the contemporary generation, the end and the means are one and the same. The point of artistic creation is self-referential and primarily concerned with critical engagement defined by the reference points of art itself. Thus, while the previous generation of artists and intellectuals extended itself toward society and used modernism as a tool for grappling with empire and postcolonial identity negotiation, the post-1990 generation became preoccupied with inclusion in a global art society organized around the dictates of transnational capital. For the 1967 generation, then, art was steeped in both local and global frames of reference. When I spoke in 2008 to Nidal Askhar, Lebanon's renowned theater director and actress, about this question of frames of reference, she explained that "Beirut at its zenith was a place where to *be* a modern Arab in the new [post-independence] era was still in the process of being defined." To Ashkar this explains why her generation could continue to be "true to its roots and resist imperialism" even as it looked westward for aesthetic inspiration. She finished off describing this period with a long and whimsical sigh: "These times were the height of modernity."[25] Any locally contrived purpose drifted beyond ideals of art for its own sake and responded directly to the audiences, language, ideologies, wars, and revolutions forming their midst. As Zeina Maasri (2020) compellingly shows in her work on Lebanon in the global 1960s, the artists of said generation were part of a circuit of Third Worldism that moved according to collective political solidarities rather than a market system of art. For the subsequent generation, this idea of the collective as being central to art's relationship to society was to be refuted, deconstructed, and reworked. It was ultimately redefined within a global art framework that encourages introspective communication between artists, prioritizes interdisciplinary knowledge exchange, raises awareness of global issues on aesthetics and politics, and provides tools to reach global audiences.[26]

Modernity as an analytical concept and normative ideal played out with varying degrees of intensity and form in Lebanon, Palestine, and Jordan. We might consider this view of modernity as "multiple modernities" that emphasizes the many historically situated trajectories toward modernity and the multitude of sociocultural backgrounds that define this experience (Aranason 2000; Delanty 2004; Eisenstadt 2002, 2004). In Jordan and Lebanon, the political regimes that took over from the colonial mandate powers (the British and the French respectively) rushed to shape their countries' sovereign identities, ushering in powerful concepts such as national identity, authenticity, and the search for cultural and religious roots that reinforced these constructions.[27] In Palestinian cities, as the sociologist Salim Tamari (2009) describes, modernity was experienced as a vibrant intellectual, political, and social exchange of ideas and initiatives in a self-conscious and secular public sphere. It enabled a generation of Palestinians to articulate a cosmopolitan identity between the demise of Ottoman rule and the violent birth of the Israeli state in 1948. Beirut's multiplicity of modernisms, as Maasri (2020) has described it, occurred roughly between the 1950s and 1970s. This period has been credited with providing the dazzling backdrop for the fiery debates that first emerged about Arabic modernism and its political dimensions in the wake of 1948 and then following suit among intellectuals in other cities of the Arab world.

These debates were felt in hinterland cities like Amman and Ramallah throughout the larger part of the twentieth century and were framed by a cosmopolitan middle class of Levantine professionals, artists, and writers who traveled across the Arab region's most dynamic cities at the time, such as Cairo, Alexandria, and Beirut. Through their travels came novel ideas relevant to the constitution of new modern identities that were in the process of being formulated. How modernity was experienced as a lifestyle and organized as a cultural and political project was arguably realized by way of a counter-hegemonic ethic intent on doing away with older traditions to confront the modern world that they were now a part of "on their own terms" in the wake of independence. In the case of the Palestinians, this project of modernity, begun in the late nineteenth century (Tamari 2009), was interrupted by Israel's forced creation and the subsequent dismantling of the Palestinian cultural and socioeconomic fabric to make way for the construction of a new Zionist identity (Doumani 2009; Tamari 2009; Azoulay 2011; Seikaly 2018). Even if modern identities and modernist cultural projects manifested in different forms in each of the settings I am concerned with, they remained a counterhegemonic frame of reference in relation to hegemonic forces of imperialism. Yet this did not mean that modernity was always experienced as a "rude imposition or inauthentic appropriation," as art anthropologist Scheid (2010: 230) put it in her writings on Lebanese artist Moustapha Farroukh, whom she describes as hoping his oil paintings of a semi-nude odalisque in *The Two Prisoners* would garner support among his fellow artists and intellectuals for a revolution against the established gender norms.

The boundaries of Arab modernity and the relationship between modernization and modernism are predicated on a dialectical interchange between process and agency (Aksikas 2009: 4–5). Modernism within this framework relates to a historical juncture and the experiences emergent from its interaction with the process of modernization. This process is defined by a set of socioeconomic and political processes that include war, strife, and identity negotiation. Modernist ideologies and counter-ideologies devised from various counterhegemonic cultural visions, values, and theories can be negotiated, then. These continue to be negotiated today. Conceiving counterhegemony in relationship to hegemony that is a "lived" process that needs to be continually renewed, recreated, and modified (Williams 1977: 112–13) means we can understand cultural actors as active agents involved in determining the contours of the debate by which cultural production will be defined and represented, even when it manifests within a framework of cultural hegemony. In other words, an active and conscious negotiation with hegemony is constantly in flux, determined by way of a sober negotiation of accepting, rejecting, or modifying what encountering the global entails. This paradigm can help us see how transcultural ideas and experiences emerged even as hegemonies were in the process of being punctured by postcolonial subjects. In alluding to her desire, along with that of her generational cohorts, to be accepted into the Western art history canon, the protesting artist at BAC I refer to above highlights this paradigm. It is this desire to be included in "the history of art at the international level," as she puts it, that I believe links generations of postcolonial subjects rewriting their histories through their own lenses.

INTROSPECTION AS DISSENT

In conversation with Stephen Wright (2006), Khbeiz—poet, essayist, journalist, and prominent commentator and actor in Lebanon's post–civil war contemporary art scene—delineates between the pre– and post–civil war generations of Lebanese artists and the new identities forged at the start of the postwar era. Bilal Khbeiz states that there existed a *total* subservience of the arts to the politics of the Arab liberation movements prior to the war:

> Where a poem may resemble a tear, a painting may amount to a scream and a novel may exceed expectations, the arts were always successful in communicating with their audience. In that context, the artist was like Rilke, the person most capable of expressing general and common emotions. (Wright 2006: 68)

Khbeiz posits the Lebanese pre–civil war generation of artists and writers on whom he is reflecting as concerned with outright political art (as opposed to politically critical art) by emphasizing its link to prevailing ideology.

Comparatively for him, the arts today have managed to "escape the edicts of politics" (Wright 2006: 68). Khbeiz is part of a generation of artists, writers, and architects, and their supporting networks and organizations in Beirut and internationally, who emerged from the rubbles of the civil war and the ambiguities of the Taif Accords that supposedly ended hostilities in 1990. Termed the "postwar artists," this group created work that responded to a very particular post-violence scenario. The particularities of their work propelled them to, first, subvert understandings of how the history of the civil war might be read and narrated; and second, to interrogate and challenge the traditional role of cultural institutions and the commercial gallery system in the creation of art often by incursions into public space, whether physically or conceptually; and third, to probe prevalent and accepted understandings of hegemony and ideology in identity formation. They did so through what they often described as an "introspective" turn, which entailed a move away from what they saw as their predecessors' tendency to "write back to the empire" within the confines of the meta-narratives of history.

In *Biokraphia* (2002), Lina Saneh and Rabih Mroué interrogate the conventional interview format common to documentary practices that often pose versions of history as conclusive. The performance (detailed in chapter 4) scrutinizes the idea of giving an eyewitness testimony of history. Oscillating between the role of victor, victim, and subject under interrogation, the protagonist—Saneh herself—stands before a glass tank full of water that hazily relays images of her face and body; she is dressed in a thin white gown set against the backdrop of thick red theater curtain (fig. 8). Alluding to television monitors and constructed narratives, the piece grapples with the indeterminacy of a fragmented identity at play within the confines of what was in 1990s and early 2000s Beirut an existent and formal hegemonic narrative propagating an amnesia of the civil war to go on living. The artists propose that their performance expand to include documentary practices that ultimately drown out the physical presence of the actors on stage. Intermeshing audio and video footage, Saneh interrogates herself in a series of intense, sometimes nonsensical and intimate questions about her life during the war.

Members of the postwar generation often articulated "introspection" or "auto-critique" to locate themselves vis-à-vis the prewar generation. This approach is aptly demonstrated in the following excerpt from the performance:

FIGURE 8. Rabih Mroué and Lina Saneh, *Biokraphia*. 2002. Photograph by Houssam Mcheimech. Courtesy of the artist.

> You're still thinking with the logic of the enemy. The enemy thinks that our work is provocative. They accuse us of being influenced by the West. Of being cerebral. Formalist. There's no story here . . . no actors . . . We have suffered and are still suffering from the homogenization of the Arab and Islamic identity. But in reality, people are not all proud of this identity. We don't remember that we're Arabs until the Americans and the Israelis bomb Beirut, the West Bank, or Iraq . . . in times of crises . . . It's only when things like this happen that this instinct in us is stirred. Our loyalty is instinctive; therefore, it's not positive. In this context, the Arab identity can be considered an issue or matter, which in itself imposes upon us the inevitability of fate and destiny.

The work touches on crucial issues regarding an artist's position in the era of globalization by tackling—head on—local political, sexual, and religious taboos. Most relevantly for this context, it attacks norms and conventions and teases out the seemingly hypocritical in Lebanese and Arab society at large. Ibrahim Abu-Rabi', scholar of Islamic and intellectual thought, argues that contemporary Arab thinkers of all hues and inclinations are wrestling with questions of modernity, postmodernity, and globalism with a twofold purpose: first, to reflect on the challenges the phenomenon of globalization has posed to the Arab world; and second, to assess the overall trajectory of the Arab world over the past century or so (2004: 186). Yet despite the added challenge of grappling with the wave of globalization and the "new world order" that pulled Lebanon in after the end of its civil war, the introspection transmitted in *Biokraphia* is part of the larger dynamics that Abu-Rabiʿ critiques.

Interestingly, the postwar artists from Beirut are often framed, especially by international onlookers, as products of a brutal war that forced a rupture with the past. This contradicts the interpretation of them as a perpetuation of a new form of introspection in cultural production that continues a longer history of war, revolution, oppression, and resistance in the region. The post–civil war generation's introspective tendency is also an integral part, in fact a continuation, of a larger movement of intellectual thought that addresses the internal workings of Arab society, mentalities, and relationship to modernity. This move was set in motion after the pre–civil war generation's cataclysmic experience of the *Naksa*. Ironically, this terminology to describe the catastrophe of the 1967 war echoes contemporary Lebanese artists' language around the Lebanese civil wars and the ruptured histories they wrought, which I discuss in more detail in chapter 4.

The novelist Elias Khoury writes about the artist's migration between places, languages, and tools: "The artists and writers of our times do not return to a place of stable values and forms. Their very being is afflicted by a crisis, searching for a significance in the only reference available to them, namely in the very artistic forms they create" (2008: 82). For artists after 1990, what the 1967 generation did and thought was to be refuted, deconstructed, and reworked within the dominant technological mode of their time, allowing, as I argue here, for a "re-visualization" of the postcolonial entity primarily vis-à-vis itself, mostly through media art, rather than a "writing-back" to the former empire in literary texts. Consequently, whether the generational introversion that Khoury describes as a crisis about artists after 1990 is symptomatic of the loss of meaning and purpose generally associated with postmodern literary and visual production, as he hints to be true, what is more relevant for our purposes is what this perception represents. In other words, Khoury's framing of the post–Cold War generation's cultural production as crisis ridden indicates the existent generational tensions over the meanings and contexts of the political. Viewed through the lens of a contentious generational divide, one may argue that cultural production—a process constituted of art production and discourse that may or may not emanate a transcendent "political"—is also a state of being that is translated and explicated in terms that are always a manifestation of the larger critical condition of society itself.

Inspired by the conversations she organized in the project in the chapter opener, Arsanios created two films that tackled the history of postcolonial nation-state building through a feminist perspective. She did so first in the single-channel video *Have You Ever Killed a Bear? Or Becoming Jamila, 2013–2014* (2014), and then through her interactive installation *Olga's Notes, all those restless bodies* (2015). In the first (fig. 9), Arsanios focuses on a woman who is preparing to star in a new film about Jamila Bouhired, one of the leaders of the Algerian anti-colonial struggle and one of the main supporting characters in *The Battle of Algiers*. Through remaking one of the original film's most famous scenes where Jamila plants a bomb in a café, Arsanios attempts a feminist reading of the role of women in political resistance and asks whether we can ever see Jamila beyond her role in the violent struggle for independence. She felt this intervention was imperative after digesting the masculine version of history that dominated the *Al-Hilal* conversations. Through the film's main protagonist, who comments on playing Jamila from the vantage point of history, Arsanios digs into how women were employed as part of the patriarchal struggles of national liberation and questions their role today. In the second film, inspired by a piece she found in *Al-Hilal* about a dance school in Cairo that Nasser set up to construct a "new body" congruent with the modern state, Arsanios asks an older, retired dancer now based in Beirut to recall the steps from a dance from years ago. In both films, Arsanios, who reflects on the flailing of Arab nationalism as a state-sponsored project for gender equality, rethinks the narrative of resistance that had been passed down to her generation. What she seems to suggest is that inserting a postcolonial feminist intersectional reading into the past might be a more productive exercise for imagining a future after a momentous revolution than rehashing old discussions about anti-colonialism, nationalism, and the failures of state building.

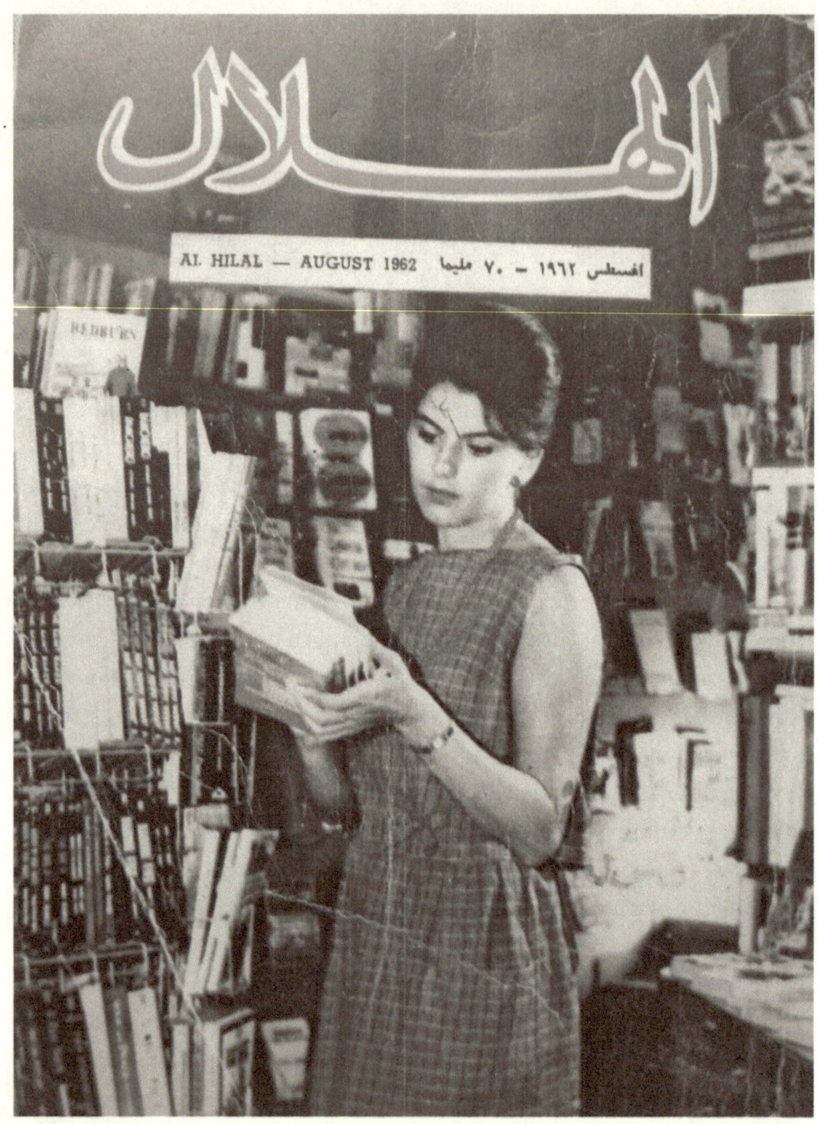

FIGURE 9. Marwa Arsanios. Reproduction of the cover of *Al-Hilal*. 2011. Courtesy of the artist.

In this chapter, I argue that post-1990 art was understood by those making and funding it to derive its new style from more subjective and self-reflexive experiences, expressed mostly in multimedia conceptual practices as opposed to the more conventional painting and sculpture that harked back to a time when art was ideologically driven. In a series of developments that began in the 1980s as part of a shift away from universalism toward particularism, global art exhibitions began to distinguish between contemporary and modern art as categories in the late 1990s. Aware that in normative art history "modernism" denotes time and delineates a formalist sensibility, exhibitions in the international fora began to distance themselves from questions of form and aesthetical practice to the ways in which modernism is appropriated as a strategy of subversion in countries on the "margins" (Meier 2010: 15). Arguably then, what distinguishes modernism from contemporary is not whether either is a strategy of counterhegemony against the grand narratives of Western progress, but rather the difference in the tools appropriated to carry out this feat. I propose that the divergent modes and mediums of the two generations I focus on be read as variations in articulations of the colonial encounter, the dissent they provoke, and their varied manifestations, across time. That is, it's not that Arsanios dissented any more or less than the anti-colonial and leftist intellectuals of the previous generation that she engaged. But how and against whom she expressed her resistance to hegemonic readings of history is informed by a different context. This indicates that the varied iterations of counterhegemony that circulate in the work of contemporary artists can be understood only within a longer history of strife and popular protest in the region that have produced differing forms of dissent.

INTERMEZZO

IN 1995, THE THEN YOUNG LEBANESE CONTEMPORARY ARTS organization Ashkal Alwan organized a group exhibition held in the public Sanaya' Gardens in Beirut. Participating artist Ziad Abillama staged a disruption within what was already perceived as a disruption of young contemporary artists probing the notion of "public" space in a supposedly peaceful postwar Beirut. As part of the curated show, invited artists were allotted space within the park to exhibit their work. For his contribution, Abillama provoked other artists by handing out a questionnaire that asked each of them to allow him to sequester thirty centimeters of their allocated spaces to produce his work for the show. Abillama proposed that, in exchange for complying with any agreement governing these thirty-centimeter blocks of space, he be allowed to exhibit what he wanted. His request was unanimously—and by many—angrily refused. For Abillama, this immaterial and ephemeral questionnaire and its results essentially became his contribution to the show. He explained:

> The piece was saying: "What do we do when as artists we are invited to behave as liberal democratic [beings]?" You have your own space, each has their own little house, we can all live together; does this not sound like the idea of a Lebanon of all the different mosaics and cohabitation—the cohabitation that failed us during the war? I was asking, "What is the connection with that

> model not only as a failure but as an idea that was refused by different actors of the Lebanese Civil War?"[1]

Abillama's discomfort stemmed from what he saw as a formal change to the way contemporary art was being lived and experienced as a site of postwar social critique. Furthermore, he observed artists neglecting to undertake the difficult feat of conceptually addressing contemporary art and its relationship to the new organizing sponsors (such as Ashkal Alwan). By interrogating the notion of territoriality in self-perceived liberal democratic spaces, which he believed were reminiscent of the wartime practice of erecting military checkpoints at the entrance of neighborhoods, he provoked crucial questions. The following chapters show young contemporary artists in post–civil war Beirut—along with the neighboring cities of Amman and Ramallah following suit ten years later—experimenting with public art in the form of installations and performances and grappling with their specific generation's place in society as their quickly neoliberalizing and securitizing cities grew in tandem. The question that animates the next chapters hones in on what conceptual reworkings were simultaneously occurring in what Jacques Rancière calls the "distribution of the sensible." That is, how did artists' physical disruptions of public space agitate against the postwar consensus, in the case of Beirut, and how was that reflected in the planning and implementation of an art show critical of the very structures that artists and their supporting organizational networks were ultimately—as Abillama implied—part of?

Abillama's disruption is crucial to the argument I make in the coming chapters about how counterhegemonic art comes to be negotiated and subsequently framed. Abillama's point was that if the role of the political in the aesthetic lies in disrupting the space designated and naturalized by the "police," then we must unpack the irony of an art show organized by a supposedly dissenting network of artists and their sponsoring organizations allotting designated space in a city long divided by military checkpoints.[2] Indeed, when looking at developments after the early 2000s, the need to question what makes processes of contemporary cultural production critical and potentially counterhegemonic becomes more pressing.

As far as I know, Abillama's intervention in the 1990s was hardly referenced in the art criticism that began to circulate in Western art journals and exhibitions more interested in the "archival impulse" of Lebanese memory and trauma-related art by the "postwar artists in the early 2000s." However, the work articulates what I propose in this book about the counterhegemonic in art being defined not solely by its ability to represent what politics appears to conceal, but also implicating the local art world's role in perpetuating this very concealment. Timothy Mitchell's description of neoliberalism as a "triumph of the political imagination [because] its achievement is double: while narrowing the window of political debate, it promises from this window a prospect without limits" (1999: 229) is helpful here. Relatedly, Abillama's wittiness is central to understanding the unfolding dynamics that I grapple with in the second part of this book. It is a certain sensibility in art that he proposes and that has in many ways inspired my thinking around how resistance to and dissent from the status quo was expressed by transnationally connected and funded artists at the turn of the millennium. In the same way, it is not whether and how artists and their supporting nonprofit organizations and initiatives pander to their funders that I set out to prove in this section. Rather, I uncover how the political function of art—that gets transnationally circulated, exposed, critiqued and funded—plays a role in shaping artists' and their organizers' self-conception as counterhegemonic even as they partake in policing the role, purpose, and meaning of art.

Part 1 of this book explores how the intricately wound-up dynamics of cultural diplomacy, counterhegemonic cultural praxis, and its aestheticization in contemporary art—and the civil society and democratization framework of funding among international development donors—contributed to an increasingly vibrant growth in the nonprofit and nongovernmental contemporary art scenes of the Arab Eastern Mediterranean after 9/11. It uncovers the cultural politics that shape perceptions of international arts funding, revealing how the historically rooted authenticity debate is tied up in the memories and contemporary realities of cultural imperialism. In effect, neoliberalized forms of support to civil society NGOs are masked under the rubric of cultural diplomacy and the detrimental effects they may have, regardless of whether they are "Arab" or "foreign." In all, the chapters of part 1 reveal the backdrop against which the art scenes of the cities I next describe play out.

The transition from part 1 to part 2 entails a shift in levels and subjects of analyses. While part 1 concerns the overall structural dynamics of cultural aid, cultural diplomacy, and epistemological and generational shifts in understanding art's counterhegemonic role, part 2 is more of a microstudy. It explores key moments in the globalizing process of contemporary art from the region. It addresses the possible meanings and reception of individual works and the artists, organizations, and South-South artist collaborations and initiatives that made them. Namely, it begins to reveal how, in contrast to the 1967 generation, the post-1990 contemporary artists conceive of the political and its manifestations as playing out within the very process in which art is made rather than the product that emerges from that process. This anti- or post-representational frame of thinking about art's resistant role fosters the idea that the counterhegemonic dimension of art is found in the democratic and open process of making an art product, whether it is a public art piece or archival based research. The chapters in part 2 shed light on works, stories, and narratives that explicate how interlinked theories and aesthetical practices operate in neoliberalized civil society contexts and emphasize the relationships among artists and the camaraderie nurtured in nongovernmental and nonprofit art initiatives as political sites that foster new forms of counterhegemonic art.

There is no quantifiable causal relationship that is intended to highlight the links between parts 1 and 2, but rather points of departure for thinking about how trends and correlations between international politics and various forms of representation and theory appropriation in the field of contemporary art sometimes embody relations of power in society and international relations. Even in seemingly "progressive" discourses of knowledge about art, resistance, and social change, ostensibly counterhegemonic cultural production cannot be evaluated without a comprehensive reference to the particularities of the processes by which works and discourses around them come into being and then get framed and discussed. Part 2 concerns these particularities. The "actors" and "objects" of focus are deliberately chosen for their embodiment of various political dynamics and certain historical moments. As such, their unfolding describes a dilemma that often emerges when articulating resistance in cultural production in postcolonial contexts: the translation and the transfer of instances of counterhegemony through "colonial difference," as Walter Mignolo puts it (2000: 173). Hence, the one thing the examples chosen and the processes described in part 2 share is that they have all been penetrated by neoliberal forces in the field of contemporary arts production through the channels of international development aid and cultural diplomacy efforts. Arguably, however, this penetration has had different effects.

The next three chapters focus on Beirut, Amman, and Ramallah consecutively. They shed light on a highly articulate and interdisciplinary contingent of activists, artists, filmmakers, writers, and poets, and the transnationally networked organizations that supported them in the aftermath of the civil war in Lebanon, the "peace" processes with Israel in Jordan, and the PNA in Palestine. Through the chapters I uncover how this contingent of cultural actors had also become by the outbreak of the Arab revolutions in 2011—whether consciously or not—constitutive of what David Harvey (2005: 39) refers to as "the construction of consent" in the consolidation of neoliberalized globalization in society and culture.[3] By this, I do not mean an explicit desire on behalf of artists to reinvent art practices complicit with neoliberal ideology. Rather I refer to the contradictions and inconsistencies inherent to neoliberal cultural hegemony and its attendant precariousness that artists and their supporting networks ended up exploring and exploiting as way of surviving it and countering it at the same time. These are reflected in the centrality of neoliberal tropes such as "choice," "accountability," and "participation" in the democratization and development practices of civil society that unfolded under the rubric of cultural diplomacy in the aftermath of 9/11. Such tropes became also central to the work of culture and art NPOs and NGOs that operate off of the belief that they can "create a different set of politics outside of the dominant system" (Touq 2016: 211).

The dynamics of how neoliberal transformations panned out is specific to each context's social, cultural, and political histories and the "base" from which they transformed into global sites of artistic production and representation. For instance, in the aftermath of the Wadi Araba peace agreement, especially following 9/11 and the subsequent war on Iraq, international civil society donors found in the Jordanian regime a willing military and political "friend of the west."[4] Jordan—whose historically sleepy Hashemite-ruled capital of Amman has been overshadowed by Beirut, Cairo, and Baghdad—became an enthusiastic recipient of democratization aid for the purpose of securing the regime's survival. Like Beirut, Amman is a neoliberal city facing an onslaught of unregulated capitalism, free trade, small government, and the marketization of virtually every aspect of life under the pretense of democratizing the political sphere and emancipating society. Yet unlike Beirut's systemic process of neoliberalization, which has increasingly united corrupt state governance and private interests toward the near collapse of the public domain (Mouawad and Bauman 2017: 66–69), Amman has not enjoyed the legacy of a long and vast history of leftist political activism and critical thought that could potentially provide—at least in theory—a countercurrent to the brutal effects of neoliberal governance and authoritarian methods of rule. Before the civil war erupted in 1975, Beirut enjoyed a liberal political climate that allowed Palestinian and Lebanese leftist parties and factions to operate freely and openly, especially after 1967, guaranteeing the city's spot as the "lightning rod for all the political movements erupting in the Arab world after Palestine's fall" (K. Boullata 2003: 24). In contrast, the newly constructed country of Jordan was living under a series of martial laws instated by King Hussein in 1967 that banned political parties and activism until 1988; the country's civil society is still recovering today.

Since the middle of the nineteenth century, Beirut's politics, society, culture, and economy have been largely determined within the matrix of a certain history and its resultant self-perception as progressive, cosmopolitan, and the most "Western" of Arab capitals. This implied a twofold assumption for some of those I interviewed during fieldwork in Beirut. First, the phenomenon of funding democratization projects in civil society under the guise of cultural diplomacy was explained away as a trend that has manifested throughout the country's history. Precisely, cultural exchange was regarded as having always been part of the country's historical social and cultural makeup. Second, tensions between authenticity as essential and pure and modernity as imported and inorganic took on a less central role in Beirut than in the contexts of Amman or Ramallah's art scenes. I did soon realize, however, that in all three contexts, the post-1990 generation's defensive counterclaims to the accusations of "inauthenticity" and "importation" directed toward them were also a knee-jerk reaction to some valid question society was asking about how contemporary artistic production was being funded, debated, and framed.

Sami Zubaida argues that "the conditions for the development of spheres of social autonomy are not only the 'withdrawal' of the state, but also an active state intervention of another kind: clear legislation and institutional mechanisms which provide the framework of rights and obligations for these spheres" (1992: 3). Beirut's art scene in general and contemporary art scene in particular lack autonomy despite the "withdrawal" of the state (Bauman and Mouawad

2017; Leenders 2012) simply because they do not function autonomously. They depend on funding and support from structures and sources external to the Lebanese state institutions and in particular the Ministry of Culture. Amman's art scene, by contrast, suffers from active state intervention. It lacks a clear framework of rights or obligations toward the sphere of cultural production and the visual arts specifically, and it intimately interacts with the patronage system of arts found in Arab monarchies, where members of the ruling families oversee the field, based on their personal interest and experience. Beirut's visual arts domain has been described as "non-institutional" or "proto-institutional," instigating various discussions around the meanings of such a predicament for the production of art.[5] Despite Lebanon's lack of conventional infrastructure for cultural institutions, and due to its capital's self-conscious positioning as a "space for congregation, debate and planning," or even a "laboratory," as artists and writers often describe it, the country's post–civil war art scene, like that of Amman's post-2000 contemporary art scene, lends itself to a reflection on the meanings embedded within what are commonly understood to be independent production processes.[6] Yet the Lebanese have also "generally known how to live outside of the State" (Salamé 1987: 52). This independence from the state is in contrast to the Jordanians for whom the political economy of regime security has meant the consistent manipulation of elections, laws, and neoliberal economic reforms that favor transnational business communities and which offer little by way of accountability and civil liberties, while at the same time maintaining a progressive air (Abu Rish: 2014). The regime's lack of intervention in the work of progressive secular cultural institutions and informal initiatives is significant for understanding the political function of contemporary art in neoliberal authoritarian systems of rule.

In the case of Palestine, the state's precarious institutional context derives essentially from its subjugation by Israel. This precariousness is manifested in two ways: first, by an inability to militarily defend its elaborate complex of state-to-be infrastructures from Israeli aggression if necessary; and second, by the dependency of its post-Oslo civil society institutions on Western aid packages (Le More 2008; Dana 2014a), which one scholar has described as a "colonial peace" (Turner 2019: 274). In place of the dense network of civil society organizations that formed one of the seedbeds of the first Intifadah, Palestinian society today is embedded in an elaborate network of mostly Western-funded

NGOs with relatively tenuous links to grassroots organizations and mobilization.[7] In turn, Palestine's contemporary art scene is vulnerable to articulating itself against common tropes of representation by mainstream media and political frameworks that preference, for instance, successive artworks inspired by the Israeli Apartheid Wall (Gronlund 2018).

Some argue that Palestinian cultural production is a form of political resistance in its own right, by virtue of its vulnerability to various forms of repression "[by] Zionist narratives, the Israeli state, Arab 'host' governments, such as Lebanon and Syria, [and] Orientalist and Islamophobic environment in the diaspora, corruption and nepotism within the Palestinian Authority (PA)" (Tawil-Souri 2011b: 470). I agree with the imperative of creating a counternarrative to attempts at Palestinian erasure, which Palestinian artists and civil society organizations have been so active in undertaking by (re) presenting their narratives and (re)negotiating their strategies of protest in the face of oppression (De Cesari 2019). Yet in accordance with many of those I interviewed and conversed with in my fieldwork, there is also a need to go beyond the framework of resistance that sees Palestinian art as a form of counterhegemony by virtue of its colonial reality. By moving beyond established paradigms we can begin to uncover how Palestinians take control of their own narratives in other ways that do not simply respond to how they are represented by others but rather how they contribute to global culture and art discourses on countering hegemony in all its other guises.

Chapter 4

BEIRUT

The Rise and Rise of Postwar Art

> I find that those practices that I identify as current, experimental, and critical in Lebanon and elsewhere are necessary because the historical relations and the natural bonds between the realm of politics and the realm of aesthetics are now again being redefined. I am neither speaking in banal journalistic terms, which in my opinion is dangerous, nor in the terms of the idiotic grassroots opposition of the aesthetic and the political, wherein the political role of the artistic is understood, purely and simply, as militant art, or art engagé. Rather, and from the onset, the question of the relationship between the realm of the artistic or the aesthetic must be understood as far more complex, where some of the complexities have only begun to unravel in the past ten years. To that effect, I would like to cite a passage from the work of a philosopher who has greatly contributed to rethinking these questions, to their actualization and their revitalization today. His name is Jacques Rancière, and he is mostly known as a political philosopher and a specialist in nineteenth-century literature.
>
> *Catherine David, "Learning from Beirut," 2002*

CATHERINE DAVID IS AN INTERNATIONALLY PROMINENT AND influential French curator who had an avid interest in contemporary artistic production from Beirut. In 2002, she lectured at the Ashkal Alwan Forum on Cultural Practices in the Region in Beirut. In her words above, she introduced her mostly Lebanese audience to the thought of Jacques Rancière, as well as the fashions of the global art scene at the time. This is not to say that audience members had no prior knowledge of Rancière and his thoughts on linking the aesthetic and the political. Her seminal

Beirut-specific lecture did confirm, however, a certain aesthetical mode of production in which she had been personally invested at the time, both curatorially and intellectually, as contemporary, critical, marginal, experimental, counterhegemonic, or in her own words "in a slight measure, what is commonly understood as contemporary art production" (2002: 33). David's advancement of a certain "political"—a subversive rather than a militant one that relates to Rancière's conception of politics and aesthetics—begs the question of how this "political" was defined in relation to the changing post–civil war and post–Cold War politics that enabled it to emerge. Considering Rancière's conceptualization of aesthetics as politics—two fields he perceives to be inherently intertwined—it is worth considering how this take on critical art that David emphasizes manifested in the context of Beirut, where a few years after her lecture Rancière was invited by Ashkal Alwan to expound on the paradoxes of political art and the notion that there was "no real that might be described as the outside of art."[1]

Critics in the first decade of the millennium largely analyzed how internationally celebrated post-1990 Lebanese artists such as Walid Raad, Akram Zaatari, and Lamia Joreige disrupt attempts at establishing linear histories through their archival work and the poetic uncertainty their meshing of fact and fiction instigates. Such a singular focus on this aspect of their production has had the effect of characterizing the larger scene to which these artists belong as perpetually dissident, perennially avant-garde, and therefore counterhegemonic. As I argue in this chapter, this group of Lebanese postwar artists became known for and for a long time remained largely focused on making critical interventions about their society's memory of violence and the role of the archive in rethinking it in the supposed aftermath of war. Missing from these critical interventions that became so pronounced by the early 2000s was a coherent attempt to deconstruct the conditions of this art scene's own making, specifically its globalization.[2] But what were the structural dynamics that shaped artistic production in the late 1990s and early 2000s when the post–civil war art scene consolidated itself within a neoliberal and globalized frame of reference? In particular, how did globalized local art platforms like festivals, forums, and exhibitions factor into local discourses on the role of art in the aftermath of violence?

POSTWAR ART AT HOME

In the immediate aftermath of the Lebanese civil wars, the specific terms of the Ta'if postwar settlement outlined an official amnesia regarding the war. Those "responsible for the war . . . became responsible for building the country" (Haugbolle 2005). The depiction of the war as a mere hiccup in the nation's history was necessary for the continued survival of this ruling class. The amnesia of the war was facilitated by the privatized postwar reconstruction logic of maximal profit that ensued shortly after the agreement was signed. Yet, as Miriam Cooke writes, "A tension arose between the need to forget this war . . . and the need to remember in order not to repeat" (2002: 400). A reversion to historic symbols of Lebanon's cosmopolitan modernity and pluralist past was intrinsic to the reconstruction process's attempts to wipe out memories of the war in preparation for the country's reincorporation into the global financial market of real estate.

In contrast, at the popular level social practices shaping interpretations of the war continued to feed into "antagonistic discourses of the 'other'" (Haugbolle 2005: 192). Rafik al Hariri—the Lebanese business tycoon and prime minister who was assassinated in Beirut on February 14, 2005—has often been credited with possessing, almost uniquely, the vision, energy, contacts, and resources to set Lebanon on the path to recovery. Yet none of it was or could have been possible without acceding to Syria's terms. Effectually, these terms were a tacit acceptance of the latter's tutelage over Lebanese affairs.[3] Hence, through his own real estate company, SOLIDERE, Hariri aggressively pushed ahead in the early 1990s and over the next fifteen years with demolishing and rebuilding what the fifteen-year civil war had left of downtown Beirut, an area that roused painful recollections of the war for so many and that was subsequently obliterated from public memory (Cooke 2002).[4]

Along with the "no victor, no vanquished" attitude, the attempt to frame the civil war as merely a rough patch in the country's recent history provoked tension between the need to forget the war and the need to remember in order not to forget. The prime minister's reconstruction plans for major highway routes, the airport, the telecommunications system, and Beirut's city center were all part of his program to turn the country into a regional center of finance and services in a post-peace Middle Eastern division of labor (Perthes

1997).[5] The new Beirut was envisaged as the Arab world's own version of Hong Kong, complete with an opulent financial center of glass tower blocks, luxury retail centers, and high-rise residences affordable only for vacationing Gulf Arabs. Various sites fell victim to Hariri's "postwar" vision: the sea view, which many of the city's residents, regardless of class, had historically enjoyed; the Old Souks where many still remember shopping, socializing, and making a living in; and the existing archaeological sites, unfortunate enough to lie on land being overturned for the new Beirut. Downtown Beirut had indeed been reborn, but as many longtime residents of the city saw it, it was reborn as a sham simulation of the unkempt yet effervescent center of culture and trade it was before the war.[6]

Saree Makdisi termed the phenomenon that gripped the city in the 1990s "Harirism," which he defined as a decisive withering of the state and common public space and the supremacy of private commercial interest and control (1997: 698). Enunciated in the Treaty of Brotherhood, Cooperation, and Coordination of May 1991, Syrian hegemony in Lebanon demanded dominance over and regulation of all fields of the economy and society. In accordance with Syrian plans to revitalize Lebanon as a stable investment and to capitalize on its tradition as a service economy harboring a relatively well-educated, cosmopolitan workforce, the country's postwar generation (sometimes dubbed the "Hariri generation") entered a labor market defined by NGO and humanitarian development projects. These included the media, advertising, graphic design, public relations, real estate, and a host of other domains tied to transnational markets and networks. Founded in 1993, Future TV, Hariri's satellite television station, was particularly active in recruiting young people trained in film, theater, and graphic design, providing them with the technical facilities to develop editing, filming, and directing skills, in addition to accessing equipment, which they could also use to develop their own artistic careers on the side.[7]

The end of the civil war in Lebanon opened up a world of once unimaginable possibilities for cultural actors such as artists, writers, poets, and filmmakers. Those I interviewed cited a number of reasons for this: the reopening of the eastern and western parts of Beirut to one another after intermittent closures during the fifteen-year war; investments in audio-visual media, with which the postwar Hariri government in particular was most concerned; and ideas, networks, and exposure brought by returnees from abroad.[8] These returnees included a number of Lebanon's now most famed postwar artists who had been studying at universities or living abroad during the period of the war. *Al-Mulhaq An-Nahar* (*The Supplement*), the Lebanese newspaper *An-Nahar*'s weekly cultural supplement, which resumed publication on March 14, 1992, was central to the postwar discussions that took place, first about the war, and then about Beirut before the war and how that period was featured in the postwar reconstruction process (K. Saghieh 2019).

These new possibilities provided much of the impetus for the changes in the interdisciplinary cultural production scene. Conscious of their city's reputation of dynamism and their place in it, young Beiruti cultural actors did not set out to revive what they understood as the old terms of ideologically driven political and cultural references, as they were under no illusions as to what it had brought their country. Both realistic and cynical about Beirut's regional status, and the continued reference to its (Phoenician and Greek) historically cosmopolitan and modern identity as part of the reconstruction process, these young men and women chose to express their manifold disagreements openly. Hence, the rebuilding of downtown became the prime focus of a generation of interdisciplinary artists and writers refusing to forget the war or to turn a blind eye to the violent ironies lying at the heart of the reconstruction process. Such sentiments were well articulated in Joana Hadjithomas and Khalil Joreige's conceptual project *Wonder Beirut* (1998–2006), in which they purposely corrupted classic images of the city (fig. 10).[9]

The subtitle of the first part of the project—"The story of a pyromaniac photographer"—refers to the fictive story about the photographer Abdallah Farah, who was supposedly "commissioned" by the Lebanese Tourist Office to make a series of twenty-four postcards of Beirut, as well as twelve images depicting Beirut's cosmopolitan identity for the official 1969 calendar. Three years after the outbreak of the civil war and following the destruction of the photographic studio where he worked, Farah began to burn his salvaged negatives from years before in an attempt to match the image with the destruction that was going on around him. As the story goes, these same postcards that show Farah's photographical and pyromaniacal work are still on sale today in bookshops, even though the places represented were almost totally destroyed during the war. Making a statement about the city's self-perception, the photos, corrupted by the artists, represent the positive side of Beirut's modernity: its

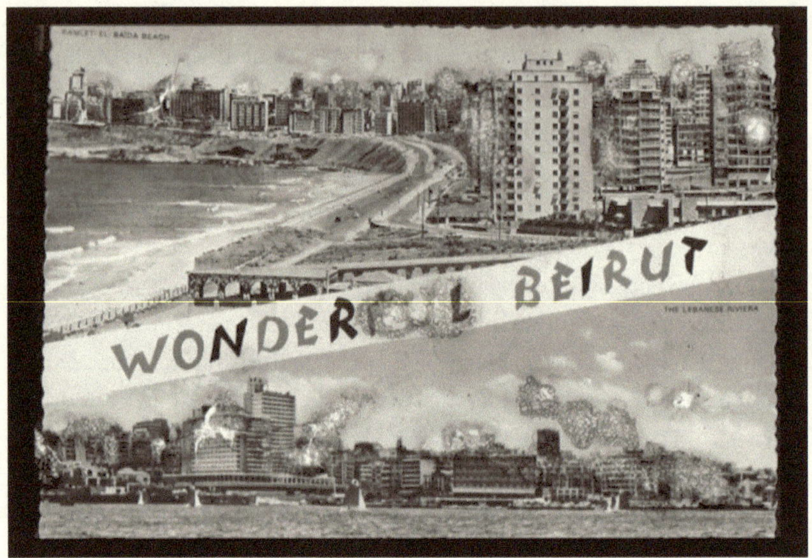

FIGURE 10. Joanna Hadjithomas and Khalil Joreige, *Wonder Beirut: The Story of a Pyromaniac Photographer.* Part I of the project Wonder Beirut (1997–2006). Mixed media (postcard detail). Courtesy of the artist.

beaches, boulevards, hotels, and sunbathers. Consumed with the power of the historical image of Beirut as the Champs Elysees of the East and the role it continues to play in the imaginations of Westerners' and its own people, the artists struck at the heart of Beirut's postwar absurdity: the lingering image of cosmopolitan Beirut sustained by the prevailing attitude that the fifteen-year civil war was a mere "disruption," a stand-alone event with no repercussions for the essentialized image that had been created. "If it was all so rosy in Beirut before the war then how the hell do we explain the war?" conveys what many of my interviewees expressed during discussions about the 1990s.[10]

The notion of Beirut's glorious past and more recent cosmopolitan modernism—embodied in SOLIDERE's logo "Beirut Madina 'Ariqa lil-Mustaqbal" (Beirut: Ancient City of the Future) and central to the *Wonder Beirut* project—was the inspiration for much of the critical work that was carried out by many other visual artists (and writers) in this period. At least initially, artists expressed themselves outside the norm of established art institutions such as the Ministry of Culture, the Lebanese Artists Association, and the gallery system.[11] This move initially provoked criticism of inauthenticity and Western importation by established art institutions. In spite of artists' commitment to addressing the new publics formed in the wake of peace, their works or the discourses they were embedded in were not able to penetrate larger structures or society in the broad sense. Arguably, this forced artists to create their own niche from which to critique established art institutions that functioned as gatekeepers for what and how cultural production was defined. This meant that many artists who had spent the latter part of the war completing their higher education in Europe or North America took it upon themselves once they returned to organize relatively small-scale art events, for which they produced and critiqued artworks. While the 1967 generation as a whole questioned the authenticity of art forms such as installation works, several actors of that generation encouraged these new forms of expression to flourish from within their already established platforms.[12]

The main media through which much of this post–civil war contemplation was carried out by the postwar artists was a hybridization of installations, urban interventions, video, photography, image-text collages, performances, and encounters, fused with historical and philosophical speculation, research, and theory. War, the trauma it left in its wake, and how to look at it, remember it, narrate it, and archive it featured prominently in most of the works. The cultural actors who understood an ill-defined and ill-structured contemporary art world as the strategic entry point for intervening in the official war narrative and the popular discourses surrounding it addressed this gateway on two levels. First, they contemplated understandings of a "shared" public space in a traditionally divided city suffering from the onslaught of a restructuring program largely oblivious to the notions of memory, the irony of the postwar identity, and trauma, such as in the examples mentioned here. And second, they deconstructed conventional forms of historiographies of the war by delving into the notion of the archive. It was especially the latter that became synonymous with the practices of this generation, as they began to travel more frequently outside of Beirut's context.

In her fifty-four-minute film, *Here and Perhaps Elsewhere* (2003), artist Lamia Joreige provokes questions that Lebanon's official postwar public discourse had elided. This discourse followed the government's decision in March 1991 to declare an official amnesty for all belligerents, which effectively left the atrocities of the war un-investigated. Joreige's film (fig. 11), now regarded as a classic of the postwar art period, along with her *Objects of War (1999–ongoing)*, was a journey of memory through Beirut as she traveled along the former Green Line that divided the city during the war. At locations that were once crossing-points on the Green Line, Joreige asks people whether they knew of anyone having been kidnapped by the militias during the war. Joreige was probing her audiences to think about how one archives the immaterial and the invisible by shifting between the factual and the poetic. She made use of archival images, such as that of the Green Line, by juxtaposing them against the conversations she triggered with her interlocuters along the way. Like *Objects of War* (fig. 12), a video and object installation where thirteen interviewees are asked by the artist to muse on an object that had some significance for them during the war, *Here and Perhaps Elsewhere* reflects the content that artists of the postwar generation became most known for internationally. It embodied her generation's attempt to interrogate the idea of constructing a linear narrative of the Lebanese war by delving into the notion of the archive and memory.

Earlier than Joreige, the internationally renowned artist Walid Raad had begun to question how to remember or narrate the violence without turning it into a chronicle of morality about good versus evil. Through an imaginary foundation, the Atlas Group "set up" by Raad sometime in the late 1990s, the artist researched, documented, studied, and produced work that sheds light on the contemporary history of Lebanon by looking for traces of war and symptoms of trauma in places where historians might not otherwise look.[13] Through this fictitious "organization," in many ways an early version of the informal, vertical, and ephemeral artist-led initiatives that soon popped up all over the region, the artist set out to systematically undermine the reliability and thereby the limitations of history's representations of Lebanon at war (Raad, Ziad, and Awada 1999).[14] *Missing Lebanese Wars* (1998), for example, is a fictitious work that documents Lebanese historians of various religious and political beliefs betting at the horse races. As the story goes, the historians would make bets not on the result of the race but on the time it would take for the official race photographer to expose the image of the winning horse once it had passed the winning post. Thus, each bet would consist of a prediction of the photographer's delay in actually taking the shot. The work, collected into an archive, was usually presented in mixed-media installations: screenings, visual essays, and

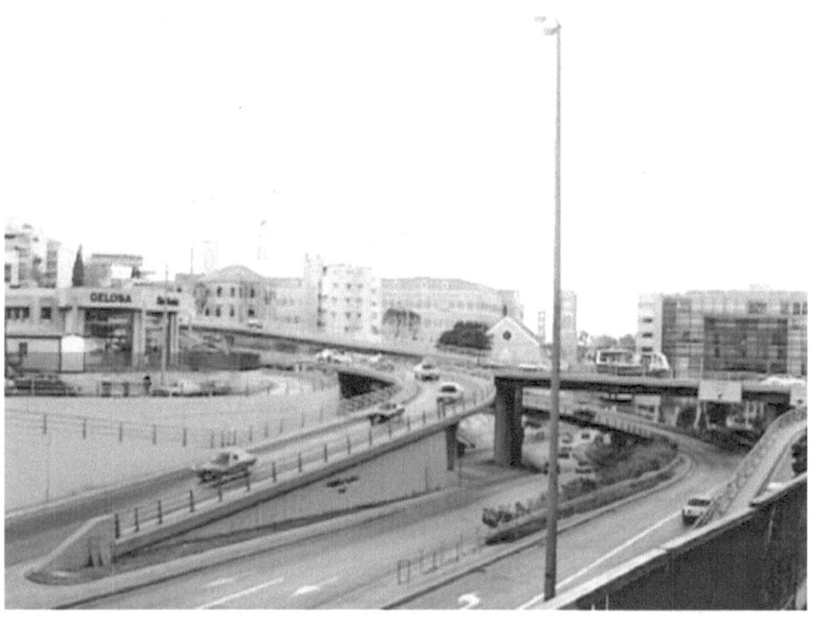

FIGURE 11. Lamia Joreige. *Here and Perhaps Elsewhere*. 2003. 54 min. HD. Screen shot. Courtesy of the artist.

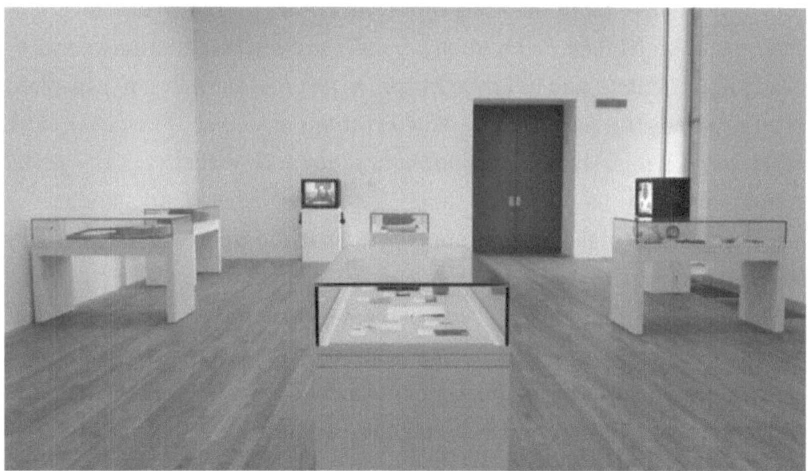

FIGURE 12. Lamia Joreige. *Objects of War 1999–Ongoing*. Installation view of exhibition at Tate Modern, 2011–2012 (Permanent Collection). Copyright of the artist.

performances that scrutinize the conceptual possibilities lodged into the city's collective and individual memory of war. The project ran a hazy and convoluted line between fact and fiction, "replacing unitary power with fragmented assemblage," as the arts magazine *Frieze* described it (Beasley 2006). On one level, the work challenged the notion of the institution as the repository of history. On another, it tackled the chasm between actual events and the impossibility of their representation, and confronted those who claimed to hold the truth by acknowledging history as a larger moral truth in the aftermath of the war. History for the Atlas Group was therefore equally constituted by the smaller lived experience of individuals. For Raad and the Atlas Group, to write history was "to daydream, to allow for the fluidity of its subject, and to relinquish the possibility of its finitude" (Mizuta Lippit 2012: 184).

Art critic Hal Foster observed "an archival impulse" in 2004 among contemporary artists who sought "to make historical information, often lost or displaced, physically present."[15] Foster suggested that the archive is a form of alternative knowledge and counter-memory. Specifically, he characterized this form of archive as "found yet constructed, factual yet fictive, public yet private" (Foster 2004: 5). In late 1990s and early 2000s Beirut, artists working on the city's post–civil war predicament were already in the midst of forming sometimes fictive (as in the Atlas Group) and other times real organizations such as the Arab Image Foundation precisely to construct alternative means to acquire, circulate, and interpret historical records (Downey 2015). Inspired in large part by the deconstructive theorizations of Jacques Derrida's *Archive Fever* (1995), which shaped the dominant ethos and aesthetics of the global contemporary art world during this period, the artists, curators and critics leading these cultural organizations conceived of the archive in the same way they did history: fragmented, nonlinear, and memory driven.

The fictional dimensions of some of the works I describe that were embedded in this deconstructive logic demanded a certain trust from their audiences—a big ask considering how deception was so clearly also a part of the work. As approached by artists in this period, the archive could be read as a counter expression to the state-directed amnesia described above. The reliance on the archive as an artistic method countered the nostalgia for the image of Beirut as the cosmopolitan and stylish Paris of the Middle East as it was propagated by official discourse, which distracted from the real need for transitional justice focused on truth and reconciliation. As such, the archival impulse in Beirut that appeared with urban development under Hariri could be read as mirroring as well as constituting the global art world's turn to the archive as a form of radical alternative knowledge. This coalescing reveals how neoliberal economic processes, in this case SOLIDERE's attempt to eradicate the memory of the war and impose an imagined historical narrative through real estate development, also contributed to shaping the very tools and language that artists with transnational links consequently had at their disposal to propose a counternarrative that was given visibility in the global art sphere.[16] On that account, art can express anti-neoliberal sentiments locally but become part of neoliberalism's cultural expression after traveling or transferring to more global platforms.

How the conversation on creating a counternarrative to the official state-imposed amnesia about the war unfolded in contemporary art practices is important to consider here. While the younger generation's approaches to the archive could be read as "political" statements that combined performance, documentation, and critical thinking, their aim was to make sense of the subjectivities of various histories within the field of contemporary art as opposed to producing any sort of objective or canonical history. This aim constituted the basis of much of the younger generation of cultural actors' take on the role of art in the postwar era and its relationship to the political. It contrasts with what they generally perceived was their older counterparts' role in the period before the war—a perception repeatedly relayed to me in interviews and informal conversations and described succinctly in an interview with Rabih Mroué on the Tate Modern's In Focus research series (Elias 2004). As chapter 3 discusses, the 1967 generation was understood as too wrapped up in the weighty image of a unified Arab voice on Palestinian suffering, dispossession, and resistance from which there seemed no escape (Elias 2004).

In an article entitled "A Matter of Words," artist, art critic, and academic Walid Sadek identifies the parameters of art posited as "politically engaged and actively protesting" as subsumed within the dynamics of an antagonistic audience tenaciously holding on to a "sacred and uninterruptible difference between the tangibility of truth in its categorical separation from its contraries" (Sadek 2002a). It is reactions to Raad's work, observed during an artist presentation he gave in 2000, that Sadek draws on in making his observations.

According to Sadek, Raad's work raised many questions regarding the politics of interpretation and canonical authority in postwar Beirut (48).[17] Hence, during the 1990s, Raad and his contemporaries posed uncomfortable questions, especially so because the state was bent on ensuring its own people's forgetfulness of what had passed. Even today in Lebanon, a search for an objective truth to recent historical events conflicts with a subjective representation that might or might not cut across generational lines. Speaking of the Atlas Group Archives, a well-known Lebanese Marxist public intellectual and historian rhetorically asked: "What is the need for faking opinions and events on the war when the real war and its events are there? They happened and actually exist."[18] Further problematizing the focus on memory in a conversation with me about global cultural discourses associated with the postwar group of artists, he argued that "memory replaces causality; you remember a trauma but you don't look for the reasons for it." I return to this point and the historian's take on transnationality at the end of this chapter. For now, however, I bring up his point because it highlights a localized context for these artworks, indicating how before their transnational circulation they were part of a localized discussion taking place on how to remember the war.

Considering the historian's thoughts, Sadek's critique in "A Matter of Words" is timely and relevant. It underlines the difference between two ways of handling a society's war memory. One entails probing the subjectivities of memory formation, while the other searches for an objective canon of real events and casualties that can be written down as history. The former points to a nonconclusiveness, the latter to a conclusive history. Added to this is the dimension of conceptual art's tendency to be regarded as set apart from broader society and culture, be it in Lebanon or elsewhere. Considering this, contemporary postwar art practices increasingly balance an aesthetics, which was presumed to bear its own politics by those making it, with a localized cultural dynamic and public, which increasingly demands to be accounted for in the making of the art and, especially, its framing upon global circulation. When the work of the historian and the contemporaries of his generation is placed within the framework of memory and post–civil war nation building that the historian outlines, the inevitability of the anxieties associated with a society in search of universal truths in the aftermath of violence is brought to light. For the 1960s generation of Marxist intellectuals from which the historian hailed, nation building in the aftermath of war is paramount. For postwar artists and other cultural actors of the post-1990 generation, it was the idea of nation building being based on a linear history and an objective truth that had to be overturned.

From early on, the aristic and cultural production of postwar artists, who were identified or self-identified as "alternative, critical, subversive, and/or countercurrent," made themselves felt through physical art installations in public spaces and bustling intellectual activity (Salti 2002: 78). This presence was paramount even if larger public engagement was sometimes lacking due to what Lebanese curator and writer Rasha Salti described as postwar art's "cold estrangement from conventional language, its defiant contemporaneity and seemingly unprejudiced borrowing of form and vocabulary from post-industrial cultures" (Salti 2002: 88). What made transnational channels for the production and presentation of new work increasingly possible were the very early efforts of nongovernmental and nonprofit cultural and arts organizations and initiatives, such as the now defunct Masrah Beirut (the Beirut Theater), Ashkal Alwan, Ayloul Festival (also defunct), the Arab Image Foundation, and Zico House, as well as a loose network of artists, architects, writers, filmmakers, and self-styled curators and cultural managers.[19] In Lebanon in the 1990s and early 2000s, the focus had been site-specific and ephemeral works that often showcased video screenings, publications, and other installations in public spaces rather than more traditional gallery venues. Each one of the public art events that temporarily took the form of an incursion into open spaces in pockets of the cityscape interrogated the very meaning of "public" space, alternative space, and institutional history versus private memory.[20] These incursions often generated counterpublic discourses among the art-going public. Prominent examples lodged into the memories of many residents of Beirut include Ashkal Alwan's early initiatives: *The Sanayeh Project* (1995), *The Sioufi Project* (1997), *The Corniche Project* (1999), and *Hamra Street Project* (2000).[21] Whether this critical thinking and experimentation reached a public beyond Beirut's cultural elite remains difficult to ascertain, even with their emphasis on public space.[22] As Sune Haugbolle relevantly questioned, "How much of the truth of the war, how many of its details, will make it into the public and become part of the nation's collective memory?" (2005: 203). Haugbolle foresaw that the answer to this question depended primarily on the links established between three crucial nodes: the populace, the cultural elites, and the political elites. His questions complicate prevalent interpretations about that time that argue that postwar Lebanese art "constitute[d] sites of emancipation with the aesthetic serving as a battleground" (Puzon 2016: 279). Haugbolle prods us to contextualize claims like these by locating them in a more nuanced complex of discursive ideas, aesthetical practices, and historical transformations.

The works of contemporary postwar artists circulated the city in an effort to locate the exhumed aesthetics of its war. Yet the more this reflection on the postwar public and public spaces circulated globally, the more criticized it was by the people who comprised the context from which it emerged. By as early as 2003, "one could speak of an inflation concerning contemporary Lebanese art whereby an increased international visibility found little impact locally," wrote Walid Sadek (2008). According to Chantal Mouffe, "public spaces are always plural and the agonistic confrontation takes place in a multiplicity of discursive surfaces" (2007a: 3), a conception that could, in theory, accommodate for the paradoxical state Sadek described. Yet the repercussions of Lebanon's divisions, based on sect and then reinforced by class and a divided physical geography, reached well into the self-described secular and liberal domain of civil society, which provided the platform for the debates that were circulating among the art scene to flourish. This meant that even for the publics, about and to whom many of the works spoke, accessibility to them was predicated on cultural capital, class belonging, and the discourses of global cultural and political identity that they were enveloped in (von Maltzhan 2018; Hamadeh 2018).

POSTWAR ART OUT IN THE WORLD

In 1997, Catherine David invited Lebanese artists to show their works in her *Documenta X* exhibition where she was the first woman ever chosen to curate the prestigious show. David famously used the platform to vocally advocate for a novel opening up of the Western art world to "non-Western art." Five years later, David embarked on her long-term project *Tamáss: Contemporary Arab Representations* by including works from Beirut in a series of exhibitions, seminars, readings, lectures, performances, and other events that took place at various European venues.[23] The show was supplemented by publications and focused on urban gentrification processes, subjective memory, and fabricated history—popular themes in 1990s and early 2000s Beirut. The project, regarded as a formative moment in the process of globalizing contemporary Arab art after 1990, brought together the works and activities of visual artists, architects, writers, poets, filmmakers, and other actors from the intellectual and cultural realm of the Arab world.[24] Her interest in the younger generation of Lebanese artists in particular lay in the centrality of their work of both the country's postwar reconstruction process and the "amnesia" that emerged after the end of the civil war. In her words: "The concern of many Lebanese intellectuals—immediately after the war—with the development and promotion of an experimental, critical contemporary Arab culture is sufficient reason to single out a group of authors who feel the need to meet and discuss a medium-term cultural project in their own city and their own context" (David 2002). Her earlier conviction that non-Western visual arts—in contrast to film and literature—could not contribute to understanding the complexities of the contemporary world was reflected in the multidisciplinary work of the artists that drifts easily between the boundaries of visual media and text she chose to work with (David 1997: 11–12).

Upon visiting Beirut in 2002 for the first time since the official end of the civil war, I was immediately struck by the buzz circulating about a phenomena I describe herein: the significant international curatorial presence, especially David's, in town for Ashkal Alwan's first Forum on Cultural Practices in the Region, titled *Home Works*.[25] Artists associated with the postwar art scene were known to congregate within Ashkal Alwan. In that year, discussions in bars and café during the preparatory phase of the forum revolved around who was commissioned to exhibit a work, which artists and intellectuals were to present a paper or lecture/performance, and why those who were not presenting were left out. Despite being an outsider to the scene at the time, I remember people being acutely conscious of this bustle occurring outside of the purview of traditional artist-supporting bodies such as galleries and state-structured organizations. The formal emphasis of the art was also new, reflecting the setting I described above: in place of painting or sculpture, a more multidisciplinary and intellectual exploration of art was being followed—a phenomena I had already witnessed on a much smaller scale between a few individual artists in Amman and Ramallah.

Although various arts-focused organizations and initiatives contributed to supporting and exposing the works of these artists, especially in the early stages of their careers, Ashkal Alwan became the most consistently associated with these artists and projects.[26] The organization was founded in 1995 by Christine Tohme and some of her friends.[27] Tohme, known as an energetic and avid networker among international representatives of the contemporary art world and funders of the local scene, remains Ashkal Alwan's director. Through its dynamic biennial forum on cultural practices, its close contact with and consistent early support from primarily the Ford Foundation, and its avid networking among other international cultural donors, Ashkal Alwan secured its place in the global art world. Although the organization was showcasing works and provoking debate on public space, memory, and the archive as early as the mid-1990s, it shot to international prominence along with a handful of artists through *Home Works*, which coincided with the Ford Foundation's sponsorship of its first forum in 2002. According to some of my interlocuters in the field, it was this turn of events that led to the organization distancing itself from Beirut's public spaces and directing its gaze beyond Lebanon's borders to a global public. Whether Ashkal Alwan's calibration to a more global platform was the reason for its perceived withdrawal from local public spaces, what it did in the process was introduce the Lebanese art-going public, Lebanese artists, and both groups' counterparts in Amman and Ramallah to a transnationally connected art world of speakers, thinkers, writers, and filmmakers. These actors became engaged in some of the most crucial debates operating at the global level, developing South-South exchanges of resources and decolonizing knowledge production in the process.

For the next fifteen years and until today, postwar artists have increasingly participated in a variety of ways in the global arts sphere. In the early 2000s, they exhibited in numerous international shows, including the Venice Biennial (2003, 2005, and 2007), *DisORIENTation: Contemporary Arab Arts from the Middle East* at the Berlin House of Cultures (2003), *Laughter* at the London International Festival of Theatre (LIFT) (2004), *Out of Beirut* at Modern Art Oxford (2006), Biennial of Contemporary Art of Seville (2006), Biennial de São Paolo (2006), Istanbul Biennial (2007 and 2009), and the Sharjah Biennial (2003, 2005 2007, 2009, 2011, and 2013). Articles and reviews also created enthusiasm for Lebanon in the global art world.[28] Most often, academics and critics based in Western cultural institutions wrote these articles, but the artists also contributed to scholarly journals, art criticisms, and exhibition catalogues by commenting about their work and its significance.

Despite their different aesthetic content and near-universal discomfort at being labeled a group, the postwar artists from Lebanon resulted in a rather consistent roster of names: Tony Chakar, partners Joana Hadjithomas and Khalil Joreige, Lamia Joreige, Bilal Khbeiz, partners Rabih Mroué and Lina Majdalanie, Walid Raad, Jalal Toufic, and Akram Zaatari. Other names that have sometimes appeared alongside the main core include Walid Sadek, Ziad Abillama, Bernard Khoury, Fouad Khoury, Marwan Rechmawi, and Paola Yacoub and Michel Lasserre.

As the global art boom took place amid a media revolution and the consequent decentralization from Western art capitals in the post–Cold War era, artists of different "ethnicities" and "cultures" from developing nations, who had been long ignored in the Western mainstream art world, were acknowledged for the first time by Western critics and able to enjoy commercial success through multicultural exhibitions and group shows (Stallabras 2004: 10–15).[29] Group shows became directly relevant to Lebanon's postwar contemporary art scene, especially toward the end of the 1990s. One prominent artist of the post-1990 generation, also a well-known art critic and professor at the American University of Beirut, cited the first edition of the Ayloul festival in 1997 as the turning point:

> Retrospectively, I think 1997 was a moment when the internationalization of Lebanese art was quickly felt not as an invitation, but rather as a havoc, almost like an interpellation—like you have to in a sense do that and I think that that impacted the work of many. Some really took on the challenge and began to organize and present their work in ways which allow it to travel, others were reluctant to do so and preferred to remain to a certain extent more bound by the context, even bound by the language and continued to work mostly in Arabic rather than translate their work.[30]

Whatever the generally perceived class affiliation may connote here, inherent in its sentiment is an inescapable assumption of a certain level of cultural and social capital and hence a proclivity toward an upward mobility within the globalized art circuit. In bifurcated societies where class largely determines culture and access to information, such attributes initially placed some artists and their supporting organizations/initiatives in a position to gain from the global art market's new focus on Lebanon's artistic production. Most funding bodies' calls for proposals tended to be in English, for instance, thereby immediately disqualifying a large number of local artists unknown to the "global" art world. Also relevant here is an art critic's analysis that many artists involved in this initiative were already working in a language and aesthetical form that Western art historians understood:

> Another remarkable thing about post-Taif Lebanese art is that most artists were very well conversant with contemporary Western art. So the form, and not necessarily the content, was often the forum for a Western audience. I know a few instances where the familiarity of the form allowed a kind of interpretation [that] is completely irrelevant to the work and the context in which it was made.[31]

Furthermore, in 2002 a professor in the Civilisation Sequence Program at the American University of Beirut assisted the House of World Cultures in Germany with preparations for the *DisORIENTation* project by researching the art scenes in both Damascus and Beirut.[32] Reinforcing the interpretations of the artist and art critic mentioned above, the professor relayed how on a visit to Syria and Lebanon representatives of the German cultural organization made it clear that despite the rich body of artwork that existed in Damascus at the time (mostly hidden in small, local ateliers), and with which the representatives were genuinely impressed, they were nonetheless not the kind of works that could be shown in Berlin due to the dominance of what they saw as more "traditional" mediums, such as painting.[33] To the professor, this incident demonstrated the degree to which the show was already loaded with preconceived ideas about how to frame contemporary art practices from the region. Confirming the professor's observation, a Beirut-based gallery owner wondered out loud to me in 2008, "Isn't it telling that there is not a single curator or arts funder who has come from abroad who is interested in painting?"[34] Such observations shed light on the way in which particular formal prejudices may have colored Western curators' and critics' understandings of the multifaceted context in which production was taking place. They might also help to explain how and why the counterhegemonic operating in a marginal space became the frame and focus of curators and critics after the early 2000s, when it continued to be the trope defining their works even after the artists began to "receive mainstream recognition on both the local and international scene" (Rogers 2008: 44).

The dissident act in art and how global art world actors framed it as part of a larger counterhegemonic force at play varied, even though these actors appeared seemingly unaware of the historical and political dynamics that shaped their acts and overly consumed with how to theorize them. Catherine David understood the postwar aesthetic quite broadly through its affective possibilities, as an "antidote against despair . . . a hope in [its] political and cultural potential" (2002: 37). Others, such as film theorist Laura U. Marks, viewed the "independent artist scene in Beirut [as] one of the strongest critical voices in the contemporary Lebanese political scene" (2004: 46). Similarly, in 2006, writer and critic Stephen Wright explained "in as much as political activism is not currently a viable option [the artists] tend to intervene in the realm of ideas, which is in itself a relatively autonomous sphere" (2006: 60). Yet another type of framing furthered the rhetoric of a subversive local art world by referring to it as "underground" (Falconer 2006). This framing extended into the early days of the 2011–2012 Arab uprisings when journalists appropriated what was happening on the streets of Cairo and Tunis and the bottom-up burst in artistic expression there; they framed postwar Lebanese artists, who were already comfortably plugged into global art circuits and already exhibiting in Western capitals, as starting "creative rebellions" (Allsop 2011). Other theorizations were more specific; they explicated, for instance, artists' chosen modes of representation by reading the liminality (such as blurring fact and faction through cross-disciplinary lines between media studies, visual cultures, and critical theory) in their works as political acts that "actively disrupt the boundaries of art" in processes that invoke "smuggling" as the "clandestine performativity of the contraband object" (S. Harvey 2006: 35–40).[35] Despite the variations on theme, depending on whether the political was read as an active process, as it is in the first three references, or interpreted as a resistant political moment on display in a global setting, there was an underlying assumption that the marginal geographical location of actors in the postwar scene produced "uncertainties" in representations of conflict.[36] These uncertainties, which blur boundaries between fact and fiction and art and nonart, were read as necessary in societies "defined by political antagonisms premised on ideological certainties" because a resort to uncertainty "clears some ground on which alternative political associations might be founded" (Faulkner 2003).

Interestingly, reading the art scene's counterhegemonic role through its uncertain aesthetics presents yet another approach that locates artists' works between "a crusading imperialism," on the one hand, and a "transnational Islamic militancy," on the other, while refusing to succumb to either in exploring the image as a means to represent conflict (Demos 2008). These framings explicate works not in relation to their own context but in the terms of the global spectator and art institution. According to this logic, the process of production they are embedded in and the works themselves are counterhegemonic because they visually and theoretically represent political content in a way that is fathomable to a global art audience, though not because they address the hegemonic institutions operating in the global art world that directly impact the way in which production is carried out in the context of the city and then transmitted to other sites of exhibition.

As I have mentioned already, most of the contemporary art practices that emerged out of Beirut were consumed with the civil war and how to remember and archive it in the brutal context of neoliberal post–civil war reconstruction. Combined with the new media employed in breaking with its past, the contemporary art scene offered an exciting new terrain for curators interested not only in Lebanon but in the politics and culture of the region as a whole. The press release for *DisORIENTation*, which was exhibited in the House of World Cultures in March–May 2003, is a case in point:

> The new generation of artists and intellectuals in the Middle East are breaking the mold in creative circles. They reject all attempts to categorize them collectively and are as critical of the Western conception of the Orient as they are of the social conditions encountered in the region. The new art is political, one which reflects on moral values and the dominant religious and political codes.

Reading this statement, it strikes me that it's almost as if through the artworks the global artworld public could have a fathomable slice of the Arab world, packaged as comprehensible, sexy, and free. It is free because it gets to reject categorizations imposed on it and sexy because it is political and new. The content and aesthetical form of what was coming out of Beirut specifically was something curators from Western art capitals could understand and respond to. The emerging works explained a lot about the history of the region in a conceptual and theoretical language borrowed from Michel Foucault, Jacques Derrida, and Jacques Rancière, which interested Western curators and their audiences could understand. The political content of works therefore continued to signify a counterhegemonic location even when they were incorporated into the global arts circuit on terms that arguably conflicted such a standing.

As already mentioned, toward the end of the 1990s, and especially after 2001, several well-known Lebanese artists participated in international biennials, gallery shows, and festivals. Much of the work exhibited abroad fell under the rubric of group shows (sometimes among a group of larger Arab artists) dedicated to exposing Western audiences to "contemporary postwar art from Beirut." Group show titles often used terminology that immediately placed the artists in preconceived frameworks of identity and strife-ridden locality: for example, *Tamás: Contemporary Arab Representations* (2002), *DisOREINTation* (2003), *Out of Beirut* (2006), *Art Now in Lebanon* (2008), *Les Inquiets: 5 artistes sous la pression de la guerre* (2008), and *Zones of Conflict: Rethinking Contemporary Art During Global Crisis* (2008–2009). These word choices highlighted the ongoing difficulty of penetrating the white cubes of established venues in Western art capitals outside of this framework.[37] Some shows, such as *Les Inquiets*, were accused of reducing artists to mere chroniclers of war (Columbus 2008: 179).[38] Others, such as the long-term project *Contemporary Arab Representations*, as well as *DisORIENTation*, were perceived as homogenizing the region's cultural production of a certain type of scene or art at the expense of highlighting its diversity (Muller 2008).[39] Others still, such as *Zones of Conflict*, were seen to fuel instead of challenge the post-9/11 propensity to place work either within an explicitly politicized or depoliticized context, even when neither the works nor the artists frame themselves within these boundaries (Farhat 2009a).

Speaking of her own experience and observations of regional and country group shows, a European curator and art critic who has observed and worked on promoting art from the region in Europe, had this to say:

> Often "regional" exhibitions in Europe, i.e. shows including work of artists from the Middle East only, take on a didactic quality. Deliberately or not. The institution of venue and curator frame the work in a specific socio-political context, which overwrites other narratives, if not aesthetics. This work is

> supposed to teach us something about Lebanon, Palestine, Egypt, etc., because that type of expectation is raised. Now of course you can perfectly curate a show without raising that type of expectation. It is disturbing because art is pushed in this narrow corner of being a historical witness or a political commentary, without considering how it operates on other levels. What is equally disturbing is that some kind of truth value is invested in it.[40]

Since most of these shows were curated by cultural actors operating out of Western art capitals, what often resulted was a view of the region that relied on Western interpretive methods for understanding the art in relation to its culture. The consequence was a number of works by a limited number of artists (of which the postwar artists constituted a significantly visible portion) that was recycled through multiple exhibitions and venues. As some observed, this occurred at the cost of overlooking the works of other artists important to the fields of new media, photography, and installation, as well as excluding a significant portion of the many artists in the region who continued to work in painting and sculpture (Farhat 2009a).[41]

Some artists took individual stands against partaking in some of these exhibitions for various reasons at different points in their careers.[42] Through my interviews I understood that the decision to exhibit was generally regarded as one that involves a process of negotiation between the artists, the curator, and the host institution. For some artists, if the show is deemed too bent on showcasing artists from Beirut in an orientalist light, they chose to opt out. For others, putting together a group show is not regarded as encompassing nodes of arbitration between two equal partners and other ways have to be found to subvert it. Significantly, for one artist in particular, known for his distancing from the postwar art scene and the main cultural organizations that supported them after being particularly active in the 1990s, these shows can be equated with the notion of humanism, which is in and of itself problematic when viewed especially within its own Western civilizational history.

> It's the artists' models which will give a face to the humanity of the Arab World. This is very important because if you accept that this humanism is triumphant and you forget that the most interesting practices in the West were questioning humanism and its implications in particular in the Second World and in the matrix of what eventually fueled a certain consensus for the creation of

> Israel . . . well . . . there is something crazy going on here. When you accept that this humanist model which as we know it has been incapable of talking about the Palestinians in an interesting way because it either sees them as victims or as terrorists then you understand that it's the same matrix of what constitutes humanity that is triumphant. Imperialism then is humanism. It [imperialism] is not just about demeaning people, but about talking to them, teaching them and about restructuring them. So we see here a productive process that leads to political and cultural practices in the last two centuries and the question I ask is, how have those practices been reshuffled in the past two decades on Lebanon? Can anyone answer me on this?[43]

The notion of humanism, as set out in the above quote, is part of the project of cultural imperialism. Interestingly, the artist's logic here fits squarely within Jessica Winegar's "The Humanity Game: Art, Islam, and the War on Terror" (2008), which critiques the universalist assumptions about humanity and the agentive capacity of art to build bridges of understanding in contexts of so-called civilizational conflict. Motivated by the rationale of building what is often referred to as a "bridge of understanding," Winegar demonstrates how art professionals who are eager to show another face of the Middle East organize special events and attract new audiences, who themselves come eager to see "another side." According to the author, such events are structured around two related assumptions: first, that "art is a uniquely valuable and uncompromised agent of cross-cultural understanding," and second, "that art constitutes the supreme evidence of a people's humanity" (652), thereby bringing everyone together. In both scenarios, Winegar questions the extent to which the agency she refers to can be realized within relations of power that encompass spaces where government officials, money, and weapons are concurrently operating to the effect of reconfiguring social relations. In particular, she asks, does the insistence on seeing rai musicians or Muslim women artists critiquing Islam "really advance Americans' 'understanding' of the Middle East, or does it merely confirm what they think they already know?" (677).

I am reminded here of an informal discussion I once had with a scholar, curator, and art critic based in the UK with an avid interest in art emerging from various war zones. Upon sharing my thoughts that the selection, evaluation, and translation of the meaning of artworks is, as Winegar argues, never "a neutral process governed by universal aesthetic principles; rather, it is deeply political" (652), the curator replied that this analysis is not necessarily relevant from his own vantage point operating out of a European capital. Moreover, he elaborated that in his selection of certain Middle Eastern works for various shows, he chooses ones that speak back to Western mainstream media, which has perpetually recycled unrepresentative images of the region. According to him, if the language contemporary artists spoke was able to transmit the message that an alternative or "third way" exists in the region, then so be it, even if this language operated within "globalized" understandings of contemporary art discourse, which are themselves in need of reflection. The message here is clear: in the world of contemporary art, the "humane" face of the Middle East depends on specific criteria determined not by itself but by the visions of mediators between two cultures operating within and also reinforcing power relations that determine what is tolerable (for a Western audience). In other words, the radical potential of the "other" art is neutralized by its assimilation into a normative center. It becomes, as Gayatri Spivak has famously argued, more that "they are like us" rather than "we are like them" (1985: 258).

BACK IN BEIRUT

Generally, the politics of representation was missing from discussions between artists and the organizations supporting them for the simple reason that participation in exhibitions of their choosing is not seen as promulgating "representation." The artists understood the works to be post-representation. The logic was that "post-modernity has no nationality," as one well-known postwar artist explained when I asked why the works were understood to transcend the politics of representation.[44] According to this reasoning, contemporary art discourse and theory do not yield to the *passé* ideological arts of representation because of the globalism of our world today—hence the shift from a focus on contemporary cultural practices from the region to one without a geographical identification but with a focus on cities, as in Ashkal Alwan's series of forums on cultural practices. This was clearly reflected in the biennial's changed title: from *Home Works: A Forum on Cultural Practices in the Region* to *Home Works: A Forum on Cultural Practices*. Yet, while national identity has been written off by participating artists and organizations, some sort of identity (specifically a new globalized one) continues to bring Lebanese and other Arab artists together in group shows for various Western audiences. As Tohme explained in 2005:

> The forum initially came out of a very honest attempt to try and explore what the region is. What is the role of Lebanon within the Arab world, and what is its relationship with regard to the Arab-Israeli conflict? But then I came to understand the incestuous side to Arab Nationalism. Do we want to go back there? No. Personally, I'm not interested. (Zolghadr 2005)

The principle guiding the 2005 edition of Ashkal Alwan's *Home Works* forum (November 17–24, 2005) was largely self-reflective—a self-proclaimed "exploration of the notion of [our] being in this world, as reconstituted in narrative and representation." The forum's mission statement continues: "We must assert the fact that we are not merely a face caught on a security camera, a stamp on a passport, a fingerprint filed in a court, a visa denied, a stereotype confirmed, or a silent misunderstanding hardened into unspeakable fact. Our faces do not implore to be saved; our faces are beautiful."[45] Central to this mission statement is a self-conscious positioning of Arab, and in this case Lebanese, identity on the world stage of cultural production. Although national identity might have ceased to be the *raison d'être* of the postwar generation's work, an identity linked to geographical boundaries, a shared history, and contemporary reality of existence as "Arabs" in a post-9/11 world continued to be the defining characteristic that allowed entry into the "global" contemporary world of cultural production. This new take on global identity then prompts us to question the complex and shifting ideological underpinnings in the realm of contemporary art whereby an object and project that is rife for consumption may also lead to rarefied conceptions, perceptions, and fetishizations.

The prevalent sentiment shared by some interviewees who were not part of the postwar art scene or its supporting networks and organizations demonstrated an uneasiness with civil war-related works exhibited on the global arts circuit, even if they used the local as a means to speak of global issues, including war, memory, and the rethinking of regional history. The question of aesthetics was almost always missing from such conversations, and works were often read as statement or analyses of the political context. One work that consumed a significant number of interviews I held was postwar artist Rabih Mroué's *I, the Undersigned* (2007), which opened at the Istanbul Bienniale the year before I began my fieldwork in Beirut. Mroué bases this performance on the story of a former militiaman who, years after the end of the civil war, makes a public apology for his actions during the conflict. Explaining that no one ever took the apology seriously, Mroué proceeds to examine the possibilities and limits inherent in a public apology by apologizing for a series of personal faults he himself committed. By interweaving "facts" from the past with subjective speculation about the present, and "individual" experiences set against those of the collective, Mroué focuses not on forgetting the war but on remembering it in all its gory detail as an active process of coming to terms with the past.

Criticisms of this work revolved primarily around anxieties concerning the logic that enables the continued relevance of the lived experience of the war regardless of time and place. The question that concerned some related to the implications of aestheticizing images and imaginings of the war and a historically exotic Beirut in the realm of the European art museum or gallery space (with its particular audiences), years after the war. Scholars have linked the reification of information and knowledge to postmodernity generally (e.g., Jameson 1991), a relevant observation here. On account of this, I would like to suggest that one defining characteristic of this reification is the blurred distinction between authentically knowing and experiencing things and a sort of surrogate knowledge/experience (Nayar 2006: 23). Underlining some of these issues, a well-known Lebanese writer and Marxist historian of the 1967 generation reflected on the content of postwar art as it circulated:

> There is a huge gap between [that] kind of artistic production and people here, so that you are actually producing for a Western audience and that's a bit difficult, because then you're producing what they would like to see or not see in a situation of violence. But you never test what you're producing with your local viewers. For instance, *Ras Beirut* would see a courageous play on the war by Rabih Mroue, but his audience is comprised mostly of those same people who are already very close to the rest of the Ashkal Alwan group and who share a lot of the same experiences. Most of them are disillusioned Leftists or Nationalists, and there are a few hundred of those. You then take that same play to Japan or wherever and audiences can see a courageous Lebanese criticizing his system[.] But you can't take this to Zgharta or Bint Jbeil . . . so then who is your public?[46]

The historian's thoughts fuse a number of important but not necessarily linked issues that were central to many of the other discussions I had with actors in the field. The need to produce work about the war is not determined solely by the whims of a Western audience and curators, as was prevalently believed, nor does it relate to why many of those interviewed expressed discomfort with the politics of representation. The postwar artists were essentially part of a much larger movement of artists and intellectuals in the country, among whom there is a conviction that to move on, Lebanon needs to address the civil war in a way that goes beyond the "forgetting but not forgiving" paradigm that today still defines the country (Fordham 2009). Yet civil war–themed works related to Ashkal Alwan and its global networks and platforms were increasingly understood, quite cynically, as being produced for the specific purpose of entry into the global art world. There are several layers here that may explain the conflation of different beliefs and practices. One relates to the discomforts often triggered by representations of war and trauma in general and the contentious politics around which they revolve. The other concerns the particularities of where contemporary global art locates itself and how it addresses its relevant "public." The final layer has to do with the power politics at play, which qualifies some forms of representations over others, as well as how they are then taken as deterministic of how contemporary art is to be understood, expressed, and debated. Essentially, the historian and others' terms of analysis seem to conflate making art about the war with their concurrently expressed opinion of the need to critically reflect on the meaning and implications of postwar art upon its attainment of international attention. Hence, the issue is not about civil war–related artworks being produced as such but about the politics that grant some works and not others visibility, while at the same time imbuing certain works and processes of production in celebratory rather than critical terms.

Relatedly, in 2009, the Beirut Art Center hosted an exhibition by architect Bernard Khoury entitled *Prisoner of War* (July 23–October 3). *Prisoner of War* drew together a body of works from the post–civil war era that systematically aestheticized war. In a provocative move, the works appropriated the most iconographic artworks from renowned contemporary Lebanese postwar artists, even titling one of its pieces *Catherine Wants to Know* (fig. 13), in reference to Catherine David, the French curator directly associated with the globalization of the postwar art scene through her several visits to Beirut and in particular her subsequent curation of *Contemporary Arab Representations*. Another piece was the installation of an "apparatus"—an ominous looking sculpture that resembles a wingless stealth bomber (fig. 14). The entire show attempted to challenge what Khoury saw as the postwar generation's consensual and dominant practice of not straying far from issues of war, identity, and memory upon the globalization of their art.[47] His main concern was how much artists had become "prisoners of war," partaking in reinforcing the gaze of Beirut as war torn, a common trope in orientalist depictions of the city (Khoury 2010). Khoury's purposefully provocative project upset several actors in the contemporary art milieu by crudely positioning Lebanese post–civil war art as bound by the whims of the global art market and its fetish for war-torn Beirut as part of a longer historical genealogy of orientalist fantasies about the East.

At the same time it was hosting Khoury's *Prisoner of War* show, the Beirut Art Center exhibited a photographic and video work, *Earth of Endless Secrets: Writing for a Posterior Time*, by renowned postwar artist Akram Zaatari.[48] This curatorial decision could be read as an answer to the phenomenon that Khoury wanted to bring to the fore by allowing a glimpse into different approaches to issues of war and the politics of art's globalization. In *Earth of Endless Secrets*, Zaatari makes the case once again that directly accessing personal histories and testimonies of civil war, occupation, and resistance is difficult, if not impossible, thereby asserting the importance of continued conversation about the multifaceted manifestations of war, regardless of the diktats of the global art market that seem compatible with local needs.[49] Thus, while one artist attempted to provoke the art scene into venturing outside of what many in the larger local cultural milieu were increasingly perceiving as a conventional and predictable form of contemporary art feeding into the global art market, another held onto the impulse of excavating the war through art.[50]

Khoury was not the first to comment on the postwar art scene's tendency to consume itself with re-presenting local politics through addressing the metaphorical manifestations of war-related catastrophes. Yet what made Khoury's contribution novel, at the time, was its pointedly crude aestheticization of a very uncomfortable question that had up to that point been discussed only in informal discussions among audience members and actors forming the larger cultural elite. Significantly, the show got no coverage from the international art journals that regularly covered the local exhibitions and happenings related to the postwar artists in those years.

My conversations with artists and cultural organizers directly associated with the postwar art scene typically touched on their frustrations that local

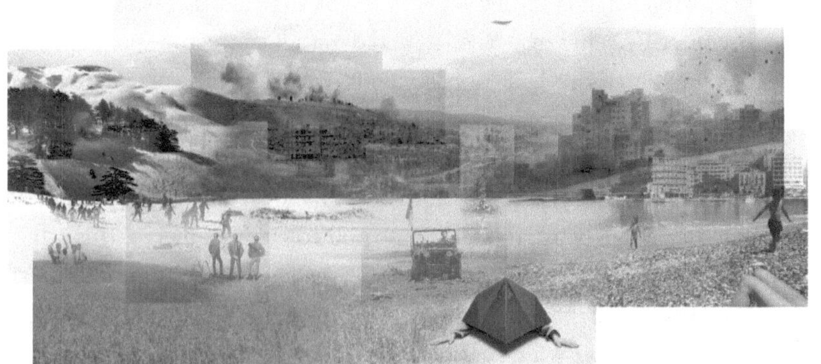

FIGURE 13. DW5/Bernard Khoury. *Catherine Wants to Know.* 2009. Installation shot. Copyright of the artist.

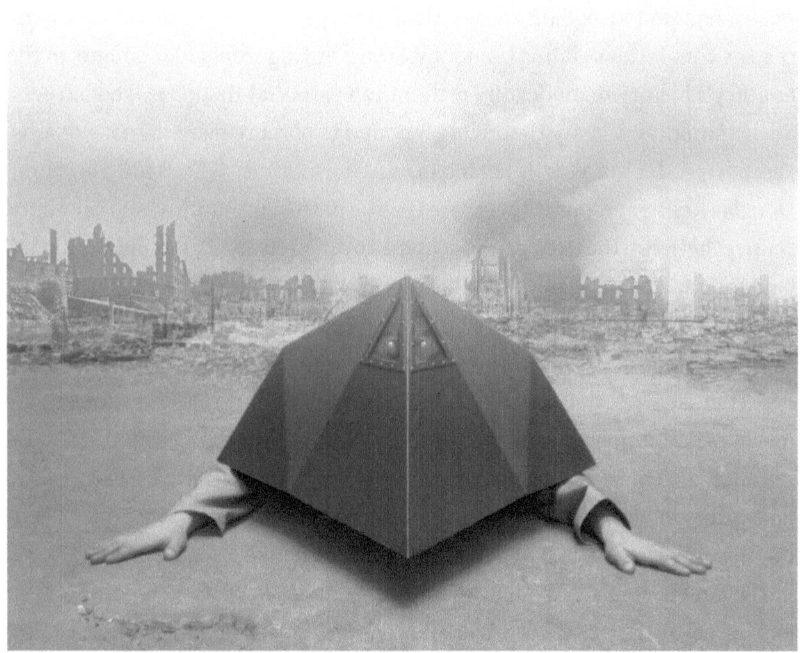

FIGURE 14. DW5/Bernard Khoury. *POW BK 001* [*Concept(s) of Operations*]. 2008. Installation shot. Copyright of the artist.

audiences largely ignored how artwork might engender a culture of theory and discourse by being read as open and dynamic in a composite field that includes the social, political, and economic. Hence, arguments on behalf of some actors in the postwar art scene push for engaging with and interpreting those works as art. Any exchange between art and the public, these arguments reason, should produce discourse and theory about art instead of remaining mired in the politics of its production and political developments. This brings to light two conceptualizations of art's role—the structuralist/materialist, which has to do with the arts-funding institutional politics of representation, versus the immaterial, which concerns the aesthetical qualities of art and its autonomy. The postwar art scene's actors saw these two conceptualizations as being at the heart of a debate on the very meaning of art and articulated them as an irreconcilable fissure between modern and postmodern discourses. Yet, as this chapter has attempted to demonstrate, historicizing two seemingly opposing ideological positions in the transformation of Lebanese, and specifically Beirut-centric, cultural production identifies the various sites of power that exist among the city's cultural elite. In other words, binaries that are understood to explain the political in art versus the politics of art can be read as contentious claims brought forward during troubled moments in the country's history of modernity rather than essential theoretical constructs. Such mutually exclusive theorizing is bound to obscure more than it explains, thereby producing a "debilitating binary normativity" (Rockhill 2014: 120). Douglas Kellner proposes that there may be both "continuities" and "discontinuities" between the two sorts of societies by referencing Raymond Williams's categorizations of "residual," "dominant," and "emergent" cultures (1990b: 275). Williams's (1977) notion of culture as an active and ongoing negotiation during periods of societal change being mediated by processes of selectivity is particularly relevant. Such reasoning further compels the question of why discourse around works and the process by which they are produced should not then also be reflected upon through the structural frameworks they are embedded in, providing they signify interpretations of how the issue of art's relationship to politics is articulated and represented.

Beirut-based art journalist and critic Kaelen Wilson-Goldie perhaps best expressed the relevance of what this chapter's opening implies: that is, that "universalist" postmodernist discourses are being appropriated in positioning the postwar art scene as a counterhegemonic site by bringing it to the center, while framing it as politically relevant in its own context. Here she wrote of Ashkal Alwan's *Home Works 5*, which took place in Beirut in April 2010:

> *Home Works* was never meant to be a sprawling international art event, a spectacle divorced from its context. When Ashkal Alwan began in 1994, its mandate was to engage the city and create artworks that tackled urgent social, economic and political issues inextricably linked to the experience of Beirut and its relationship to the region and the world. *Home Works* was an alternative to big-budget biennials and splashy arts festivals well before either of those models was even plausible or desired in a place like Beirut. For better or worse, in its fifth incarnation, *Home Works* became the very thing it never needed or wanted to be: an art-world power summit, an occasion for lavish lunches, dinners and after parties, an event with little to no local audience or consequence that rolls into town, makes a lot of noise, blows a lot of hot air and disappears. (2010b)

If Wilson-Goldie's remarks are true at all, then they do not describe a situation that developed suddenly in 2010. Rather, they denote what this chapter and the previous section of the book demonstrate started in the late 1990s and became consolidated by the early 2010s. In this chapter, we saw how the global culture funded art scene in Beirut reflected the contentious politics of neoliberal globalization and how it interplayed with more localized histories and narratives. The next chapter looks at how these same neoliberalized sources of funding, art making, and critique produced a different effect in Amman by triggering a multiplication of art sites with varied meanings of their political and social functions.

Chapter 5

AMMAN

Uneasy Lie the Arts

IN 2009, A THIRTY-SOMETHING-YEAR-OLD WOMAN IN A CRISP, white button-down shirt got up on a podium in the middle of a vegetable market in downtown Amman to deliver a speech in flawless Arabic (fig. 15). Shoppers and pedestrians went about their business as Samah Hijawi, whose voice began reluctantly, spoke in a progressively more authoritative and dramatic tone about the United Arab Republic (UAR), the federation between Egypt and Syria that lasted between 1958 and 1961. During the speech, Hijawi, a Jordanian artist of Palestinian descent, reconstructed and randomly sewed together twelve of former Egyptian leader Gamal Abdel Nasser's speeches on Arab unification between 1959 and 1963. She repeatedly enunciated terms associated with his legendary figure in the region's recent political history and the centrality that Palestine held there. Words like "unity," "solidarity," "struggle," and "imperialism" strung together her cobbled sentences, until they began intermeshing into one another, making it impossible for anyone trying to make sense of the speech to fully comperehend it.[1] The artist never revealed to her audience that her speech was taken from Nasser's speeches. Nor did she ever indicate the aim of her performance: to see how the public would react to a made-up speech tapping into their recent history. "Do[es] [the public] recognize it?" she asked, "Do they find it funny, ridiculous, absurd? Does it resonate at all?" (Hijawi 2015). In the tradition of artists of her generation, as examined in chapters 3 and 4, Hijawi probed the contemporary relevance of past ideological narratives.

This scene is from a series performed in different public and private venues in Amman (and later Ramallah). The events make up a project of Hijawi's, titled *Where Are the Arabs?*, or in Arabic, *Wayn Al'Arab?*—after a well-known rhetorical question of protest about the Arab regime's lack of reaction to Israeli colonization of Palestine: Hijawi (2015) described the project's intentions:

> People in the region have a tendency to dwell on a glorious past, in *Where Are the Arabs?* I wanted to investigate the public's relationship with its recent political history, and the collective Arab identity, while pointing to Palestine as a focal point for understanding the region's identity politics.

At various points, she invited those watching to read from her speech. According to the artist, others who were present, and the video documentation of the first day of the performance in the famous Souk Mango (Mango Market),

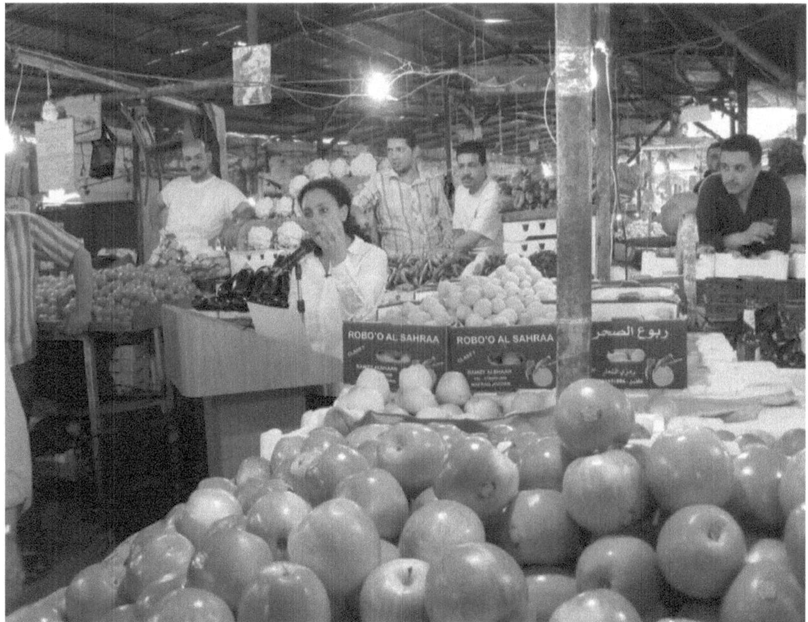

FIGURE 15. Samah Hijawi. *Where Are the Arabs?* 2009. Performance view, Mango Market, Amman. Photograph: Ali Saadi. Courtesy of the artist.

the reactions from the public ranged from shock and ridicule to amusement and utter disbelief at her boldness. According to the artist, the audience was initially unsure of what to make of the performance, but as it proceeded, they seemed to get more comfortable. Some encouraged the artist to run for parliament, promising they would vote for her if she did; others questioned the performance, yet agreed to come up to the podium to read from the speech.

The artist considered the project a success—even though she did not know what the audience actually thought about their recent political history or whether they truly considered it as a "glorious" phase, as she describes. Bear in mind that when reference to a glorious Arab past, or *al 'asr il thahaby* (a golden age), is made in Arabic it is often in relation to the more distant past, such as Muslim rule in the Iberian Peninsula in the Middle Ages, for example, and not the period of twentieth-century postcolonial nation-state building. Significantly, before launching the project, Hijawi was required to get a special permit from Amman's General State Security (GSS) through the Royal Film Commission. Considering the GSS's notoriously tight control of public spaces in the country, this was considered a feat. It did not stop the GSS, however, from attending three of the performances and asking for a copy of the script on the final day.

In requesting permission, Hijawi framed her project as one segment of a larger film project instead of an art project. In effect, she was tapping into one of the regime's soft spots: the construction of a film industry in Jordan, a project spearheaded by members of the royal family.[2] The relative ease with which Hijawi implemented her public art project demonstrates how the regime in Jordan cooperates on matters of cultural production, which might highlight its supposed democratic ideals of tolerance and freedom of expression, indicating how modern national institutions of power have productive and coercive means of power that often work at the same time (Masaad 2001). In other words, in the eyes of the regime, Hijawi's ephemeral work in a public site did not pose any real threat to security, despite its public probing of political expression in Arabic—a combination that often lands artists in hot water.[3] Viewed within this frame, the project arguably reinforced the regime's self-image, mainstream international media coverage, and diplomatic circles' representation of it as modern, liberal, and progressive, as inimitably emblematized in Queen Rania of Jordan herself.[4] The acceptance of *Where*

Are the Arabs? by the regime's progressive face impels question of how we understand the political function and social relevance of contemporary art to the local public in a context where the ruling regime preaches the counsel of piecemeal reform and gradualism, which rarely, if ever, delivers major change (Larzillière 2016).[5] An analysis of contemporary art's relationship to regime politics in Amman and the politics of representation in the global art sphere helps illustrate the ways in which cultural production's role is always multiple and contradictory; its reception and meaning varies across social and class lines, as Hijjawi's project demonstrated, and it is always intimately linked to and shaped by the dynamics of the political and ideological projects of states, political, and cultural elites.

Despite the work's intrusion into daily life and its being part of the artist's larger oeuvre, which deals with readings of the construction of national identity and interpretations of the past, the project was neither critiqued nor written about in any of the local dailies that normally cover art events, except to list it as a cultural happening. On the other hand, the myriad English-language visual art journals, magazines, and website publications concerned with contemporary art from the region engaged more closely with the work.[6] In addition, segments of it were presented in performance lecture format at a group show at the Museum of Modern Art (2014) in New York City. The exhibition was dedicated to showcasing public art from the region and was inspired by the then recent revolutionary events. It borrowed its title from Hijjawi's work.[7] I am interested in the unlikely interface between two seemingly unrelated domains: the global art world's interpretation of the project and the local regime's appropriation of it, and the ways that this dynamic can be used as a tool for understanding the larger relationship between the political economy of globalized art and local cultural politics in Jordan. This aligns with my aims expressed in the introduction to the book, where I suggest using art as a starting point for understanding the transnational politics of countries in the region through a global frame of reference, rather than starting with domestic politics and then locating the art inside of that frame (Scheid 2020).

From its inception, *Where Are the Arabs?* was concerned with how art interplays with affective encounters in public space as well as sensorial and emotional politics. These themes have concerned theorists such as Jacques Rancière (2004, 2009, 2010), Chantal Mouffe (2006, 2007a), Judith Butler

(2015), Sara Ahmed (2004), and a growing body of Middle East-focused scholars since the onset of the Arab uprisings of 2011–2012 (Winegar 2012, 2016; Tripp 2013; Pearlman 2013; Hasso and Salime 2015). The project seemingly interrogated, in political theorist Jacques Rancière's (2004) terminology, the "distribution of the sensible" through its interaction with the public and its emphasis on active spectatorship to probe what we think we see and therefore experience. The French philosopher proposes the fostering of a radical and emancipatory democratic politics as a site that encompasses "what is seen and what can be said about it, around who has the ability to see and the talent to speak" around ways of "doing and making" as a shared sense of the "common" (Rancière 2004: 12–13). Yet as I propose in this chapter, the cooperation of the GSS and regime politics more generally complicate Rancière's proposal, one that over the past ten years has gained him much popularity in the globalized contemporary art world partly because "it tells the art world what it wants to hear about itself; it reinforces the glowing stereotype that the art world fancies for itself—that is, as an inherently political and almost subversive place" (Wright 2008: 5).

Questions about the body and its place vis-à-vis the publics and public space concern many artists, social studies scholars, and art critics of the region. Consider a piece published in the journal *Afterall* that analyzes how young Arab artists are dealing with the legacy of pan-Arabism. The writer begins the piece by referring to Hijawi's uncovered hair in public space during *Where Are the Arabs?* (Stefan Weiner 2015). Crucially, whether Hijawi's hair was covered during her performances was beside the point to the larger performance. Neither in her conversations with me about her piece nor in any of the descriptions of the work did the author ever refer to the question of the veil or even her female body in public space—questions that have historically consumed Western scholars in a different way than they have the women of the region. According to the artist, the public and private venues she chose to perform in are those she often frequented as a resident in the neighborhood of nearby Dawar il Thalith (Third Circle). She felt relative ease circulating through these spaces as an unveiled woman, like many other women in that area, and conceived of her project in the terms of an active citizenship she was participating in on an equal footing.[8] If anything, what was probably more interesting than whether she was veiled was the fact that her "tongue-in-cheek" choice of venue for the first performance was Souk Mango, one of the longest running souks in downtown Amman known for selling women's lingerie.[9]

The form of representation that the author of the article employs indicates how readings of public art end up bestowing on art a counterhegemonic quality by virtue of its content and supposed ability to provoke affective encounters with the audience alone. Likewise, the role of the local audience and the frame through which they interpreted the artwork is elided, even in the projects of the most well-intentioned artists. This gives us insight into the often-ambiguous relationship between the artist and local audience. For instance, I was reminded several times during my fieldwork that art students at Jordanian universities use the Internet for research because of the dearth of Arabic printed material in their libraries. This dimension of their studies already limits their possible exposure to and inclusion in a virtual global conversation on artwork discussed about a context in which they live. This also complicates the idea of capacities often triggered by art that determine "what is seen and what can be said about it, around who has the ability to see and the talent to speak" (Rancière 2004: 12–13). If most writing about the project, which was concerned with localized histories and spaces, are only in English, then whose "voices are being heard" and who is "doing and making?" By extension, certain forms and contents may be emphasized over others when art begins to circulate globally.

While the capacities set in motion by art are necessary and indeed a crucial component of critical and resistant cultural production, they do not suffice alone as a paradigm for understanding the layers that define art's role in counterhegemony. Taken in isolation this paradigm, seen repeatedly in the coverage, reinforces a gestural politics or a tendency to frame the political in art as merely an ontological exploration. The perpetuation of this paradigm, I suggest, is based on a belief in the transnationally connected and internationally funded contemporary art world that a reconceptualization of the world around us is enough to confer a counterhegemonic role for art and the artists making it. In this scenario, the presumption is that all one must do is confirm that there *is* a place to "speak" or "feel" for that place to actually exist.[10] Yet the challenge in Amman, as well as in Beirut and Ramallah, also lies in creating and then reflecting on the conditions that privilege some speech and action over others. As I argue in this section of the book more generally, Rancière's formulation of politics as intrinsic to aesthetics because of its affective possibilities—a formulation so popular in the global and mostly English-speaking contemporary art world—does offer us entry into rethinking art's role as utopian and resistant to capitalist hegemony. In concrete terms, this enables the viewer of an artwork to affectively react to the atrocities of the region's wars, ideologies, and the inaccuracies of the official histories related to each, including the mutability of memory and more recently the violence of populism and religion. Yet, simultaneously, the viewer may be rendered incapable of recognizing the very same violent relations of power that connect capital and the selective circulation of some images and not others in the global arts circuit.[11]

Considering the relationship between the regime and civil society in Jordan, I query the extent to which the emancipatory claims of contemporary global art may articulate a relevant form of localized counterhegemonic politics in complex domestic contexts, like Jordan's, that alternate between political authoritarianism and economic liberalization disguised as democratization (Robinson 1998; Lucas 2003). This point is notwithstanding, of course, that contemporary art, often in its immaterial form as when Hijawi (re)presented her work in global venues, is sometimes most alive when it is traveling. For as a creative transcultural act, this art embodies the global and thus feels most at home there (Clifford 1997).[12] Yet, as I indicate in the introduction to the book, despite the globality of contemporary art and its supporting institutions, I nonetheless understand the local and the global to be interwoven in such a way that they each take shape through their interaction with one another. Even if the locally flavored art is often eclipsed in discourses on global culture, it is still part of globalization's very makeup. Accordingly, I suggest that the legacy of the Hashemite-ruled kingdom in Jordan as a benevolent autocracy—tolerant only of some forms of regime-sanctioned anti-establishment rhetoric—complicates potential counterhegemonic contemporary arts production. This legacy makes it difficult for contemporary art, and especially public art, that experiments with new form and content to disentangle itself from the regime's current policies on political reform, cultural development, intercultural dialogue, and education in line with international pressures and its own cultural diplomacy strategies. Such policies are intended to bring about democratization and cede some power to the people—but only "the right kind of people" (Goldberg 2013), leading to what has been termed as the regime's "defensive democratization."[13] This is significant because it complicates the contested field where artists create with varying degrees of compromise, and in turn, regimes respond by constructing façades of tolerance (Cooke 2007; Wedeen 1999). A third player is also added to this two-way relationship: the community of artists that produces art with a self-conscious knowledge of belonging to a global art world defined by its neoliberal circuits of production and global cultural funds that are part of the larger aid dependency structure that defines Jordan's political economy.

ANATOMIES OF ART

It is impossible to fully understand Hijawi or other similar public art projects that took place in Amman in the first decade of the millennium without reading the role of the cultural space Makan, where many young artists of middle- to upper-class backgrounds congregated at the time. It is helpful if we also undertake this reading against the backdrop of the older, more established nonprofit and nongovernmental institution of art and culture: Darat al Funun (Arabic for "home of the arts") in Amman. Darat al Funun is a self-funded institution, founded and funded in 1988 by Suha Shoman and her husband, the late Palestinian businessman and art collector, Khalid Shoman, to support contemporary Arab artists.[14] Makan opened ten years later as a contemporary art space founded by the then twenty-nine-year-old Ola El-Khalidi with precarious funding and a collective ethic. Defunct as of 2015, Makan's space is just down the street from Darat al Funun's. Both of these initiatives played a leading role in the early 2000s and beyond in introducing the publics in Amman to discourses, theories, and concepts of art rooted in global aesthetics. In the process, both initiatives distinguished themselves from the galleries or museums that were until the early 2000s the most common types of arts venues in the country.[15] Yet, while Darat was founded on a platform dedicated to creating a regional hub for contemporary art and artists, and was particularly attentive to promoting a more localized conversation in Arabic on arts and cultural production more broadly,[16] it was also committed to weaving itself into the already existing cultural fabric of the city through the architectural preservation of the 1930s and 1940s buildings that housed it.

Makan instead relied on international donor funding from organizations such as the European Cultural Foundation and the Ford Foundation, or one of the host of funding organizations active also in neighboring Beirut and Ramallah, such as the brainchild of the Ford Foundation-Young Arab Theatre Fund. Like other initiatives in Beirut that perceived themselves as "independent" (e.g., Zico House, Ashkal Alwan in its early years, and the now defunct Art School Palestine in Ramallah), Makan was more committed to providing an open space where younger generations of artists could experiment more fluidly and democratically in both the content and forms of their production than they would in more "mainstream venues with more orthodox standards" (El Ahmad 2003).

These different orientations of Makan and Darat were reflected not only in each initiative's audience but also in their architectural forms and aesthetical focuses. Darat Al-Funun indicated a structure rooted in the local community where Jordanian university students, artists, writers, and the broader public could come to read about their cultural past and global modern and contemporary art in its library and rethink their presence and imagine their futures in the series of workshops, artist talks, artist residencies, music festivals, and poetry readings it hosted by local and international artists, poets, critics, and curators of different generations. The Darat also played a decisive role in establishing a home for Iraqi art in Jordan, especially after the 1991 Gulf War. Makan (Arabic for "place") paradoxically exuded a sensibility that did not restrict itself to anything or anyone. The founder said of why she chose this name: "I wanted people to create their own feelings in it" (El Ahmad 2003). Makan was understood by the collective of artists that formed its core group as well as all the younger corpus of musicians, activists, writers, bloggers, and visual artists that frequented its events and workshops to be an open, unregulated, and nonhierarchical space. The question of aesthetics and its relationship to the public was defined through experimentation and a series of trials and errors instead of commissioned exhibitions, exactly as in *Where Are the Arabs?*, which was supported and finalized in conjunction with Makan.[17]

Walking into Makan on any afternoon of the workweek, one was sure to find the often bilingual and well-traveled artists, writers, and bloggers who came to rent studios in Jebel el Weibdeh, drinking tea and smoking cigarettes on a cozy balcony overlooking the hills of Amman or installing an art show in the facility's modest but uniquely designed exhibition space (fig. 16). This

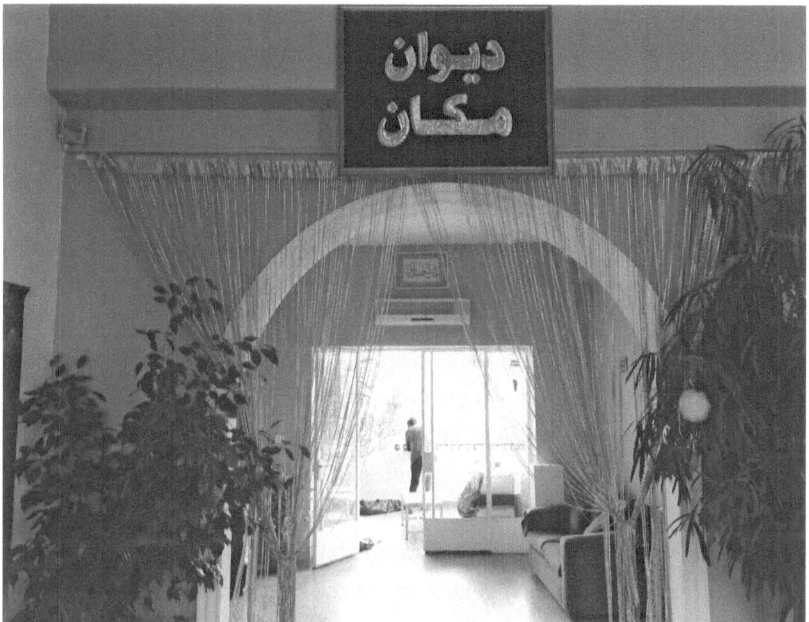

FIGURE 16. Makan main entrance, exhibition space and balcony overlooking downtown Amman. Copyright Oraib Toukan.

group, along with a growing number of visiting artists from the region and Western cities, increasingly inhabited what is now the gentrified and hip landscape of the neighborhood. Jebel el Weibdeh is known today for being the cultural heart of Amman, along with those neighborhoods adjacent to it: the First and Second Circles, which possess some of the most beautiful palatial 1920s and 1930s houses in the city as well as a host of galleries such as Dar Al Anda, the much loved and now renovated and upgraded Jordan and National Museum, and various important European cultural institutions, such as the French Cultural Center and the Spanish Cervantes Institute.

The artists who frequented Makan in those early years were a noticeably different crowd than the ones lounging on the chairs in the Darat's original terraced café, sipping its famous mint lemonade or a cup of Turkish coffee by its arabesque-style water fountain.[18] The crowd at the Darat tended to be made up of mostly Arabic-speaking artists, poets, and writers of various generations, along with a cohort of art students from various universities in the country, who during the first decade of the millennium were more inclined to practice painting and sculpture as opposed to media arts. In the early 2000s, there was still a clear demarcation between locally educated painters, sculptors, artists, and often Western-educated artists more interested in and working on interdisciplinary multimedia production. As the 2000s wore on, multimedia practices became more ubiquitous, when artists who practiced painting and sculptor began to more freely experiment with digital media and public platforms. Other visitors to the Darat in those days, and even more today, included tourists who were often attracted by the exhibitions on display at the venue and the space's more "authentic" feel and architecture. With time, there was more crossover between the two crowds as it became increasingly clear that Darat and Makan were complementary rather than competitive nodes. It was clear from the outset, however, that Darat's presence in the country since 1988, in addition to its sustainable source of self-funding through a private endowment, meant it was free to define its own agenda. In the early 2000s, this extended to catering to the growing media-based contemporary art scene generally led by the younger generation in the country and the region more broadly. Concurrently, the Darat was free to continue with its tradition of keeping art about Palestine and Palestinian artists at the core of its programming initiatives.[19] According to the director of the Jordan National Gallery of Fine Arts, also a well-known painter, the continuation of this tradition was meaningful at a time when, in his opinion, the centrality of Palestine in the works of young, transnationally linked contemporary artists was waning because of their concerns with tackling how the nation and nationalism has affected the personal through a more theoretically and conceptually informed aesthetic that critiques collective causes and ideas.[20]

Suha Shoman, a sometimes feared, yet always highly respected woman with social and political connections, was quick to remind me in conversation that contemporary artists in Amman and neighboring cities in the region have predecessors. They did not emerge from a tabula rasa of art or criticism, as she rightfully believes art writing on the region often indicates and as the artists themselves often imply.[21] Sifting through the substantial digitized archive of events and publications published by the Darat and looking back at the events I was able to attend, such as Adonis and Haidar's (2007) exhibition and talk *Adonis and Haidar: A Dialogue Between Collage and Drawing*, it became clear that the Darat was pushing for a conversation on locating contemporary Arab art within its own teleology of art history. This decolonizing mission, which has now matured into a concerted and ongoing effort by scholars of global art history with a focus on the Middle East (some of whom I refer to in the introduction to this book), responds to the gap in the literature that Shoman and others cultural workers in the regions frustratingly pointed to during my fieldwork.

The younger artists and curators whom I interviewed were most consumed with documentary, photography, archival research, and collectively based and process-oriented work informed by the educational turn in art that encouraged pedagogical experimentation as a form of knowledge production. They understood their practices to emanate from an entirely different art historical and political reference. This reference bluntly contradicted formalist notions of beauty and the sublime in art that were understood by the younger generation of artists as also being linked to articulations of a national identity. One of Jordan's now well-known painters of the post-1990 generation expressed to me that as an Arabic-speaking painter from the Palestinian camps in the country he felt more comfortable in the early 2000s drinking Turkish coffee on the Darat's patio speaking to older artists than he did drinking tea on Makan's balcony. In the artist's view, Darat allowed him to remain true to who he was—an Arabic-speaking painter interested in a conversation about painting—while Makan's discourse and global connections forced him to partake in a conversation he felt was more interested in pursuing an audience outside of Jordan.

While Darat did not initially set out to cater to the younger post-1990 generation of artists, by the early 2000s it had become one of the most important platforms and markers of success for that group of artists, whether they practiced painting or worked with multimedia. As Shoman reminded me on the two occasions we spoke, she did not rely on external source funding and was therefore free to strategize and prioritize in accordance with the society's needs rather than funders' whims. With the help of established art historians and curators such as Sarah Rogers and Eline Van der Vlist acting as advisors and artistic directors, Darat was able to carefully refashion itself into one of the leading hubs of cultural production, a position it consolidated with the beautiful renovation and construction of the LAB, a platform set up in 2011 in three old renovated houses for younger experimental artists to support their practices and exchanges, stimulate critical discourse, and research, document, and archive Arab art.[22] Many of the artists associated with Makan interacted with this institution, and some eventually exhibited there. Even before the establishment of the LAB, Darat had given emerging artists from the younger generation like Hani Alqam, Saba Innab, Oraib Toukan,Ala Younis, and Sima Zureikat working in Amman, the opportunity to produce their first solo shows, present lecture performances, attend one of the many workshops, and even offer their own sometimes. With Shoman's self-governed vision and financial resources, Darat also invited some of the biggest names in contemporary art from the region to exhibit in Amman: these included Palestinian artists Emily Jacir and Mona Hatoum, as well some of Lebanon's most well-known postwar artists, such as Walid Raad and Akram Zaatari. There was a consistent effort in those years to introduce the works of younger and established Arab artists residing abroad, or in "exile," to the communities living in the contexts that often inspired their works. More important perhaps was the South-South connection that was being emphasized in these cultural exchanges across the region through workshops, festivals, and courses.

Amman, unlike Ramallah or Beirut, was not a hub for international curators interested in recruiting Arab artists for shows and festivals to be held in Western capitals, and it never was. In contrast, Palestine has always been a historical place of fascination in the Western imaginary. Its domination by Israel, and the headline coverage it received as a result, meant that Palestinian cultural production, as I highlight in the following chapter, became a cause for Western liberals to champion, sometimes at the expense of art practices elsewhere in the region.[23] Likewise, Lebanon's postwar memory generation and Beirut's historical appeal to Westerners as the "Paris of the East" ensured its place on Western curators' itineraries. The international focus on Beirut's art scene therefore piqued the interest of many artists from Ramallah who were unable to enter Lebanon and attend its contemporary art festivals and workshops, which Jordanian artists could because they had no restrictions on entering the country. Hence, Darat in Amman provided Palestinian artists with a preserve of expression and learning about global art.

When the work of younger-generation artists such as Samah Hijawi, Saba Inab, Oraib Toukan, Alaa Younis, and Sima Zureikat began to circulate in international exhibitions, it was never framed as representing "Jordanian" art but as emphasizing globally relevant themes. For example, Innab's work foregrounded architecture and space, Toukan's focused on institutional critique and the inscription of memory in our lives, and Younis's emphasized narratives and personal histories. This arguably positive development of making artists visible on the terms of their own research rather than their perceived exotic, national belonging tells of how funding from private endowments and corporations may provide an alternative form of representation and discussion about art's role in society and to whom it speaks. Once again, this points to the argument I make at the beginning of chapter 1 about how in Arabic *tamwyl ajnabi*, or funding, is not a neutral term as it is in English. Rather, it is steeped in memories of empire and the ongoing Arab experience of neo-imperial violence now legitimated by neoliberal culturalism. Hence, these sensitivities around funding and the questions they provoke even from those who receive such funds are not simply a competition between the forces of darkness and light, as the journalist Youssef Bazzi laid out (2007). What they indicate instead is a body of proactive subjects determining the very contours of the debate by which cultural production will be defined and represented—an act of negotiated "cultural sovereignty" (Winegar 2006: 281).

Makan arguably has earned its place in the city's short history of contemporary art among many younger artists, international curators, and art funders, despite never intending to institutionalize like Darat, and in spite of the founding collective of artists' knowledge of its ephemerality. The space introduced the idea that art was as much about the object produced as it was about the democratic process of making and exhibiting it. As Toleen Touq, artist, cultural activist, and writer, put it in an interview on the role of young artists in Jordan during the 2011–2012 uprisings and the impact it had on her generation in Amman, "We have to recognize and remember that their resistance was present before 2011, and now they continue to support critical movements" (Guevera 2012). Touq was specifically referencing the assumption often made that it was the Arab uprisings alone that triggered the nonprofit and nongovernmental art scene to invest in more decentralized and collaborative projects.

Touq's own project, cofounded with Noura Al Khasawneh, consists of an annual three-month art residency program known as Spring Sessions, which was founded to explicitly "address the absence of critical and experiential art education in Jordan." Spring Sessions unfolded from conversations that took place in Makan, and it relocated to its building after Makan closed in 2015.[24] The program invites fifteen to twenty international and local artists to create a collaborative environment for artistic exchange between cultural practitioners. Conceived every spring as a 100-day program of workshops, mentoring sessions, research excursions, and other activities in Amman, the organizers' purpose is to question existing paradigms by experimenting outside of traditional modes of learning, while consciously engaging with communities and institutions to create a fluid cultural landscape.

Two questions that emerge are how and to what end initiatives such as Makan and Spring Sessions invest in a "relational aesthetics"? (Gottesman 2010). In his reflective piece, Eric Gottesman draws on Nicolas Bourriaud's (1998) well-known theory about art being defined by the whole of human relations and their social context, rather than by the independent and private spaces that enable their work. Gottesman does so to expound the idea that artist-led initiatives are powerful precisely because they do not define themselves in terms of their art. Rather, in artist-led initiatives the art extends itself in a horizontal and informal way to its audiences, the communities from which it emerges, and the social structures that sustain each. How are these projects, then, related to the political in Jordan? And by the political here I mean how do the practices Makan supported intervene in the space of state-society relations defined by community, subjectivity, citizenship, institutional change, and political imagination? Within this framework, the audience takes on a central role in the production of work and the construction of its meaning, even if it is never visible on its own account and almost always spoken for by artists and elements of its supporting structures such as critics and funders. Hence, what complicates this dialectic between the composition of Amman's contemporary art scene and the political is the fact that most of the initiatives, organizations, and projects inspired by Makan insist that they work outside of any institutional hierarchy and protocols. Instead they emphasize the process of friendships, passion, and camaraderie between each other and with their audiences in the making of art rather than its aesthetical production, audience size, and impact. I discuss this conceptualization in the next section.

"DO WE REALLY NEED AN AUDIENCE?"

One warm summer afternoon in 2009, I met up with Ola El-Khalidi for a discussion about her work and my research. El-Khalidi is an old friend whose prescient verve for creating an alternative arts space was something we began discussing informally as far back as the winter of 2002. When El-Khalidi and I first spoke about her plans and the possibilities Makan might have for obtaining international funding—knowing full well that she would never be able to obtain local public funds for such a project—she had just returned to Amman after completing first a bachelor's degree at the American University of Beirut and then a master's degree in management from the University of Surrey in the UK. In the late 1990s, she was one of a group of people who worked at Blue Fig café, one of the earliest known restaurant cafés in Amman to host a blend of musical concerts, experimental arts exhibitions, and poetry readings, along with a fusion food menu. El-Khalidi also worked at Beirut D.C., an NGO in Lebanon founded to support the growing cadre of independent Arab filmmakers overcoming the constraints of independently minded Arab cinema. She was also a close friend of the founder and working associate at Zico House in Beirut, one of the city's first independent art spaces. During her time there, El-Khalidi was increasingly intrigued by the potential an informal art space might have in a smaller and less culturally diverse and cosmopolitan city like Amman.

El-Khalidi felt she needed to engage more closely with young, multimedia-based artists and musicians if she was going to provide a platform in which they could exhibit their work and facilitate interaction with the local public, from whom they often felt estranged. Aware that the region's wars in the post-9/11 world were changing the society around her as well as attracting international interest in the region, El-Khalidi did not know whether the combination of her feelings and experiences could launch a functioning space, but she decided to try. Armed with the blessings and financial support of close families and friends, Makan finally opened its doors on 21 Mallah Street in April 2003, a few houses down from Darat al Funun and next door to the Dar Al Anda Gallery. As the story goes, when Makan finally opened, "Ola sat at her desk with a cup of sweet tea (she still had sugar in her tea then), and waited. Organizing and re-organizing papers, opening fresh files, not knowing where all of this was going" (Khasawneh 2010). She eventually began to meander her way through the streets of her new neighborhood and eventually the larger city, making connections, meeting artists, and planning projects. In the words of El-Khalidi and Dialah Khasawneh, an artist, writer, and early partner in the project,

> day after day, this organic creature went discovering the world around it, meeting people, embarking on projects, acquiring experiences, some expected, some full of surprises, learning with each one. Makan did not stop at its physical boundaries, but went onto the street (Maha Abu Ayyash, Oraib Toukan,

> Lina Saoub), took performacafé to a café, a bar, and a vegetable market (Samah Hijawi), filled the National Gallery park with music (electronic music festival-*100 Live*), and exhibited work in an abandoned pasta factory (Yasmin Ayyashi). The space also collaborated with other cultural institutions such as Al Balad Theater and Darat al-Funun, and worked with tcaféarpenter, café owner, and the vegetable vendor, as well as the hip hop performer. (2010)

Initially, its conservative working-class neighbors and a nearby mosque did not warmly welcome Makan. The space by contrast attracted members of the many humanitarian aid organizations; the growing precarious class of freelance writers, bloggers, artists, architects, and urban planners; and university students. From early on, it also became known as a safe haven for visitors of marginalized sexual orientations and identities. I remember attending events in its early years, like films shown on very basic projectors whose sounds were intercepted by calls to prayer at the mosque next door, although outside of the official hours in which the mosque calls to prayer. This was the mosque's way of expressing disapproval at the young, mixed groups of people standing outside of its front gates and pouring onto its streets, smoking and chatting during intermissions and exhibition openings. Eventually, Makan won over the community by commissioning services like upholstery and woodwork, needed in the work of the many local and international artists who held residencies at the space itself or rented studio space in the streets adjacent to it. The neighborhood in which Makan was located—Jebel el Weibdeh, or simply "Weibdeh," as it is more commonly known by residents of the city—today is known café its bohemian cafés and easygoing lifestyle. In the early 2000s Weibdeh's streets, however, were not yet filled with the variety of quaint cafés, painted murals, street markets, and little handcraft shops interspersed with artist studios that they are today. But Makan and the artists who gravitated to it in search of cheap rent and interesting urban spaces to produce their work most definitely played a leading role in putting the neighborhood on the city's cultural map.

The political scientist Jillian Schwedler (2010) has shown that the neoliberal onslaught on Jordan unexpectedly brought with it new sites of participation and engagement, where cosmopolitan young Jordanians learned how to transgress entrenched class boundaries in ways that might not necessarily be emancipatory but that tell of new ways to negotiate hegemonic power structures, through what she describes as practices of survival, creativity, and re-imagination" (549). Hence, in Jordan, the opening up of the cultural production scene, including theater, visual arts, and music, with the help of international donors, allowed for an emancipatory sensibility and mood to emerge among artists of the post-1990 generation and the communities in which they thrived.

As the sun began to set that summer afternoon during my meeting with El-Khalidi, we moved from her bright and minimally decorated office that housed a small bookshelf of mostly English art publications to the balcony for a cup of tea. We had an open conversation about the workings of culture in an economically and culturally segregated society, such as Amman's, where two parts of the city—West Amman and East Amman—are virtually walled off from each other. Though over the years El-Khalidi and I had enjoyed many conversations about art and funding after 9/11, especially in the months leading up to Makan's official opening when she did not have any money or a clear strategy, this was the first time we spoke in the context of what was my PhD field research at the time.[25] Our disagreement that day had to do with the prevalent understanding in the nonprofit and nongovernmental arts sector that while the actors in the sector might not agree with what they perceive to be their international patrons' political agendas, they had no choice but to work with them. Notwithstanding, El-Khalidi, and others I interviewed in the field, concerned with the rigid confines of international funding for nonprofits and NGOs, could still create a local and relevant discourse on art's relationship to society and intervene in the political space of thought, knowledge production, and cultural representation.

A few days after our meeting, I called a number of artist friends and freelance curators for an informal focus group of tea drinking and chatting on Makan's balcony. I wanted to discuss some of the questions that were arising from my fieldwork. One of the issues we thought through that day was what they described as the conspiratorial thinking prevalent in society that contemporary art was categorized an inauthentic Western import and that as a generation of cultural producers they were "neither here nor there." They explained that they were neither artists interested in producing paintings for a gallery nor artists who cared about whether the general public believed that what they were doing was relevant to wider national conversations on politics and culture.[26] Their choices, logics, and aesthetical tastes, I was told, were deemed by the rest of society to stem from different historical and political references, which would inevitably lead to their irrelevance to local audiences who were challenged to relate to their conceptual language and frame of thinking, even if the artists were addressing issues relevant to the wider public, like urban gentrification, identity, and citizenship.

Earlier on, between 2004 and 2007, Meeting Points, an interdisciplinary contemporary arts festival organized in conjunction with Makan, was instrumental in putting Amman on the contemporary Arab arts circuit.[27] The different iterations of the festival toured with cities in the region and featured theater, contemporary dance, music, and visual artists. Its intention was to provide South-South meeting points for artists, art spaces, art operators, and audiences. As well as producing works of art, the event promoted the mobility of artists within the region and created a network among the many nonprofit and nongovernmental art spaces that were quickly emerging. Meeting Points encouraged well-known European curators to finally come to the city and reach out to its artists through studio visits and planned collaborations. Until that point, most curators used Amman only as a stopover on the way to the West Bank or bypassed it altogether and just went straight to Beirut. The then newly published English-language, Middle East–focused arts publication *Bidoun* reported on Meeting Points in its third issue titled "Hair":

> This year's [2004] *Amman Meeting Points*, organized by the Brussels-based Young Arab Theatre Fund and the Makan gallery space, created a stir of unprecedented activity in the capital. The event served as a novel forum for both local and international artists to meet, while its theme was rooted in notions of borders and travel—fitting given the geographic situation of the Jordanian capital as an historic crossroads. . . . Importantly, the use of new media in Meeting Points provided local audiences with incredible exposure to alternative art forms. Egyptian Amal Al Kenawy stunned audiences with two powerful installations, *The Journey* and *The Room*—both exploring the body as a zone of potential rupture. Alexandrian Wael Shawky presented his video installation *Asphalt Quarter* in a revamped, simpler form—a multimedia exploration of the problematic poetics of modernization. (Khasawneh 2005)

In early 2000s Amman, there existed a mood similar, not in scope but in principle, to what I have tried to convey about Beirut of the 1990s. This sentiment embodied a breaking with the recent past by using new media as a tool to do it. One Jordanian American artist trained in drawing and photography told me in an interview many years later in Berlin that the advice she received from globally focused curators and cultural managers in Amman at the time was to redirect her work to video art so that she could gain exposure outside of Jordan. Thinking retrospectively after I asked her to, the artist didn't think this advice necessarily pandered to funders' interests but rather reflected an aura that increasingly pervaded among her generation and that questioned the traditional function of art in society and its role as form of critique of authority. In her words, "video art and public art was understood as critical and more sensitive to its changing audience, painting as old and irrelevant and sort-of 'domestic.'"[28]

Bidoun's framing of Meeting Points as providing audiences with "incredible exposure to alternative art forms" underscores, once again, how local audiences are spoken for and about, despite being central to the artworks' conceptualizations. In the quote above, who the audiences were, how they encountered the art, and what they thought about it were invisible, even though they are mentioned as being introduced to new art forms. As I show in the previous chapter, in the framing of the new forms of art and organizational structures that were appearing in the early 2000s, there was an underlying assumption that such festivals were "independent," "alternative," and "novel" because of how they approached public space and publics by demanding that art be extracted from its quarantines in conventional art world structures of museums and galleries and be released on to the streets.

These assertions go a long way in helping us understand what supporters, funders, and commentators on the art scenes in the region in the early 2000s were telling us about what they would like to see as the role of the aesthetic in society and how to construct it as a space of freedom in countries' march toward democratization. This enmeshment between how proponents of the scenes described them and what they wished to attain from them gives rise to questions concerning the possibility of funders, critics, and art organizations actually supporting art with the mandate of social engineering rather than a comprehensive consideration of the intricacies involved in the evolving role of art as more than merely a social agent. Hence, the way in which the "impact" of art was being articulated may actually have been to the detriment of supporting and allowing "Art for Art's sake" to take its own course. For allowing art to follow its own path would have been contradictory to the very logic that drives arts funding from international donors to local civil organizations to invest in what they refer to "as art for social change" or "art for democratization" through developing the "culture market" and relevant audiences.[29]

Other art festivals organized by Makan also focused on public art projects and outreach. The Shatana Art Workshop (2007) was funded in part by the Ford Foundation's Triangle Arts Trust, whose mission is to move art from capitals to new, often remote, communities by organizing a retreat for international and local artists to produce site-specific work. In Shatana, a village of 150 people located in northern Jordan 70 km outside of Amman, the locals became very involved in the artistic process of making site-specific works. For two weeks, artists occupied the village, reinvigorating its local economy by buying food and other materials required for the art installations that were being constructed. The residents, with the assistance of their local Catholic Church, offered their houses as accommodations for the duration of the workshop in return for the renovation and maintenance of the old stone houses the tiny village is known for.

In the words of one of the organizing artists of the workshop:

> It was interesting to realize that, despite the stereotype, while some visitors from Amman, the capital and main city of "culture" of Jordan, where there are galleries and cultural events take place, were puzzled by this event and stood ill at ease in front of the installations and acts of intervention, the visitors from Shatana itself, in their Sunday clothes, related to the work, saw familiarity in it and interacted with it. (Khasawneh 2007)

Another relevant project was the Utopian Airport Lounge (2010), curated by Juliana Irene Smith, curator in residence at Makan that year, and funded by Pro Helvetia, the Goethe-Institut Jordan, the European Cultural Foundation, the Young Arab Theatre Fund, and the Ford Foundation's International Institute of Education. Like the Shatana Art Workshop, the Utopian Airport Lounge emphasized public art interventions and site-specific works as a form of communicating with local audiences. The centerpiece of the show was Saba Innab's installation of bird cages in front of a mosque in the neighborhood of Abdali, within an area of the popular Amman Friday flea market. Inspired by Le Corbusier's visual and abstract approach to utopia in combination with Marc Auge's hypothesis on the formation of identities in nonplaces such as airports, superstores, and highways, Innab's work caused some stir among the usual working-class market clientele and the mosque nearby.[30] At the time of Innab's intervention, the market was under threat of relocation by the municipality, which was trying to "clean up" the market area whose land prices had shot up because of the Abdali regeneration project launched in 2005. The aim of the project, which has now been completed, was to develop the 384,000 square meters of land at the estimated cost of five million US dollars into a "smart district" catered toward businesses, high-end housing, and tourists. Since then and after much controversy, the market closed and relocated.

Innab's project, which she had been researching as part of her larger oeuvre on neoliberalism and the restructuring of Amman's urban space, experimented with how residents "question/rethink" their space in a city when dislocated by neoliberal regeneration projects.[31] She wanted to see how sellers and the usual Friday customers would reposition themselves, their interactions, and their normal shopping routes in the context of their changing environment. She placed her colorful art cage installation at a side entrance to the market because she was not able to obtain a permit (fig. 17). In her words, "I reshaped the entrance of the market by creating a path, kind of a maze with the walls made from the cages . . . the users of the market adjusted with the change immediately, and even started to mark their position to others referring to the new Land mark, 'I am next to the bird cages,' a man on the phone directing his friend!"[32] The sheikh of the mosque accused Innab's installation of blocking

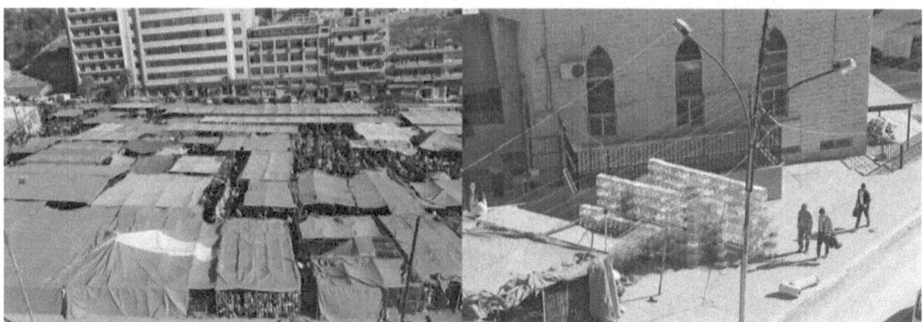

FIGURE 17. Saba Innab. *Up the Hill Down the Hill.* 2010. Installation view. Courtesy of the artist.

the entrance to the mosque on Friday prayers. He threatened to expose the artist during his Friday ceremony later that morning if she did not remove the installation. "Of course I did," she said. In reality, no one could reserve a location in the market unless they paid extra or had insider connections. Innab and the team of artists helping her install the work were told that she wasn't blocking the entrance but her art project occupied a spot where the sheikh sold knickknacks in an unofficial capacity. A few weeks after Innab's show, the mosque had a wall built around the space.

How the organizers of Shatana and Annab conceptualized the audience in the process of creation is arguably attuned with the genealogy of participatory artistic work in the West that can be traced back to the May 1968 revolts and its concomitant avant-garde experimentation. For some, this genealogy even goes as far back as futurist, Dada, and surrealist counter-bourgeois art (Bishop 2012). Beyond involving people, both artistic experiments I highlight addressed the public by featuring a political critique of contemporary society, as underscored in terms like "socially engaged art," which have been described as constituting "the social turn" in art (Bishop 2006).

Hence, framing projects like the Shatana International Workshop and Utopian Airport Lounge in terms of their emancipatory potential for evolving democracies as they were articulated in curatorial statements, artist-generated material, and funders' strategic missions was always going to be a precarious undertaking. But this is not necessarily because of the Western genealogical tradition that is assumed to underpin these practices. Some art historians have argued that the Middle East has its own long tradition of communal and interactive art that reaches back beyond modern times (Karimi 2016: 1). This undertaking is precarious, I propose, because such projects are impossible to measure, especially in terms of the kind of social change cultural elites and liberal funders are looking to impact with public interventions.[33] It is also because the questions that have already been asked about public participatory art and its relationship to both audience and democracy in Europe—such as "were the artworks for the people" and "do they encourage participation," "do the works relinquish elitism" and "are they accessible" (Deutsche 1992: 34)—are equally relevant to the context I describe.

As the curator and organizer of another annual event of contemporary art in the city somberly reminded me in conversation:

> We always talk about audience and outreach, and we all want that, but this is impossible to measure. What kind of "outreach" are we talking about? What is it that we want the people to do in response to our work? Who are the public and can we really change our society when there is no common language?[34]

It is due to my belief that the ultimate contribution of the works and projects I describe lies in their apt insistence that urban subjects not occupy space in a passive manner, that I question the methods and language used by artists to translate this idea into praxis. By extension I also question the tendency for critics, curators, and funders to too quickly read such instances of art making as emancipatory acts of resistance as opposed to expressions of resistance. As public art interventions claim to speak with or for the publics they interact with, how do we move beyond the framework of "romanticizing resistance" (Abu-Lughod 1990) in self-reflective artist-generated material to understanding how the cultural and aesthetic is actually being experienced by subjects in the site of the political?

NEGOTIATING ART, PERFORMING POLITICS

A couple of weeks after I held my focus group and on the suggestion of one group participant, I met with Jordan's then minister of culture for an interview. I wanted to hear what she and her associates at the Ministry thought of contemporary art, specifically public art. From this, I took away a clear understanding that the contemporary arts and more, the artists and the organizers of this scene, were viewed as unworthy of financial support, not because experimental forms of art were deemed too Western, as was relayed during the meeting at Makan, but because monetary investment would not have returns. Considering the meager budget of the Ministry compared to other public bodies, such as the Ministry of Defense or Public Security, this was an important point of consideration. I use the word "unworthy" here because in my conversation with the minister that day, she used terms such as "local," "relevant," and "national identity" to describe the importance of the more traditional institutions of cultural production that the Ministry supported in cooperation with the Greater Amman Municipality, like the regionally established Jerash Festival, the King Hussein Cultural Center, and the Royal Cultural Center. The Ministry also partnered with other grandiose governmental cultural institutions to fund events such as the Karama Human Rights

Film Festival and regional theater festivals, which were known to attract larger and more diverse audiences. She elaborated that the smaller Euro-American funded initiatives were more interested in experimental video and film than folkloric work. She also indicated that experimental art forms attracted elite audiences of locals and expats who communicated in English about subject matters that were not always relevant to the wider publics. More, their transnational links made them less of a priority for Jordan as the Ministry distributed its already tight annual budget of around four million Jordanian dinars between various civil society groups.

Much like representatives of other organizations whom I interviewed in Amman and Beirut, the minister described a clear donor interest in funding "alternative" or "non-mainstream" cultural practices that experimented with new form and content, specifically, video-art, performances, and films that deal with more cutting-edge topics. Based on these realities, the minister relayed that the reason she focused on more locally relevant cultural practices was not because she was "suspicious" of contemporary artists for what the larger society might deem their Western-influenced styles but because they had the capacity to gain support elsewhere. In other words, the regime's arm of public diplomacy understood the need to invest in arts and culture, yet it was not interested in using its meager funds to pay for projects that alienated the majority of the population.

As I listened to the words of the minister of culture, I, perhaps superficially, read them as articulating the real and ongoing tension between the regressive and progressive elements of society that I argue continue to artificially compose the constructed binary between the authentic/traditional and the modern/Western, which I discuss in chapters 1 and 2. In retrospect, who to fund and why was for the Jordanian minister of culture a practical question of visibility. The minister was right to identify the relatively small audience comprised of expatriates and bilingual or trilingual Western-educated persons from middle- to upper-income brackets who attended events that showed works inspired by local contexts expressed in a global conceptual language. The visual aesthetic portrayed at these events often relied on new media and film/video that the funders and the local cultural organizations encouraged as a form of cultural development. Adila Laïdi-Hanieh has already written about this phenomenon so eloquently, focusing on the Khalil Sakakini Cultural Center in Ramallah and its relationship to its international funders and local audience in the early 2000s

(Laïdi-Hanieh 2006). Attracting a diverse and regular audience remains a challenge, even today, with the shift toward local art patronage, funding, and arts education in each of Beirut, Amman, and Ramallah. Communication around contemporary art practice is often in English, although tellingly, since 2011 cultural practitioners have repeatedly stressed the need for work to be translated into Arabic. However, the problem of the general public's estrangement from contemporary art does not lie only in the issue of language, as I argue in the previous chapter on Beirut, although language is a central component.

While the minister's predilections were not inaccurate, I didn't believe that they were entirely practical. I wondered whether the Ministry's ideals were anchored in the need to present culture as authentic for a political purpose. For framing certain forms of cultural production as towing the line of the Hashemite monarchy's modern identity as Arab, Jordanian, and Muslim as it is enshrined in the constitution demonstrates that the modern nation-state is productive as much as it is repressive (Massad 2001). Culture is defined in the 1990 Jordanian National Charter as encompassing Islamic heritage, religion, beliefs, customs, traditions, conventions, laws, and the Arabic language and literatures (Al Khatib et al. 2010). What is not enshrined in the National Charter but is central to the Hashemite regime's survival is public diplomacy and, in particular, cultural exchange with its friends in the West. In that sense, the minister worked within well-defined parameters of expression that could be expanded and contracted according to the regime's whims. The Hashemite Kingdom of Jordan, regarded as one of the moderate monarchies in the region, is considered a key US partner in the Middle East and a historical partner in global counterterrorism operations. It has historically juggled between the geo-strategic interests of the US and Europe. At the same time, it maintains a domestic population rife with tension between its two major constituents: Jordanians of Palestinian origin and native Bedouins. The monarchy has imposed austerity measures and neglected issues of corruption, unemployment, poverty, poor government services, and increasingly difficult living conditions for the majority of the population.[35] The cost has been termed a "reluctant" or "hesitant" democratization, a turbulent combination of repression and censorship in the name of regime security and, since the launch of the global war on terror, the fight against extremism.

In a period of defensive nation building in the aftermath of the 1970 civil war between the Palestinian guerillas and King Hussein, the 1970s and 1980s saw the rise of institutional cultural infrastructure, as well as populist nationalist music and folkloric practices (Massad 2001). The country, however, has witnessed a significant shift since King Abdullah II presented his economic liberalization plans in 1999. As part of this turn, a growing cultural production scene has been transmitted through cultural diplomacy channels to place Jordan on the global culture and tourism map. From the building of its new Jordan Museum to regime investment in the film and multimedia sector, as well as the increase of funds for national and international art festivals, the arts are increasingly taking center stage as the human face of the regime (Ali and Hijawi 2010: 98). Yet the artists associated with contemporary arts nonprofit and nongovernmental initiatives with whom I spoke remain on the margins.

Since the Arab uprisings of 2011–2012, Jordan has experienced an exceptionally contentious decade. Youth are demonstrating and protesting visibly and more than they ever have in the country's short history. This mobilization has not generated a mass movement but it has arguably resulted in what Asef Bayat (2013) has termed "social non-movements": the collective actions of dispersed and unorganized actors who do not strategically or directly aim at political democracy and broader demands for social justice but at claim making, especially in public space.In Jordan, "social non-movements" have amounted to intermittent demonstrations by youth, veteran activists, labor unions, and members of the impoverished classes, demanding an end to austerity measures, government corruption, rising fuel and bread prices, unemployment, and electoral and constitutional reforms. At the same time, however, these constituents have engaged in non-movements where they directly practice what they preach in their everyday actions instead of tending to ideologically driven mobilization like more classical social movements. Landmark projects, like the Hashtag Debates between businessmen, politicians, and younger member of the public initially held at Makan's location, meant that artists and activists were carving out a site of protest in conjunction with what was happening all around them.

As a result, Jordanians are facing a series of renewed onslaughts on their civil liberties, driven essentially by the withering away of the historical social contract between the regime and the people, which surrenders the latter's political rights in return for the state's provision of public sector jobs, free education, healthcare, and subsidized food and fuel.[36] The impact of this suppression has included arrests of government critics using social media, the clamping down on the right of Jordanians to freely assemble and organize independently (whether in a demonstration, public meeting, or in a small group), government vetting of NGOs, and revising of the press and publications laws to prevent online and print media disparaging the regime.

Yet for any veteran visitor to Amman today, the city, especially West Amman, the more affluent and politically connected part of the city, looks and feels shockingly more open and liberal than it did even five years ago. Art making, circulation, and reception, as demonstrations of "claim making," have become visual proof of these changes. West Amman today is filled with parks, galleries, museums, theatcafé craft shops, art cafés, English and Arabic bookshops, specialty retail shops by local designers, beautifully and minimally designed restaurants, and nightclubs frequented by a growing class of consumers. These thriving venues give the city the sense of liberal flair, urbanism, and cosmopolitanism it was always looked down on by neighboring countries for not possessing. During the summers, the cultural itinerary of the Amman municipality is filled to the brim with commissioned outdoor street art and seemingly rebellious graffiti, music and design festivals, art exhibitions, book festivals, and upscale food and crafts street markets, often funded through resources allocated by the office of Queen Rania or one of her many social, welfare, and youth NGOS, and/or the host of European donors present in Amman, such as the French Cultural Center, the Goethe Institute, the Spanish Cervantes Institute, and the British Council, which have historically presided over the cultural production scene in the city.[37] Even downtown Amman has seen rejuvenation in its once deadbecafénd ignored historical cafés and bookshops. The visual landscape of neoliberal Amman is accordingly dotted with high-end malls, business towers, and gated communities, such as the Jordan Gate project and Abdali, that drive out the poorer segments of society to the city margins in what Rami Daher (2013) refers to as "newly zoned heterotopias." Nestled in between all these changes in the urban and social landscapes—and especially in the larger area of downtown Amman, known locally and in Arabic as Al-Balad to designate the area connecting some of the city's oldest sites—is a mushrooming scene of alternative nonprofit arts and culture spaces located in beautifully renovated 1920s and midcentury modernist buildings, often founded by new graduates returning from university studies in Beirut or patronized by a growing class of rich sponsors.[38] Corporate investment in urban heritage along with a smaller but growing committed class of cultural patrons and architectural activists have enabled much of the gentrification of the once neglected older parts of the city (Daher 1999, 2014).

In her contribution to an edited volume on cultural institutions in the Arab world, Toleen Touq (2016) concluded that despite challenges of funding and a lack of sustained public audience, Amman's art scene is still the only site in the country where true critical discourse and experimental artistic practices occur. Like most of the actors in this scene, Touq emphasizes this emerging sector's potential for playing a role in developing democratizing projects that function independently of traditional sources of knowledge in society. On a similar note, the anthropologist Aseel Sawalha, who has begun work on the first and much-needed anthropological study of art in Amman, has argued that because women run and attend the majority of the booming art scene in the city, the "presence of women in public arenas and their noticeable presence in public events (gallery, openings, running cultural cafés, and selling arts and crafts in street markets), challenge the dominant image of the docile, oppressed Arab woman" (Sawalha 2018: 459).

Analyses like these are indispensable to our understanding of how, why, and by whom such scenes emerge in the first place. Sawalha's (2018) framing of these formations as women sites only is particularly crucial to recognize. Not only in Amman, Beirut, and Ramallah, but in most cities the entire for-profit and nonprofit art scenes that are growing have been, for the most part, led by middle- to upper-class women. Despite this emancipatory dimension, however, I admit to being uneasy with the celebratory normative assumptions the gendered focus employ about the role contemporary and particularly transnationally connected and funded cultural production play in gender politics, identity politics, and the politics of resistance without the class and capital dimension being simultaneously addressed. As I have tried to show in this chapter, class affiliation and cultural capital directly impact how artists relate to their audiences and how local audiences feature in Western representations about them. More, the regime's omnipresence, combined with the neoliberal process that has attempted to harness art and culture as well as more organically evolved arts activities and spaces in Amman, has encouraged a multiplicity in new sites of production and ways of reading art's relationship to its audiences. Accordingly, this complicates our understanding of what counts as hegemony and whether in reality there is ever a single locus of hegemony, and, by extension, counterhegemony.

Chapter 6

RAMALLAH

The Paintbrush Is Mightier than the M16

Specifically Ramallah is a different situation, it's not like, let's say, Bethlehem, Hebron or Jenin or Nablus exactly because . . . there is a kind of urban density with people, with diversities even though they're under occupation. So what we are trying to understand is that if specifically for Ramallah, there is a possibility for a Palestinian counter-project, something that we can call resistance or just another form of co-optation. Because we can say that perhaps in Jenin, Hebron, they do the same thing more-or-less, but they are not built in the same way, for the same reason and they don't have the power. This is the basic thing about Ramallah, no? That in a way, because there is the Palestinian Authority, they have the power to speak for everybody, in other words they are representative of power.

Alessandro Petti, "It Has Become a Small Nucleus of Palestinian Society" 2009

Together with the artists, we try to escape the double bind of Israeli colonialism and the current Palestinian political regime. We have a passion for inscribing our loyalties and allegiances within our "cultural idioms" and in the spirit of our history. This escape from a discourse of "action" and "reaction" recharges our political imagination and modes of resistance and is based on what you [the author] referred to as "local forms of knowledge and ways of knowing that have historically been carried across geographies and time." It is the only way that is resourceful enough to transform our "learned helplessness" to "learned optimism."

Yazid Anani, 2014, in conversation with author

ONE LATE SUMMER EVENING IN 2013, I SAT WITH FRIENDS AND acquaintances who were artists and curators working in Ramallah. Our setting was Beit Aneeseh, a now defunct trendy bar and café opened in a turn-of-the-century stone house a few years earlier as an urban cultural project and business endeavor. Against the background of this favorite spot for foreign and local activists and a younger generation of Palestinian elites with its vintage PLO posters–lined walls, graffitied parking lot, and stunning outdoor garden, I partook in an informal conversation about a recently published novel. This novel irked the sensibilities of many members of Ramallah's cultural elite for what they regarded as its distasteful writing style, vulgar depiction of the city, and Islamist leanings in its representation of the city's cosmopolitan elements.[1] In *Blonde Ramallah* (2012), by Ramallah alShaqraa', protagonist Abbad Yahya is a young Palestinian journalist who wrestles from the perspective of an insider who feels like an outsider with what he portrays as a highly fractured, classist, and quickly changing neoliberal identity in post-Oslo Ramallah. Moving through the city—its streets, cafés, and many cultural events—the protagonist conveys what he sees from daily interactions, thoughts, and sensations between Palestinian residents of the city and the many Westerners living and working among them in the constellate of international NGOs, government representative offices, diplomatic peace-making outfits (like the infamous Peace Quartet), UN institutions, and the many visiting political tourists. He observes the "foreign" presence, as metaphorically referenced in the title word, "Blonde" and unabashedly writes about his distress over it.

One reason the novel provoked intense feeling in some members of the art world is because its protagonist attends the much-touted *Picasso in Palestine* art project opening, which I discuss further in this chapter. Another part that irked readers in the cultural milieu was the novel's representation of those attending Slavoj Žižek's talk at the Franco-German Cultural Center in Ramallah, which occurred as part of a series of events loosely organized in tandem with the *Picasso* opening. What Yahya essentially articulates as a "Ramallah bubble" in his bleakly written novel in a crude literary form and often identitarian tone is his and his city's reckoning with a burdened Palestinian context lying at the heart of the impasse between the binaries of colonial/postcolonial and global/local, which the two chapter-opening quotations allude to in different ways. The first quote strikes at the meaning of Ramallah as a cosmopolitan and economically liberal city open to experimental art practices and business ventures, constructed in the wake of the Oslo peace process under the PNA and because of it as well. The second thinks about how a curatorial project can respond to this politically impossible situation. Both quotes, part of bigger curatorial projects, were voiced against the backdrop of the complex bureaucratic nature of Oslo and the new phase of colonization it initiated that the novel indulges. Under this setup, the Palestinian National Authority (PNA) did not gain full sovereignty but became the middleman of the occupation, managing security and repressing Palestinian dissent through its own internal military and intelligence apparatus. Simultaneously, the PNA has taken on the role of the legitimate head of a state-to-be in the international diplomatic sphere, a role that necessitates partaking in cultural diplomacy and improving the image of Palestine in the international community.[2] Yahya's novel, congruent in form to Sonallah Ibrahim's *Dhat*, questions the limits of journalism as well as its fusing with fiction to describe his perceptions of lived realities unfolding in the space of an impossible impasse caused by the ambiguities of living in Ramallah, among the international diplomatic community, and in PNA's post-Oslo-constructed capital city at a time when settlement expansion in the West Bank continues unabated while Israeli politics turn increasingly right wing and racist.[3] The Palestinian leadership is divided, and an unaccountable and corrupt PNA acts as Israel's police force in the West Bank. This quandary is compounded by social fragmentation, economic decline, and political disillusionment with established factions, including leftist factions. Bashir Makhoul, writing about the sociopolitical context of Palestinian video art, has succinctly described the situation as resulting in "constellations of diverse identity formations through the insignia of occupation" (2013: xvii). This chapter reveals how this context ultimately framed the different interpretations of the *Picasso* project I study.

I admit to agreeing with my friends and acquaintances in our conversation that evening. Abbad's nostalgic reminiscing over Ramallah's simplicity before the neoliberalization of economic, social, and cultural life in the post-Oslo era was somewhat naïve and based on the binaries of West/East, global/local, and authentic/inauthentic, which the first part of the book discusses in more detail. At the same time, like others in the conversation, I was aware of the neoliberal development and democratization paradigms that dominated donor-funded civil society NGOs; these have been described as the "missionaries of the new era" (Merz 2012) and criticized for leading to the emergence of a Palestinian globalized elite (Hanafi and Tabar 2002). I well understood Yahya's critique of the aid industry and the formation of the globalized cultural elite as an assertion of agency. Like others of his generation, Yahya had come of age around the turn of the millennium with the outbreak of the Second Palestinian Intifada in September 2000; he experienced the changes in the NGO-ization of the Palestinian national liberation project firsthand.[4] I was therefore very uncomfortable with his being branded an "extremist," instead believing we should decode his ideas about the cultural production scene in Ramallah and how it relates to larger post-Oslo politics that provoked these reactions in the first place. The conversation that evening was rife with tension: first, because Israel's ongoing oppression of Palestine provides the material for impassioned attacks on the globality that has come to define Ramallah as the embodiment of the failures of the Oslo peace process; and second, because they exemplify an active general and not just a contemporary art-going public willing to renegotiate and reconfigure the terms of how globalized art is to be processed, practiced, and represented in their own context.

In this final chapter, I analyze the A to Z of the art project that Yahya saw as embodying post-Oslo politics: *Picasso in Palestine*. I do this to disentangle the micro-dynamics of producing a work of contemporary art about a transfer of a modernist art piece, which was conceived to reveal art production under colonial occupation and the conceptualization of imagination as central to the emancipatory project of bringing a Picasso painting to Palestine. In contrast to Lebanon, where the state is weak, and Jordan, where the state is omnipresent, Palestine today is a nation-state-to-be. It lives under ongoing colonial rule facilitated by the PNA's state-building project of constructing a coercive security state (Milton-Edwards 1998). This chapter intends to show, by way of *Picasso*, how the Palestinian experience of contemporary art making in the West Bank is a microcosm of the larger dynamics at play in international politics and domestic cultural politics. It should be read against the underlying forces discussed in the first part of this book—from uncovering the layered meaning of cultural diplomacy, to the neoliberalization of civil society through the support of NGOs as part of larger democratization programing in the international development sphere—and thought of in terms of the varied understandings of how art features in counterhegemony. Palestinian artists such as Emily Jacir, Larissa Sansour, Yasir Batniji, Mona Hatoum, Raeda Saadeh, and Sharif

Waked, among many others, have been instrumental in wresting a transnational Palestinian art history by repossessing the past from the dominance of hegemonic interests. By focusing on an alternative mode of thinking about art in this chapter, one that goes beyond nationhood, narration, and representation, I reveal just how difficult it is to produce projects that comprehensively bring together global and local dimensions of contemporary art in fraught contexts. Art historian Kamal Boullata wrote in 2009 that the "elephantine budgets cultivated a new breed of artists who were co-opted into becoming professionals of a post-Oslo clientalism that eventually contributed to giving a new shape to cultural expression" (233). The debate over whether and how far this is true still rages in Palestine. In a much-discussed public speech as part of the Young Artists of the Year Award, hosted annually by the Abdel Mohsen Qattan Foundation, one of Ramallah's most prominent cultural institutions, its director openly reproached the failure of the Palestinian and artistic milieu in the era of Oslo to produce any meaningful dialogue or questions about the demise of the Palestinian national project.[5] According to those present, the director, Omar Al-Qattan, had just returned from a trip to Gaza where he saw the destitution there so closely; as a result, he seemed to lash out at the entire cultural scene of Ramallah. Despite the generalization in tone and content, Al-Qattan arguably expressed the discomfort that many if not most members of the public, including writers, intellectuals, and artists, feel in the West Bank and Gaza about the extent to which cultural work, and especially the visual arts, have been able to engage with the collective Palestinian experience of oppression and the historical and political subjects that are often at the heart of the questions that haunted most of my interlocutors in Ramallah.

Like in Amman and Beirut (and many Western cultural capitals, as was often pointed out to me by artists in conversations), audience size and public attendance continues to occupy center stage in debates around art's place in the political. As already mentioned in chapter 3, what has been referred to as contemporary art's "cold estrangement" from local audience is often regarded as the reason art events continue to attract mostly the expat community of international development funders, journalists, and cultural tourists, who come for a specific time to attend set events, as well as a relatively small culture-going community of artists, writers, scholars, and members of the general public. For some cultural practitioners in Ramallah, art and its benefits to social change and political struggle are reaped only once it is mainstreamed in the national education curricula and related to by the publics, not as an NGO project but as an ongoing process that makes its own localized meaning and relevance beyond its global reach and presence (Belting 2009: 12).[6] However, this is a mean feat. Besides the Al Qattan Foundation and the Welfare Association, most arts projects in Ramallah, like in Amman and Beirut, are funded only for their specific duration and often in response to funds disbursed in response to a call for proposals put out by an international funder. Except for the Ford Foundation, which had at the time of writing withdrawn its entire support program for Palestine, most funders do not cover running costs of the nonprofit institutions and initiatives they support, preferring instead to work on a project-by-project basis, such as was the case with the *Picasso* project.[7] In these cases, long-term sustainability and grassroots investments in arts education in a setting like Palestine's unique one, where the entire political governing administration relies on donor funding, become a near impossibility.

The art scene today in Ramallah, like that in Amman and Beirut, increasingly includes private patrons who take on the mission of grassroots and informal arts education, private galleries, and PNA-funded museums, all of which are perceived to be marginalizing smaller art nonprofits and art collectives engaged in what they deem to be more radical work.[8] Interestingly, in the first decade of the millennium, of which I like to think of *Picasso* as somehow being the culmination, nonprofit cultural heritage projects normally associated with the state's hegemony found a radical edge in the Palestinian context through a commitment to visually telling the story of Palestinians' loss and rich heritage, as well as filling the gap left by the destruction of the dense network of the civil society organizations that had been the seedbeds of the first Intifadah until Oslo laid them to rest. This required a negotiation between international funders (and their focus on NGO-ization and democratization) and cultural production dynamics that always had to be negotiated at two levels: the domestic and the global. These issues all came alive in *Picasso.*

For this reason, I selected this project among other art projects in Palestine to use as an anchor to recap the arguments I make throughout the book. I acknowledge that this was a very difficult decision for me to make. History has put Palestinians in the absurd situation of perpetually having to convince the rest of the world of their very existence. In response, scholars, artists, and filmmakers working in and on Palestine, interested in countering orientalist tropes representing the Palestinian as terrorist, victim, or romantic revolutionary, are slowly building a formidable visual archive of the historical fact and experience of ongoing dispossession and displacement, but also continued survival on the land. So much of this production, as *Picasso* demonstrates, has been concerned with reworking Palestinian cultural heritage into critical practices of narration and memory rooted in the local Palestinian aesthetical, architectural, territorial, and even culinary experience, while being driven by questions and frameworks determined in the global art world.[9] More, so much of it has taken place in the transcultural Palestinian experience itself—that is, on Palestinian soil, even as it is transnationally linked and globally framed in ways that may contradict some of the works' original purpose (Makhoul 2013). All of these layers of art making in and about Palestine inspired me to uncover how nationalism, institutions, and international donor aid—constructs that play out in different ways in the neoliberal contexts of Beirut and Amman—do so in Ramallah. I unravel these layers by honing in on a single project as a site of research. I acknowledge that this methodological choice leaves me vulnerable to possible criticisms of ahistoricity. However, I found that it was the only way to intricately grapple with the issues raised throughout the book.

IMAGINATION UNDER OCCUPATION

On the afternoon of June 24, 2011, Picasso's 1943 portrait of his lover Francoise Gilot, *Buste de Femme*, was exhibited on the grounds of the International Academy of Art Palestine (IAAP) in Ramallah. Transporting Picasso's *Buste de Femme* to Ramallah resulted from a collaborative effort between the IAAP and the Van Abbemuseum in Eindhoven, the Netherlands, a relationship begun at the Middle East Summit held at the Dutch museum in 2008. The exhibition's opening at the IAAP, as well as the process of bringing it to Ramallah under the title *Picasso in Palestine*, attracted hordes of international and local artists, curators, cultural managers, scholars, diplomats, television and newspaper reporters, the usual art-going publics, many ordinary members of the public who would not normally attend art events, and some very proud PNA officials. Among these officials was Salam Fayyad, the PNA's then prime minister, who gave an opening speech on that memorable day. The exhibition opening also included a display of klashen-clad PNA security forces, official speeches, dignitary processions, traditional *dabke* dance and folk singing, and the sale of *Picasso in Palestine* paraphernalia, such as mugs and t-shirts. For some who attended that day, the dress in pomp and ceremony of the band performing on the grounds of an institution in an occupied territory was ironically reminiscent of postcolonial state-led identity formation adaptations of national symbols. Along with an electric organ rendition of John Lennon's *Imagine*, the opening events marked the culmination of the exhibition, which had been in the making for well over two years.

The project attracted more celebratory local and international media attention, conversation, and analyses than any other art project in the history of contemporary Palestinian art. It was conceived and largely implemented by Khaled Hourani, a well-known Palestinian artist and, at the time, director of the internationally funded IAAP.[10] From its inception, the project was heavily grounded in and framed by not so much its affective qualities or the visceral reactions it might evoke in spectators as a contemporary work of art that intervenes in the social world as it claimed, but, as I proposed in the previous chapters, in discourses of power and the representation of global cultural values and identities.

Through the process of realizing this multipurposed project, a captivating tale of ingenuity emerged. Yet this tale also strikingly reflects, rather than necessarily interrogates, the convoluted and deceptive nature of post-Oslo Palestine's reality under Israeli colonization (Hanieh 2013b). This predicament, which has been described as living in a "Post-Colonial Colony" is largely defined by the bureaucratic paradoxes of living in a state without sovereignty in the West Bank and Gaza under the guise of a supposed diplomatic and fair process leading toward a two-state solution (Massad 2000: 311). Further, this shift in the dynamics of colonial control enabled by the Oslo peace treaty in 1993 may have had, as it's widely argued, the effect of disciplining Palestinian resistance to Israel by stripping it of its political content through the NGO-ized professionalization of the practice and emphasizing the benefits of a specifically "nonviolent" discourse by watering down the collective Palestinian experience and identity to gain friends in the international sphere (L. Khalili 2007; Qumsiyeh 2011; Ṭabar and al-ʿAzza 2014; Shweiki 2014).

In Hourani's words, *Picasso* primarily aimed "to probe mechanisms, procedures, obstacles and requirements in getting a painting of this kind to Palestine." In doing so, the project "sheds light on the contemporary reality of Palestine and gives the project the power of the impossible" (quoted in *Van Abbemuseum* 2011).

The impossible Hourani refers to is the very act of bringing a Picasso painting to Palestine, a state that does not technically exist. "Why shouldn't a Picasso go to Palestine? . . . Why wouldn't Palestine be like any other country that Picasso would visit?" queried Hourani (Tolan 2011). He initially proposed the idea of bringing Picasso to Ramallah at one of a series of meetings held at the Van Abbemuseum. Participating were several key figures from the Middle Eastern art world, there to discuss contemporary art practices and cultural identity in relation to the museum's future vision. By rendering what seemed to be an impossible mission into a possibility and indeed a reality, Hourani hoped to provoke Palestinian imagination through his artwork into flirting with the very idea of an independent state, its cultural production, relationship to modernity and modernism, and cultural identity in a global world (Hourani, Toukan, and Miller 2010). Specifically, Hourani's project probed his fellow Palestinians in the Occupied Territories to imagine having a state. By doing so, they could creatively envision how art and the notion of a national museum could play a role in the minds of a people struggling to fathom the troubled history of modernity and its links to colonialism, while forging the nascent institutions of a state, in reality still undergoing an anti-colonial struggle.

As such, the journey reflected the thorny politics of Oslo. Hourani and his fellow organizers had to wrestle with established international protocols defining museum loan traditions that normally dealt only with sovereign countries and the bureaucratic measures defining "peace" agreements, checkpoints, airports, international insurance requirements, and finally, the inability to fulfill—at least at first—the environmental conditions necessary for the painting to sit at the Art Academy in Ramallah for three weeks (humidity and temperature control) (Esche 2012). As framed by the mainstream media coverage of the project and discussed in various influential contemporary Western art journals that devoted significant coverage to the project, *Picasso in Palestine* was about its means—the process of the painting's transfer and all that it exposed along the way—rather than its end—its exhibition at the IAAP in Ramallah. Subsequently, the project has been lauded internationally as an instance of art's ability to transcend political realities—even for a moment—showing "that the paintbrush" is indeed "mightier than the M16" (C.S. 2011).

PICASSO IN PALESTINE AND THE WORLD

Reflecting on the signification of Picasso in an interview, Hourani explained:

> Picasso is the most famous modern artist; if I asked my mother to name one modern artist, she would name him. Of course, other artists were also conceivable—Marcel Duchamp, for example—but I was keen to bring over a work by an early Modernist, since we are not in a contemporary situation here yet—at least, not in terms of our discourse. We need to have the discussion around Modernism first. (Hourani, Toukan, and Miller 2010)

In line with this logic, which points toward a linear and monolithic path to modernity, Charles Esche, the director of the Van Abbemuseum, asserted that the *Picasso* project, and specifically the exhibition of *Buste de Femme* in Ramallah, was an "auspicious" occasion. More than its confirmation "of an already long-standing relationship between the Van Abbemuseum and the IAAP," he writes, the project "represents a symbolic connection between European modernity and contemporary Palestinian culture: a connection that can serve, if understood well, as a way to imagine cultural globalism as mutuality rather than conformism to a single worldview" (Esche 2012). Further, Esche reminds us that modernity as seen from Europe is associated with its violent colonial history, as much as it is embodied in the liberating representations of the artistic avant-garde. Proceeding from this reasoning, Esche goes on to claim that "change is afoot, modernity is over and the *reactive* Palestine of the past is becoming *step by step* a proactive community, taking on the burdens of national and cultural responsibility along the way" (Esche 2011; my emphasis).

Subsequently, *Picasso*'s much-touted achievement was defined by what it interrogated and exposed through the process of the painting's transfer. It revealed the structural, bureaucratic, and legal paradoxes of the Occupied Territories' relationship with Israel as well as the relevance (or not) of the European museum and its loan regulations in today's global world. Arguably these findings contributed a novel attempt at institutional art critique as it is commonly understood in Western visual art theory and as it was applauded. Yet as I posit here, the project embodied, rather than interrogated or subverted, the very contentious conditions that it sought to reveal to achieve its goal of calling on the imagination to "reconstitute the reality in Palestine through alternative means" (Fatima Abdul Karim, quoted in Conio 2011: 31).

These conditions divide into three interrelated phenomena. First are the ongoing Israeli colonial practices. Cultural exclusion and military domination are supported by an architecture of bureaucratic hurdles and procedures aimed at maintaining a costly occupation in the Occupied Territories that necessitates the control of Palestinian life (inside and outside Israel) under a carefully designed system of legalized, institutionalized, and indeed normalized racial discrimination that *Picasso* sought to transcend through a plea to the imagination. Second is the complex bureaucratic nature of Oslo and the new phase of colonization it paved the way for. Third is the European museum's historically universalizing mission of acquiring, conserving, and displaying aesthetic objects with the goal of educating and enlightening non-European cultures that have historically sat at the heart of the modernity project. Lying at the core of this mission, and as per Anderson's groundbreaking "imagined communities," is the central role imagination plays in the delineation of national and other identities through the construction of institutions essential to the modernity project such as the map, the museum, and the census (B. Anderson 1991: 164). I read the contested interpretations, and therefore the meanings and functions, of the *Picasso* within this framework of interrelated phenomena.

The image (fig. 18) that accompanied reports of the exhibition in the international media showed the painting flanked by two armed security guards from the PNA. Ultimately, this photograph visually represented the process of bringing a multimillion-dollar Picasso work to Ramallah under the auspices of its allegedly legitimate Palestinian national government as a way of probing Palestinians' imagination on what their nation might one day look like. The image provokes us to interrogate the nature of the relationship between the modern Palestinian colonial subject, European modernity, the object of imagination, and the apparatuses of the Oslo security state. The question most pronounced is whether and to what extent the modernist and "universalist" tendencies that were intended to be critiqued by the *Picasso* project ended up

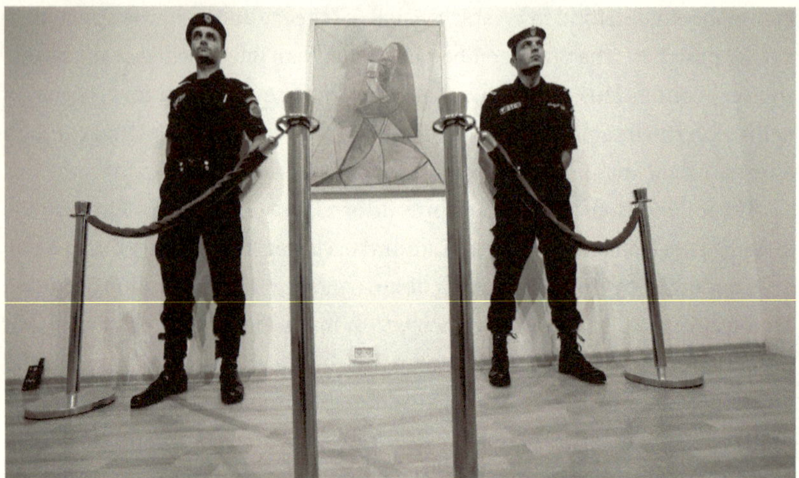

FIGURE 18. Hourani Khaled. *Picasso in Palestine*. 2010. Photo by Khaled Jarrar. Copyright of the artist, courtesy of the artist.

being ironically employed in the positioning of the project and those involved in it as an indubitable space of dissent and transgression. If so, to what extent has this positioning been accomplished by naturalizing artistic "resistance" when (re)presenting the work on a global level? In other words, and to use Esche's logic, to what extent was the project really pushing us to "imagine cultural globalism as mutuality rather than conformism to a single worldview" (2012)? Or, as Gayatri Spivak has famously argued, how far was it a case of "they are like us" rather than "we are like them"? (1985: 258).

Answers to such queries are necessary for the normative implications they carry, especially as control over discourse is a vital source of power. Furthermore, rather than considering what is commonly understood as critical art to be an indubitably counterhegemonic act, as Lila Abu-Lughod (1990) suggests in her warning against romanticizing resistance, it is the question of what other possible meanings can be understood from exploring the convoluted relationship between cultural politics, aesthetics, and notions of resistance in cultural production that is more urgent. The answers might tell us a great deal about how colonial subjects situate their respective "postcolonial" discourses vis-à-vis dominant economic and political orders within increasingly integrated global systems.

THE CULTURAL POLITICS OF RESISTANCE

I consider *Picasso* as a site of cultural politics where imagination is emphasized in the artwork as a form of resistance. I draw my inspiration from Deleuze's (2004) understanding of the imagination as constructed by determinants that legislate and authorize notions of taste rather than being an innate and emancipatory quality in and of itself. Relevant here is not why *Picasso*'s organizers called on the imagination and inserted themselves into the lived realities of everyday politics; instead, it is understanding how the project was perceived to relate to the assemblages of objects, sensations, emotions, and people that it purported to converse with and about as a way of organizing conceptions of resistance in cultural production (Deleuze and Guattari 1987). The approach to reading the project that I propose queries the negotiation of language, the construction of frames, as well as the delineation of boundaries of what is to be included and what is to be excluded from the public discourse on the aesthetical practice and meaning of resistance in the production of contemporary art.

Concurrently, this Deleuzian-inspired framework, which sees particular understandings of aesthetical resistance as a diagnostic of power, also counters the normative assumptions about the celebratory role of contemporary cultural production in international relations and specifically cultural diplomacy in the Middle East that have tended to prevail especially in the aftermath of September 11, 2001, and then more recently with the onset of the Arab revolutionary process in 2011. It sheds light on the complexity of empirical evidence and the "instability of empirical 'facts'" on which normative theories relating to cultural diplomacy efforts in the Middle East (and elsewhere) often uncritically depend (Rao 2010: 30). Central to this analysis is understanding post-Oslo Palestine's bifurcated discourse regarding the changing nature of its own resistance to Israeli domination and how it is to represent this struggle internationally if it is to gain and maintain legitimacy among global solidarity activists and in the international media. One arm of this discourse that is dominant in diplomatic circles can be understood within the framework of the US-Israel-led "peace" process along with their regime and civil society partners in the region. This so-called conflict resolution within a two-state solution paradigm is increasingly being countered by horizontally organized international solidarity based around an anti-apartheid movement. The latter aligns with the mounting call for a true and just solution in Palestine, undertaken by transnational and local civil society activists and intellectuals critical of the Oslo sponsored "two-state" solution.

CRITIQUING THE INSTITUTION, CRITIQUING MODERNITY

In many ways, *Picasso* did exactly as its project visionaries and organizers intended. First: a work by one of the world's most famous modern artists was brought to Ramallah and exhibited to a Palestinian audience. Moreover, as an icon of European m,odernism, the work asked the Palestinian public to imagine what kind of rapport the two could have with one another. As Michael Baers (2012) explains, what would have normally been a standard loan procedure between two institutions had to be rethought due to the nature of the PNA's relationship with Israel.[11] Protocols were bent and legal frameworks relating to insurance, transportation, and imports into the West Bank were reconfigured. *Picasso* also temporarily gave Ramallah a modern art museum in the form of the IAAP and asked its public to consider what sorts of institutions the city could invest in along with Western support as part of thestate-building process (Baers 2012). Finally, for the Van Abbemuseum organizers, the project investigated the possibilities for Western museums to significantly engage in such a politically volatile terrain.

Significantly, it was the Norwegian Ministry of Foreign Affairs that mainly funded the IAAP, along with smaller financial support from the PNA, the Ford Foundation, the British Council, the Heinrich Boll Foundation, the Palestinian Investment Fund, and individual contributors. This setup was intertwined with *Picasso* from the start. The IAAP, one of Palestine's most important pedagogical experiments in arts education of recent years, had an explicitly national developmental mission and diplomatic role, which it gleaned from Norway's historical role as the host of the Oslo Accords. In a speech given at the opening of the IAAP, Norwegian Minister of International Development Erik Solheim said: "Art is of vital importance in national identity-building. It helps to build bridges, plays a part in social development and inspires people to reflect on their situation. This is why the opening of the Academy in Ramallah is such an important occasion" ("Launch of the International Academy" 2006).

Due to the financial constraints under which it operated, the IAAP heavily relied on visiting lecturers to supplement its two permanent staff members. It is well regarded today for having brought a rich diversity of internationally acclaimed artists and lecturers to visit and teach at the academy, many volunteering or asking only for travel/subsistence costs. Some of these acclaimed artists and academics played important roles in exposing young Palestinian contemporary artists who are not part of the diaspora to the critical language and aesthetics of the global art world. From the course syllabi to the networks and contacts needed by artists to have their work exhibited in more significantly global platforms than Ramallah, the IAAP advanced the interests of young artists. Yet some regarded this very globalized contemporary art structure as limiting the creation of a generation of critically minded artists. This point, which I heard from a number of educators whom I interviewed during fieldwork, resounded most fervently in the conversation I had with the then director of the IAAP in August 2012. In a very nuanced analysis, she explained how the Academy provided the cultural capital, financial capital, and technical know-how needed for marginal Palestinians to expand and invest in global arts careers. Reproducing neoliberal logic, she identified the IAAP as a source of diversification and democratization of the field of art. The director argued, however, that because of how the market operated—international curators who zoomed in and out of the West Bank to entice selected artists with glamorous opportunities, like travel and exposure—elements such as the language, form, and aesthetics of critical art are decided outside of Palestine (fig. 19). What is regarded as critical, she argued, is often driven by market forces. The "slickness of global art is picked up and thought of as critical by young artists. . . . The process of experimentation and discovery is gone, students want the finished glossy product. The process of art-making is stunted in this process. All work done is 'for an exhibition' and an audience elsewhere.'"[12]

As had been noted about the Academy and its role in Ramallah by one of its visiting lecturers:

> Lots of questions abound. Which aesthetic, language, discourse, and art history are our artists being professionalized with, and why? What to make of students' constant desire for identity politics as material? How to formulate an arts education that's more interdisciplinary, without compromising the autonomy of an arts education itself? How to celebrate equally moments of ambiguity, fragility, and indecision in a political context that we salute for its clarity and perseverance? And how to maintain an institutional memory of the fact that conceptual art unfolded over "there," coincidentally, just as anticolonial movements were being fought over "here," and elsewhere. (O. Toukan 2014)

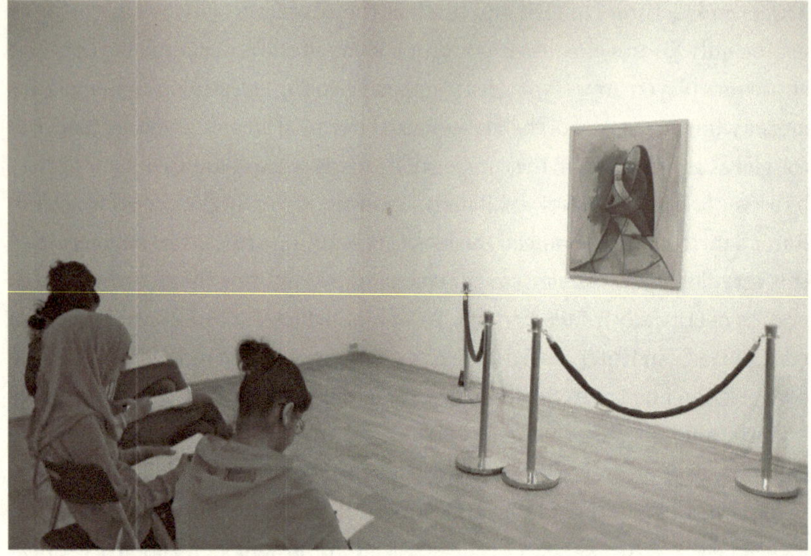

FIGURE 19. Hourani Khaled. *Picasso in Palestine*. 2010. IAAP studio art class. Photo by Mamon Eshreteh. Copyright of artist, courtesy of the artist.

Questions like these foreground our perception of what we deem urgent, relevant, and generally counterhegemonic art in anti-colonial movements. To be exact, in the same way critical theory rejects the given world and looks beyond it, "when theorizing art," writes the cultural theorist Gene Ray, "we need to distinguish between uncritical, or affirmative, theory and a *critical* theory that rejects the *given* art and looks beyond it" (Ray 2009: 79). In other words, and in the context of *Picasso*, the role of a critical theory of art or a critical work of art is not simply to critique modernity but to offer a critique of that critique of modernity.

In the circumstance that Ray (2009) describes as "art under capitalism," the democratic values of freedom, plurality, participation, choice, transparency, critical thinking, and majority consensus in art practices constitute liberal democracy's disciplining of resistance through cultural production. In *Picasso* this may be translated as art becoming the expression of freedom, where the project imagines a future Palestinian State at peace with its occupier through newly founded civil society institutions and related cultural projects.[13] To be exact, *Picasso* did address if not also somewhat explore the conditions of its own production. It also arguably did this within a "democratic" framework. First, the decision to choose *Buste de Femme* was made by the students of the IAAP along with Hourani, who saw *Buste de Femme* as resonating with Palestine's historical reference to the woman as the symbol of nationhood, resistance, and *ṣumūd* (steadfastness)—an arguably gendered symbol that functions on normative constructions of femininity. Second, the negotiations over the transfer of the painting and the aims of the project held between the IAAP led by Hourani and representatives of Van Abbemuseum were always consensual, involving long-winded and tense discussions. Third, the project, according to the repeated claims of its organizers, possessed popular appeal that attracted a significant local audience: the "subaltern" public, so to speak.[14] Finally, the project may also be read as transparent since it incorporated a look into its own making. As part of the exhibition in Ramallah, the curators displayed for their audience a portion of the body of documentation amassed along the way from the tedious and convoluted negotiations it undertook with the Van Abbemuseum in Eindhoven. It also from the onset documented the two-year process of the actualization of the project through commissioning Palestinian filmmaker Rashid Masharawi to visually record the process. In the days following the opening of the exhibition in Ramallah, a series of programs, including lectures and panels about the significance of the project held by members of the Palestinian literati, as well as many international speakers and guests titled *Picasso Talks* were held in Ramallah with virtual connections to East Jerusalem and Gaza. Additionally, the Palestinian art foundation *Al Maʿmal* in East Jerusalem held an exhibition of the documentation relating to the process of bringing the painting to Ramallah.

If seen within the described framework and from the context of the global art world's reference points as evidenced by the celebratory descriptions of the project in various platforms,[15] *Picasso* was a conceptual art project. It was also a democratic exercise in institutional critique in its classical sense of seeking to expose the ideologies and power structures underlying the organized circulation, display, and discussion of art. According to the Dutch organizers, that *Picasso* required a rereading of the Oslo Accords and a rethinking of the international protocols defining museum loan traditions indicated an act of subversion against the institution in its own right. This act was one directed at the European system of regulations that continues to define the movement of cultural products. Through an aesthetical intervention, which drew on a particular formal, conceptual, and visual language, *Picasso* placed itself at the heart of the bureaucratic entanglement that defines Israel's relationship to the West Bank and the many manifestations that emanate from it. These include the distorted dynamics of so-called sovereignty while still technically living under occupation, the intention to make Ramallah the capital of a future Palestinian State, and the effects of the modern European museum's interest in experimenting with devolving its power base to societies on the margin.

Yet, like much institutional critique in art that emerged from and became articulated in Western art capitals and that tends to launch its attacks from the very place it aims to deconstruct, *Picasso* needed the Van Abbemuseum's consent as well as technical and financial support to expose the Israeli State to the international community, visually symbolize the dismantling of European modernity, and normalize the situation in Ramallah by extending itself out of the art world. It also required the PNA's willingness, as well as Israel's direct cooperation and approval, to facilitate the process of the painting's transfer. This meant that the art activity commissioned by those institutions and artists that may themselves become the "self-critical, flexible, and creative subjects of production" (Chukhrov 2014) remained unquestioned.

In the global art world, the debate on the contradictions inherent to institutional critique have demanded enunciations of a third generation critique, one distanced from either the politics of the art institution and its relationship to the state as in the first generation, or as in the case of the second generation, the politics of representation in the art world articulated in the wake of cultural studies, feminist, and postcolonial epistemologies.[16] But in Palestine, where an anti-colonial war is being fought, identities are constantly shifting, institutions are in the process of being formed, and modernities are still being defined, institutional critique may take on other possible meanings that were not entertained in the interpretation of *Picasso*'s significance for Palestine in a transnational context.[17] Particularly, from a "local" perspective, as the below section demonstrates, the project operated from start to finish on the premise of the diplomatic two-state solution and the widely unpopular Oslo Accords. Hence the project's hopes, first, of putting "the political reality of Palestine into contact with the world of contemporary art," and second, of exhibiting a modernist masterpiece at an international standard to "construct Palestinian art institutions" and help "reform [Palestinian] culture" (Hourani, Toukan, and Miller 2010) through appealing to the imagination come to embody the very history and logic that it sought to interrogate. This history refers to the European cultural institution's missionary role as mediator, teacher, and transporter of universal values and collective moral progress to communities on the margin. This embodiment is facilitated by way of the partnership between the Oslo regime and the international community that works to normalize the effects of the occupation through the diplomatically defined two-state solution and the development and humanitarian interventions that it comes with.[18] The function of cultural production in this context is to arbitrate social change rather than to critically intervene. "It's not that you are here some stupid limited culture. No, you are the universal: enemies are making you particular!" claimed Slavoj Žižek in a recorded discussion with the Palestinian and Dutch organizers of the project in 2011. Žižek was pointing to the fact that while Palestinians do indeed have a humane face, the occupation and its representation has defaced it. In other words, through an art project that focuses on the bureaucracy of the occupation, Palestinians do not divert attention from their cause as they have been accused of doing by local critics; instead, they ask the world to look at the lived reality of people in the region. Yazid Anani, curator and professor of architecture at Birzeit University in Ramallah, has cynically queried this need to imagine Palestine as a universal human condition through art (Anani 2013). This logic, according to Anani "support[s] the equivocal postcolonial ideology of post-Oslo state building and the right of Palestinians to be part of the universal. Art projects from this category deal with the imagination of the future state as an amalgamation of nationalistic edifices and infrastructure" (Anani, quoted in H. Toukan 2015).

Relatedly, at stake in Žižek's emphasis on the project's universalizing potential and Anani's cynicism toward the normalization of Palestine are issues that pertain to art's presumed civilizing mission, its tool in cultural diplomacy, and its role in what has been termed the "humanity game," in reference to "universalist assumptions about humanity and the agentive capacity of art to build bridges of understanding in contexts of so-called civilizational conflict" (Winegar 2008: 651).

Accordingly, the project could be read as entwined within the politics of the PNA's contested bid for statehood, which was first attempted at the level of the Security Council in 2011, and then later in November 2012 when it was finally granted non-observer member status by the UN General Assembly.[19] The transfer of the painting came at a time when Palestine's position in the world was under scrutiny. The exchange took place just two months before the UN's General Assembly in September 2011, where Palestine would request admission as a member state, calling for international recognition of the 1967 borders with East Jerusalem as a capital. Interestingly, the Dutch minister for foreign affairs at the time stated that the Netherlands would not support unilateral Palestinian statehood, instead calling for a return to negotiation. In a paper issued by the Institute of Cultural Diplomacy on the *Picasso* project, Mahmoud Abbas, the chairman of the PLO, stated that the Netherlands' close links with Israel "doesn't disturb [Palestine] at all," citing instead the Palestinians' appreciation of their help. While the Netherlands may not officially recognize the state of Palestine, it is, as the paper claims, still supportive of the people and the issues surrounding the bid (Hoogwaerts 2012). According to the author of the paper, "The exchange essentially allowed Palestine to image itself as a modern nation that appreciates modern art thereby promoting values that can be universalized." Through initiatives such as these, "Palestine slowly elevates its image internationally commanding respect through means other than economic and military elements" (10).

According to the project's organizers, "By physically transgressing boundaries the *Picasso in Palestine* project not only imagine[d] a different world, but [made] it possible" (Van Abbemuseum 2011). Yet despite its plea to the people of the West Bank to "imagine" a normalized situation, the project placed the ceiling on Palestinian imagination by containing the questions it asked about the role of art in the future Palestinian State's capital, Ramallah. In effect, the project interrogated the definitions of territory, so-called legality, and justice already determined by the international diplomatic order led by the US and Israel along with the PNA and its other regime partners in the region. The integration of Palestine into the global contemporary art sphere, by way of Picasso's journey to an exhibition in an experimental museum in an occupied territory, becomes allegorical of Palestine's possible recognition by the UN and thereby the world community.

Hence, the supposed facility of art to render the impossible possible through a humane and universal language that references imagination ends up affirming the idea of the modern and democratic state ordered along the lines of the increasingly illegitimate two-state solution. More crucially, within this logic and returning to the words of the director of Van Abbemuseum quoted earlier, "the reactive Palestine of the past is becoming step by step a proactive community, taking on the burdens of national and cultural responsibility along the way" (Esche 2011). The indirect reference to Palestine's past of revolutionary armed resistance in the comment and its insinuation that the once "reactive" Palestine has been replaced by a mature entity willing to join the international community on entirely different terms dismisses one of the project's main aims: to critique modernity. Historically, resistance to the dark side of modernity, along with its foreign invasions, colonization, territorial partitions, rude demographic displacements, and extraterritorial violations, has not been sanctioned or accepted in international diplomatic circles.

Buste de Femme left Eindhoven and traveled to Amsterdam and Tel Aviv before arriving in Ramallah. Escorted by Israeli police from Tel Aviv to the infamous Qalandia checkpoint that divides Palestinians between the West Bank, East Jerusalem, and Israel, the painting was driven for around 4 kilometers without Israeli or Palestinian police due to stipulations connected to the Oslo Accords. On a whim, and in accordance with what Hourani termed the "imaginative thinking" of one of his fellow Palestinian organizers when faced with the refusal of the Dutch insurance company to cover the supposed no man's land 4 kilometers after passing Qalandia, Hourani invited international media to follow the painting. The idea was that the constant surveillance would increase the painting's security. The insurance company agreed, and this became one of the project's most advertised highlights: its ability to disrupt the course of established insurance regulations and the role of media as merely news coverage. Yet, as many of those I spoke with in the field were quick to remind me when I raised this point, the Israeli Army has never needed or obtained special permission to enter Ramallah through this supposed no man's land, whether it is to arbitrarily arrest a "terror" suspect or to remind Palestinians in the West Bank who is really in charge.[20] Additionally, as was also ironically pointed out to me several times, the project's insistence that it was successfully able to transport an epic modernist painting into the West Bank by imaginatively meandering around the confines of Israel's Occupation stands in stark contrast to the refusal to allow Noam Chomsky, the world renowned radical intellectual and political dissident, into the West Bank to deliver a speech to Birzeit University less than a year before. Hence, according to those questioning the idea that the transfer was indeed disruptive, if anything, the art object in the moment of transfer was not a disrupter of established protocols on museum loan traditions and global cultural flows, but rather a pawn in Israel's show of commitment to the agreement it made under Oslo and its supposed tolerance for the cultural rights and economic development of the Palestinian people.

Once in Ramallah, the painting came under the armed guard of PNA security and remained so until its removal from the Academy three weeks later. The project's completion was in part possible because of Israel's benevolent waiver of a mandatory 15 percent security deposit on important works of art. In other words: the "IDF helped the PA Exhibit a $4.3 million Picasso" (Ronen 2011). For local critical voices who happened to come across this information, the fact fueled their cynicism. According to the Israeli Army blog, as well as some others related to Israel's public relations campaigns, the Israeli Civil Administration announced that it was "pleased to contribute to the [Picasso] endeavour and will continue to assist in all future artistic and cultural efforts" (Ronen 2011). The Israeli Army describes the Israeli Civil Administration as "a government and IDF body, which runs local Palestinian civil matters and cares for their well-being." On the day of departure, an Israeli Civil Administration international liaison officer, Dutch diplomats, and Van Abbemuseum representatives ensured, according to the Army blog, "the orderly passage of the painting toward its destination" (Ronen 2011).

Significantly, while Israelis, expats, and international diplomats were able to visit the exhibition that was held in tandem in Jerusalem, most Palestinians living in the West Bank, including Hourani, could not attend due to Israeli-imposed travel restrictions to the city. Consequently, the question of Jerusalem and its function in the larger project, according to individuals from the local art scene critical of the project, was not only glossed over but also left unaddressed in the conceptualization of the project.[21] Arguably, the role of Jerusalem in the project—while meant to expose Israeli segregation practices against the Palestinians and show how Palestinians transcend these realities by "doing art" there anyway—ended up instead reinforcing the ruptured mental geography of a whole generation of Palestinians who are barred from entering

Jerusalem. This policy in effect has severed Palestinians from each other and from Israelis since the onset of the second Intifada. Despite being one of the most vexing challenges Palestinians undergo living under Israeli domination, the inability to physically access Jerusalem is also the most clichéd. Hence, for those critical of the project, the intention to expose Israel's control over access to Jerusalem was but a mere media publicity stunt intended not for the Palestinian audience who see and experience this reality as the most mundane of occupation restrictions, but for a global art audience as a "Palestine 101," as one of my interlocutors cynically put it.

The presence of Salam Fayyad (the then prime minister who most personifies the PNA's reputation as the financial and security manager of Israel's colonial project) at the opening of the exhibition came to define local interpretations of the art project's function as a political one, rather than a formally experimental one. The PNA's logic of taking its demand for statehood to the UN is based on the great strides it believes it has made toward meeting the criteria of a sovereign state, including improvements in governance, security, and physical infrastructure as indicators of the state's readiness. Fayyad's boasting of the PNA's efficient security system that enabled the protection and secure transfer of *Buste de Femme* that day on the grounds of a private higher education institute provoked various aesthetic and non-aesthetic responses alike.[22]

Accordingly, one may suggest that the emphasis on imagination as an affective tool in overcoming the hard political realities of occupation is a positive spin on the term. However, it's one that also dangerously disregards imagination's possible simultaneous function as a site of cultural politics that organizes our perceptions and understanding of what the dissenting dimension of art looks like. Specifically, *Picasso* imagined Palestinian artistic production as neutral, friendly, and nonreactionary, yet also globally relevant, critical of and resistant to linear European modernity and its concomitant institutions. Managed and enabled by the project organizers, this imagining blurred the discursive boundaries between cultural globalism, state building, resistance, imagination, and the role of institutional critique in each. Thus, *Picasso* was framed as a counterhegemonic moment precisely because of the project's reference to the imagination as a formal tool to critique the institution of occupation and thereby subvert the structural challenges it sets in place.

To return to Yahya's *Blonde Ramallah*, the narrator attends Žižek's talk about the role of film in political struggle, advertised in English and carried out in English without translation. He gives this as one example of how a people can be excluded from a global liberal discourse about struggle and revolution in their own context by propagating what he candidly describes as a rigid cultural globalism—as well intentioned as it might be. Further, when he ventures to the grounds of the art academy on the day of the *Picasso* opening, he is confronted with Picasso's original *Buste de Femme* painting. He bluntly states at the end of his notes that the work is ugly and has no relevance to Palestine at this juncture in its modern history, debunking the myth of universalism and European multiculturalism that has arisen from postmodernism's obsession with salvaging the former from its colonial history. More, he is incensed at the three million dollars it cost to exhibit the painting on the grounds of the academy to show that Palestine is and can be part of the global community. Like other Palestinian art projects, and indeed contemporary works of art in other contexts too, *Picasso* drew on the relationship between art, the production of knowledge, and its mediation. As such, I understand the objecting voices in *Picasso*, from members of the public, to cultured elites, to scholars, writers, and activists to be subjects standing at the nexus of the colonial/postcolonial who insist nonetheless to impose their agency. Through the process they strike at the fundamental challenges facing contemporary art anywhere. Armed with their knowledge of the other side of the story of globalized Palestinian art and the political context from which it emerges they broke out of the shackles of the representational frames they are normally defined by, and thus, intruded into the site of claim making.

With that complexity in mind, I posit that *Picasso* illuminated the tendency for contemporary global art discourses to elide the micro-realities of contemporary art in their own contexts. In the process, however, it gave rise to multiple localized discussions, publications, and interventions, demonstrating that Palestine was able to shed off the "burden of representation" that the project was ultimately embedded in (Mercer 1990).[23] The multilayered project intervened in the globalized contemporary art conversation on what constitutes relevant and timely art, if only for a brief moment. These discussions might not have been carried out by the general public, and they were not even highlighted in the many representations and discussions about the project in the international media, but they existed, even if they were not archived or recorded. Significantly, they also embodied what Raymond Williams described in relation to the formation of counterhegemony as the dependent relationship between dominant, residual (as in remnants of traditional forces), and emergent cultural forces in an ongoing process of exchange, confrontation, and assimilation on all fronts within the hegemonic sphere (Williams 1970: 110).

As I have tried to show throughout the pages of this book, postmodern-inspired notions of diversity, multiplicity, fragmentation, and illusory subjectivity with which the theoretical notion of the immaterialization of the art object is associated have allowed for the visibility of marginalized historical subjects. As *Picasso* demonstrates, broader homogenizing (and vulgarly materialist) meta-narratives rarely allowed this visibility in the same way. Yet I propose that paradoxically it is also these post-modern notions that carry within them the potential to erase structural historical dynamics, such as disparities in power, the inequalities of class, and the violent persistence of geopolitics. This quagmire is, if anything, a somber reminder of the difficulties of contemporary art making embedded in postmodern discourses in colonial/postcolonial contexts like Ramallah, as well as Amman and Beirut. It is also a reminder of what writing about, processing, and then framing the "other" in neoliberalized forms of production, representation, and circulation actually entail.

CONCLUSION

At the Opening of a new museum of modern and/or contemporary Arab art in a Arab city, a proud local resident rushes to the entrance only to find that he is unable to proceed. Was it the thugs that shielded the ruling dynasty (attending the event en masse along with their newly contracted western and eastern celebrity-friends, to showcase their benevolence and refined sensibilities, pubescent-future-rulers in tow) that prevent his access? No. Was it his casual wear at an event announced as a black-tie affair? No. He simply feels that were he to walk in, he will certainly "hit a wall." On the spot, he turns to face the rushing crowd and screams: "Stop don't go in. Be careful." Within seconds he is removed from the site, severely beaten and sent to a psychiatric facility.

My sense is that a similar event will unfold sometime between 2014 and 2024 in Beirut/and or Amman and/or Abu Dhabi and/or Doha and/or elsewhere in the region. We may even read in newspapers the following day the headline: "Demented Man Disturbs Opening: Claims World is Flat." Consequently, an opening in the world will have been disturbed in more ways than anticipated.

Walid Raad, Miraculous Beginnings, 2010

IN 2018, I PRESENTED PARTS OF CHAPTERS 2 AND 3 OF THIS BOOK at a luncheon seminar series at Brown University, where I was visiting assistant professor at the time. During the Q and A period, a professor of comparative literature asked a question whose reasoning was familiar to me. Why and how, he asked, does studying the contemporary artworks of a younger generation, seemingly out of touch with their own societies, matter? And, by extension, who does it matter for? I had received queries like this during my fieldwork, usually from older intellectuals in the cities I studied. These intellectuals believed that the younger generation's seeming alienation from local public debates in the traditional understanding of the role of *al-muthaqaff* was due to their precarious financial dependency on freelance art writing for international art journals that served the demands of a mostly English-language global culture industry that emphasized the visual over the textual dimensions of cultural production. By extension, this meant that any chance they had at becoming organic intellectuals, in the sense that Antonio Gramsci (1971) put forward and Edward Said (1994) after him subscribed to, became nearly impossible. Like the professor who wanted to know what studying a globally oriented, seemingly elite group of artists implied methodologically, the critics were concerned with researchers like myself who relied too heavily on an unrepresentative sample of cultural actors to explain the cultural history and political developments of the region and the role critical thinkers play in each.

This issue touches on one of the major concerns I had while writing this book. The anxieties consuming scholars in the Western academy and the region's older public intellectuals informed a part of my thinking from the beginning. Their concerns centered on not being able to easily locate research about contemporary art in the established disciplines like art history and Islamic art or political science and international relations. They also revolved around their own perceptions of a quickly changing society that could not be explained by existing consensual regimes of thought around the demarcation of disciplines and theories between—to borrow from Rancière's thinking on boundaries—"the sayable and unsayable, the proper and the improper, the legitimate and illegitimate" (Bosteels, quoted in Rockill and Watts 2009: 160). While the local anxieties about the disproportionate attention received by multimedia contemporary artists were not unfounded, as I explain all through the book, I have grappled with their social function rather than their aesthetics. As outlined in the introduction, I did not see art and politics as either separate *or* one and the same. Rather, I saw the nexus at which they met as contingent on the histories and societies in which they are both experienced (Rockhill 2014). In the same way, I wanted to understand why an interdisciplinary project like mine could offend some steeped in the disciplinary confines of Western universities, which I am a product of myself. I wanted to show that a research about the politics of art and the international political economy of its making was first and foremost committed to being genuinely interdisciplinary. It was equally responsive to the subject of its research, which was itself also multivalent and ultimately hybrid. I partially grounded myself in political theory, political economy, and international relations by touching on topics related to cultural diplomacy, development, international institutions, and the Cold War and the global war on terror. At the same time, however, I attempted to show the kinds of relations and ideas forged when individuals in different cities, who operate through globally oriented institutions, converge. In this respect, I was influenced by the work of international relations theorist Christine Sylvester (2009) and sociologist of globalization Peggy Levitt (2015), both of whom focused on art and museums. My goal was not to produce a definitive comparative account of multiple cities but to study phenomena experienced in three cities at the same point in time.

Driving this book was a pursuit to find new frames of thinking and new methods for analyzing cultural production in the Arab world in a globalized context and transnational frame. The analytic goal was to slow down and explain what happens when what is migrating transnationally passes through certain nodes on its circuit and also what happens when we use art as the starting point to understand social transformations. This book contributes to the conversation by reading the political economy of cultural production from and about Arab cities in the Eastern Mediterranean as a discourse analysis of the global art world by investigating aspects of the multilayered micro-dynamics of the local cultural politics that constitute it. It does not rely in any way on positivist methodology. As I have tried to show throughout these pages, the notion of a free and neutral global art space is more complex than it appears; certain narratives fall out of view as certain representations are privileged over others.

When I began my ethnography in 2009, most work on contemporary art practices from the region had been undertaken within the ambit of art writing in mostly English-language journals, which dedicated themselves to single practice reviews of what international development civil society funders referred to as "young Arab artists" already enjoying much exposure in the global arts circuit. As such, my political economy approach to art sometimes provoked ambivalent reactions from members of the cultural elite benefiting from global exposure and funding, as well as from representatives of global cultural funding organizations. It became increasingly obvious to me that this research was implicated in a predetermined dichotomy because it was intertwined with the challenges that some actors in the post-1990 generation seemed to reject as a reaction to what they perceived as locally contrived, overdetermined material conceptions of art. They saw these conceptions as driving an ideological rather than aesthetical interpretation of their works. This dichotomy framed art as located either within the gambits of postcolonial nationalism or within a Westernized liberalism. The ensuing status quo pitted two camps against each other, with one deemed to be associated with the remnants of colonialism and the other, a self-perceived counterhegemonic reaction to the former's propensity toward meta-narratives. The fact that the latter benefited from a postpolitical atmosphere of seemingly altruistic international funding and support, where ideological preferences were supposedly buried with the Cold War and the regional political and economic reformulations that came with it, further reinforced its self-perceived counterhegemonic location in relation to lingering nationalist, socialist, and Arabist ideologies. Further, discussions with some of those benefiting from transnational links and international funding quite often steered clear of confronting what cultural funding, the growing Gulf art industry, and globalization might signify for aesthetics. Within the atmosphere described, what was understood as critical and alternative post-2000 contemporary art production, which had its more immediate roots in the politics and structures of the late 1990s and early 2000s, continued to thrive amid a growing celebratory global art world seemingly uninterested in commenting on the structural changes that were concurrently occurring.

But then, in 2008, Walid Raad, the most internationally recognized Lebanese postwar artist, initiated a project about the history of contemporary and modern art in the Arab world. I was already a few months into my field interviews when he presented the first installment of his research results under the title *Scratching on Things I Could Disavow: A History of Art in the Arab World / Part 1_Volume1_Chapter 1 (Beirut: 1992–2005)*, which was first exhibited at Beirut's Sfeir Semler Gallery and later traveled globally. In this show, Raad takes viewers on a journey through the multilayered terrain of the quick emergence of art spaces and institutions in the Arab world of the past ten years. In addition to the new physical infrastructure that includes Middle Eastern branches of the Guggenheim and Louvre, this infrastructure also contains internationally linked workshops, festivals, art funds, art schools, white cube galleries, large museums, journals, and the surge in private and public collectors. Raad built on the writings of fellow Lebanese postwar artist and theorist Jalal Toufic (2000), who conceptualized "the withdrawal of tradition past a surpassing disaster" to question whether and how culture and tradition in the Arab world may have been affected, either materially and/or immaterially, by the violence of the region's wars and accompanied growth in Arab art popularity. Through his aesthetical translation of these circumstances by the depiction of "curious" occurrences such as the flattening of art spaces, white cube walls, the contraction of artworks, and the accenting of various forms, Raad's project set out to locate the ideological, economic, and political scope of the recent changes in the world of Arab art. This opening in the research terrain was timely and critical in that it discursively aestheticized what was very quickly becoming too difficult to ignore.

This book attempts to capture the role of three cities in contributing to what Raad aestheticizes, by playing a part in constructing, perpetuating, and sometimes resisting it. I began the book by foraying into the world and legacy of *Hiwar* to unravel one often overlooked aspect of the globalized contemporary art scene, that is, the often ambiguous and always tense relationship between cultural production and "external" sources of funding. Situating the narratives around the story of *Hiwar*'s demise and its place in the memory of cultural elites, all within the context of a longer history of cultural diplomacy manifested in various guises in the region's modern history, was a way to highlight how the contentious relationship to non-Arab or nonlocal sources of funding conceal a more pertinent issue. This issue concerns a class politics that has given way to identity politics in liberal cultural circles. It had the effect of congealing critique into a form of consensual acceptance of neoliberal forms of funding and circulation in art because they appear as neutral and democratizing forces of change, be they the links of nonprofit and nongovernmental art organizations and initiatives to international aid or to the growing Gulf art industry. From there, I demonstrated the structural changes in both civil society practices and the larger terrain of cultural production by examining the changes that were taking place at the same time between visual and textual forms of art as dominant forms of critique in the region in the context of the post-1990s generation's conceptions of the encounter with modernity and modernism. After an intermezzo, I dedicated the subsequent three chapters to uncovering the stories, works, and experiences of making art in each individual city. I showed how a globally oriented generation of cultural actors appeared to be contesting the weight given to official versions of history and prevalent imaginings of it. This generation saw themselves as the latest in a set of critiques of Orientalism (Said 1978), perceived as far too focused on the binaries of good and evil, East and West. In its place, they pushed a new political that articulated the role of critical art as counterhegemonic in a postmodern and deconstructivist language and aesthetic. This new political was more rooted in concepts of difference, ambivalence, and hybridity (Bhabha 1990) as tools to combat dominant discourses and structures of power, wherever those may lie, whether in the "East" or "West." These critiques, which targeted essentialist readings of history in favor of more Foucaultian and Lacanian readings of identities as signifiers at play in cultural fields, rendered the societies around them ill at ease. Yet at the same time they garnered global admiration for their ability to explain their complex histories and positionalities in an aesthetical language understood by the global art world.

Whether artists were confined to working under the state in Jordan, or within civil society institutions that knew very well how to "live outside of the state" in Lebanon (Salamé 1987: 52) or as part of the highly aid dependent culture NGO sector in Palestine, the vulnerability of intercepting the meaning and framings of work was most true of those aesthetical forms that were most at ease in, and most celebrated by the circuits of global capital. This was never a one-way process, however, and always depended on the content of the negotiations. Locating pockets of dissent, resistance, and revolt in unconventional spaces has become a hallmark of contemporary postcolonial discourse; in other words, "Hegemonies are never completed projects, they are always in contention. There are always cracks and contradictions—and therefore opportunities" (Hall, Massey, and Rustin 2013: 17). Accordingly, this complicates our understanding of what counts as hegemony and whether a single locus of hegemony ever really exists. By extension, if it complicates hegemony, then it must complicate counterhegemony, and how it changes form and meaning depends on context. Together, the chapters illustrate how seemingly anti-hegemonic cultural production sometimes ends up, ironically and often unwittingly, reinforcing discourses that are hegemonic in a different space and time. It is ultimately ideological dogma and power relations that decide in advance of context, and in advance of an examination of the balance of forces in a particular situation, how and what to frame as the force against which to resist.

THE MANY AFTERLIVES OF REVOLUTION

In the spring of 2011, the artist collective Dictaphone Group invited participants from the public to board a small motor-powered fishing boat to explore the nature of ownership on the Beirut seafront, the laws that govern it, and the political practices of those who use those areas. Once on board, the participants were taken along the shoreline of Beirut from the Ein el-Mreisse fishermen's port to Dalieh and then to Ramlet el-Baida beach, where participants shared stories oftheir own experiences with the sea. The project above all centered around ethnographic work that included collaboration with several fishermen, a collection of oral histories relayed during the boat ride. Equally significant, it analyzed detailed accounts of the particularities of land ownership, the laws that govern them and the practices of its users.

It did so through a critical action-oriented, site-specific, and interventionist mode. Almost as though purposefully breaking with the tendency of the post-1990 generation of artists to shy away from representations of history by insisting on its fabrication as opposed to its truth, Dictaphone Group's project maintained that resistance requiredthe blunt representation and articulate framing of the historical fact of urban memory erasure. This insistence on urgency, collectivity, objectivity, and participation echoed the demands of the 2011–2012 revolutionaries.[1] It also clearly broke away from the post-1990s generation's overreliance on theory and introspective reflection as a form of dissent.

In the early years of the Arab uprisings when citizens of the Arab world rose up in unison to demand an end to the authoritarian violence that has dominated the region for the most part since independence, Lebanese, Palestinians, and Jordanians of all generations watched and cheered from the sidelines at the momentous changes taking place in the larger neighboring countries of Egypt, Syria, Bahrain, and Libya. The mass activism and broad social movements that soon followed inspired especially the younger generation of these societies to agitate against their own then stable but equally contentious and largely resented ruling elites.

In Lebanon, an entrenched political elite relying on sectarianism and clientalism to maintain control over public resources that facilitate trade, real estate, construction, and banking thwarted the early rumblings of a bottom-up, horizontally organized and Arab Spring inspired anti-sectarian movement.

This movement centered around public appeals for social justice, higher wages, and the need for electricity, running water, and other basic necessities that the state has consistently failed to provide (Hermez 2011). The mobilization, which dwindled for a couple of years, came rushing back with full force in late 2019 until it was quelled again by the very real but also very convenient threat of the corona virus pandemic. This showed us, yet again, that revolutions are almost always processes and hardly ever just one-off events. In Jordan, what came to be known as *al Hirak al Shababi*, or the March 24 Shabab Movement (youth movement), a horizontally and loosely organized group of mostly younger unaffiliated activists shaped the changing landscape of civil resistance in the contexts of regional revolutionary fervor. Building a campaign comprised of demonstrations, sit-ins, strikes, and boycotts, the movement dubbed simply *al-Hirak* (the movement), maintained a small but consistent pattern of protests that crossed established lines of criticism of the Hashemite monarchy and even the king himself that lasted well into 2015 and beyond. In typical regime fashion, the response was guarded and calculated. It allowed protestors enough freedom to encompass the waves of popular discontent shaping the region but, at the same time, never wavered from the counterrevolutionary trope of security and stability at the cost of freedom (Ryan 2018). Although *al-Hirak* has not managed to achieve even the short-term goals of its campaign to hold public officials accountable for the urban economic inequality in the capital, it nonetheless triggered changes in how discourses of discontent, opposition, and political engagement were to be articulated. The Palestinians for their part also shared the sentiments of injustice and anger that drove the mass revolts in the region. Yet, despite some initial show of support in the form of demonstrations, mostly from youth groups and independent activists, "the spatial, political, and affective conditions of the Palestinians did not facilitate mass-scale mobilization" (Pearlman 2016).

It is these dynamics of change, evolving networks of activism, and novel styles of mobilization that inspired a new "post" generation of artists and artworks, such as Dictaphone Group's *This Sea is Mine*. Among other civil society formations like women's groups, human rights activists, and youth movements, this post-2011 generation of activists and artists has emerged from the euphoria of revolution and the ugly violence of the counterrevolutions after 2012 as one of the most prominent and visible voices for change. From Amman to Beirut and Ramallah, what are understood as bottom-up, horizontally and informally organized art spaces, initiatives, and activist groups are dominating the artistic landscape and emerging alongside a globally and locally funded and patronized art scene that is using the arts as an alternative form of politics. As a prominent businessman and major art patron in Amman described to me in the spring of 2018, "Politics is no longer done the way it used to be, the rules of the game are changing and we can now do politics from within art. Local patronage can shape new societies and ways of thinking."[2]

If cultural nonprofit organizations funded by Western donors under the umbrella of cultural diplomacy dominated the visual arts production scene from the 1990s until roughly the outbreak of the revolts in 2011–2012, since then a growing number of domestic arts patrons with strong business ties to the Gulf are seeing the need to invest in an arts infrastructure that goes beyond the self-interest of cultural diplomacy and Western donor aid to the nongovernmental sector. This begs the question, to what extent will these new forms of funding, which are even more intricately bound up with global capital, push for a truly dissident, critical, and radical cultural production, one that reaches far beyond merely supporting art to express discontent with the status quo?

Writing about the arts in 1990, Cornel West argued that intellectuals should be engaged in a "new cultural politics of difference" (West 1990). For him, this involved the alignment of cultural creators and theorists with disempowered minorities and the creation of artworks that focus on themes of gender, race, difference, and empowerment. It is safe to say that many contemporary artists from the Mashriq, like other artists from the Global South, have achieved what West called for all those years ago. Today, from the Arab Gulf to the countries of the Mashriq and Maghreb, and reaching far into Europe to cities like London and Berlin to which so many Arab artists are escaping from the crushing weight of counterrevolutionary authoritarianism, the art of difference has become the norm. True, this art of difference has resulted, a lot of the time, in an otherwise articulated set of lingering neo-orientalist mentalities in the re-presentations and framing of works. But that we can even have this discussion is ultimately a sign of not only the serious effort to make visible particularity and diversity but also of its relative success in becoming mainstreamed in both the region and Western capitals. Activist initiatives focused on decolonizing the most powerful institutions operating in the global art world, such as the now well-known Decolonize This Place, have taken up a notch this conversation about diversification. In the process, they are revealing how the celebration of diversity and particularity is not enough; in fact, it can help perpetuate the very violent colonial relationships it purports to address.

In the Middle East today, the cultural politics of diversity and multiple modernities is paid lip service by some of the most authoritarian yet internationally, diplomatically connected of the monarchial Gulf Arab regimes, along with the eager and sometimes highly questionable support of powerhouse US and European curators and art directors (Sahakian 2018). This new wave of state-supported institution building and renovation, underway largely in Saudi Arabia, Qatar, the Emirates, Lebanon, Egypt, Kuwait, and Jordan, are instances of top-down, globally attuned national identity formation, state-led societal development, and soft power and public diplomacy.[3] In most cities a strong effort is being made to build with the combined efforts of business art patrons, conservative government funding, and international development funders, all the elements of a strong art scene in the region. This includes investment in the artists, museums, nonprofits, collectors, patrons, curators, alternative pedagogical art programs, and everything in between.

In the words of the decolonial theorist Walter Mignolo, writing about the Qatari Museum of Islamic Art in Doha: "What is happening is not merely an imitation of westernisation, but an enactment of de-westernisation in that western cultural standards are being appropriated and adapted to local or regional sensibilities, needs and visions. In the sphere of civilisations and museums, this is a significant departure" (2013a: 11–12). The suggestion that he and others have made is that prosperous and stable Arab capitals like Doha, Dubai, Abu Dhabi, and Muscat have the capability to redraw the global cultural map by redefining the Arab capital in a manner that is neither "Eurocentric nor Europhobic; neither retrograde nativist nor rootless cosmopolitan" (Dabashi 2017).

There is something to these celebratory and hopeful takes on art infrastructure in the cities of the Arab Gulf. Yet, to my thinking, glaringly absent is an examination of how tangled these spaces are in regional geopolitics, economic diversification strategies, and military alliances with Western powers (evidenced not least by the location of military bases such as those of France in the UAE or the US in Qatar). This examination is necessary especially because this new art infrastructure is understood to be de-Westernizing art discourses and collecting practices by re-routing the direction of travel and sales of each. Decolonial claims do not seem to factor into the corporate power that often shapes the conversations that take place in and about museums, even if these museums—especially as in the case of the Gulf museums—are able to reverse art market trends by paying more for artworks than traditional Western art patrons are able to today.

The Lebanese poet and critic Abbas Beydoun once warned of the consequences of transforming art into a technical subject by disconnecting it from larger protest movements. By not renewing its form of protest, art end ups living "in a time when culture becomes a secondary issue, and maybe, an additional credit for the politicians and the bureaucrats and even the priests and the mullahs" (2003: 30). I posit that since the headiness of the 2011 Arab revolutions and the subsequent violence of the continued protest movements and violent counterrevolutions of the 2010s, a renewal of protest in art from and in about the region is taking place. This strife is occurring in multiple sites, in the region and outside of it, wherever Arab artists, writers, and intellectuals are residing. But for the latest protest renewal to endure beyond an expression of unrest, it cannot leave unaddressed its interruption by the discourses and practices embedded in neoliberal art world structures and their concomitant supporters in international diplomatic channels. If sustained through neoliberal ethics and capital, multiplying sites of cultural production are bound to have competing elements and visions that should not—and indeed cannot—follow a consensus-based course if they are to create a new radical language that responds to the right-wing resurgence we are living. What I imagine instead, perhaps naively, is a locus where artists as much as audiences and publics force their way through the cracks in the walls that hegemony imposes by disturbing the world in more ways than anticipated. With the coronavirus pandemic being the backdrop against which I write these words in isolation at home, thinking about how its aftereffects will aggressively aggravate neoliberalism's preexisting injustices and paradoxes, I dare say that the revolution in art is yet to come, in the region I study and elsewhere. What I keep returning to in my mind—even after the research I present in this book—is some version of China Miéville's response to the global rise of nationalism in *The Last Days of New Paris* (2016). This response is a call not for a revolt in politics but for a dissonant revolt from within art.

Notes

INTRODUCTION

1. The NSRD carries out research and analysis of defense and national security issues for the US and allied defense, foreign policy, homeland security, and intelligence communities and foundations and other nongovernmental organizations that support defense and national security analysis. Some of RAND's research output on art and culture in the Arab world includes, for example, Zellman, Martini, and Perlman (2011); Schwartz et al. (2009); and Helmus and Kaye (2009).

2. See, e.g., Berger et al. (2008). See also Bouquerel and El Husseiny (2009); Isar (2014); and informal discussion blogs, such as Helmus and Dassa Kaye (2009). See also Hyesun (2013) and especially De Perini (2017) for interesting accounts of the different historical phases that EU intercultural policy dialogue with the Mediterrean countries went through: emergence, consolidation, professionalization.

3. See, e.g., Snider and Faris (2011) on youth and technology. For a debunking of such myths, see Selim (2013).

4. For a list of such spaces, see Koenig and Omareen (2018).

5. Several cultural hegemonies are at play in the region, some of which are violent and destructive. Hence, while I could choose from several donor relationships in the countries I researched (e.g., Iranian support of Hizbullah in Lebanon and the Syrian regime in Syria or the Qatar-Saudi rivalry and their attendant support of different Islamist cultural organizations across the Arab and Muslim world), I was most

interested in the relationship that was a function of a specifically neoliberal take on global culture. This relationship has its recent roots in historical Western cultural relations to the global south; it is arguably the model of Western cultural diplomacy and art as modern and civil that is the legacy of Cold War diplomacy that reigns in the region today.

6. See also Wade (1991).

7. Joseph Nye (2004) developed the idea of "soft power" in the context of international relations theory. The term, now widely used in international affairs by academics, analysts, and political leaders, refers to the ability to obtain what one wants through cooption and attraction, rather than the hard power of coercion and punishment.

8. For example, Stonor Saunders (2013), which briefly mentions the funding of *Hiwar* in Lebanon. See also Von Eschen (2004); Wilford (2008); Finn and Couvée (2014); Iber (2015).

9. A key exception is Rubin (2012).

10. Two examples are Demos (2009), on the well-known Palestinian artist Emily Jacir, and Cotter (2009), on renowned Lebanese artists Akram Zaatari and Walid Raad, whom she featured in her show *Out of Beirut* (Cotter 2006).

11. See Saadawi (2020) for an elaborate critique of this tendency. Atrissi (2009) is a notable exception. Atrissi's short essay focuses on the influences on and the development of graphic design in the Arab world as a contemporary form of visual art. He looks at the recycled Arab visual elements and icons appropriated by young twentieth-century artists that transformed vernacular art into high art, urban art, and visual identities.

12. I use the term "cultural" loosely here to describe these diverse organizational formations. In the Arabic language, the term *thaqafa*, which is translated into English as "culture," refers to a social framework, and so is related to the traditional practices, language, cultural heritage, and artistic productions of society.

13. I use the term "secular" with trepidation. As some literature argues, secularism has no conceptual coherence and has become a signifier for very different sorts of accommodations between religion and state in different places that needs to be understood as a historical construct (Taylor 2007). Yet I employ the term here and throughout the book in its most basic sense to distinguish between civil society organizations that consider faith core to their missions and activities and those that do not.

14. The terms "global," "transnational," and "international" are sometimes used interchangeably. I employ them recognizing that choosing one over the other may hide the tenacity of the politics of unequal relations that still defines each (DeVereaux and

Griffin 2006). I talk about international (or regional) funding to describe the funding for culture and civil society programs that comes from outside the borders of Lebanon, Palestine, or Jordan that is part of the neoliberal structure of civil society that has been occurring. I use "transnational" to describe the movement of capital, people, ideas, and art across different borders. And I use "global" to refer to the platforms of representation and circulation of works that take the global audience, discourses, and aesthetics as their frames of reference.

15. See, e.g., Awad (2006); Al Sayyid (2007); Bazzi (2007a, 2007b); Muna (2008). A notable exception is Omar Amiralay, a filmmaker and human rights activist who resists a "he said, she said" approach, instead evaluating the interest of funders as well as how they might be affecting local cultural scenes in the Arab region. See Amiralay (2009).

16. See Erskine-Loftus, Penziner Hightower, and Ibrahim Al-Mulla (2016); Matar (2015). For a dynamic approach to understanding museums' roles as sites of cosmopolitanism in an increasingly transnationalized and global world, see Levitt (2015).

17. In the twentieth century, the distinction between artworks and the conditions of their making prevailed, leaving discussions of the organizational practices involved in art making to the sociology of art (Tanner 2003). Jonathan Harris argues that in part the field of visual culture itself was a proposition that "became used emphatically to indicate a specific rejection of traditional art history" (2004: 63–75). Despite these changes, questions of pure aesthetics persisted as a "return to aesthetics" or a "return to beauty." For the autonomy of art, see Zangwill (2002).

18. My reasoning here is inspired in part by the focus on the relationship between technique and political orientation in Walter Benjamin's 1934 essay "The Artist as Producer" (Benjamin 1998).

19. Interview with the author, February 17, 2009, Beirut.

20. Makhoul (2013), for instance, has argued that the boundaries between what is and what is not visual art have become so blurred that they are barely discernible. Generally, "contemporary art" is a broad term used to describe art produced after the Second World War, and especially since the 1960s and 1970s. It is not as easily classifiable as modern art and is essentially critical of the historical meta-narratives and idealism associated with modern art. See Aranda, Kuan Wood, and Vidokle (2010) for different practitioners' interpretations that start from the premise of the difficulty of "pinning it down." For a more comprehensive approach to understanding the multilayered dynamics conditioning contemporary art and the implications for its meaning today that I ascribe to here, see Stallabras (2004).

21. See Daher (2011) for an analysis of cultural heritage NGOs working in the domain of art and architectural preservation in Palestine, Lebanon, and Jordan. He provides a thorough account of the new young class of cultural entrepreneurs and patrons of the arts who are taking over what should normally fall under the state's jurisdiction.

22. Jordan and Israel officially warred for decades. Israel took control of the West Bank, which had previously belonged to Jordan, in the Six-Day War of 1967. Relations before the signing of a 1994 peace treaty were not formalized, but despite outward violence, Jordanian Hashemite kings had strong ties to Jewish leaders through secret backchannels.

23. See, e.g., Carothers (2003).

24. I scare-quote these terms to highlight their contested nature, especially in the way they have been appropriated by international development practitioners to push forth their transition to democracy theory. The use of such terminology demarcates the category of secular civil society activists that donors traditionally dealt with from their Islamic civil society counterparts but with whom they do not generally collaborate. As I write these words, it seems neither camp in this dual conception of Arab civil society has played a leading role in bringing about the revolutionary movements sparked first by the Tunisian uprising of January 2011 and then again in 2018–2019. The current rebellions in the Arab world are largely horizontal, and participation has encompassed the entire demographic and social spectrum cutting across national, ethnic and religious lines. How these events will unfold remains to be seen, but in the past ten years it has become increasingly obvious that the Washington- and EU-led formula of civil society and democratization in the region has failed to achieve what it set out to do. See Cavatorta and Durac (2010) for a comprehensive study on how civil society and democratization promotion had the opposite effect of propping up the very authoritarian regimes that it purportedly set out to undermine.

25. I elaborate in detail on this point in chapter 1.

26. At the time of writing, the global coronavirus pandemic has canceled an entire way of life aong with structures of support for many contemporary artists, for whom international travel has been a central pillar in their careers. How this increased difficulty in traveling and the reliance on going digital will affect the content of artwork, its funding structures, and exhibition possibilities in the long term is yet to be seen.

27. See Hanssen and Safieddine (2016: 194).

28. For how the losses of 1967 impacted the form and content of art, see especially Boullata (2009: chap. 3)

29. The generations I designate here are partly drawn from how social actors in my fieldwork referred to each other. These delineated categories are also artistic milieus in Bourdieu's sense of socially stratified patterns of perception, classification, and thinking that shape a specific lifestyle. In his approach, the link between age and generational cohort is not the defining feature of a generation but is how each is marked by a shared worldview and defined by what happens when actors arrive to a field and enter its habitus (1984, 1990). To be clear, I use the term "generation" throughout the book to denote the range of Arab cultural actors who share certain sensibilities often defined by ideological, generational, and experiential habitus, but I do so with trepidation and in full recognition that sometimes these generations fuse on more than one level. There are two reasons for this: first, because these categories of identity are not static, and second, because conversations and collaborations between members of the two groups are fairly very common. Yet for all the fluidity of the generational interactions, there is a difference in how the relationship to transnational circuits of art and Western sources of funding are perceived. I will delve more into this in chapter 3 where it becomes obvious that historical ruptures around 1967 and 1990 and then again 2011 (a period I do not treat in this book) triggered changing outlooks on how to understand resistance in cultural production. How the media revolution influenced artistic and literary expressions and their circulation is of fundamental importance between the post-1967 and post-1990 generational categories. I am aware that artistic practices in Lebanon, Palestine, and Jordan, for instance, can be further categorized in ways that correspond to domestic and regional political landscapes. But my interest here is in the macro-historical ruptures in epistemological frames and lived realities of cultural actors that came first with 1967 and then after the end of the Cold War. For a thorough description of how the 1967 and 1990 generations and their outlooks are split and reflected in similar literature, see Halabi (2017). On visual art, see Rahman (2015: 4–9).

30. For more on Foucault's thinking on techniques by which a society is rendered governable, see Foucault et al. (1991). Most literature on neoliberalism takes a critical stance on its principles of global capitalism and the destruction of the welfare state (e.g., Chomsky [1999]; Touraine [2001]; Hermansen [2005]; Saad-Filho and Johnston [2005]; Plehwe, Walpen, and Neunhöffer [2006]).

31. Philip Marfleet, for example, argues that the events that began in 2010–2011

were part of a process under way for many years during which Arab citizens—against all odds—created space for self-expression. For more on the study of political agency and new ways of understanding Arab politics in the wake of the revolutionary process, see Marfleet (2016). See also Hanafi (2012) and Kraidy (2016) for a rethinking of political resistance through the site of the Arab body.

32. US interests in Lebanon are centered around maintaining a strategic buffer between war-torn Syria and Israel. Lebanon is also regarded as a tactical front against terrorism in the region, starting with its own complicated relationship to Hezbollah. The US has provided Lebanon more than $1.5 billion in military assistance since 2006. See "Pentagon to Keep Backing Lebanon Military, Despite Hezbollah Gains," *Reuters*, May 11, 2018, https://www.reuters.com/article/us-lebanon-election-usa-military/pentagon-to-keep-backing-lebanon-military-despite-hezbollah-gains-idUSKBN1IC2BD. See also Lia (2007); "Lieutenant General Keith Dayton: United States Security Coordinator," *Ma'an News Agency*, March 30, 2010, http://www.maannews.com/Content.aspx?id=265173; Bedein (2009); Bureau of Near Eastern Affairs (n.d.).

33. Daher further argues that the circulation of global capital (such as surplus oil revenues) in search of high-yielding investments, combined with excessive privatization, has transformed urban reality, inflated property values, fueled speculation, and altered the nature of public.

34. Interview with the author, June 9, 2013, Amman.

35. Interview with the author, May 17, 2017, Ramallah.

36. For a review of the entire project, see Harb, Hijjawi, and Touq (2018).

CHAPTER 1

1. For a firsthand account of some of these debates as they are expressed in art writing by artists and art critics, see Lenssen et al. (2018). See also Faisal Darraj's (2013) essay on the relevance of these debates for modern and contemporary Arab art.

2. Yousef Bazzi is a Lebanese poet and journalist who worked with the Saudi-backed Lebanese Future Movement political party–supported print newspaper *Al Mustaqbal*; as of 2019 the paper is only in online form. Bazzi is part of a generation of Lebanese leftists turned liberals in the aftermath of the civil war. These writers are vocal critics of what they perceive to be Arab culture's tendency to forgo individual freedom and political democracy for the purpose of armed resistance, anti-imperialism, provincialism, and nationalism.

3. For a summative analysis of the "foreign funding debate" with particular regard to Egyptian women's rights and the NGOs where these debates are most hotly contested, see Al-Ali (2000).

4. A good example of how this binary is drawn on historically is found in Boullata (2009: 126), in which he describes two intellectual currents among literary forms and magazines reflected in the visual arts. The first current called for an engaged literature as popularized in the immediate post–World War II era by French existentialists such as Jean Paul Sartre. The second emanates from artists whose figurative language perpetuated a narrative pictorial art that seemed to echo the metaphorical imagery popularized by the poetry introduced in the pan-Arabist *Al-Adab*, founded and edited by the writer and literary critical Suhail Idriss. The poets associated with *Shi'r*, on the other hand, valorized the more abstract and experimental artists.

5. See Sayegh (2001 [1995]) for an understanding of the concerns and thinking of this generation. See also Kassab (2009).

6. For a thorough and polemical take on cosmopolitanism as ideological warfare, see Brennan (1997). On how conceptions of cosmopolitanism and nationalism shape identity and protest, see Rao (2010).

7. Discussion, April 12, 2015.

8. For more on this debate, see Mohammed (1989) and Sabry (2010: 29). For the preoccupation with *assala* (authenticity) in artistic production today, see especially Winegar (2006: chaps. 1–3). Through a critique of three major pan-Arab conferences that took place in the Arab world after 1967 as part of Arab intellectuals' introspective turn, Elizabeth Suzanne Kassab (2009) provides a comprehensive take on the place of authenticity and tradition in the post-1967 intellectual scene, arguing that these notions are often de-historicized while simultaneously idealized by cultural elites.

9. In *Trials of Arab Modernity*, literary scholar Tarek El-Ariss makes similar suppositions about the experience of encountering modernity as an experience rather than as a representation (of an event). He reframes Arab modernity as a somatic condition shaped through "accidents and events (*adth*) emerging in between Europe and the Arab World" (El-Ariss 2013: 3).

10. The formation of subjectivity in relation to power has been tackled by theorists interested in the interface between psychoanalytic theory and emancipation. Examples include Butler (1997) and Žižek (1999). Through the repertoires of Lacanian psychoanalysis, Derridian deconstruction as well as postmodern notions of mimicry and performance, Homi Bhabha seeks to locate the meaning of culture in the marginal

spaces lying between the dominant symbolic order. He has proposed rethinking nationalism, representation, and resistance by positing "ambivalence," "hybridity," and "liminality" as central sites of colonial contention (1994: see esp. chap. 1).

11. Samah Idriss, founding editor of *Al-Adab*, a Lebanese Arabic language arts and culture journal, and son of the late literary giant Suhail Idriss, who was deeply involved in confronting *Hiwar*'s role in the cultural Cold War, cynically wondered in conversation with me how it was that Tawfik Sayigh's journal suffered the fate it did, while today an entire industry is built around the politics of Western funding for culture and the arts "with hardly any questions asked by the generation building it."

12. A comprehensive report on cultural policies in the Arab world shows how the language of development, civil society, and democratization is interwoven with arguments about the politics of arts production in the region (Al Khatib et al. 2010).

13. Soft power describes the ability of a political body, such as a state or its civil society, to indirectly influence, through trust and mutual understanding, the behaviors or interests of other political bodies through ideological means of persuasion rather than coercion. For more, see Nye (2004).

14. An interesting read in this regard is Tim Rivera's (2015) report on cultural relations or cultural diplomacy in reference to the British Council. See also Bátora (2005); Melissen (2005); and Cull (2009).

15. In this reading, Williams tries to break down the analysis of culture into three terms; ideal, documentary, and social. Ideal refers to lives, works, and values; documentary is the body of the intellectual work (i.e., the actual evidence of the culture); and social is the description of a particular way of life. The social element could refer to traditions or language. Williams also ascertains that the dependent relationship between dominant, residual (as in remnants of the traditional), and emergent cultural forces is an ongoing practice of exchange, confrontation, and assimilation on all fronts within the hegemonic sphere. These three elements invariably and selectively co-opt each other (Williams 1977: 110).

16. Interview with the author, May 2, 2008, Beirut.

17. Interview with the author, May 2, 2008, Beirut.

18. Interview with the author, April 28, 2008, Beirut.

19. This definition is taken from the Institute of Cultural Diplomacy's website, which is interesting because it uses the definitions of international relations theorists and its own practical work to construct a meaning that is very much tied up with its

own policies and projects that aim to use cultural diplomacy as a form of soft power (Nye 2004).

20. Interview with the author, August 29, 2017, Amman.

21. The concept of power in public diplomacy has been explored in Rasmussen's discursive influence model of normative power (2009). These normative frameworks have been criticized in Pamment (2011). See Sylvester (2009) for an alternative view that utilizes feminist and poststructuralist approaches to account for the role of culture in international politics.

22. For an excellent analysis of Mitchell's piece, see the introduction of his republished chapter in Preziosi (2009).

23. For more on the world exhibitions, see both Allwood (1977) and Benedict (1991). See also Çelik (1992).

24. To see how the power relations inherent to cultural diplomacy are elided by framing the practice as an enjoyable dimension of public diplomacy that values free cultural expression, see Schneider (2004).

25. For an interesting take on how the terms "internationalism," "transnationalism," and "globalism" have configured into this history of cultural hegemony as practices by many of the cultural institutions I consider in this book, see DeVereaux and Griffin (2006).

26. In the aftermath of the attacks of September 11, 2001, a plethora of articles, reports, and op-ed pieces appeared, giving attention to how the US and its values, culture, and policies are perceived abroad and how it can improve those perceptions. Among the recommendations were calls for increased efforts in the area of cultural diplomacy. Ironically, the renewed interest in cultural diplomacy comes at a time when the country's resources and infrastructure are at their lowest levels. Since 1993, budgets have fallen by nearly 30 percent, staff has been cut by about 30 percent overseas and 20 percent in the US, and dozens of cultural centers, libraries, and branch posts have been closed. "Arts and Minds: Cultural Diplomacy amid Global Tensions" (presentation, Columbia University, New York, NY, April 14– 15, 2003), https://www.americansforthearts.org/by-program/reports-and-data/legislation-policy/naappd/arts-and-minds-cultural-diplomacy-amid-global-tensions.

27. Schneider (2004) details these changes in funding focus.

28. The Barcelona Conference, which took place on November 27–28, 1995, brought together representatives from twenty-seven countries (all fifteen EU member states at the time, in addition to Algeria, Cyprus, Egypt, Israel, Jordan, Lebanon, Malta,

Morocco, Syria, Tunis, and the Palestinian Authority) (Euro-Mediterranean Committee 1995).

29. See, for instance, the 1950 Bureau of the Budget memorandum quoted in Aguilar (1996: 54): "Culture for culture's sake has no place in the US Information and Education Exchange Program. The value of international cultural interchange is to win respect for the cultural achievements of our free society, where the respect is necessary to inspire cooperation with us in world affairs." See also Schneider (2004) for an elaborate overview of the shifting policies and priorities of US cultural diplomacy efforts.

30. Arguably, this is changing, especially since the "migration crisis" has become an issue for politicians in the EU. The gap between the political realities of the EU and the wishes of those invested in culture continues to widen. The ambiguity of the European approach to dialogue has continued to invoke the common cultural heritage of the Mediterranean basin and, at the same time, firm policies of security, migration, and enlargement, which draw a clear frontier in the middle of the Mediterranean.

31. See, for instance, Rogers (2011).

32. In this period before Oslo, Palestinians living under occupation did not have the privilege of accessing international diplomatic missions, cultural centers, and institutes that could support their art. According to artists Vera Tamari, Suleiman Mansour, and Nabil Anani, access to Amman's airport and cultural centers and embassies at this point was an important base for artists to access art encounters outside of Palestine; this was especially the case after 1982 when the PLO was expelled from Beirut after Israel's invasion of Lebanon.

33. See especially Sukarieh (2012, 2016).

34. It's interesting, for instance, that AMIDEAST, the US nonprofit organization that has historically worked to strengthen mutual understanding and cooperation between Americans and the people of the Middle East, has expanded in recent years from educational service provision in public schools to training the Jordanian military personnel to read weapons manuals in English, and also to international business language provision training.

35. James Zogby's poll after 9/11 from mid- to late April 2002 reveals that contrary to popular perception in the US, the negative view of the country in the region does not relate to an inability to grasp the American way of life or Western culture, but to US foreign policy in the region.

36. A researched account of the journal can be found in Holt (2013), which significantly adds to Issa J. Boullata's modest but focused contribution on the journal and its editor. Zeina Maasri (2020) offers the most comprehensive contextual and historical

analysis of the journal's significance by placing it within her account of cosmopolitan Beirut and global solidarity during the 1960s.

37. Visual cultures scholar Zeina Maasri writes that "unlike its predecessors in Arabic literary journals, *Hiwar* forged an aesthetic interface between modernist literary and visual arts, hitherto separate and hierarchically organized aesthetic practices privileging the former. In so doing, it instituted a model of visuality in the Arabic literary and cultural publications that followed" (2020: 65). For more on the complex ways in which local actors contributed to creating a transcultural visual and literary aesthetic, and were not merely duped into playing into the Americans' cultural Cold War, see Maasri (2020: esp. chap. 2).

38. According to Elizabeth Holt (2013: 94), over the course of its short life, *Ḥiwar* published both emerging and more established authors, critics, novelists, and poets of the 1960s. This list of authors included Badr Shakir al-Sayyaab, Ghaadah al-Samman, Albert Hourani, Jabraa Ibraahim Jabraa, Suhayr QalamaawiialWaliid al-Khaalidi, Samir Khalaf, Zakariyya Tamir, Layla Baʿalbaki, Sạlaḥʿ Abdal-Sụbur, Salmaal-Khaḍraʾ al JayyusiaySạbriḤafiz,Luwịs ʿAwaḍ, Ibrahim Mansur, Ibrahim Asḷan, al-Tạyyib Saliḥ, and Yusuf Idris. The journal was also known and today remembered for featuring translated interviews with major international cultural figures such as T. S. Eliot, Ezra Pound, Arthur Miller, Ernest Hemingway, Jean-Paul Sartre, and Pablo Picasso.

39. In my interviews, the word *faḍyḥah* was used on numerous occasions to describe the shock that came with discovering the journal's source of funding. Tarek El-Ariss explains the Arab defeat by Israel in June 1967 as a *faḍyḥah*—a scandal that ultimately "exposed [the] instability and vulnerability" of Arab projects of modernity, yet that pushed many to rethink the nature and role of literature in society (Ariss 2012: 521). See El Baroni (2011).

40. In the words of Peter Coleman, one of its historians, the CCF "was America's principal attempt to win over the world's intellectuals to the liberal democratic cause" (1989: preface).

41. The Iowa Writers' Workshop, a renowned creative writing program, was founded in 1936 by a group of writers and poets. Since 1967, it has run its international program in collaboration with the State Department. Writers from all over the world have attended in recent years, including well-known writers from Palestine such as Sahar Khalifeh and Najwan Darwish, and Iman Humaydan from Lebanon. Funded by the State Department, the workshop's international program had a stated cultural diplomacy direction. The goal, according to Bennett, was to discourage the abstract

theorizing and systematic social critiques to which the radical literature of the 1930s had been prone. Instead, the program favored a focus on the personal, the concrete, and the individual. While workshop administrators such as Paul Engle and Wallace Stegner wanted to spread American values, they did not want to be caught imposing a particular ideology on their students for fear of appearing to use the same tactics as the communists (Bennett 2015).

42. See Frascina (2003).

43. An exception to this one-sided, historiographical lens is highlighted in an interview by Michael Vazquez with Achal Prabhala, former editor of the CCF's Indian journal *Quest*, in which Vazquez notes the considerable role that *Hiwar* played in 1960s Arabic literary culture (Vazquez 2012). *Ḥiwar* also comes up in studies of global literature and the Congress for Cultural Freedom (Rubin 2012: 59). Timothy Mitchell briefly discusses *Ḥiwar* and its connections with the CIA, as well as a far larger edifice of American intelligence that was shaping the region's intellectual production (2002: 337). See also Lockman (2016). In Arabic cultural memory, the scandal has been reignited in recent years, particularly with the publication of letters and diary entries.

44. As quoted in Holt (2013: 94), Sayigh declared the journal's objectives on the very first page of the first issue of *Hiwar*. In his words, the journal's "ambition was to observe developments in the field of culture in other countries," while simultaneously remaining committed to the Arab nationalist cause. See *Ḥiwar* 1, no. 1 (1962): 2.

45. In the words of Ounsi el Hajj, Lebanese poet and contributing writer to *Hiwar*: "The journal *Hiwar*, was, then, a traitorous journal. And we, all of those whose names appeared in it, are traitors as well. Out of ignorance or knowledge of the matter, there is no difference" (el Hajj 1966: 19, as cited in Holt 2013: 98).

46. See the introduction to the recent publication of Sayigh's diary notes around this tense period in Shurayḥ (2011). Shurayh's introduction relays the details of the intense period of controversy that engulfed the journal before and after Idriss's rejection of the award. He conveys the sense of urgency and humiliation that came with the slandering of the magazine in the various Arab cultural journals.

47. But even before then, the anti-imperial sentiment in the region colored the cultural milieu's reception of the journal. According to Shurayḥ, that the journal was mired in controversy from the beginning must be read as part of Western "aggression" toward the Arabs in that period (Shurayḥ 2011: 4).

48. In 1957, poets Yousef el-Khal and Adonis (regarded as the leaders of the modernist movement in Arabic poetry) founded and edited *Shi'r*, a magazine that inaugurated modern Arabic poetry. For the years between 1957 and 1970, the magazine struggled

against what it perceived to be outdated and archaic poetic theory and practice. This propelled the beginnings of a reflection on the role of Arab nationalism in relation to Palestine's 1967 defeat. Adonis, who was never fully trusted by Arab nationalists, later launched the daring literary journal *Mawaqif*, in which he and his colleagues reassessed the poetic style of the previous two decades and of the very language and vocabulary of politics of the time.

49. In 1951, the American Friends of the Middle East (AFME), a pro-Arabist organization critical of US support for Israel and run by three covert CIA officers in the 1940s and 1950s, was established with the hope of forming an alliance with the Arab countries as they emerged under the sway of Britain and France. As the Cold War gathered momentum, the organization saw that the best way to keep the region within the US orbit and protect its access to oil was to encourage a positive attitude toward Arabs in the US and to foster a mutual cultural relationship. A component of the AFME's work consisted of publishing newsletters, books, and pamphlets; sponsoring a library; and taking part in lectureship exchanges, goodwill missions, and artist exchanges. For more on AFME activities, see Wilford (2013: esp. chap. 9).

50. These artists include Jawad Selim from Iraq, Fateh Moudarres from Syria, and Jirair Palamoudian from Egypt. They are listed in Al Qassemi (2017a). The full list of artists and funded exhibits between the period of 1956 and 1966 include Iraqi Latif Al Ani, Tunisian Jalal Gharbi, and Sudanese artists Hassan Bedawi Omer and Mohammed Omer Khalili. The list can be found in the AFME's archive at the Berman Jewish Policy Archive, https://www.bjpa.org/bjpa.

51. The history of committed literature in Arabic went hand in hand with the adoption of literary ideas of socialism and French existentialism. The literary journal *Al-Adab*, which was founded in Beirut in 1953 and distributed nearly all over the Arab world, based its interpretation of commitment on Jean-Paul Sartre's idea of *littérature engagée*. *Al-Adab* succeeded in creating a common platform for the leftist and/or nationalist literary circles in Lebanon, Syria, Egypt, Iraq, and Jordan. For more on this, see Klemm (2000). For the way in which committed literature has manifested in different fields of cultural production since its inception in the 1950s, see Pannewick and Khalil (2015).

52. Interview with the author, February 14, 2009, Beirut.

CHAPTER 2

1. See the chapter "New World Order" of Stallabras (2004).

2. There is a strong case to be made for a reemergence of a collectively driven

activist art with overt political purpose that is vocally critical of the effect of neoliberal capitalism that emerged in the Arab world after its 2011–2012 uprisings.

3. For an excellent analysis of the series of AHDR reports, the politics of their production, and the ensuing debates in the Arab world, see Bayat (2010: chap. 2).

4. Bayat argues that the "'elitist' approach of the report derives not only from a distrust of 'politics from below' it also relates to the authors' liberal perception of the 'state' as the neutral apparatus representing public interests, a notion deeply embedded in the conceptual paradigms which inform the general visions of the UNDP and World Bank" (2010: 39).

5. Painting was increasingly "*passé*" and represented "styles that have long since lost their edge and relevance" (Wilson-Goldie 2005).

6. Interview with the author, August 28, 2008, Amman. The Lebanese star Haifa Wehbe is one the Arab world's most iconic modern and commercial pop singers. Known as the Star of the East or (Kawkab al-Sharq), Umm Kalthum is regarded as the greatest Arabic singer in history and remembered for her mythical voice and length of songs addressing the universal issues of postcolonialism, nationalism, war, and love.

7. See, for example, Wilson-Goldie (2006: 87): "[The] works that critical contemporary artists are producing in postwar Lebanon, whether they attract the attention of a wide audience or not, are actually affecting the way people speak, move, construct their identities and conduct their daily lives in Beirut by formulating a visual language that rings true to those experiences, adequately represents them, and at the same time calls attention to the limitations imposed on them."

8. I return to this wording and framing in more detail in chapter 4.

9. See Hanafi and Tabar (2002).

10. Nada Doumani, interview with the author, September 7, 2008, Amman.

11. This refers to the explicit common agenda of funders and fund recipients, which are linked to agendas of fighting global terrorism and reducing the appeal of extremism and fundamentalism.

12. Interview with the author, February 14, 2009, Beirut.

13. I feel compelled to note here what I believe is a telling observation regarding this self-perception as unaffected and neutral. In fieldwork in Ramallah and Amman, artists were generally more open to discussing the dynamics of aid and what it might imply for their works and the scenes in which they circulate. I recall here especially my conversation with Tina Sherwell in Ramallah in August 2012, the then director of the now defunct International Academy of Art Palestine project. Sherwell openly

communicated anxieties about how the early global exposure of young art students to star curators and guest lecturers who visited the school affected both the content and the form of works produced. To explain the disparity in openness artists had to having this conversation, I hypothesized that perhaps in Lebanon most artists believed themselves separate from the larger NGO-ization process taking place because they were more conscious of themselves belonging to a longer genealogy of global art that is part of their cosmopolitan history.

14. Interview with the author, May 3, 2008, Beirut.

15. The classic text in this regard is Ferguson (1994).

16. See, for instance, the recorded and published discussion of artist Oraib Toukan with her students at the International Academy of Art Palestine on contemporary arts discourse, the English language, its circulation, and its relation to its audiences (O. Toukan 2011).

17. For a thorough overview of how Palestinian resistance and the struggle for liberation has aesthetically featured in Palestinian art of the twentieth century, see Samia Halaby (2004) *Liberation Art of Palestine: Palestinian Painting and Sculptor in the Second Half of the Twentieth Century.* NY : H. T. T. B. Publications.

18. In this regard, artist Khaled Hourani's 2019 novel investigates the Palestinian fine art scene since the 1970s, including the challenges those artists experienced, and the conditions of their work and artistic production through the tales and stories about the trajectory of this lost and then remade iconic painting.

19. As large, state-led infrastructure projects failed, donors grew disillusioned with governments as key development actors, and NGOs were a welcome replacement. See Iriye (2004: 130), on how the global loss of faith in government and the vacuum it created gave civil society the opportunity to assert itself.

20. Indian novelist and activist Arundhati Roy (2014) was probably one of the first to use the term "NGO-ization" to refer to the potential of NGOs to depoliticize discourses and practices of activism and mobilization around issues of social and political justice. In Middle East Studies, Asef Bayat and Islah Jad have written extensively on the detrimental effects of NGO-ization on grassroots mobilization around issues of women rights and urban development. See also Abdelrahman (2004); Carapico (2000); Fisher (1998).

21. For a general reading on the discursive repertoires of NGOs, see Hilhorst (2003).

22. Interview with the author, July 16, 2008, Beirut.

23. Interview with the author, August 11, 2009, Amman.

24. Interview with the author, June 4, 2008, Beirut.

25. This generally remains the case today but is slowly changing. The one obvious exception is the Arab Fund for Arts and Culture, which requests that applications be submitted *only* in Arabic. Many applicants in this period wrote their applications in English and then had them translated into Arabic. The reason cited for this was often to do with the challenges of finding the equivalent in Arabic of the contemporary art terms they use in their applications.

Interview with the author, April 28, 2012, Ramallah.

26. Also the critique of the English language as the dominant means of communication in a supposedly global yet also postcolonial art world is one that various artists outside of the Arab region have engaged with to gauge the meaning of universal language in the global art world. This includes Croatian artist Mladen Stilinović's (1994) piece *An artist who cannot speak English is no artist*, which I borrow for the title of this chapter. A contextualization of the project can be found in Erjavec (2014). See also Levine and Rule (2012). For a recorded conversation with art students in Ramallah on the place of the English language in the global circuits in which Palestinian art circulates, see O. Toukan (2011).

27. Conference organized by *Zawaya Magazine*, the now defunct leading contemporary Arab-language cultural magazine published in Beirut, November 15–16, 2005. See also Al-Turk (2005).

28. In 2003, the Ford Foundation was critiqued by US news service Jewish Telegraphic Agency, among others, for supporting Palestinian NGOs that were accused of promoting anti-Semitism at the 2001 World Conference Against Racism in Durban. Under pressure from members of US Congress, the Ford Foundation apologized for its NGO partners' backing of resolutions that equated Israeli policies with apartheid during the conference. Following this, Ford was very quick to adopt more stringent funding criteria by asking its grantees to condemn in signature "violence, terrorism, bigotry or the destruction of any state."

29. From the Roberto Cimmetta Fund's mobility program, acting on a par with the European Agenda for Culture, to Mophradat, a collective of regionally focused nonprofit cultural organizations funded by various nongovernmental US and European cultural foundations, such as the Ford Foundation and the Andy Warhol Foundation, the mobility of artists is recognized as one of the fundamental pillars of contemporary cultural production.

30. Salwa Mikdadi and Nada Shabout have called for stronger arts education and training in the region and posit that without disciplinary scholarly production in

the arts and without "a local theoretical construct and in the absence of academic discourse or critical art reviews, art of the region will remain wide open to misinterpretation and conjecture" (Mikdadi and Shabout 2009: 10).

31. Mikdadi and Shabout (2009: 10). In settings where there is a clear division between classes due to a historically smaller middle class, the intimidation is exacerbated by the outward appearance and social background of the cultural operator.

32. The UAE also lent support to Hosni Mubarak's regime in Egypt until just before his forced resignation.

33. These details are from a discussion with one of the organizers of the protest who preferred not to be identified. In our conversation, she emphasized how hard it was to enlist fellow artists, especially Arab artists, in her and her collaborators' protest because they viewed themselves as guests who had no business to fight the Emirati government without the permission of its own people to do so.

34. Email conversation with the artist, April 12, 2011.

35. Taking a swipe at Sharjah's art world participants, one artist put into email circulation a supposed press release of the online arts journal *e-flux* (which he named *e-fux*), which stated that an artistic action committee that had been set up by "born-again activists is advocating the return of more than $10,100,600 in donations Sharjah Biennial artists received from the Ruler of Sharjah this year because they now realize Ruler means Dictator." The author of the email was getting at the art world's seemingly naïve shocked reaction at the dismissal knowing full well that ultimately the UAE is an authoritarian state and that censorship is always a threat.

36. See, for instance, O. Toukan (2014).

37. See Shannon (2012) for an overview of the development and the differences between Dubai and Sharjah as global art centers.

38. Gulf Labor, for example, is a coalition of international artists working to ensure that migrant worker rights are protected during the construction of museums on Saadiyat Island in Abu Dhabi. For a thorough analysis of Gulf Labor's progress and setback since its inception, see especially Azimi (2016).

39. For example, Gokulan (2009).

CHAPTER 3

Adapted partly from Hanan Toukan, "Whatever Happened to *Iltizam*? Words in Arab Art after the Cold War," in *Commitment and Beyond: Reflections on/of the Political in Arabic Literature since the 1940s*, ed. Friederike Pannewick and Georges Khalil (Wiesbaden: Dr. Reichert Verlag, 2015).

1. For Arsanios, one of the most interesting aspects of the magazine was noticing the move toward more popular and consumerist content after 1967, along with the change from illustrations to image photography.

2. The magazines became the basis of a series of thought-provoking aesthetical experiments in reading rituals, video works, art installations, and book displays.

3. Saghieh especially represents the band of thinkers in the Arab region who hold Arab intellectuals themselves responsible for the plight of their societies. Other journalists and scholars in Lebanon belonging to this school of thought include Hazem al-Amin, Youssef Bazzi (mentioned already in chapter 1), and Bashar Haydar. Saghieh is often placed within the body of thought regarded by some Western observers as staunchly self-critical and unapologetic in contrast with what Edward Said has been accused of by his foes. Other Arab authors that Saghieh is bracketed with include Bassam Tibi, Fouad Ajami, and Kanan Makiya. Saghieh has consistently made the argument that the Arab world as a whole needs to reconsider its tendency to conflate modernity with imperialism. See, for instance, H. Saghieh (2007). For a critical and relevant reading of manifestations of a fledgling individualism that has stunted cultural development in the Arab Middle East, see Saghie (2002).

4. For a republished sample of some of the invitees' reflections, see *Al Musatqbal Newspaper*, April 29, 2011, 9–12.

5. 98weeks research project/space is an artists' organization and project space founded by Marwa Arsanios and Mirene Arsanios on October 31, 2007. It was conceived as a research project that shifts its attention to a new topic every 98 weeks. Focusing on artistic research, combining both theoretical and practical forms of inquiry, 98weeks' projects take multiple forms such as workshops, community projects, seminars, reading groups, publications, and exhibitions. The space was eventually lost to the gentrification process of Beirut's Mar Mikhael neighborhood.

6. John Chalcraft (2016) has argued the mass uprisings of 2011–2012 had their surprising and creative dimensions precisely because they emerged without any preceding state breakdown, and they underscored the people as a sovereign subject in a way distinct from anti-colonial nationalism

7. For a thorough reading of some of these debates and how they unfolded in the context of socialist Lebanon, a Marxist organization that saw itself as part of a global people's struggle, see Bardawil (2016). For how the 1967 defeat spurred the thinking, media, journals, and art of radical left organizations, which has influenced activists in the post-2011 Arab world, see Haugbolle (2017).

8. Interview with the author, July 31, 2008, Beirut.

9. In popular discourse, the revolution or *al-thawra* is commonly associated with the 1967 generation and the culture of anti-colonial resistance it helped generate.

10. The appropriation of writing in the form of quotations, words, and single letters has historically appeared in the works of many Arab artists. Iraqi Ghani Alani; Egyptian Ahmed Mustafa; Lebanese Samir Al-Sayegh, Etel Adnan, Aref el Rayyes, and Salwa Raouda Choucair; Palestinian Kamal Boullata; Syrian Mahmoud Hamad; and Algerian Rachid Koraichi are among the many others who have explored the rich literary tradition of the region and transformed it into sculpture, painting, drawing, etching, book art, and, more recently, performance and video art. For more on the use and power of the written word in the works of Middle Eastern artists today, see the online archive of the British Museum's 2006 exhibition *Word in Art: Artists of the Modern Middle East* (http://www.british museum.org/wordintoart/). See also the contributions of Mejcher-Atassi (2007, 2012, 2016) concerning the topic of textuality and visuality in art and literature.

11. On the condition of migrant labor in the Gulf, see Roth (2019).

12. See Al Qassemi (2017b), in which the Emirati businessman and Twitter commentator cum arts collector writes "'I see the UAE as also being an Athens of the Arab world.' What distinguished the ancient Greek city was its investment in culture, architecture, education and theatre as well as its radical democratic experiment. Today Abu Dhabi and the UAE match Athens in all these aspects save for the political structure. In fact in terms of culture the UAE has gone a step further by not only investing internally but venturing internationally from the very beginning of its foundation." What Al Qassemi leaves out in his obsequious analysis is how intertwined cultural and political structures have always been.

13. Interview with the author, August 13, 2017, Amman.

14. I want to emphasize here that this mocking is not in any way a relinquishing of the centrality Jerusalem in Palestinian history. It is more a critique of how the city as a symbol has been appropriated by political forces from all sides, thereby contributing to the formation of a nostalgic rather than a political discourse about the city. In a nod to this history, the 2018 opening show of the Palestinian Museum in Birzeit, *Jerusalem Lives* (*Tahya Al Quds*), dealt with how artists throughout history have approached Jerusalem outside of the nostalgic commemorative framework.

15. This phenomenon has had the effect of marginalizing the visual heritage of both the Ottoman Empire and the vast Indo-Persian artistic tradition from mainstream representations of the region's culture (Boullata 2015; Laïdi-Hanieh 2008).

16. The issue of the intellectual is similarly taken up by Egyptian artist, writer, and musician Hassan Khan (2010).

17. For a thematically based approach to understanding the influence of theory and its confluence with new media, diversity, and everyday visual culture in contemporary critical art practice, see Robertson and McDaniel (2016: chap. 1). For a critique of the idea of critical art practice, see Ray (2009).

18. See Boullata (1970a, 1971), the latter of which was translated by Katharine L. Halls as "Art in Time of the Palestinian Revolution" and published in Lenssen, Rogers, and Shabout (2018). See also Maasri (2020: chap. 5) for an elaborate analysis of how this call for the intense revolutionary art shaped the 1967 generation's worldviews and how they configured it in their own societies.

19. For an example of this engagement with Western political philosophy, see El Baroni, *Fifteen Ways to Leave Badiou* (2011). For this project, Egyptian artist El Baroni, cofounder and former director of the Alexandria Contemporary Arts Forum, invited a group of artists from the Middle East to produce works responding to Alain Badiou's text in a wider reflection on questions of universality and truth in relationhip to art-topics that Badiou has written extensively but most recently and famously summarized in his "Fifteen Theses on Contemporary Art."

20. For an idea of how the artist as diplomat manifested in the artworks and the role of the artist in host societies in the Middle East, see Rogers (2011).

21. Lebanese curator and writer Rasha Salti has dealt with this issue in several publications. In an older key text reflecting on both the insights of the postwar generation of artists as well as their local critics, Salti describes a "cold" reception of local audiences to her friends' "subversive" production in the following terms: "Unfortunately, this audience has, for most of the time, remained frozen in its misapprehension of the unfamiliar and obscure. On the other hand, the technicity and the craftsmanship invested in creating such works, the cold estrangement from conventional language, its defiant contemporaneity and seemingly unprejudiced borrowing of form and vocabulary from post-industrial cultures, has rendered the perception and judgment of conceptual art and its kin forms as imported "postmodern" forms, unfit for expression within Lebanese society." According to Salti, it is as a result of the above scenario that a conceptual or installation piece "becomes laden with pointless interrogations on the authenticity of expression and representation and ultimately, on identity" by those uneasy with the logic, framing and production of new works (Salti 2002: 88).

22. The roundtable, which took place on June 24, 2009, was part of a series of events titled *On Lebanese Wars* curated by Lamia Joreige and Manal Khader for the Beirut Art Center. The roundtable referred to here discussed the works in the adjoining exhibition, *The Road to Peace: Paintings in Times of War*, curated by Saleh Barakat, June 17–July 14, 2009.

23. Interestingly, the exception to this rule is the growing Gulf market for Arab art, which includes, for example, the Sharjah Biennial for contemporary arts. These all attract global art world elites, from gallery owners and curators to art writers and critics.

24. Notable academic interventions in these prevalent perceptions include scholarly work that I mention in the introduction. This has been compounded by the investments in establishing informal art schools and educational programs offered by nonprofits such as the MMAG Foundation and Spring Sessions in Amman, the International Art Academy in Palestine, the AM Qattan Foundation in Palestine, the now defunct International Art School Palestine and Ashkal Alwan in Beirut. Rasha Salti and Kristine Khouri's painstakingly researched *Past Disquiet: Narratives and Ghosts from the International Art Exhibition for Palestine, 1978* revisits the making of the International Art Exhibition for Palestine, which opened in Beirut in the spring of 1978 and which comprised some 200 works donated by artists in solidarity with Palestine from nearly 30 countries. For the curators' description of the project and its content, see Khouri and Salti (2016). The collection of essays in Lenssen, Rogers, and Shabout (2018) demonstrates that there existed not only a regional but also a global movement of ideas, resources, and works from and about artists in the region throughout the twentieth century.

25. Interview with the author, June 19, 2008, Beirut.

26. I was informed many times by artists in all three contexts that the reality they have to confront is that contemporary art belongs only to an international network, which, in the words of a filmmaker, photographer, and archival artist from the postwar generation, an artist "either stands within or outside of, and if it is the latter then the artist will become increasingly insignificant." Interview with the author, September 18, 2008.

27. On the Jordanian state and society formation, see in particular Massad (2001). On Lebanon, see especially the standard reference of Salibi (2005) and Fawwaz Traboulsi's political economy and social history approach in Traboulsi (2007).

INTERMEZZO

1. Interview with the author, June 17, 2009, Beirut.

2. Jacques Rancière (2004) argues that politics involves a "distribution of the sensible," where this is understood as a legitimization of ways of seeing, feeling, acting, speaking, and being in the world with one another. For Rancière, aesthetic practices are political to the extent that they play a key role in the "distribution of the sensible."

3. See D. Harvey (2005: chap. 2). Harvey takes what Antonio Gramsci calls "common-sense" to answer the question of "how neoliberalism was accomplished and by whom." For a shift of such magnitude to occur, he shows, a construction of consent was needed to guarantee cooperation by appealing to cultural socialization conceived as rooted in long-standing traditions.

4. The Jordanian monarchy has traditionally been a precious Western ally in the region. As some have argued, the Hashemite dynasty was able to remain in power partly because of the very open support provided by both the US and Britain at crucial times in its troubled history (Cavatorta and Durac 2015).

5. For example, see Wright (2006: 58).

6. See, for instance, Elias Khoury on Lebanon's cultural and political role in the region: "The main role of Lebanon today is to be a place where all the democratic forces in the Arab World can congregate, debate and plan the future of the Arab World. This is the real meaning of the country, if we want to give it any meaning" (1993: 136). See von Maltzhan (2018) for a study of the forces shaping the relationship between the Ministry of Culture and cultural actors in Lebanon.

7. During the years of the first Intifadah, these artists inserted into their paintings materials and objects from the tropes of 1980s art, such as the village landscape and harvest season. New Directions orchestrated a breakthrough in existing art traditions. It brought "the political" in its symbolic material form—mud, hay, leather, wood, and shards from Jaffa—inside the artwork. New Visions responded to the shifts in political predicaments and became a platform and model for later contemporary art practices.

CHAPTER 4

1. Rancière presented his paper "Some Paradoxes of Political Art" at *Home Works III: A Forum on Cultural Practices*. For the full text, see Charafeddine, Refka, and Tohme (2005).

2. On the role of "Artist as Historian" in historical representation and photography, see in particular Godfrey (2007).

3. See especially W. Harris (2006: chap. 8).

4. SOLIDERE's plan envisions the reconstruction of Beirut as a global city and a center for trade and tourism located among restored churches and mosques, gardens, and ruins. See its website: http://www.solidere.com.lb. For critical evaluations of SOLIDERE, see Larkin (2010); Makdisi (2006); Nagel (2002); Sarkis (1993).

5. Hariri has been both credited with and blamed for the reconstruction of the city. See Gavin and Maluf (1996).

6. Through the mid- to late 1990s, and at the cost of massive expansion of public debt and a highly skewed income distribution, Hariri stabilized the currency, lowered inflation, sponsored a construction boom, and achieved annual growth rates of 5 to 7 percent, thus securing Lebanon as a stable and profitable area for investment, for its own business elites as well as Syrian and other investors.

7. One of Lebanon's most well-known post-1990 artists, Akram Zaatari, for example, made the documentary video *All Is Well on the Border* (1997) while he was working at Future TV. Rabih Mroué has also spoken about his early experiments with video and in particular how the media manipulated images, coming out of his experience working at Future TV in the early 1990s (Elias 2015).

8. Two influential workshops were mentioned by several artists in Amman, Ramallah, and Beirut for having affected the media arts landscape in the region: in particular, to encourage it being seen as an art form in its own right. The first was held by Lebanese-Canadian artist Jayce Salloum and Lebanese artist Walid Raad in Beirut in 1992. The other was a 2001 workshop organized by Akram Zaatari and Mahmoud Hojeij, who organized a more regional workshop entitled "Transit Visa" where artists like Mais Darwazeh from Jordan and Lubna Huddad from Syria attended.

9. A full description of *Wonder Beirut* can be found on the artists' website: http://www.hadjithomasjoreige.com.

10. This rhetorical question was asked by a well-known Lebanese Marxist historian and writer during a conversation, May 29, 2009, Beirut.

11. Some cultural actors I spoke with about this period articulated their difference in terms of where they stood in relation to Lebanon's oldest and largest culture festival, the Baalback International Festival. The festival, which takes place in the Roman ruins of Baalbek in the Beqaa Valley of Lebanon, is famed for hosting of some of the Arab world's most famous singers, such as Fairuz, Umm Kalthoum, and Sabah, as well as other theater, music, and dance shows. Today it is seen as an event hosting commercial and classical culture.

12. One important example is Masrah Beirut (The Beirut Theater) and the Ayloul festival that evolved from it.

13. The project's constantly changing date of establishment plays on the very idea of an established linear history.

14. Some films that tackled war in the same way from the period of the 1990s include Jocelyn Saab's *Once Upon a Time: Beirut* (1994), Jayce Salloum's *This Is Not Beirut* (1994), and Danielle Arbid's *Alone with War* (2000). These films demonstrate resistance to interpretations that rely on linear narratives of the war that endorse a moral nationalist discourse. For a review of memory, violence, and subjectivity in postwar cinema, see Khatib (2008: chap. 7).

15. Similarly, Mark Godfrey observes that "there are an increasing number of artists whose practice starts with research in archives, and others who deploy what has been termed an archival form of research" (2007: 142–43). Godfrey refers to Walid Raad/The Atlas Group as an example.

16. For a discussion of the archival turn in the contemporary practices of art from Lebanon and the wider Arab region, see Downey (2015).

17. In footnote 5 of Walid Sadek's "A Matter of Words" (2002a), he explains that "Raad's approach . . . challenged the audience's notion of what is a believable document, and thus, by presenting what he terms as a 'hysterical document' raised many issues on the politics of interpretation and canonical authority."

18. Interview with the author, May 29, 2009, Beirut.

19. This list is by no means exhaustive. Beirut DC (a film collective that runs Ayyam Beirut al-Cinemaiyya, a biennial festival of independent Arab cinema from which emerged Cinema Metropolis, an alternative art house cinema), Né à Beyrouth (which organizes an annual festival of Lebanese film, BiPod (an international dance platform), Espace SD (now closed), the Beirut Art Centre, and collectives such as 98 Weeks Research Project (a curatorial collective that arranges workshops and symposia), BiPod (an international dance platform), and AIW:A in Aley and Batroun Projects in Batroun. Extending contemporary practices outside of the capital are just a sample of the many organizations and initiatives established in the ten-year period after 1999 and the entry of various international donors. For a detailed analysis of some of these organizations and initiatives, see H. Toukan (2012).

20. See, for example, Sadek (2007) for an account of the reactions abetted by the Hamra Street Project (2000), whose artists engaged with the continued "mythical" significance of the street as a center of cosmopolitanism brimming with political

and cultural significance during Beirut's heyday in the prewar years. This Ashkal Alwan commissioned project took place amid tension over SOLIDERE's downtown reconstruction process. Downtown's newly manicured commercial center was in stark contrast to the diminishing significance of Hamra's historical role in the city, thereby provoking artists into interrogating the street's mythical standing as progressive, modern, and cultured in the Arab cultural psyche.

21. For an idea of some of these events and how they were received in the Arabic media, see, for example, Bazzi (2000). See also Al-Hujeiry (2000).

22. Peter Rowe and Hashim Sarkis argue that intervening in public space through public art installations was a means to partake in a conversation that was being silenced in official discourse (1998: 10).

23. The exhibition first opened in 2002 at Fundació Antoni Tàpies in Barcelona and later traveled to Witte de With in Rotterdam and the BildMuseet in Umeå.

24. See Lafuente (2007) for an elaborate summary of the show's content and form that reflected David's aim to produce and disseminate knowledge that represented a concrete cultural and political situation in the region that conflicted with dominant views in the West, especially in the aftermath of 9/11.

25. See Abi Saab (2002) for a description of that first forum and how it was presented in the media.

26. I discuss these and other initiatives during this period more comprehensively in H. Toukan (2012).

27. These include Marwan Rechmawi (artist), Rania Tabarra (designer), Mustafa Yammout (cultural events organizer), and Leila Mroueh (communications director).

28. Samples of this writing can be found in *Parachute* no. 108 (March 2003), issue on Beyrouth-Beirut; *Tamass: Contemporary Arab Representations, Beirut, Lebanon*, exhibition catalog (2002); *Out of Beirut*, exhibition catalog (2006); *Art Journal* 66, no. 2 (2007), issue on Lebanon; three editions of *Ashkal Alwan Home Works Forum* catalog (2002–2005); as well as articles in various magazines devoted to contemporary culture in the Middle East: *Artforum*, *Bidoun*, *Canvas*, *Flash Art*, *Frieze*, and *Ibraaz: Contemporary Culture in North Africa and the Middle East*; in addition to *Discourse: Journal for Theoretical Studies in Media and Culture* (2002) and the *Drama Review* (2006).

29. On the persistence of exoticism and identitarian referencing amid the multicultural turn in the Western art world, see Oguibe (2004).

30. Interview with the author, February 17, 2009, Beirut.

31. Interview with the author, February 17, 2009, Beirut.

32. *DisORIENTation Contemporary Arab Art Production from the Near East—Egypt, Palestine, Lebanon, Jordan, Syria and Iraq* was exhibited in the House of World Cultures in March–May 2003. The press release for the show stated: "The new generation of artists and intellectuals in the Middle East are breaking the mould in creative circles. They reject all attempts to categorize them collectively and are as critical of the Western conception of the Orient as they are of the social conditions encountered in the region. The new art is political, one which reflects on moral values and the dominant religious and political codes."

For the full press release, see *DisORIENTation: Contemporary Art from the Middle East*, 23 March–April 3, 2003, https://archiv.hkw.de/en/presseinfos/pressemitteilungen/DisORIENT2/c_index.html.

33. Interview with the author, June 11, 2009, Beirut.

34. Interview with the author, August 5, 2008, Beirut.

35. The uncertainties that come with crossing boundaries are made in reference to the works of artists Paola Yacoub and Michel Lassere, and architect Bernard Khoury, who have combined art, architecture, and archaeology in their works.

36. The critic Stephen Wright writes: "All these disciplinary border fudging's mirror the geopolitical border conflicts that are the plight of so many lives" (2006: 58).

37. Writing in the *Guardian*, Antonia Carver, editor of *Bidoun* magazine, a quarterly forum for Middle Eastern art, states that "only a handful of Middle Eastern artists have had the privilege of seeing their work defined by terms other than its, or their, geographical origin." Carver lists Walid Raad, Akram Zaatari, Joana Hadjithomas, and Khalil Joreige (2006: 31).

38. *Les Inquiets* brought together a group of five Israelis, Lebanese, and Palestinians in an exhibition that explores aspects of life under the Arab-Israeli conflict.

39. See also an interesting discussion with Catherine David and others on the Contemporary Arab Representations project in Dagher et al. (2007).

40. Skype interview with the author, May 25, 2010.

41. The same point was made to me in interviews with other curators and artists in Beirut, Ramallah, and Amman, especially those working with art and artists they regarded as "underrepresented."

42. See, for instance, the notes of Jack Persekian, curator of *DisORIENTation*, which speak of artist Walid Sadek's declining to take part in the show. For Sadek, the words of Benjamin Franklin celebrating a time when any philosopher will be able to go anywhere on this earth and say "this is my country," inscribed at the entrance of the House of

World Cultures, "spoke eloquently, albeit hyperbolically, of a nascent and ambitious Modernity, itself a project which posited, in spite of many contradictions, the future subject of a universal civic society" (Parsekian 2003). For more on this, see the House of World Cultures archive of the event, https://archiv.hkw.de/en/dossiers/disorientation/.

43. Interview with the author, June 17, 2009, Beirut.

44. Interview with the author, July 9, 2009, Beirut.

45. Published on the organization's website: http://www.ashkalalwan.org.

46. Interview with the author, May 29, 2009, Beirut. Zgharta, a town in North Lebanon, is a Maronite stronghold that fought a violent war with the Palestinians between 1975–1977 as well as a series of fratricidal conflicts between warring Maronite families. Bint Jbeil is the second largest town in the South of Lebanon, and the city represents the resistance against Israel. It was first occupied in 1978 and again 1982 until 2000.

47. See Khoury (2010) in which he elaborates on these points.

48. Akram Zaatari based *Earth of Endless Secrets* on the letters and photographs of a former Lebanese prisoner in Israel named Nabih Awda, who joined the Lebanese resistance as a member of the Communist Party in 1986 and took part in several military operations against the Israeli army in southern Lebanon.

49. See the London-based *Frieze* and the Dubai newspaper the *National* for reviews of only Akram Zaatari in the joint exhibition at the Beirut Art Center (and Sfeir Semler in the case of Zaatari) (Saadawi 2009; Wilson-Goldie 2009a).

50. The two artists' different takes on the matter are relayed in Gilbert (2009).

CHAPTER 5

1. The videos can all be found on the artist's website: https://www.samahhijawi.com/blank.

2. Jordan's burgeoning film industry is defined by the Royal Film Commission's (2003) now defunct Red Sea Film School, which was set up in the early 2000s. The aim of the school was to create a proper film industry in Jordan and to help any filmmakers who came from inside or outside the region to film in the country. See Ginsberg and Lippard (2010: 222).

3. On this issue, see Hijjawi (2015), in which she reveals through an analysis of various public art projects from a historical perspective that it's not the form but the content, combined with the Arabic language and the physical location of the art's installation and its potential to draw attraction by the general public, that censors find most threatening.

4. For more on the way in which the Jordanian regime, media, and policymakers alike have propagated the view of the first lady as empowered and modern to suit their political agendas, see Sukarieh (2015). For an example of the typical Western mainstream media presentation of the royal family as modern and progressive, see the *60 Minutes* Australia segment "The Modern King and Queen of Jordan, Abdullah and Rania," published March 7, 2019, https://www.youtube.com/watch?v=meL1oLnOyoY.

5. See Larzillière (2016), in which she describes how the regime has relied on "defensive democratization," "paradoxical liberalization," and "authoritarian elections," completely rejecting any possibility of a countermodel of class struggle and revolution.

6. See Mikdadi (2015); see also "Where Are the Arabs?—Documentation" (2009), http://theoaklandstandard.museumca.org/where-are-arabs-documentation.

7. "Where Are the Arabs?" MOMA PS1, https://www.moma.org/calendar/events/3271.

8. Interview with the author, July 22, 2019, Amman.

9. Interview with the author, July 22, 2019, Amman. The artist chose Souk Mango to launch her project ultimately because of its foot traffic and open space. That it also was a famous lingerie section of the souk, in her view, added a dimension of intrigue to the project that was picked up by those who were acquainted with downtown Amman and its history.

10. For Rancière, the politics in aesthetics lie primarily in the potential to disrupt and antagonize the recognized order (2004: 12–13).

11. See Downey (2011) for another example of the appropriation of the Rancièrian paradigm to understand the 2011–2012 uprisings in the Arab world and their link to the political role of art featured at the 54th Venice Biennial in advancing what will soon be referred to as "the Former Middle East" according to the author. Downey, the curator of the Arab segment of the Biennial, *The Future of a Promise*, emphasized the featured art's role in redefining modes of civic engagement by being involved in a redistribution of the sensible. Yet nowhere does he identify the framework through which the art featured will link up to the civil society structures, networks, and organizations that will in reality realize the "Former Middle East."

12. I am referring here to James Clifford's (1997) proposition that travel is where modern culture reveals itself in the most nuanced ways.

13. On the contradictions of democratization in Jordan, see Cavatorta and Durac (2010: chap. 5). See also Robinson (1998). For how this has manifested in the works of public art tolerated by the regime, see Hijjawi (2015), herself reflecting on the practices

of her peers and their relationship to the political in the country where she gives a glimpse in to the regime's mindset. In a nutshell, when the language of the art is Arabic and when it is placed in public sites with much foot traffic, projects are not tolerated. When they unfold in private spaces and especially in the English language, and are frequented by expats and diplomats, then the margin of freedom is expanded.

14. The story of the founding of Darat is one of family love and passion for social change. Parts of the story span decades and are set amid some of Jordan's and the larger region's most turbulent moments in the twentieth century. This story was relayed to me by Shoman over a coffee and long chat in one of the beautiful 1920s buildings that was painstakingly renovated as part of Darat's formation. This story has been told and retold in various iterations in interviews and coverage of both the Khaled Shoman Collection and Darat itself, so I will not repeat it here. The most elaborate description of how the organization came to be is told by Rogers (2012).

15. Darat Al Funun is in large part run on the funds of the Khaled Shoman Foundation, set up by Suha Shoman and her children in honor of her husband and the founder of the Arab Bank, Khaled Shoman. Makan, like other initiatives of its kind in the country and the region, relied mostly on organizations such as the Ford Foundation, the Young Arab Theatre Fund (itself funded by the Ford Foundation), and the Hivos Insitute, among others.

16. At the opening of Darat al Funun in 1993, the performing arts were celebrated with a concert by soprano Tania Nasir, who sang poems in Arabic by Jabra Ibrahim Jabra, and was accompanied by pianist Agnes Bashir and modern ballet dancer Rania Qamhawi. Soon afterwards, Suha Shoman and her team organized solo exhibitions for Samia Halaby in 1995 and Kamal Boullata in 1998. They hosted the play *Lights of Jericho*, based on Ghassan Kanafani's "Men in the Sun," directed by Sawsan Darwazeh and performed by Samar Dudin in 1995. They also presented a play titled *Al Zaroub*, based on al-Nakba stories by Samia Al Bakri from Akka. In addition to hosting exhibitions and performances, talks by prominent writers such as Jabra Ibrahim Jabra and Abdul Rahman Munif were held, as well as poetry recitals by the famous father and son Mourid and Tamim Barghouthi.

17. For a thorough review of the conception of the architectural space, how it came to be in the spot in occupied on Nadim al Mallah Street, and what it meant for those who worked most closely to it, see its publication produced by Makan and funded by the Ford Foundation. It details passion, love, and commitment: *The Balcony: An Idea in a Void* (2010).

18. The painstaking process and story of renovating the three buildings that now make up the Darat can be found on its website, https://daratalfunun.org/. See also van der Vlist (2012).

19. While the Darat supported Jordanian and all Arab art in general, it reserved a special place for Palestinian art at a time when it was losing its central place in the discourse about the role of art and political change among the younger generation, who while remaining committed to Palestine became increasingly concerned with aesthetically exploring the political and economic issues that defined their daily lives in their increasingly neoliberalized cities. As early as 1992, the work of the experimental Palestinian New Vision Group was brought to Amman in an exhibition. Held that same year was an exhibition for three artists from Gaza: Laila Shawa, Kamel al Mughanni, and Fayez Al Hasani. In 2017, the Darat dedicated its annual exhibition and events program, which marked 100 years since the Balfour Declaration, 70 years since the 1947 UN partition resolution, and 50 years since the 1967 war, to exhibiting Palestinian civilization and cultural heritage under the title *Falastin al Hadara* (*The Civilization of Palestine*). Among the most memorable and large-scale events that same year was the year-long program that launched with archeological talks on the early settlements of Jericho in Palestine and Ain Ghazal in Jordan and extended to exhibitions on early Palestinian press and radio. The exhibition included the art of Karimeh Abboud, the first Palestinian and Arab woman photographer, and talks on Palestinian photography, writings, cinema, and music. The *Pioneers* segment of the program exhibited works by Nicolas Saig, who opened the first studio in Jerusalem in the thirties, and Zulfa al Sa'di, who received an award for her art at the 1933 First National Arab Fair. For more on the very extensive program, see "30th Anniversary Inaugural Exhibition Booklet," published by Darat al Funun-The Khaled Shoman Foundation, 2018.

20. Interview with the author, August 13, 2017, Amman. I was not surprised to find that the director's thoughts were almost identical to those quoted by a member of the rap group Katiba 5 in Richter-Devroe and Salih (2014). That a director of a national gallery and a rap singer are observing the same phenomenon is testament to the changing forms of cultural production in the past twenty years. For more on these changing attitudes in other forms of art like music, see especially Maira (2013).

21. In published writing, it is specifically Beirut's group of postwar artists that have been held up as an example of a body of work emerging out of a tabula rasa. According to Sarah Rogers, "the dominant critical paradigm for Beirut is a locale in which the violent history of the civil war produced a tabula rasa for visual practices"

(2008: 191). Portraying Beirut's art scene as "proto-institutional," Western critics have promulgated an understanding of an art scene operating in a void (Wright 2002). Scholarly work like Shabout (2007) that indicated that there is a lack of art criticism specialized in the language of visual criticism may have perpetuated these sorts of stereotypes that emphasis a Western genealogical tradition in their analyses of what art practices and art writing exist in the region. Such ideas have now being corrected with publications such as Lenssen, Rogers, and Shabout (2018).

22. For more on the Lab, see https://daratalfunun.org/?page_id=33#lab.

23. For more on the well-intentioned yet problematic interest in Palestinian art within the context of "Arab" or "Middle Eastern" art in politically turbulent times, see, for instance, Farhat (2009b); C. Ferguson (2004). See also Winegar (2008).

24. The program Noura Al Khasawneh and Toleen Touq founded brings together international artists and young and emerging artists for participatory workshops and collaborative sessions. On average, there are eighteen participants per year from across the globe. The artists and practitioners chosen to lead the sessions share a strong focus on collaboration, prioritizing alternative pedagogies, and critical methodologies. Participating artists have included Basma Al Sharif, Rheim Alkadhi, Michael Rakowitz, the design collective åbäke, Hong-Kai Wang, James Webb, Bahbak Hashemi Nezhad, and more recently the Cairo Institute of Liberal Arts and Brian Conley. Several of these artists have returned to the space to continue projects they have started in Amman. As such, the program opens up a two-way exchange: to cultivate critical thinking and develop methodological approaches to art making for participants; and, for the resident artists leading the sessions, Amman itself has offered a new site of creative praxis.

25. El-Khalidi's opening event was a concert by the well-known singer Makadi Nahhas. The few events after were focused on giving a platform to experimental musicians in the city. In those early days, El-Khalidi was entertaining the thought of working solely with the country's growing alternative music scene.

26. It is interesting that *An Idea in a Void* is precisely about this ill definition.

27. Meeting Points was created by Tarek Abdel Fotouh of the then Young Arab Theatre Fund in Brussels. The Young Arab Theatre Fund was originally set up to serve independent young artists living and working in the Arab world. The YATF's main areas of funding were production, touring, travel, art events, and alternative spaces. The YATF, which changed its name to Mophradat in 2015, has been registered as an international nonprofit association in Belgium since 2004. It receives its core funding from the Ford Foundation and other project funders such as the Goethe Institute, the

European Endowment for Democracy, the Open Society Institute, and the Heinrich Boll Foundation, among others.

28. Interview with the author, June 28, 2019, Berlin.

29. For example, the British Council, the UK-based Morris Hargreaves McIntyre Consultancy, and the EU National Institute of Culture (EUNIC), which have compiled a market-driven study of culture in Jordan, published the Audience Atlas Report in 2017. See also the project Media and Culture for Development in the Southern Mediterranean Region's mission to support the efforts of the Southern Mediterranean countries in building deep-rooted democracy and to contribute to their sustainable economic, social, and human development through regional cooperation in the fields of media and culture. https://www.euneighbours.eu/en/south/stay-informed/projects/media-and-culture-development-southern-mediterranean-region.

30. See the publication launched with the opening of the exhibition of the interventions at Makan art space in Amman on December 5–26, 2010, which gives a platform to the contributing artists' musings on their work and the curatorial mission.

31. Personal communication with the author, June 1, 2016.

32. Personal communication with the author, June 1, 2016.

33. See, for instance, the language used in Helly and Lane (2014). The authors write of Mercy Corps and others' work in the process of building what they call a knowledge society based on public wealth achieved largely through the arts to enact the community development needed.

34. Toleen Touq, Interview, July 2015, Amman.

35. In contrast to state-formation in neighboring countries, the founding of the Hashemite Kingdom of Jordan was not preceded by an indigenous nationalist movement for independence, a historical fact that has tainted its reputation as a British construct, especially among nationalists of all persuasions.

36. For an excellent, if dated, account of the limitations of democracy in Jordan and the state's social contract role, see Wiktorowicz (1999). For a more recent analysis of the Gulf Cooperation Council's role in maintaining the social contract, see Helfont and Helfont (2012). See also Abu Rish (2014).

37. For the Jordanian government and the Ministry of Culture having official international and locally funded artists draw murals and spray graffiti on designated parts of the quickly gentrifying city in hip areas catering to the international community and their local counterparts of middle-class educated young professionals and students has become a central project of theirs, such as the international Baladak

Grafitti Festival they fund to act as a marker of both democratic practice and a tolerance to dissent, especially in the wake of the Arab Spring. Yet any murals on the condition of the Syrians need to get official municipal approval. Anything too provocative doesn't get approved as several NGO-funded, Amman-based graffiti artists I spoke with informed me.

38. The Abu Ghazaleh MMAG foundation in Amman is the most recent example of this trend. The Ivy League-educated children of Mohammad and Mahera Abu Ghazaleh took over and renovated three old houses to establish a center on a hilltop overlooking downtown Amman in an art-led, gentrifying area. It features permanent gallery spaces and a public library, and hosts exhibitions, programs, talks, screenings, and workshops. The foundation is currently working on developing a free art school. In an informal conversation with their son in Amman, he discussed his passion and commitment to making "politics happen," a central driving force behind his work there. As he explained it, politics has become stale, and art is the only place left to make a difference. Of course, this to me was reminiscent of the many funders whom I met in my fieldwork who expressed this same need to invest in the arts to bring change to the region.

CHAPTER 6

Adapted from Hanan Toukan, "Picasso is Mightier than the M16: On Imaging and Imagining Palestine's Resistance in the Global Community," *Cultural Politics* 13, no. 1 (2017): 101–23.

1. This was articulated in the context of what some residents of Ramallah regard as its historical cosmopolitanism. Even if it was always a small city, a suburb of Jerusalem where the wealthy spent their summers for its fresh, mountainous air, for many the early missionaries and travelers who traversed Jerusalem for centuries also contributed to neighboring Ramallah's modernity, dynamism, and diversity, which its residents often contrasted with the social and religious conservatism of cities like Nablus, Jenin, and Hebron (Taraki and Giacaman 2006: 50). It is ironic that Yahya's second novel, *Crime in Ramallah* (2017), was actually banned by the PNA for its "indecency" that threatened public morality. Abbad's text included explicitly sexual content and homosexual characters.

2. Commented Salam Fayyad, the former PNA prime minister, in the 2009 PNA state-building plan: "Palestine will be a peace-loving state that rejects violence, commits to coexistence with its neighbors, and builds bridges of cooperation with the

international community. It will be a symbol of peace, tolerance and prosperity in this troubled area of the world" (cited in Jawad 2014).

3. Like in *Dhat*, the story is not only the story of the protagonist. Rather it is a collective one that represents the transformation that Ramallah underwent after Oslo, like Egypt did in the 1970s, to becoming a private sector–oriented and international investment–friendly setting that transforms urban space at the material and social levels through the new flows and sites of global capital.

4. For a detailed account of what this generation has been born into and how it has impacted their view of the world and their place in it, see Maira (2013: esp. chap. 2).

5. The Young Artist Award, named after the late artist Hassan Hourani, is one of the most important events in the visual arts calendar of Palestine and has been organized on a biennial basis by the A.M. Qattan Foundation since 2000. For some who were present at the award ceremony, Al-Qattan's words were harsh generalizations that overlooked the real achievement in getting Palestine onto the world cultural map. For others, Al-Qattan was pushing his audience to think honestly and critically about the global political economy of arts production that Palestinian artists, like artists elsewhere, have had to negotiate, often at the expense of effacing local historical and ongoing processes of resistance. See Hamdan (2016). Al-Qattan (2018) offered a detailed response to the *Al-Akhbar* piece, which he saw as wrongfully representing his statement.

6. While I heard this point that Hans Belting (2009) rightfully makes from many cultural practitioners and artists whom I spoke to in Ramallah, I discussed this point at length in an interview with art historian and educator Vera Tamari, first on August 5, 2012, and then on May 28, 2017, in her home in Ramallah. Tamari, who had lectured in Islamic art and architecture at Birzeit University and who founded and directed the Ethnographic and Art Museum at Birzeit for many years, in addition to serving as advisor and board member on many institutions, is also a prolific artist. Although Tamari and I had the occasion to meet informally numerous times on my trips to Ramallah, it was in those two interviews with her that I truly understood how much her role as educator informs her practice and vice versa. She knew the Ramallah context well and has watched the post-Oslo generation come of age as it transitioned into a global space for the production of art. She promoted and partook in many of globally connected, funded, and critiqued projects, and believed that despite their value, it is investment in arts education at the grassroots level that was truly needed for these projects to have impact.

7. See the published interview of the well-known Palestinian curator and arts manager Jack Parsekian on this topic in Downey (2016b).

8. This point was raised several times during my interviews in Palestine and especially in interviews I conducted between 2015 and 2018. Even though I do not cover this period in this book, it is an important and interesting development that I would like to make note of. After the Arab revolutions and the diminishing of Palestine as a central issue for activists and political parties in the region, international funders decreased their funds to cultural projects in Ramallah. This opened the way for the A.M. Qattan Foundation, a well-established organization, to become the main player and disburser of funds allocated to it from its own sources or European funders. The EU in "External Relations Palestine Report" highlights the foundation as the "main player in cultural policy and appears even to have taken on to some extent the role of the Minister of Culture" (M. Schneider 2014).

9. Reema Salha Fadda (2016) provides a thorough account of the negotiations Palestinian cultural institutions must undertake to claim legitimacy and remain visible in the face of Israeli erasure of the Palestinian identity and at the same time the politics of international funding and linkages that come with their own neoliberalized conditions.

10. A Pioneering Institution in Palestine concerned with developing and advancing the practice and knowledge of contemporary visual arts, through learning, capacity building, resource networks, and innovative programs, the IAAP was funded through a seed grant from the Ministry of Foreign Affairs, Norway, and the Ford Foundation for its overall running cost and core expenditure. In addition, over the following years it received funds for student exchange programs and visiting lecturers from other bodies such as the British Council, the Henrich Boell Foundation Kiel, the Belgian Consulate, the Palestinian Investment Fund, and individual contributors (Butler 2012).

11. See Michael Baers's fascinating 2014 account of the *Picasso* project as narrated through illustrated renderings based on his interpretations of the ethnographic research he undertook of all the individual characters the project involved in both Palestine and the Netherlands.

12. Interview with the author, August 22, 2012, Ramallah.

13. For an account of Norway's role as democratic and civilized peacemaker in today's world, see Witoszek (2013) and Jumana Manna and Sille Storhile's *The Goodness Regime* (21 min, 2013), a video projection with sound, for a creative take on Norway's

culture of consensus and its link to performing the benevolent in facilitating peace talks by the PLO and Israel in 1993.

14. Baers's (2014) thorough account of the event elaborated significantly on this point by relaying the thoughts of several local interviewees on this particular matter.

15. With the exception of Baers (2014), coverage of the *Picasso in Palestine* project, whether in mainstream representations in the international media (such as the *Economist*, *Al-arabiya*, and *Al-Jazeera*) or the more "critical" analyses usually found in academic circles and art journals was by and large celebratory in content. Whether praised as a triumphant moment of art's ability to conquer grim reality through a transcendent imagination, a prime example in cultural diplomacy, or an intelligent moment in the history of institutional critique, what was consistently left unaddressed is the possible meanings of the project in the context of Palestine's history of art and cultural production and especially its post-Oslo institutionalization and NGO-ization and the relationship of each to Palestinian histories of resistance and identity construction in a global context and transnational frame. See, for instance, Gangat (2017); Esche (2012); Tolan (2011). See the film made by Rashid Masharawi and Khaled Hourani *Picasso in Palestine* (2011), debuted in *Documenta 13*.

16. For a thorough study of the history, development, and current status of institutional critique, see Raunig and Ray (2009).

17. For an interesting take on what institutional critique could mean in the historical context of Palestine and the rest of the Arab region, see O. Toukan (2014). Toukan questions the meaning of the term and its paradoxical relationship to ideology and intellectualism, national liberation struggles, and nation building.

18. The body of literature concerned with this topic is too vast to cite here, but some of the most prominent and recent interventions on the humanitarianization and/or NGO-ization of Palestine's civil society include Dana (2014b); Feldman (2018); Feldman and Ticktin (2010); Khalidi and Samour (2014); Nakhleh (2012); and Turner (2007).

19. Anthropologist Chiara De Cesari (2012) has written of this tendency for artists and cultural heritage NGOs to mimic nation-state institutions in a more critical and defiant way.

20. The Israeli army enters the supposedly "independent" West Bank (or area A in Oslo terminology, which refers to the supposed full civil and security control granted by Israel to the PNA as part of the Accords) and arrests or kills civilians on almost a daily basis. Whether to enact curfews, carry out nighttime raids to supposed terror suspects, intimidate local farmers, or thwart big demonstrations

such as those that took place in the aftermath of the war on Gaza in the summer of 2014, the Israeli army enters freely and always under the pretense of national security consideration.

21. Prominent critics, curators, artists, architects, and writers mostly all expressed these critical views of this aspect of the project in interviews I undertook in the summer of 2012, with most asking me to leave their names anonymous if I were to publish my findings.

22. One of these, for instance, came in the form of an artist collective's illustrated (re)-presentation of *Picasso* as part of a small publication thrown into public circulation. The illustrations are playful, and there is one in particular where ex-US security coordinator for the PNA and Israel, Keith Dayton, sits beside *Buste de Femme*. The artists seemed to suggest that Palestinian art and its circulation in global spaces be looked at through the critical lens of the convoluted histories of modernity, the military, and colonialism in Palestine precisely to avoid the over-fetishization of Palestinian art as indubitably resistant (Abbas, Abu Rahme, and Haj-Yahya 2012).

Further interventions came from prominent and well-networked members of the Palestinian contemporary cultural production scene, such as curator Yazid Anani, as well as Yazan Al-Khalil, a visual artist. Both intercepted mainstream analyses of the project floating around in English-speaking art journals through humor and the power of the absurd in the fuss made over the painting's ability to supposedly transcend the shackles of occupation through recourse to the imagination. In both texts, the security state, its relationship to art, and the constructed image of Palestine as an independent entity featured heavily in the critique offered. In Khalili's words, writing in the journal *Ibraaz*, "I came to look at Picasso, only to find myself confronted with the State itself" (2011).

23. I borrow this term from Kobena Mercer (1990), who first used it in reference to black artists who were forced to carry an expectation that imposed on them the responsibility to speak in the name of their entire culture and national belonging.

CONCLUSION

1. I have elaborated on this work and its significance in more detail elsewhere (see H. Toukan [2019]).

2. Interview with the author, May 23, 2018, Amman. John Chalcraft (2016) has convincingly argued that the mass uprisings of 2011–2012 had their surprising and creative dimensions precisely because they emerged without any preceding state

breakdown, and they underscored the people as a sovereign subject in a way distinct from anti-colonial nationalism.

3. See, for instance, Erskine-Loftus, Penziner Hightower, and Ibrahim Al-Mulla (2016); and Matar (2015). Levitt (2015) offers a dynamic approach to understanding museums' roles as sites of cosmopolitanism in an increasingly transnationalized and global world.

References

Abaza, Mona. 2013. "Walls, Segregating Downtown Cairo and the Mohammed Mahmud Street Graffiti." *Theory, Culture & Society* 30 (1): 122–39. http://doi.org/10.1177/0263276412460062.

Abbas, Basel, Ruann Abu-Rahme, and Raouf Haj Yahya. 2012. "The Stories of Uncle Dayton." *Uncle Dayton* (blog). uncledayton-blog.tumblr.com/post/19239810282#note-container.

Abdelrahman, Maha. 2004. *Civil Society Exposed: The Politics of NGOs in Egypt*. London: Taurus Academic Studies.

Abi Saab, Pierre. 2002. "Ashkal alwan tabdaa' ashghaliha al fanniya al-yawm fi beyrut: tajarub fanniya mushara'a a'ala al-as'ilah wa-ali'htimalat" (Homeworks Begins Today in Beirut: Artistic Experimentation Open for Questions and Possibilities). *al-Hayat*, April 2, 2002.

Abourahme, Nasser. 2009. "The Bantustan Sublime: Reframing the Colonial in Ramallah." *City: Analysis of Urban Trends, Culture, Theory, Policy, Action* 13 (4): 499–509.

Abu Rish, Ziad. 2014. "Protests, Regime Stability, and State Formation in Jordan." In *Beyond the Arab Spring: The Evolving Ruling Bargain in the Middle East*, edited by Mehran Kamrava. Oxford: Oxford University Press.Abu-Lughod, Lila. 1990. "The Romance of Resistance: Tracing Transformations of Power Through Bedouin Women." *American Ethnologist: Journal of the American Ethnological Society* 17 (1): 41–55. https://doi.org/10.1525/ae.1990.17.1.02a00030.

Abu-Rabi', Ibrahim M. 2004. *Contemporary Arab Thought: Studies in Post-1967 Arab Intellectual History*. London: Pluto.

Adorno, Theodor W. 1991. *The Culture Industry: Selected Essays on Mass Culture*. Edited by J. M. Bernstein. London: Routledge.

Aguilar, Manuela. 1996. *Cultural Diplomacy and Foreign Policy, German American Relations 1955–1968*. Studies in Modern European History 19. New York: Peter Lang.

Ahmed, Sara. 2004. *The Cultural Politics of Emotions*. Edinburgh: Edinburgh University Press.

Aksikas, Jaafar. 2009. *Arab Modernities: Islamism, Nationalism and Liberalism in the Post-Colonial Arab World*. New York: Peter Lang.

Al Khatib, Reem, et al. 2010. *Cultural Policies in Algeria, Egypt, Jordan, Lebanon, Morocco, Palestine, Syria and Tunisia: An Introduction*. Brussels: Al Mawred Al Thaqafy.

Al Qassemi, Sultan Sooud. 2017a. "How the CIA Funded Arab Art to Fight Communism." *Newsweek*, April 21, 2017. https://www.newsweek.com/how-cia-funded-arab-art-help-win-cold-war-587218.

———. 2017b. "The Athens of the Arab World." *EDA Reflection*. Emirates Diplomatic Academy. September 2017. http://www.eda.ac.ae/docs/default-source/Publications/eda_reflection_the_athens_of_arab_world_eng.pdf?sfvrsn=2.

Al Said, Shakir Hassan. 1953. "Hawla al-Ma'rad al-Fanni al-Thalith fi al-Ma'had al-Thaqafi al-Britani fi Baghdad." *Al-Adab*, no. 10, 77–79.

Al Sayyid, Nazem. 2007. "Al tamwil al gharbi lil thaqafa fil lubnan: ma al badeel al thaqafy muqabil al aaml'ah al saa'bah?" *Al-Quds Al-Arabi*.

Al Zaatari. 2010. "Amman 'Asimat al-Intithaar al-Abady." *Al-Akhbar*, December 15, 2010.

Al-Ali, Nadje. 2000. *Secularism, Gender and the State in the Middle East: The Egyptian Women's Movement*. Cambridge: Cambridge University Press.

Al-Hujeiry, Mohammad. 2000. "Oustouratou Shari' Marthiyyatou'Ahd" ("The Myth of a Street, the Elegy of an Era"). *as Safir*, November 21, 2000.

Ali, Nawal, and Samah Hijawi. 2010. *Cultural Policies in Algeria, Egypt, Jordan, Lebanon, Morocco, Palestine, Syria and Tunisia*. Amsterdam: Boekmanstudies, Culture Resource (Al Mawred Al Thaqafy) and European Cultural Foundation.

Ali, Wijdan. 2001. "Modern Painting in the Mashriq." In *Colors of Enchantment: Theater, Dance, Music, and the Visual Arts of the Middle East*, edited by Sherifa Zuhur. Cairo: American University in Cairo Press.

Alibhai-Brown, Yasmin. 2011. "Cultural Revolution: How Artists Have Been Inspired by the Arab Spring." *Independent*, July 15, 2011. https://www.independent.co.uk/

arts-entertainment/art/features/cultural-revolution-how-artists-have-been-inspired-by-the-arab-spring-2314807.html.

Allsop, Laura. 2011. "Rabi' Mroue, the Lebanese Artist Starting a Creative Rebellion." *CNN*, April 12, 2011. http://edition.cnn.com/2011/WORLD/meast/04/05/lebanon.artist.mroue/index.html.

Allwood, John. 1977. *The Great Exhibitions*. London: Studio Vista.

Al-Qattan, Omar. 2016. "(Cultural) Palestine Will Not Die." A.M. Qattan Foundation, December 6, 2016. http://qattanfoundation.org/en/qattan/media/news/omar-al-qattan-cultural-palestine-will-not-die.

Al-Ragam, Aseel. 2014. "The Politics of Representation: The Kuwait National Museum and Processes of Cultural Production." *International Journal of Heritage Studies* 20 (6): 663–674.

Al-Turk, Jihad. 2005. "nadwa li-jami'at ashkal alwan fi masrah al-madina: al-ijaba al-mutaa'thirah al tasau'lat al-kabira" [A Workshop for Organizations at Ashkal Alwan in al Madina Theatre: The Impossible Answer to Very Big Inquiries]. *Al-Mustaqbal*, November 20, 2005.

American Friends of the Middle East. 1952. *First Annual Report of the Executive Vice President to the Board of the Directors and the National Council for the American Friends of the Middle East, Inc. May 15, 1951 to June 30, 1952*. New York: AFME.

Amiralay, Omar. 2009. "Al da'am al ajnabi lil thaqafah wal fonoon fil 'alam al 'arabi" [Foreign Support for Art and Culture in the Arab World]. *al- Safir*.

Amirsadeghi, Hossein, Salwa Mikdadi, and Nada M. Shabout, eds. 2009. *New Visions: Arab Contemporary Art in the 21st Century*. London: Thames and Hudson.

Anani, Yazid. 2013. "In the Shadows of Contemporary Palestinian Art." *This Week in Palestine*, no. 186, 4–5.

Anderson, Benedict. 1991. *Imagined Communities: Reflections on the Origin and Spread of Nationalism*. London: Verso.

Anderson, Betty S. 2011. *The American University of Beirut: Arab Nationalism & Liberal Education*. Austin: University of Texas Press.

Appadurai, Arjun. 1996. *Modernity at Large: Cultural Dimensions of Globalization*. Minneapolis: University of Minnesota Press.

Aranda, Julieta, Brian Kuan Wood, and Anton Vidokle, eds. 2010. *What Is Contemporary Art?* New York: Sternberg Press.

Arendt, Hannah. 1998. *The Human Condition*. 2nd ed. Chicago: University of Chicago Press.

Arnason, Johann P. 2000. "Communism and Modernity" *Daedalus* 129 (1): 61–90.

Arndt, Richard T. 2005. *The First Resort of Kings: American Cultural Diplomacy in the Twentieth Century.* Lincoln: Potomac Books.

Atrissi, Tarek. 2009. "The Transformed Vernacular New Language Design." In *New Visions: Arab Contemporary Art in the 21st Century*, edited by Hossein Amirsadeghi, Salwa Mikdadi, and Nada M. Shabout. London: Thames and Hudson.

Awad, Maysa. 2006. "Mann yumawil al thaqafa fi lubnan wa hal yasnaa'ha al mal al ajnabi?" *al- Safir.*

Azimi, Negar, 2016. "The Gulf Art War." *New Yorker*, December 19–26, 2016.

Azoulay, Ariella. 2011. *From Palestine to Israel: A Photographic Record of Destruction and State Formation, 1947–1950*. London: Pluto Press.

Baers, Michael. 2012. "No Good Time for an Exhibition: Reflections on the Picasso in Palestine Project, Part I." *e-flux* 33. https://www.e-flux.com/journal/33/68274/no-good-time-for-an-exhibition-reflections-on-the-picasso-in-palestine-project-part-i/.

———. 2014. "An Oral History of Picasso in Palestine." *Haus der Kulturen der Welt*. http://berlindocumentaryforum.baers.hkw.de/content/download/An-Oral-History-of-Picasso-in-Palestine%C2%AD_Baers_2014_HKW.pdf.

Barakat, Halim. 1993. *The Arab World: Society, Culture and State*. Oakland: University of California Press.

Bardawil, Fadi A. 2016. "Dreams of a Dual Birth: Socialist Lebanon's World and Ours." *boundary 2* 43 (3): 313–335. https://doi.org/10.1215/01903659-3572854.

Barthel, Pierre-Arnaud. 2010. "Arab Mega-Projects: Between the Dubai Effect, Global Crisis, Social Mobilization and a Sustainable Shift." *Built Environment (1978-)* 36 (2): 132–45. http://www.jstor.org/stable/23290061.

Bátora, Jozef. 2005. "Does the European Union Transform the Institution of Diplomacy?" *Journal of European Public Policy* 12 (1): 44–66.

Bayat, Asef. 2005. "Transforming the Arab World: The Arab Human Development Report and the Politics of Change.'" *Development and Change* 36 (6): 1225–37.

———. 2010. *Life as Politics: How Ordinary People Change the Middle East.* Stanford, CA: Stanford University Press.

———. 2013. *Life as Politics: How Ordinary People Change the Middle East.* 2nd ed. Stanford, CA: Stanford University Press.

Bazzi, Youssef. 2000. "Tajheez Shari' Al-Hamra Am Woukoufun Ala Atlalihi" [Installing Hamra Street or Contemplating Its Ruin?]. *al- Mustaqbal*, December 1, 2000.

———. 2007a. "A Short History of the Relationship Between Lebanese Arts Production and Foreign Funding." *Babelmed*, July 18, 2007. http://eng.babelmed.net/article/6256-a-short-history-of-the-relationship-between-lebanese-arts-production-and-foreign-funding/.

———. 2007b. "We Can Now Talk about an 'Alternative' Arab Culture that Is in the Process of Taking Shape." *Babelmed*, July 12, 2007. http://eng.babelmed.net/article/6255-we-can-now-talk-about-an-alternative-arab-culture-that-is-in-the-process-of-taking-shape/.

———. 2010. "The Styles of Language." In *Kitabat alkitabah*. Translated from the Arabic by Iman Humaydan. Beirut: ARRAWI.

Beasley, Mark. 2006. "Walid raad/The Atlas Group." *Frieze*, March 17, 2006. frieze.com/article/walid-raadthe-atlas-group.

Becker, Carol. 2002. *Surpassing the Spectacle: Global Transformations and the Changing Politics of Art*. Lanham: Rowman & Littlefield.

Becker, Howard. 1982. *Art Worlds*. Berkeley: University of California Press.

Bedein, David. 2009. *The Implications of United States Military Training of Palestinian Security Forces*. Center for Near East Policy Research. https://emetnews.org/documents/Implications_of_US_Military_Training_of_Palestinian_Security_Forces.pdf.

Bell, Alistair, ed. 2018. "Pentagon to keep backing Lebanon military, despite Hezbollah gains." *Reuters*, May 11, 2018. https://www.reuters.com/article/us-lebanon-election-usa-military/pentagon-to-keep-backing-lebanon-military-despite-hezbollah-gains-idUSKBN1IC2BD.

Belting, Hans. 2009. "Contemporary Art as Global Art: A Critical Estimate." In *The Global Art World: Audiences, Markets, and Museums*, edited by Hans Belting and Andrea Buddensieg. Ostfildern: Hatje Cantz.

Belting, Hans, Andrea Buddensieg, and Peter Weibel. 2013. *The Global Contemporary: The Rise of New Art Worlds after 1989*. Cambridge, MA: MIT Press for ZKM, Karlsruhe.

Ben Jannat, Zuhair. 2005. "Developmentalist Strategies Between Local Requirements and Globalized Constraints." *Insaniyat*. https://journals.openedition.org/insaniyat/5292.

Benedict, Burton. 1991. "International Exhibitions and National Identity." *Anthropology Today* 7 (3): 5–9.

Benjamin, Walter. 1998 (1934). "The Author as Producer." In *Understanding Brecht*, translated by Anna Bostock, 85–103. New York: Verso.

Bennett, Eric. 2015. *Workshops of Empire: Stegner, Engle, and American Creative Writing During the Cold War.* Iowa City: University of Iowa Press.

Berger, Maurits, Els van der Plas, Charlotte Huygens, Neila Akrimi, and Cynthia Schneider. 2008. "Bridge the Gap or Mind the Gap: Culture in Western Arab Relations." *Clingendael Diplomacy Papers*, no. 15.

Beydoun, Abbas. 2003. "Culture and Arts; Re: The Actual." In *Home Works: A Forum on Cultural Practices in the Region, Egypt, Iran, Iraq, Lebanon, Palestine, and Syria, April 2–7, 2002*, edited by Ghenwa Hayek et al. Beirut: Ashkal Alwan.

Bhabha, Homi K. 1990. *Nation and Narration.* New York: Routledge.

———. 1994. *The Location of Culture.* London: Routledge.

Bishop, Claire. 2006. "The Social Turn: Collaboration and Its Discontents." *Artforum International* 44 (6): 178–83.

———. 2012. *Artificial Hells: Participatory Art and the Politics of Spectatorship.* London: Verso.

Bloembergen, Marieke. 2006. *Colonial Spectacles: The Netherlands and the Dutch East Indies at the World, 1880–1931.* Translated by Beverly Jackson. Singapore: Singapore University Press.

Borchardt-Hume, Achim, ed. 2010. "In Search of the Miraculous: Walid Raad and Achim Borchardt-Hume." In *Miraculous Beginnings: Walid Raad.* London: Whitechapel Gallery.

Boullata, Issa J. 1973. "The Beleaguered Unicorn: A Study of Tawfīq Ṣāyigh." *Journal of Arabic Literature* 4:69–93.

———. 1990. *Trends and Issues in Contemporary Arab Thought.* Albany: State University of New York Press.

Boullata, Kamal. 1970a. *Nahwa Fan 'Arabi Thawri'. Mawaqif*, June 9, 1970, 26–44.

———. 1970b. "Towards a Revolutionary Arab Art." In *The Palestinian Resistance to Israeli Occupation*, edited by Naseer Arouri. Wilmette, IL: Medina University Press.

———. 1971. "Al-Fan fi Zaman al-Thawra al-Filastiniyya." *Mawaqif*, January 13–14, 1971, 176–79.

———. 2003. "Artists Re-Member Palestine in Beirut." *Journal of Palestine Studies* 32 (4): 22–38. http://doi.org/10.1525/jps.2003.32.4.22.

———. 2009. *Palestinian Art: From 1850 to the Present.* London: Saqi.

———. 2015. "Notes on Verbal Dominance and Visual Expression in Arab Culture." In *Imperfect Chronology: Arab Art from the Modern to the Contemporary*, edited by Omar Kholeif. New York: Prestel.

Bouquerel, Fanny, and Basma El Husseiny. 2009. "Towards a Strategy for Culture in the Mediterranean Region. EC Preparatory Document. Needs and Opportunities Assessment Report in the Field of Cultural Policy and Dialogue in the Mediterranean Region." 2009. http://www.alfpolska.org/public/editor/file/report_mediterranean_region.pdf.

Bourdieu, Pierre. 1984. *Distinction: A Social Critique of the Judgment of Taste*. Cambridge, MA: Harvard University Press.

———. 1990. *The Logic of Practice*. Stanford, CA: Stanford University Press.

———. 1993. *The Field of Cultural Production: Essays on Art and Literature*. Cambridge: Polity.

Bourriaud, Nicolas. 2010. *Relational Aesthetics*. Translated by Simon Pleasance and Fronza Woods. Dijon: Les Presses du Reel.

Brennan, Timothy. 1997. *At Home in the World: Cosmopolitanism Now*. Cambridge, MA: Harvard University Press.

Brones, Sophie, and Amin Moghadam. 2016. "Beirut–Dubai: Translocal Dynamics and the Shaping of Urban Art Districts." In *The Transnational Middle East: Peoples, Places, Borders*, edited by Leïla Vignal. London: Routlege.

Bureau of Near Eastern Affairs. n.d. "Project 70: Evaluating U.S. Security Assistance in the Middle East and North Africa." IUPI: School of Public and Environmental Affairs. Assessed October 20, 2020. https://scholarworks.iupui.edu/bitstream/handle/1805/12527/Project_70_presentation.pdf?sequence=2&isAllowed=y

Burgat, Francois. 2003. "Issues and Trends in Global Re-Islamization." In *Modernizing Islam: Religion in the Public Sphere in Europe and the Middle East*, edited by Francois Burgat and John L. Esposito. New Brunswick, NJ: Rutgers University Press.

Burger, Peter. 1984. *Theory of the Avant-Garde*. Minneapolis: University of Minnesota Press.

Burns, Aileen, Johan Lundh, and Tara McDowell. 2018. *The Artist As*. Berlin: Sternberg Press.

Butler, John. 2012. "International Art Academy Palestine (IAAP) Quality Enhancement Institution Review." April 2012. The Oslo National Academy of the Arts & the Ministry of Foreign Affairs Norway.

Butler, Judith. 1997. *The Psychic Life of Power*. Stanford, CA: Stanford University Press.

———. 2015. *Notes toward a Performative Theory of Assembly*. Cambridge, MA: Harvard University Press.

Carapico, Sheila. 2000. "NGOs, INGOs, GO-NGOs and DO-NGOs: Making Sense of Non-Governmental Organisations." *Middle East Report* 30 (214): 12–15.

Carothers, Thomas. 2003. "Is Gradualism Possible? Choosing a Strategy for Promoting Democracy in the Middle East." Carnegie Endowment for International Peace Working Papers, no. 39. https://carnegieendowment.org/pdf/files/wp39.pdf.

Carver, Antonia. 2006. "Don't Force Middle Eastern Artists into an Identity Strait-jacket." *Guardian*, September 6, 2006. https://www.theguardian.com/commentisfree/2006/sep/06/arts.visualarts#comments.

Cavatorta, Francesco, and Vincent Durac. 2010. *Civil Society and Democratization in the Arab World: The Dynamics of Activism*. Abingdon, UK: Routledge.

———. 2015. *Politics and Governance in the Middle East*. Basingstoke: Palgrave Macmillan.

Çelik, Zeynep. 1992. *Displaying the Orient: Architecture of Islam at Nineteenth-Century World's Fairs*. Berkeley: University of California Press.

Central Intelligence Agency. 2008. "Origins of the Congress for Cultural Freedom, 1949–50." Last updated June 27, 2008. r sdfsdfs/95unclass/Warner.htmance.dea of " to introduce this link.n'u'more about introducing what the CCF did than the debatehttps://www.cia.gov/library/center-for-the-study-of-intelligence/csi-publications/csi-studies/studies/95unclass/Warner.html.

Chalcraft, John. 2016. *Popular Politics in the Making of the Modern Middle East*. Cambridge: Cambridge University Press.

Chalcraft, John, and Yaseen Noorani, eds. 2007. *Counter-Hegemony in the Colony and Postcolony*. London: Palgrave Macmillan.

Channick, Joan. 2005. "The Artist as Cultural Diplomat." *American Theatre* 22 (5): 4.

Charafeddine, Chaza, Masha Refka, and Christine Tohme, eds. 2005. *Home Works III: A Forum on Cultural Practices, November 17–24*. Beirut: Ashkal Alwan.

Charlesworth, J. J. 2013. "Global versus Local." *ArtReview Asia*, November 2013. https://artreview.com/features/november_2013_feature_global_versus_local_by_jj_charlesworth_1/.

Chatterjee, Partha. 1993. *The Nation and Its Fragments: Colonial and Postcolonial Histories*. Princeton, NJ: Princeton University Press.

———. 2004. *The Politics of the Governed: Reflections on Popular Politics in Most of the World*. New York: Columbia University Press.

Chenal, Odile, et al., eds. 2008. *An Alternate Gaze: A Shared Reflection on Cross Mediterranean Cooperation in the Arts*. Amsterdam: European Cultural Foundation.

Chomsky, Noam. 1999. *Profit Over People: Neoliberalism and Global Order.* New York: Seven Stories Press.

Chukhrov, Keti. 2014. "On the False Democracy of Contemporary Art." *e-flux* 57 (September). https://www.e-flux.com/journal/57/60430/on-the-false-democracy-of-contemporary-art/.

Clifford, James. 1997. *Routes: Travel and Translation in the Late Twentieth Century.* Cambridge, MA: Harvard University Press.

Coleman, Peter. 1989. *The Liberal Conspiracy: The Congress for Cultural Freedom and the Struggle for the Mind of Post-War Europe.* London: Free Press Collier Macmillan.

Collier, Stephen J. 2009. "Topologies of Power: Foucault's Analysis of Political Government beyond 'Governmentality.'" *Theory, Culture & Society* 26 (6): 78–108.

Columbus, Nikki. 2008. "Past Imperfect: Nikki Columbus on Home Works IV in Beirut." *ArtForum International* 46 (10): 179–80.

Conio, Andrew. 2011. "Picasso in Palestine: A Diagram." *A Prior*, no. 22, 27–40.

Cooke, Miriam. 2002. "Beirut Reborn: The Political Aesthetics of Auto-Destruction." *Yale Journal of Criticism* 15 (2): 393–424.

———. 2007. *Dissident Syria: Making Oppositional Arts Official.* Durham, NC: Duke University Press.

Cotter, Suzanne, ed. 2006. *Out of Beirut.* Oxford: Modern Art Oxford.

———. 2009. "The Documentary Turn: Surpassing Tradition in the Work of Walid Raad and Akram 2009. Zaatari." In *Contemporary Art in the Middle East*, edited by Paul Sloman. London: Black Dog.

C. S. 2011. "Picasso in Ramallah: The Paintbrush Is Mightier than the M16." *Economist*, June 27, 2011. http://www.economist.com/prospero/2011/06/27/the-paintbrush-is-mightier-than-the-m16.

Cull, Nicolas J. 2009. *Public Diplomacy: Lessons from the Past.* Los Angeles: Figueroa Press.

Cummings, Jr., Milton C. 2009. "Cultural Diplomacy and the United States Government: A Survey." Americans for the Arts (formerly Center for Arts and Culture). https://www.americansforthearts.org/sites/default/files/MCCpaper.pdf.

Dabashi, Hamid. 2012. *The Arab Spring: The End of Postcolonialism.* London: Zed Books.

———. 2017. "Rethinking the Arab Capital through Art." *Al Jazeera*, April 10, 2017. aljazeera.com/indepth/opinion/2017/04/rethinking-arab-capital-art-170409105111270.html.

Dabbous-Sensenig, Dim. 2002. "From Defending 'Cultural Exception' to Promoting 'Cultural Diversity': European Cultural Policy and the Arab World." In

"Globalization, Audiovisual Industry and Cultural Diversity" edited by Joan Manuela Tresserras, special issue, *QUA-DERNS*, September–December, 33–44.

Daccache, Soline. 2006. "Mobility to Do What?" In "The Challenges of Artistic Exchange in the Mediterranean: Made in the Mediterranean." Fonds Roberto Cimetta, Fondation René Seydoux Pour le Monde Méditerranéen, Relais Culture Europe, and the European Cultural Foundation. http://www.cimettafund.org/documents/EN/FRC-E-.pdf.

Dagher, Sandra, Catherine David, Rasha Salti, Christine Tohme, and T. J. Demos. 2007. "Curating Beirut: A Conversation on the Politics of Representation." *Art Journal* 66 (2): 98–119. https://doi.org/10.1080/00043249.2007.10791258.

Daher, Rami. 1999. "Gentrification and the Politics of Power, Capital and Culture in an Emerging Jordanian Heritage Industry." *Traditional Dwellings and Settlements Review* 10 (2): 33–45.

———. 2007. *Tourism in the Middle East: Continuity, Change, & Transformation*. Bristol: Channel View.

———. 2008. "Global Capital, Urban Regeneration, and Heritage Conservation in the Levant." Special edition, *Viewpoints*, "Architecture and Urbanism in the Middle East," 22–24. http://eprints.soas.ac.uk/20494/1/Architecture_and_Urbanism_in_the_Middle_East.pdf.

———. 2011. "Families and Urban Activists as Emergent Local Actors in Urban Rehabilitation in the Mashreq: Re-defining Heritage/Re-Writing the City." In Daher and Maffi, *Politics and Practices*.

———. 2014. "Neoliberal Urban Transformations in the Arab City: Meta-narratives, Urban Disparities and the Emergence of Consumerist Utopias and Geographies of Inequalities in Amman." *Environnement Urbain/Urban Environment* 7. http://journals.openedition.org/eue/41.

Daher, Rami, and Irene Maffi, eds. 2011. *The Politics and Practices of Cultural Heritage in the Middle East: Positioning the Material Past in Contemporary Societies*. London: I. B. Tauris.

Dana, Tariq. 2014a. "Disconnecting Civil Society from Its Historical Extension: NGOs and Neoliberalism in Palestine." In *Human Rights, Human Security, National Security: The Intersection*, edited by Saul Takahashi. Santa Barbara: Praeger Security International.

———. 2014b. "Palestine's Capitalists: A Group of Palestinian Activists Are Profiting off Occupation." *Jacobin*, February 2014. https://www.jacobinmag.com/2014/02/palestines-capitalists/.

———. 2015. "The Structural Transformation of Palestinian Civil Society: Key Paradigm Shifts." *Middle East Critique* 24 (2): 191–210.

Darraj, Faisal. 2013. "The Peculiarities of Arab Modernity." In *Arab Art Histories: The Khalid Shoman Collection*, edited by Sarah A. Rogers and Eline van der Vlist. Amman: Khalid Shoman Foundation.

David, Catherine. 1997. "Introduction." In *Documenta X, Short Guide*. Ostfildern-Ruit: Cantz Verlag

———. 2002. "Contemporary Arab Representations, Beirut/LebanonSunday 15 September—Sunday 24 November 2002." Witte de With Center for Contemporary Art. https://www.wdw.nl/en/our_program/exhibitions/contemporary_arab_representations_beirut_lebanon.

———. 2003. "Learning from Beirut: Contemporary Aesthetic Practices in Lebanon: Stakes and Conditions for Experimental, Cultural and Aesthetic Practices in Lebanon and Elsewhere." In *Home Works: A Forum on Cultural Practices in the Region, Egypt, Iran, Iraq, Lebanon, Palestine, and Syria, April 2–7 2002*, edited by Ghenwa Hayek et al. Beirut: Ashkal Alwan.

Davidson, Christopher M. 2011. "The Making of a Police State." *Foreign Policy*, April 2011. http://www.foreignpolicy.com/articles/2011/04/14/the_making_of_a_police_state

De Cesari, Chiara. 2012. "Anticipatory Representation: Building the Palestinian Nation (-State) through Artistic Performance." *Studies in Ethnicity and Nationalism* 12 (1): 82–100. https://doi.org/10.1111/j.1754-9469.2012.01157.x.

———. 2019. Heritage and the Cultural Struggle for Palestine. Stanford, CA: Stanford University Press.

de Pirini, Pietro. 2017. *Intercultural Dialogue in EU Foreign Policy: The Case of the Mediterranean from the end of the Cold War to the Arab Uprisings*. Abingdon, UK: Routledge.

Deeb, Lara. 2006. *An Enchanted Modern: Gender and Public Piety in Shi'i. Lebanon*. Princeton, NJ: Princeton University Press.

Defillippi, Robert, Michael Arthur, and Valerie Lindsay. 2006. *Knowledge at Work: Creative Collaboration in the Global Economy*. New York: John Wiley & Sons.

Del Sarto, Raffaella A. 2005. "Setting the (Cultural) Agenda: Concepts, Communities, and Representation in Euro-Mediterranean Relations" *Mediterranean Politics* 10 (3): 313–30.

Delanty, Gerard. 2004. "Multiple Modernities and Globalization." *ProtoSociology* 20:165–85. http://doi.org/10.5840/protosociology20042010.

Deleuze, Gilles. 2004. "The Idea of Genesis in Kant's Esthetics." In *Desert Islands and Other Texts 1953–1974*, edited by David Lapoujade. Translated by Mike Taormina. Los Angeles: Semiotext(e).

Deleuze, Gilles, and Felix Guattari. 1987. *A Thousand Plateaus: Capitalism and Schizophrenia*. Translated by Brian Massumi. Minneapolis: University of Minnesota Press.

Delgado, L. Elena, and Rolando J. Romero. 2000. "Local Histories and Global Designs: An Interview with Walter Mignolo." *Discourse* 22 (3): 7–33.

Demos, T. J. 2008. "Image Wars." In *Zones of Conflict: Rethinking Contemporary Art During Global Crisis*, 3–11. New York: Pratt Manhattan Gallery.

———. 2009. "Desire in Diaspora." In *Contemporary Art in the Middle East*, edited by Paul Sloman, 42–49. London: Black Dog.

Derrida, Jacques. 1996. *Archive Fever: A Freudian Impression*. Chicago: University of Chicago Press.

Deutsche, Rosalyn. 1992. "Art and Public Space: Questions of Democracy." *Social Text* 33:34–53.

DeVereaux, Constance, and Martin Griffin. 2006. "International, Global, Transnational: Just a Matter of Words?" *Eurozine*, October 11, 2006. https://www.eurozine.com/international-global-transnational-just-a-matter-of-words/.

DeVlieg, Mary Ann. 2008. "Why Does the Euro-Med Need to Support and Develop Contemporary Art and Exchange?" *Babelmed*, May 23, 2008. http://eng.babelmed.net/article/6948-why-does-the-euro-med-need-to-support-and-develop-contemporary-art-and-exchange/.

DisORIENTation: Contemporary Art from the Middle East. 2003. March 23–April 3, 2003. Press Release. https://archiv.hkw.de/en/presseinfos/pressemitteilungen/DisORIENT2/c-index.htm.

Doumani, Beshara B. 2009. "Archiving Palestine and the Palestinians: The Patrimony of Ihsan Nimr." *Jerusalem Quarterly* 36:4–12.

Downey, Anthony. 2011. "Beyond the Former Middle East: Aesthetics, Civil Society, and the Politics of Representation." *Ibraaz* 001/1 (June 1). http://www.ibraaz.org/essays/8.

———. 2014. *Uncommon Grounds: New Media and Critical Practices in North Africa and the Middle East*. London: I. B. Tauris.

———. 2015. *Dissonant Archives: Contemporary Visual Culture and Contested Narratives in the Middle East*. London: I. B. Tauris.

———, ed. 2016a. *Future Imperfect: Contemporary Art Practices and Cultural Institutions in the Middle East*. Berlin: Sternberg Press.

———. 2016b. "Collective Institutions: The Case of Palestine." In *Future Imperfect: Contemporary Art Practices and Cultural Institutions in the Middle East*, edited by Anthony Downey. Berlin: Sternberg Press.

Drennan, Daniel. 2010. "A Black Panther in Beirut." Counterpunch. https://www.counterpunch.org/2010/01/13/a-black-panther-in-beirut/.

Eagleton, Terry. 1990. *The Ideology of the Aesthetic.* Oxford: Blackwell.

———. 1996. *Literary Theory: An Introduction*. 2nd ed. Oxford: Blackwell.

———. 2000. *The Idea of Culture*. Oxford: Blackwell.

———. 2016. *Culture*. New Haven, CT: Yale University Press.

Eisenstadt, Shmuel N., ed. 2002. *Multiple Modernities*. Piscataway, NJ: Transaction.

———. 2004. "La modernité multiple comme défi à la sociologie." *Revue du MAUSS* 24 (2): 189–204.

El Ahmad, Serene. 2003. "Makan: A Place of Creativity." *Star*, May 29, 2003.

El Baroni, Bassam. 2011. *Fifteen Ways to Leave Badiou*. Alexandria: Alexandria Contemporary Arts Forum.

El Hajj. 1966. "The Issue of the Journal Hiwär." *Mulhaq al-Nahär*. El-Ariss, Tarek. 2012. "Fiction in Scandal." *Journal of Arabic Literature* 23:510–31.

———. 2013. *Trials of Arab Modernity: Literary Affects and the New Political*. New York: Fordham University Press.

Elias, Chad. 2015. "Interview with Rabih Mroué." *In Focus: On Three Posters 2004 by Rabih Mroué*, edited by Chad Elias. Tate Research Publication. https://www.tate.org.uk/research/publications/in-focus/on-three-posters-rabih-mroue/interview-with-rabih-mroue.

———.2018. *Posthumous Images: Contemporary Art and Memory Politics in Post-Civil War Lebanon*. Durham, NC: Duke University Press.

"Electronic Prying Grows: C.I.A. Is Spying for 100 Miles Up; Satellites Probe Secrets of the Soviet Union." 1966. *New York Times*, April 27, 1966.

Erjavec, Aleš. 2014. "Eastern Europe, Art and the Politics of Representation." *Boundary 2* 41 (1): 51–77.

Erskine-Loftus, Pamela, Victoria Penziner Hightower, and Mariam Ibrahim Al-Mulla, eds. 2016. *Representing the Nation: Heritage, Museums, National Narratives and Identity in the Arab Gulf States*. Abingdon, UK: Routledge.

Esanu, Octavian. 2012. "What Was Contemporary Art?" *ARTMargins* 1 (1): 5–28. https://doi.org/10.1162/ARTM_a_00003.

Esche, Charles. 2011. "Picasso in Palestine." *de Keuken* (blog), Van Abbemuseum. June 27, 2011. http://thekitchen.vanabbe.nl/2011/06/27/picasso-in-palestine/.

———. 2012. "A Picasso in Search of a Context." *Artezine*, Fall 2012. http://arteeast.org/quarterly/a-picasso-in-search-of-a-context/.

Escobar, Arturo. 2011. *Encountering Development: The Making and Unmaking of the Third World*. Princeton, NJ: Princeton University Press.

Euro-Mediterranean Committee. 1995. "Barcelona Declaration and Euro-Mediterranean Partnership." November 27–28, 1995. http://eur-lex.europa.eu/legal-content/EN/TXT/?uri=LEGISSUM%3Ar15001.

Falconer, Morgan. 2006. "The Long and Wounding Road." *Times*, May 2, 2006.

Farhat, Maymanat. 2009a. "Circuit Breaking: New Approaches to Art in the Arab World." *Contemporary Practices: Visual Arts from the Middle East* 4. http://www.contemporarypractices.net/index.html.

———. 2009b. "Imagining the Arab World through Art." *Callaloo* 32 (4): 1223–31.

Faulkner, Simon. 2003. "'Asylum Seekers,' Imagined Geography and Visual Culture." *Visual Culture in Britain*, April 2003.

———. 2009. "The Green Line, Running the Border." *Simon's Teaching Blog: History of Art and Visual Cultural Teaching at London Metropolitan University*. Last modified December 27, 2009. http://simonsteachingblog.wordpress.com/2009/12/27/traveling-the-green-line-and-the-aesthetics-of-uncertainty.

Fayyad, Salam. 2009. "Ending the Occupation, Establishing the Palestinian State." Program of the Thirteenth Government. www.un.int/wcm/webdav/site/Palestine/shared/documents/Ending%20Occupation%20Establishing%20the%State%20(August%202009).pdf.

Featherstone, Mike. 1995. *Undoing Culture*. London: Sage.

Feigenbaum, Harvey B. 2001. *Globalization and Cultural Diplomacy*. Washington, DC: Center for Arts and Culture.

Feldman, Ilana. 2018. *Life Lived in Relief: Humanitarian Predicaments and Palestinian Refugee Politics*. Oakland: University of California Press.

Feldman, Ilana, and Miriam Ticktin, eds. 2010. *In the Name of Humanity: The Government of Threat and Care*. Durham, NC: Duke University Press.

Ferguson, Coco. 2004. "Islamic Art at a Crossroads." *Bidoun: Arts and Culture from the Middle East* 1/2:52–55.

Ferguson, James. 1994. *The Anti-politics Machine: "Development," Depoliticization, and Bureaucratic Power in Lesotho.* Minneapolis: University of Minnesota Press.

Finn, Helena K. 2003. "The Case for Cultural Diplomacy: Engaging Foreign Audiences." *Foreign Affairs* 82 (6): 15–20.

Finn, Peter, and Petra Couvée. 2014. *The Zhivago Affair: The Kremlin, the CIA, and the Battle Over a Forbidden Book.* New York: Pantheon Books.

Fisher, Julie. 1998. *Nongovernments: NGOs and the Political Development of the Third World.* Sterling: Kumarian Press.

Fisher, William. 1997. "Doing Good? The Politics and Antipolitics of NGO Practices." *Annual Review of Anthropology* 26:439–64.

Fisk, Milton. 2005. "Multiculturalism and Neoliberalism." *Praxis Filosofica* 21:21–28.

Fitzpatrick, Kathy R. 2011. *U.S. Public Diplomacy in a Post-9/11 World: From Messaging to Mutuality.* Los Angeles: Figueroa Press.

Fordham, Alice. 2009. "Lebanon's Movement to Remember." *National*, April 11, 2009. http://www.thenational.ae/news/worldwide/middle-east/lebanons-movement-to-remember.

Foster, Hal. 2004. "An Archival Impulse." *October* 110:3–22. http://www.jstor.org/stable/3397555.

Foucault, Michel. 1990 (1978). *The History of Sexuality.* Vol. 1, *An Introduction.* Translated by Robert Hurley. New York: Vintage.

Foucault, Michel, Graham Burchell, Colin Gordon, and Peter Miller. 1991. *The Foucault Effect: Studies in Governmentality: With Two Lectures by and an Interview with Michel Foucault.* Chicago: University of Chicago Press.

Frascina, Francis. 2003. "Institutions, Culture, and America's 'Cold War Years': The Making of Greenberg's 'Modernist Painting.'" *Oxford Art Journal* 26 (1): 71–97.

Fukuyama, Francis. 1989. "The End of History?" *National Interest*, no. 16: 3–18. http://www.jstor.org/stable/24027184.

Gangat, Rafique. 2017. "An Artist with a Cause—and Effect." *GulfNews*, April 19, 2017. https://gulfnews.com/entertainment/arts-culture/an-artist-with-a-cause--and-effect-1.2014089.

Gavin, Angus, and Ramez Maluf. 1996. *Beirut Reborn: The Restoration and Development of the Central District.* London: Academy Editions.

Gilbert, Ben. 2009. "War Themed Art Is Popular in Lebanon but Many Are Tired of the Fixation on Their Troubled Memory." *MinnPost*, September 23, 2009. http://www.minnpost.com/globalpost/2009/09/23/11803/warthemed_art_is

_popular_in_lebanon_but_many_are_tired_of_the_fixation_on_their_troubled_history.

Ginsberg, Terri, and Chris Lippard. 2010. *Historical Dictionary of Middle Eastern Cinema*. Lanham, MD: Scarecrow Press.

Godfrey, Mark. 2007. "The Artist as Historian," *October* 120:140–72. https://doi.org/10.1162/octo.2007.120.1.140.

Gokulan, Dhandusha. 2009. "Cultural Diplomacy in Focus at Art Forum." *Khaleej Times*, March 21, 2009. https://www.khaleejtimes.com/article/20090320/ARTICLE/303209972/1002.

Goldberg, Jeffrey. 2013. "The Modern King in the Arab Spring." *Atlantic*, April 2013. https://www.theatlantic.com/magazine/archive/2013/04/monarch-in-the-middle/309270/.

Gottesman, E. 2010. "ANYSPACE: Whatever." In *The Balcony: An Idea in a Void*, edited by Diala Khasawneh. Amman: Makan. See esp. "How It All Started: A Condensed History of Makan."

Gramsci, Antonio. *Selections from the Prison Notebooks*. Edited and translated by Quintin Hoare and Geoffrey Nowell Smith. London: Lawrence Wishart, 1971.

Gronlund, Melissa. 2018. "'Solidarity' and What It Means in Palestine's Art Scene." *National*, October 14, 2018. https://www.thenational.ae/arts-culture/art/solidarity-and-what-it-means-in-palestine-s-art-scene-1.780482.

Gruber, Christiane. 2019. *The Praiseworthy One: The Prophet Muhammad in Islamic Texts and Images*. Bloomington: Indiana University Press.

Gruber, Christiane, and Sune Haugbolle. 2013. *Visual Culture in the Modern Middle East: Rhetoric of the Image*. Bloomington: Indiana University Press.

Guevera, Paz. 2012. "Curating in Times of Need: Political and Cultural Changes in Jordan." *Nafas Art Magazine*, September 2012. https://universes.art/en/nafas/articles/2012/toleen-touq/.

Habib, Mohammed. 2011. "The Question of Independence in Contemporary Arab Theater." College of Fine Arts, University of Babylon, Iraq. June 17, 2011. http://www.uobabylon.edu.iq/uobcoleges/service_showarticle.aspx?fid=13&pubid=2138.

Halabi, Zeina G. 2017. *The Unmaking of the Arab Intellectual: Prophecy, Exile and the Nation*. Edinburgh: Edinburgh University Press.

Halaby, Samia. 2004. *Liberation Art of Palestine: Palestinian Painting and Sculptor in the Second Half of the Twentieth Century*. New York: H. T. T. B. Publications.

Hall, Stuart, Doreen Massey, and Michael Rustin, eds. 2013. *After Neoliberalism? The Kilburn Manifesto*. London: Soundings.

Hamadeh, Dima. 2018. "Bridges, Hearts, Cash: Neoliberal Markets of Cultural Understanding." *Contemporary Journal* 1 (10). https://doi.org/10.31411/TCJ.01.01].

Hamdan, Tarek. 2016. "Omar Al-Qattan: Bakae'ya Muta'akhira . . . Walakin" [Omar Al-Qattan: A Belated Jeremiad . . . or Not]. *Al Akhbar*, October 26, 2016.

Hamid, Shadi. 2010. "Civil Society in the Arab World and the Dilemma of Funding." Brookings Institute, October 21, 2010. https://www.brookings.edu/articles/civil-society-in-the-arab-world-and-the-dilemma-of-funding/.

———. 2011. "The Struggle for Middle East Democracy." Brookings Institute, April 26, 2011. https://www.brookings.edu/articles/the-struggle-for-middle-east-democracy/.

Hammami, Rema. 1995. "NGOs: The Professionalization of Politics." *Race & Class* 37 (2): 51–63.

Hanafi, Sari. 2012. "The Arab Revolutions: The Emergence of a New Political Subjectivity." *Contemporary Arab Affairs* 5 (2): 198–213. http://dx.doi.org/10.1080/17550912.2012.668303.

Hanafi, Sari, and Linda Tabar. 2002. "NGOs, Elite Formation and the Second Intifada." *Between the Lines* 2 (18): 31–37.

———.2007. "The Emergence of a Palestinian Globalized Elite: Donors, International Organizations and Local NGOs." *Journal of Refugee Studies* 20 (1): 154–56. https://doi.org/10.1093/jrs/fel037.

Hanieh, Adam. 2011a. *Capital & Class in the Gulf Arab States.* London: Palgrave Macmillan.

———. 2011b. "The Internationalisation of Gulf Capital and Palestinian Class Formation." *Capital & Class* 35 (1): 81–106. http://doi.org/10.1177/0309816810392006.

———.2013a. *Lineages of Revolt: Issues of Contemporary Capitalism in the Middle East.* Chicago: Haymarket Books.

———. 2013b. "The Oslo Illusion." *Jacobin*, April 21, 2013. https://www.jacobinmag.com/2013/04/the-oslo-illusion/.

Hanssen, Jens, and Hicham Safieddine. 2016. "Lebanon's al-Akhbar and Radical Press Culture: Toward an Intellectual History of the Contemporary Arab Left." *Arab Studies Journal* 24 (1): 194–228.

Harb, Shurug, Hijjawi, Samah, Touq, Toleen. 2018. "The River Has Two Banks: 2012–2017." Documentation. https://3fc9a313-0103-433b-8f03-70ce8e89c99e.filesusr.com/ugd/91f697_ad7505fc7fd7457182cb2b0148a91980.pdf

Harding, Jason. 2017. "'Our Greatest Asset': Encounter Magazine and the Congress for Cultural Freedom." In *Campaigning Culture and the Global Cold War: The Journal of the Congress for Cultural Freedom*, edited by Giles Scott-Smith and Charotte Lerg. London: Palgrave Macmillan.

Harlow, Barbara. 2012. "Resistance Literature Revisited: From Basra to Guantanamo." *Journal of Comparative Poetics* 32. http://www.jstor.org/stable/41850736.

Harris, Jonathan. 2001. *The New Art History: A Critical Introduction*. London: Routledge.

———. 2004. "Putting the 'Culture' into Visual Culture: The Legacy and Challenge of Raymond Williams." *Visual Culture in Britain* 5 (2): 63–75.

Harris, William W. 2006. *The New Face of Lebanon: History's Revenge*. Princeton, NJ: Markus Wiener. See esp. chap. 8.

Harvey, David. 2005. *A Brief History of Neoliberalism*. Oxford: Oxford University Press.

Harvey, Simon. 2006. "Smuggling Practices into the Image of Beirut." In *Out of Beirut*, edited by Suzanne Cotter. Oxford: Modern Art Oxford.

Hasso, Frances S., and Zakia Salime. 2005. "Public and Private Memory of the Lebanese Civil War." *Comparative Studies of South Asia, Africa and the Middle East* 25 (1): 191–203.

———, eds. 2013. *Freedom without Permission: Bodies and Space in the Arab Revolutions*. Durham, NC: Duke University Press

Haugbolle, Sune. 2005. "Public and Private Memory of the Lebanese Civil War." *Comparative Studies of South Asia, Africa and the Middle East* 25 (1): 191–203.

———. 2017. "The New Arab Left and 1967." *British Journal of Middle Eastern Studies* 44 (4): 497–512.

Hawthorne, Amy. 2004. "Middle Eastern Democracy: Is Civil Society the Answer?" Carnegie Papers: Middle East Series, no. 44. http://carnegieendowment.org/files/CarnegiePaper44.pdf.

Hay, Colin. 2013. *Why We Hate Politics*. Hoboken, NJ: John Wiley & Sons.

Helfont, Samuel, and Tally Helfont. 2012. "Jordan: Between the Arab Spring and the Gulf Cooperation Council." *Orbis* 56 (1): 82–95.

Helly, Damien. 2017. "Cultural Diplomacy and Cooperation in the Mediterranean: A Constant Investment." *IEMed Mediterranean Yearbook 2017*. https://www.iemed.org/observatori/arees-danalisi/arxiusadjunts/anuari/med.2017/IEMed_MedYearbook2017_cultural_diplomacy_cooperation_Helly.pdf/.

Helly, Damien, and Phillipe Lane. 2014. *Jordan Country Report for 2012*. Preparatory Action "Culture in EU's External Relations." European Commission. https://ec.europa.eu/assets/eac/culture/policy/international-cooperation/documents/country-reports/jordan_en.pdf.

Helmus, Todd C., and Dalia Dassa Kaye. 2009. "Fighting Terror the Cold War Way."

RAND Blog, RAND. October 14, 2009. https://www.rand.org/blog/2009/10/fighting-terror-the-cold-war-way.html.

Hermansen, Tormod. 2005. "Den nyliberalistiske staten." *Nytt Norsk Tidsskrift* 21:306–19.

Hermez, Sami. 2011. "On Dignity and Clientalism: Lebanon in the Context of the 2011 Arab Revolutions." *Studies in Ethnicity and Nationalism* 11 (3): 527–37.

Hijawi, Samah. 2015. "Interventions as Performative Gestures for Political Engagement in Jordan." *Ibraaz* 009_00 (May 28). https://www.ibraaz.org/essays/129.

Hilhorst, Dorothea. 2003. *The Real World of NGOs: Discourses, Diversity, and Development.* London: Zed Books.

Holborow, Marnie. 2015. *Language and Neoliberalism.* London: Routledge.

Holt, Elizabeth M. 2013. "'Bread or Freedom': The Congress for Cultural Freedom, the CIA, and the Arabic Literature Journal Hiwär (1962–67)." *Journal of Arabic Literature* 44:83–102.

Hoogwaerts, Leanne. 2012. "What Role Do Museums and Art Institutions Play in International Relations Today and Specifically in the Development of What Joseph Nye Called 'Soft Power'?" Institute for Cultural Diplomacy, August 14, 2012. http://www.culturaldiplomacy.org/academy/content/pdf/participant-papers/2012-08-acd/what-role-do-museums-and-art-institutions-play-in-international-relations-today-leanne-hoogwaerts.pdf.

Hourani, Khaled. 2019. *Al Bahth 'an Jamal Al Mahamel* [In Search of Jamal Al-Mahamel]. Amman: Dar Al Ahliyah.

Hourani, Khaled, T. Z. Toukan, and Daniel Miller. 2010. "Ramallah: City Report." *Frieze*, January 1, 2010. https://www.frieze.com/article/ramallah/.

Huntington, Samuel P. 1993. "The Clash of Civilizations?" *Foreign Affairs* 72 (3): 22–49. http://doi.org/10.2307/20045621.

Hyesun, Shin. 2013. "Post-9/11 International Artist Exchanges Between the United States and the Middle East." *Journal of Arts Management, Law, and Society* 43 (4): 203–14.

Iber, Patrick. 2015. *Neither Peace nor Freedom: The Cultural Cold War in Latin America.* Cambridge, MA: Harvard University Press.

Ibrahim, Sonallah. 1992. *Dhat.* Cairo: Dar al-Mustaqbal al-'Arabi.

Innab, Saba. 2008. "Abdali—A Personal Experience." *Amkenah.*

———.n.d. "City of Events: A Close Look at Al Abdali Bus Terminal and Beyond." City Sharing. http://www.citysharing.ch/invited-projects~68.html.

Iriye, Akira. 1991. "Culture and International History." In *Explaining the History of*

American Foreign Relations, edited by Michael J. Hogan and Thomas G. Paterson. Cambridge: Cambridge University Press.

———.2004. *Global Community: The Role of International Organizations in the Making of the Contemporary World.* Berkeley: University of California Press.

Isar, Yudhishthir Raj. 2014. *Engaging the World: Towards Global Cultural Citizenship.* Preparatory Action "Culture in EU External Relations." European Commission. https://www.cultureinexternalrelations.eu/cier-data/uploads/2016/12/Engaging-The-World-Towards-Global-Cultural-Citizenship-eBook-1.5_13.06.2014.pdf.

Jad, Islah. 2004. "The 'NGOization' of the Arab Women's Movements." *Review of Women's Studies* 2:42–56.

———.2007. "NGOs: Between Buzzwords and Social Movements." *Development in Practice* 17:622–29.

Jameson, Frederic. 1991. *Postmodernism, or, The Cultural Logic of Late Capitalism.* Durham, NC: Duke University Press.

Jawad, Rania. 2014. "Aren't We Human? Normalizing Palestinian Performances." *Arab Studies Journal* 22 (1): 28–45.

Jeffrey, James F., and Michael Eisenstadt. 2016. "U.S. Military Engagement in the Broader Middle East." Part I. Washington Institute for Near East Policy. Policy Focus 143, March 2016. https://www.washingtoninstitute.org/uploads/Documents/pubs/PolicyFocus143_JeffreyEisen-4.pdf.

Jora, Lucian. 2013. "New Practices and Trends in Cultural Diplomacy." *Romanian Review of Political Sciences and International Relations* 10 (1): 43–52.

Kamat, Sangeeta. 2004. "The Privatisation of Public Interest: Theorizing NGO Discourse in a Neoliberal Era." *Review of International Political Economy* 11 (1): 155–76.

Kanafani, Ghassan. 1999. *Men in the Sun and Other Palestinian Stories.* Translated by Hilary Kilpatrick. London: Lynne Rienner.

Karabell, Shellie. 2018. "Beirut's Art Scene Returns in Full Force." *Galerie*, January 24, 2018. https://www.galeriemagazine.com/beiruts-art-scene-returns-full-force/.

Karimi, Pamela. 2016. "Effective on the Ground and Invisible to the Global Art Market: Participatory Art in the Middle East." *Ibraaz* 010_02 (June 15).

Kassab, Elizabeth Suzanne. 2009. *Contemporary Arab Thought: Cultural Critique in Comparative Perspective.* New York: Columbia University Press.

Kellner, Douglas. 1990a. "Critical Theory and the Crisis of Social Theory." *Sociological Perspectives* 33 (1): 11–33.

———.1990b. "The Postmodern Turn: Positions, Problems and Prospects." In *Frontiers of Social Theory: The New Synthesis*, edited by George Ritzer. New York: Columbia University Press.

Khalidi, Raja, and Sobhi Samour. 2011. "Neoliberalism as Liberation: The Statehood Program and the Remaking of the Palestinian National Movement." *Journal of Palestinian Studies* 40 (2): 6–25.

———. 2014. "Neoliberalism and the Contradictions of the Palestinian Authority's State-Building Program." In *Decolonizing Palestinian Political Economy: De-development and Beyond*, edited by Mandy Turner and Omar Shweiki. Basingstoke: Palgrave Macmillan.

Khalidi, Rashid. 1998. *Palestinian Identity: The Construction of Modern National Consciousness*. New York: Columbia University Press.

Khalili, Laleh. 2007. "Heroic and Tragic Pasts: Mnemonic Narratives in the Palestinian Refugee Camps." *Critical Sociology* 33 (4): 731–59.

Khalili, Yazan. 2011. "How I Became a Politician, or, How Theft Turned Me into an Artist." *Ibraaz* 2 (November 1). https://www.ibraaz.org/essays/20.

———. 2013. *Scouting for Locations: Film Title: Traces of a Screem*. https://www.lawrieshabibi.com/artists/139-yazan-khalili/works/1867-yazan-khalili-scouting-for-locations-2013/.

Khan, Hassan. 2010. "In Defense of the Corrupt Intellectual." *e-flux* 18. https://www.e-flux.com/journal/18/67447/in-defense-of-the-corrupt-intellectual/.

Khasawneh, Diala. 2005. "Amman Meeting Points." *Bidoun: Hair*.

———. 2007. "23 Artists from Different Countries Created Site-Specific Works in the Village of Shatana, Jordan." *Nafas: Universes in Universe*, August 2007. https://universes.art/en/nafas/articles/2007/shatana-workshop.

———, ed. 2010. *The Balcony: An Idea in a Void*. Amman: Makan. See esp. "How it All Started: A Condensed History of Makan."

Khatib, Lina. 2008. *Lebanese Cinema: Imagining the Civil War and Beyond*. London: I. B. Tauris. See esp. chap. 7.

———. 2012. *Image Politics in the Middle East: The Role of the Visual in Political Struggle*. London: I. B. Tauris.

Khouri, Kristine, and Rasha Salti. 2016. "Past Disquiet: From Research to Exhibition." *Artl@s Bulletin* 5 (1): art. 8.

Khoury, Elias. 1990. "The Unfolding of Modern Fiction and Arab Memory." *Journal of the Midwest Modern Language Association* 23 (1): 1–8. http://doi.org/10.2307/1315033.

———.2008. "In Defense of Metaphor." *Belonging and Globalisation: Critical Essays in Contemporary Art and Culture*, edited by Kamal Boullata. London: Saqi.

———.2010. "Beirut, a Faceless Present." *TAR* 3:80–81. https://www.bernardkhoury.com/uploads/TAR-pdf.pdf.

Kim, Hwajung. 2017. "Bridging the Theoretical Gap between Public Diplomacy and Cultural Diplomacy." *Korean Journal of International Studies* 15 (2): 293–326.

Klemm, Verena. 2000. "Different Notions of Commitment (*Iltizam*) and Committed Literature (*al-adab al-multazim*) in Literary Circles of the Mashriq." *Arabic & Middle Eastern Literature* 3 (1): 51–62.

Koenig, Thierry, and Zaher Omareen, eds. 2018. "Independent Art and Culture Spaces in the Arab World." Young Arab Theatre Fund. http://mophradat.org/wordpress/wp-content/uploads/2018/01/Independent-Arts-and-Culture-in-the-Arab-World.pdf.

Kraidy, Marwan. 2016. *The Naked Blogger of Cairo: Creative Insurgency in the Arab World*. Cambridge, MA: Harvard University Press.

Kunkel, Jenny, and Margit Mayer. 2011. "Introduction: Neoliberal Urbanism and Its Contestations: Crossing Theoretical Boundaries." In *Neoliberal Urbanism and Its Contestations: Crossing Theoretical Boundaries*, edited by Margit Mayer and Jenny Kunkel. Basingstoke: Palgrave Macmillan.

Lafuente, Pablo. 2007. "Art and the Foreigner's Gaze: A Report on Contemporary Arab Representations." *Afterall: A Journal of Art, Context and Enquiry*, Spring/Summer.

Laïdi-Hanieh, Adilah. 2006. "Arts, Identity, and Survival: Building Cultural Practices Under Occupation." *Journal for Palestine Studies* 35 (4): 28–43.

———.2008. "Paradigm Shift: Building Inclusive Cultural Practices." In *An Alternate Gaze: A Shared Reflection on Cross-Mediterranean Cooperation in the Arts*, edited by Odile Chenal et al. Amsterdam: European Cultural Foundation.

Landeau, Clemence. 2015. "Disseminating the Cultural Cold War in Arabic—Interview with Elizabeth Holt." WeberWorldCafé. https://wwc.hypotheses.org/1227.

Larkin, Craig. 2010. "Remaking Beirut: Contesting Memory, Space and the Urban Imaginary of Lebanese Youth." *City and Community* 9 (4): 414–42.

Larner, Wendy. 2003. "Guest Editorial: Neoliberalism?" *Environment & Planning: International Journal of Urban and Regional Research* 21 (5): 509–512. http://doi.org/10.1068/d2105ed.

Larzillière, Pénélope. 2016. *Activism in Jordan*. Translated by Cynthia Schoch. London: Zed Books.

"Launch of the International Academy in of Art Palestine." 2006. *Electronic Intifada*,

November 29, 2006. https://electronicintifada.net/content/launch-international-academy-art-palestine/687.

Le More, Anne. 2008. *International Assistance to the Palestinians after Oslo: Political Guilt, Wasted Money.* London: Routledge.

Leenders, Reinoud. 2012. *Spoils of Truce: Corruption and State-Building in Postwar Lebanon.* Ithaca, NY: Cornell University Press.

Lenssen, Anneka. 2020. *Beautiful Agitation: Modern Painting and Politics in Syria.* Berkeley: University of California Press.

Lenssen, Anneka, Sarah Rogers, and Nada Shabout, eds. 2018. *Modern Art in the Arab World: Primary Documents.* Durham, NC: Duke University Press.

Leslie, Esther. 2006. "Add Value to Contents: The Valorization of Culture Today." European Institute for Progressive Cultural Policies. http://eipcp.net/transversal/0207/leslie/en/print.html.

Levine, David, and Alix Rule. 2012. "International Art English." *Triple Canopy.* https://www.canopycanopycanopy.com/contents/international_art_english.

Levitt, Peggy. 2015. *Artifacts and Allegiances: How Museums Put the Nation and the World on Display.* Berkeley: University of California Press.

Lia, Brynjar. 2007. *Building Arafat's Police.* London: Ithaca Press.

Lockman, Zachary. 2016. *Field Notes: The Making of Middle East Studies in the United States.* Stanford, CA: Stanford University Press.

Lucas, Russell E. 2003. "Deliberalization in Jordan." *Journal of Democracy* 14 (1): 137–44.

Maasri, Zeina. 2009. *Off the Wall: Political Posters of the Lebanese Civil War.* London: I. B. Tauris.

———. 2020. *Cosmopolitan Radicalism: Beirut in the Global Sixties.* Cambridge: Cambridge University Press.

Maira, Sunaina. 2013. *Jil Oslo: Palestinian Hip Hop, Youth Culture, and the Youth Movement.* Washington, DC: Tadween.

Makdisi, Saree. 1997. "Laying Claim to Beirut: Urban Narrative and Spatial Identity in the Age of Solidere." *Critical Inquiry* 23 (3): 661–705. http://www.jstor.org/stable/1344040.

Makdisi, Ussama. 2006. "Beirut, a City Without History?" In *Memory and Violence in the Middle East and North Africa,* edited by Ussama Makdisi and Paul Silverstein. Bloomington: Indiana University Press.

Makhoul, Bashir, ed. 2013. *Palestinian Video Art: Constellation of the Moving Image.* Jerusalem: Palestinian Art Court, Al Hoash.

Makhoul, Bashir, and Gordon Hon. 2013. *The Origins of Palestinian Art*. Liverpool: Liverpool University Press.

Manovich, Lev. 2001. *The Language of New Media*. Cambridge, MA: MIT Press.

Marfleet, Philip. 2016. "The Political Subject in the 'Arab Spring.'" *Contemporary Levant* 1 (1): 4–11. http://dx.doi.org/10.1080/20581831.2016.1148456.

Marks, Laura U. 2004. "The Ethical Presenter or How to Have Good Arguments Over Dinner." *Moving Image*, 4 (1): 34–47.

Massad, Joseph. 2000. "The 'Post-colonial' Colony: Time, Space, and Bodies in Palestine/Israel." In *The Pre-occupation of Postcolonial Studies*, edited by Fawzia Afzal-Khan and Keplana Geshadri-Crooks. Durham, NC: Duke University Press.

———. 2001. *Colonial Effects: The Making of National Identity in Jordan*. New York: Columbia University Press.

Matar, Hayfa. 2015. "Museums as Signifiers in the Gulf." In *Cities, Museums and Soft Power*, edited by Gail Dexter Lord and Ngaire Blankenberg. Washington, DC: AAM Press.

Mehrez, Samia, ed. 2012. *Translating Egypt's Revolution: The Language of Tahrir*. Cairo: American University in Cairo Press.

Meier, Prita. 2010. "Authenticity and Its Modernist Discontents: The Colonial Encounter and African and Middle Eastern Art History." *Arab Studies Journal* 18 (1): 12–45.

Mejcher-Atassi, Sonja, ed. 2007. "Writing: A 'Tool for Change.' Abd al-Rahman Munif Remembered." Special issue, *MIT Electronic Journal of Middle East Studies* 7. http://web.mit.edu/CIS/www/mitejmes/intro.htm.

———. 2012. *Reading Across Modern Arabic Literature and Art*. Wiesbaden: Reichert.

Mejcher-Atassi, Sonja, and Muzaffar, May. 2010. *Rafa Nasiri: Artist Books*. Milan: Skira.

Melissen, Jan, ed. 2005. *The New Public Diplomacy: Soft Power in International Relations*. London: Palgrave Macmillan UK. See esp. chap. 8, "Culture Communicates: US Diplomacy that Works."

———. 2017. "Public Diplomacy." In *Diplomacy in a Globalizing World: Theories and Practices*, edited by Pauline Kerr and Geoffrey Wiseman. Oxford: Oxford University Press.

Mercer, Kobena. 1990. "Black Art and the Burden of Representation." *Third Text* 4 (10): 61–78. https://doi.org/10.1080/09528829008576253.

Merz, Sibille. 2012. "'Missionaries of the New Era': Neoliberalism and NGOs in Palestine." *Race & Class* 54 (1): 50–66. http://doi.org/10.1177/0306396812444820.

Miéville, China. 2016. *The Last Days of New Paris*. New York: Del Rey

Mignolo, Walter. 2000. *Local Histories/Global Designs: Coloniality, Subaltern Knowledges, and Border Thinking*. Princeton, NJ: Princeton University Press.

———. 2011. "Epistemic Disobedience and the Decolonial Option: A Manifesto." *Transmodernity: Journal of Peripheral Cultural Production of the Luso-Hispanic World* 1 (2): 44–66.

———. 2013a. "Enacting the Archives, Decentering the Muses: The Museum of Islamic Art in Doha and the Asian Civilisations Museum in Singapore." *Ibraaz* Platform 006, 11–12. http://ibraaz.org/usr/library/documents/main/enacting-the-archives.pdf.

———. 2013b. "Re-emerging, Decentering and Delinking: Shifting the Geographies of Sensing, Believing and Knowing." *Ibraaz* Platform 005, 1–15. https://www.ibraaz.org/usr/library/documents/essay-documents/re-emerging-decentring-and-delinking.pdf.

Mikdadi, Salwa. 2008. "Arab Art Institutions and Their Audiences." *Middle East Studies Association Bulletin* 42 (1/2): 55–61.

———. 2009. "New Trends in Arab Art." In *New Visions: Arab Contemporary Art in the 21st Century*, edited by Amirsadeghi Hossein, Salwa Mikadi, and Nada Shabout. London: Thames & Hudson.

———. 2015. "Art and the Arab Citizen: Raising Public Consciousness Through the Arts." *Guggenheim USB Map* (blog), Guggenheim Museum. January 20, 2015. https://www.guggenheim.org/blogs/map/art-and-the-arab-citizen-raising-public-consciousness-through-the-arts.

Mikdadi, Salwa, and Nada Shabout. 2009. "Introduction." In *New Visions. Arab Contemporary Art in the 21st Century*, edited by Hossein Amirsadeghi, Salwa Mikdadi, and Nada Shabout. London: Thames & Hudson.

Milton-Edwards, Beverly. 1998. "Palestinian State-Building: Police and Citizens as Tests of Democracy." *British Journal of Middle Eastern Studies* 5 (1): 95–119.

Mirgani, Suzi. 2017. "Introduction: Art and Cultural Production in the GCC." *Journal of Arabian Studies* 7 (1): 1–11.

Mirzoeff, Nicholas. 1999. *An Introduction to Visual Culture*. London: Routledge.

Mitchell, Timothy. 1989. "The World as Exhibition." *Comparative Studies in Society and History* 31:217–36.

———. 1990. Everyday Metaphors of Power. *Theory and Society* 19 (5): 545–77. https://www.jstor.org/stable/657563.

———. 1999. "Dreamland: The Neoliberalism of Your Desires." *Middle East Report*, no. 210, 28–33. http://doi.org/10.2307/3012500.

———. 2000. "The Stages of Modernity." In *Questions of Modernity*, edited by Timothy Mitchell. Minnesota: University of Minnesota Press.

———. 2002. *Rule of Experts: Egypt, Techno-Politics, Modernity*. Berkeley: University of California Press.

———. 2012. *Ex-Cinema: From a Theory of Experimental Film and Video*. Berkeley: University of California Press.

Mohammed Al-Jabri, Abed. 1989. *Ishkaleyat al-Fikr al-Arabi al-Mua'ssir*. Casablanca: Banshara.

Mouawad, Jamil, and Hannes Baumann. 2017. "Wayn al-Dawla: Locating the Lebanese State in Social Theory." *Arab Studies Journal* 25 (1): 66–90.

Mouffe, Chantal. 2000. "Deliberative Democracy or Agonistic Pluralism?" *Reihe Politikwissenschaft / Institut für HöhereStudien, Abt. Politikwissenschaft* 72:1–17.

———. 2005. *On the Political* (*Thinking in Action*). Abingdon, UK: Routledge.

———. 2006. "Which Public Space for Critical Artistic Practices?" In *Cork Caucus: On Art, Possibility & Democracy*, edited by Tara Byrne. Cork: National Sculpture Factory & Revolver Press, 2006: 149–71.

———. 2007a. "Artistic Activism and Agonistic Spaces." *Art & Research: A Journal of Ideas, Contexts and Methods* 1 (2). http://www.artandresearch.org.uk/v1n2/mouffe.html.

———. 2007b. "Public Spaces and Democratic Politics." *LAPS*. https://laps-rietveld.nl/?p=829.

Muller, Nat. 2008. "18000 Words Please: On the State of Contemporary Art Please." *Lab for Culture*. http://www.labforculture.org/en/users/site-users/site-members/nat-muller/51308/27792.

Muna, Ziad. 2008. "al-Fajr il-kathib fi al-ufuq: mu'asasat al-thaqafah al-arabiyah" [The False Dawn in the Horizon: Arab Cultural Institutions]. *Al-Adab* 56 (1): 96–98.

Nagel, Caroline R. 2002. "Reconstructing Space, Re-creating Memory: Sectarian Politics and Urban Development in Post-War Beirut." *Political Geography* 21 (5): 717–25.

Nakhleh, Khalil. 2012. *Globalized Palestine: The National Sell-out of a Homeland*. Trenton: Red Sea Press.

Nayar, Pramod K. 2006. *Reading Culture: Theory, Praxis, Politics*. New Delhi: Sage.

Nederveen Pieterse, Jan. 2010. *Development Theory: Deconstructions/Reconstructions*. London: Sage.

Noorani, Yaseen. 2007. "Redefining Resistance: Counterhegemony, the Repressive Hypothesis and the Case of Arabic Modernism." In *Counterhegemony in the Colony and Postcolony*, edited by John Chalcraft and Yaseen Noorani. New York: Palgrave Macmillan.

Nye, Joseph, Jr. 2004. *Soft Power: The Means to Success in World Politics*. New York: Public Affairs.

———. 2010. "The New Public Diplomacy." Project Syndicate, February 10, 2010. https://www.project-syndicate.org/commentary/the-new-public-diplomacy?barrier=accesspaylog.

Oguibe, Olu. 2004. *The Culture Game*. Minneapolis: University of Minnesota Press.

Oshinsky, David M. 1989. "Cranky Integrity on the Left." *New York Times*, August 27, 1989.

Pamment, James. 2011. *The Limits of the New Public Diplomacy: Strategic Communication and Evaluation at the US State Department, Foreign & Commonwealth Office, British Council, Swedish Foreign Ministry and Swedish Institute*. Stockholm: Department of Journalism, Media and Communication (JMK), Stockholm University.

Panebianco, Stefania. 2004. "The Euro-Mediterranean Partnership in Perspective: The Political and Institutional Context." In *A New Euro-Mediterranean Cultural Identity*, edited by Stefania Panebianco. London: Frank Cass.

Pannewick, Friederike, and Georges Khalil, eds. 2015. *Commitment and Beyond: Reflections on/of the Political in Arabic Literature since the 1940s*. Wiesbaden: Reichert Verlag.

Parsekian, Jack. 2003. "Disorientation. A Diary of Disorientation: Part 1." House of World Cultures. https://archiv.hkw.de/en/dossiers/disorientation/kapitel9.html.

Paschalidis, Gregory. 2009. "Exporting National Culture: Histories of Cultural Institutes Abroad." *International Journal of Cultural Policy* 15 (3): 275–89.

Paynter, November. 2011. "Sharjah Biennial: 10 Plot for a Biennial (16 March–16 May 2011) and Art Dubai (16–19 March 2011)." Art Agenda, March 24, 2011. http://www.art-agenda.com/reviews/sharjah-biennial-10-plot-for-a-biennial-16-march-16-may-2011-and-art-dubai-16-19-march-2011/.

Pearlman, Wendy. 2013. "Emotions and the Microfoundations of the Arab Uprisings." *Perspectives on Politics* 11 (2): 387–409.

———. 2016. "Palestine and the Arab Uprisings." In *Civil Resistance in the Arab Spring: Triumphs and Disasters*, edited by Adam Roberts, Michael J. Willis, Rory McCarthy, and Timothy Garton Ash. Oxford: Oxford University Press.

Perthes, Volker. 1997. "Myths and Money: Four Years of Hariri and Lebanon's

Preparation for a New Middle East." *Middle East Report*, no. 203, 16–21. http://doi.org/10.2307/3012641.

Petti, Alessandro. 2009. "It Has Become a Small Nucleus of Palestinian Society." *Ramallah Syndrome* (blog). http://ramallahsyndrome.blogspot.com.

Plehwe, Dieter, Bernard Walpen, and Gisela Neunhöffer, eds. 2006. *Neoliberal Hegemony—A Global Critique*. London: Routledge.

Pratt, Nicola. 2006. "Human Rights NGOs and the 'Foreign Funding Debate' in Egypt." In *Human Rights in the Arab World*, edited by Anthony Tirado-Chase and Amr Hamzawy, 114–26. Philadelphia: University of Pennsylvania Press.

Preziosi, Donald, ed. 2009. *The Art of Art History*. Oxford: Oxford University Press.

Puzon, Kataryzyna. 2016. "Memory and Artistic Production in a Post War Arab City." In *Post-Conflict Performance, Film and Visual Arts: Cities of Memory*, edited by Des O' Rawe and Mark Phelan. London: Palgrave Macmillan.

Qumsiyeh, Mazen B. 2011. *Popular Resistance in Palestine: A History of Hope and Empowerment*. London: Pluto.

Raad, Walid. 2010. *Miraculous Beginnings: Walid Raad*. London: Whitechapel Gallery.

———.2009. *Scratching on Things I Could Disavow: A History of Art in the Arab World /Part 1_Volume 1_Chapter 1 (Beirut: 1992–2005)*. Los Angeles: Redcat, the California Institute of the Arts.

Raad, Walid, Abdullah Ziad, and Farah Awada. 1999. "Missing Lebanese Wars." *Public Culture* 11 (2): i–xiv.

Rabie, Kareem. 2013. "Ramallah Bubbles." *Jadaliyya*, January 18, 2013. https://www.jadaliyya.com/Details/27839.

Rahman, Najat. 2015. *In the Wake of the Poetic: Palestinian Artists After Darwish*. Syracuse: Syracuse University Press.

Ramadan, Dina. 2004. "Regional Emissaries: Geographical Platforms and the Challenges of Marginalisation in Contemporary Egyptian Art." *Proceedings of Apex Conference* 3. http://apexart.org/conference/ramadan.htm.

Rancière, Jacques. 2004. *The Politics of Aesthetics: The Distribution of the Sensible*. Translated by Gabriel Rockhill. London: Continuum.

———.2005. "Some Paradoxes of Political Art." Public lecture on Monday, November 21, 2005. *Home Works III: A Forum on Cultural Practices*, November 17–24, Beirut.

———.2009. *The Emancipated Spectator*. Translated by Gregory Elliot. London: Verso.

———.2010. *Dissensus: On Politics and Aesthetics*. Translated by Steven Corcoran. London: Continuum.

Rao, Rahul. 2010. *Third World Protest: Between Home and the World.* London: Oxford University Press.

Rasmussen, Steffen Bay. 2009. "Discourse Analysis of EU Public Diplomacy: Messages and Practices." Netherlands Institute of International Relations 'Clingendael.' https://www.clingendael.nl/sites/default/files/20090700_cdsp_discussion_paper_115_Rasmussen.pdf.

Raunig, Gerald, and Gene Ray, eds. 2009. *Art and Contemporary Critical Practice: Reinventing Institutional Critique.* London: MayFly Books.

Ray, Gene. 2009. "Toward a Critical Art Theory." In *Art and Contemporary Critical Practice: Reinventing Institutional Critique*, edited by Gerald Raunig and Gene Ray. London: MayFly Books.

Richter-Devroe, Sophie, and Ruba Salih. 2014. "Cultures of Resistance in Palestine and Beyond: The Politics of Art, Aesthetics, and Affect." *Arab Studies Journal* 22 (1): 8–27.

Ritzer, George. 1996. *The McDonaldization of Society.* Thousand Oaks, CA: Pie Forge Press.

Rivera, Tim. 2015. *Distinguishing Cultural Relations from Cultural Diplomacy: The British Council's Relationship with Her Majesty's Government.* Los Angeles: Figueroa Press.

Roberto Cimetta Foundation, Fondation René Seydoux. 2006. *The Challenges of Artistic Exchange in the Mediterranean: Made in the Mediterranean.* Edited by Adriano Farano. Roberto Cimetta Foundation, Fondation René Seydoux Pour le Monde Méditerranéen, Relais Culture Europe, and the European Cultural Foundation. https://www.cimettafund.org/~cimettaf/content/upload/file/Made-in-the-Med-FRC-En.pdf.

Robertson, Jean, and Craig McDaniel. 2016. *Themes of Contemporary Art: Visual Art After 1980.* 4th ed. Oxford: Oxford University Press. See esp. chap. 1.

Robinson, Glenn E. 1998. "Defensive Democratization in Jordan." *International Journal of Middle East Studies* 30 (3): 387–410.

Rockhill, Gabriel. 2014. *Radical History and the Politics of Art.* New York: Columbia University Press.

Rockhill, Gabriel, and Philip Watts, eds. 2009. *Jacques Rancière: History, Politics, Aesthetics.* Durham, NC: Duke University Press. See esp. chap. 10.

Rogers, Sarah. 2007. "Out of History: Post-War Art in Beirut." *Art Journal* 66 (2): 9–20.

———. 2008. "Post-War Art and the Historical Roots of Beirut's Cosmopolitanism." PhD diss., Massachusetts Institute of Technology.

———. 2011. "The Artist as Cultural Diplomat: John Ferren in Beirut, 1963–64." *American Art* 25 (1): 112–23. http://doi.org/10.1086/660035.

———. 2012. "The Khaled Shoman Private Collection and the Founding of Darat Al Funun." In *Archives, Museums and Collecting Practices in the Modern Arab World*, edited by Sonja Mejcher-Atassi and John Pedro Schwartz. Farnham: Ashgate.

Ronen, Gil. 2011. "Picasso in Ramallah: IDF Helps PA Exhibit $4.3 Million Picasso." *Arutz Shiva 7*, July 21, 2011. israelnationalnews.com/News/News.aspx/145967.

Roth, Kenneth. 2019. *World Report 2019: Events of 2018*. US: Human Rights Watch. https://www.hrw.org/sites/default/files/world_report_download/hrw_world_report_2019.pdf.

Rowe, Peter, and Hashim Sarkis eds. 1998. *Projecting Beirut: Episodes in the Construction and Reconstruction of a Modern City*. Munich: Prestel.

Roy, Arundhati. 2014. "The NGO-ization of Resistance." *Massalijn*, September 4, 2014. http://massalijn.nl/new/the-ngo-ization-of-resistance/.

Rubin, Andrew N. 2012. *Archives of Authority: Empire, Culture, and the Cold War*. Princeton, NJ: Princeton University Press.

Ryan, Curtis R. 2018. *Jordan and the Arab Uprisings: Regime Survival and Politics Beyond the State*. New York: Columbia University Press.

Saadawi, Ghalya. 2009. "Akram Zaatari." *Frieze*, August 4, 2009. frieze.com/article/akram-zaatari-1.

———. 2011. "Post-Sharjah Biennial 10: Institutional Grease and Institutional Critique." *e-flux* 26. http://www.e-flux.com/journal/view/239.

———. 2019. "Rethinking the Witness: Art After the Lebanese Wars." PhD diss., Goldsmiths, University of London.

———. 2020. "A Book Review in the Form of a Polemic Chad Elias's Posthumous Images: Contemporary Art and Memory Politics in Post-Civil War Lebanon and the Old New World Order." *ARTMargins* 9 (3): 69–86.

Saad-Filho, Alfredo, and Deborah Johnston, eds. 2005. *Neoliberalism: A Critical Reader*. London: Pluto Press. http://doi.org/10.2307/j.ctt18fs4hp.

Sabry, Tarek. 2010. *Cultural Encounters in the Arab World: On Media, the Modern and the Everyday*. London: I. B. Tauris.

Sadek, Walid. 2002a. "A Matter of Words." *Parachute* 108:34–49.

———. 2002b. "From Excavation to Dispersion: Configurations of Installation Art in Post-War Lebanon." In *TAMÁSS Contemporary Arab Representations Beirut/*

Lebanon 1, edited by Catherine David and Fundació Antoni Tàpies. Rotterdam: Witte de With.

———. 2007. "Place at Last." *Art Journal* 66 (2): 35–47. https://doi.org/10.1080/00043249.2007.10791253.

———. 2008. "Peddling Time When Standing Still; Art Remains in Lebanon and the Globalization That Was." October 13, 2008. http://www.ghassansalhab.com/press/Peddling%20Time%20When%20Standing%20Still.pdf.

Saghie, Hazim, ed. 2002. *The Predicament of the Individual in the Middle East.* London: Saqi Books.

Saghieh, Hazem. 2007. "The Arab Defeat." Open Democracy, June 11, 2007. http://www.opendemocracy.net/the_arab_defeat.

Saghieh, Khaled. 2019. "1990s Beirut: *Al-Mulhaq*, Memory, and the Defeat." *e-flux* 97. https://www.e-flux.com/journal/97/250527/1990s-beirut-al-mulhaq-memory-and-the-defeat/.

Sahakian, Rijin. 2018. "A Coalition of the Willing: How Saudi Arabia and US Arts Institutions Partnered on a Cultural Diplomacy Offensive." *Hyperallergic*, November 1, 2018. https://hyperallergic.com/468850/saudi-arabia-and-us-art-institutions/.

Said, Edward. 1978. *Orientalism*. New York: Pantheon Books.

———. 1994. *Representations of the Intellectual: The 1993 Reith Lectures*. New York: Vintage Books.

———. 1996. *Peace and Its Discontents: Essays on Palestine in the Middle East Peace Process.* New York: Vintage Books.

Salamé, Ghassan. 1987. *The Foundations of the Arab State: Nation, State, and Integration in the Arab World.* Vol. 1. London: Routledge.

Salha Fadda, Reema. 2016. "Playing Against Invisibility: Negotiating the Institutional Politics of Cultural Production in Palestine." In *Future Imperfect: Contemporary Art Practices and Cultural Institutions in the Middle East*, edited by Anthony Downey. Berlin: Sternberg Press.

Salibi, Salibi. 2005. *A House of Many Mansions*. London: I. B. Tauris.

Salti, Rasha. 2002. "Framing the Subversive in Post-War Beirut: Critical Considerations for a Social History of the Present." Paper presented at *Home Works: A Forum on Cultural Practices in the Region: Egypt, Iran, Lebanon, Palestine, and Syria*, Beirut, April 2–7, 2002.

San Juan, E. 2003. "Antonio Gramsci on Surrealism and the Avantgarde." *Journal of Aesthetic Education* 37 (2): 31–45. http://doi.org/10.2307/3527453.

Sarkis, Hashim. 1993. "Territorial Claims: Post-War Attitudes towards the Built Environment." In *Recovering Beirut: Urban Design and Post-War Reconstruction*, edited by Samir Khalaf and Phillip Khoury. Leiden: E. J. Brill.

Sawalha, Aseel. 2018. "Gender, Art, and the Reshaping of the Urban in Amman, Jordan." In *The Routledge Handbook of Anthropology and the City*, edited by Setha Low. Abingdon, UK: Routledge.

Sayegh, Anis, ed. 2001 [1995]. *Al-muthaqaff al-arabi: humumuh wa ata'ouh* [The Arab Intellectual: Challenges and Concerns]. Beirut: Markez Dirasat al-Wihdah al-A'rabiyah.

Schäfer, Isabel. 2007. "The Cultural Dimension of the Euro-Mediterranean Partnership: A Critical Review of the First Decade of Intercultural Cooperation." *History and Anthropology* 18 (3): 333–352. http://doi.org/10.1080/02757200701469733.

Scheid, Kirsten. 2005. "Painters, Picture-Makers, and Lebanon: Ambiguous Identities in an Unsettled State." PhD diss., Princeton University.

———. 2010. "Necessary Nudes: Ḥadātha and Mu'āṣira in the Lives of Modern Lebanese." *International Journal of Middle East Studies* 42 (2): 203–30. http://www.jstor.org/stable/40784723.

———. 2020. "Start with the Art: New Ways of Understanding the Political in the Middle East." In *Routledge Handbook of Middle East Politics: Interdisciplinary Inscriptions*, edited by Larbi Sadiki. New York: Routledge.

Schiller, H. I. 1976. *Communications and Cultural Domination*. New York: Sharp.

Schmitt, Carl. 2007. *The Concept of the Political*. Chicago: University of Chicago Press.

Schneider, Cynthia. 2004. "Culture Communicates: US Diplomacy that Works." *Diplomacy*, no 94, Netherlands Institute of International Relations Clingendael. http://www.culturaldiplomacy.org/academy/content/articles/e-learning/read/a1/Culture_Communicates-_US_Diplomacy_that_works-_Cynthia_Schneider.pdf.

Schneider, Mirjan. 2014. *Palestine Country Report*. "Preparatory Action: Culture in the EU's External Relations." European Commission. https://www.cultureinexternalrelations.eu/cier-data/uploads/2016/08/Palestine_report56.pdf.

Schwartz, Lowell H., Todd C. Helmus, Dalia Dassa Kaye, and Nadia Oweidat. 2009. Barriers to the Broad Dissemination of Creative Works in the Arab World. MG-879-OSD. Santa Monica, CA: RAND.

Schwartz, Lowell H., Dalia Dassa Kaye, and Jeffrey Martini. 2013. *Artists and the*

Arab Uprisings. Santa Monica: Rand Corporation. https://www.rand.org/pubs/research_reports/RR271.html.

Schwedler, Jillian. 2010. "Amman Cosmopolitan: Spaces and Practices of Aspiration and Consumption." *Comparative Studies of South Asia, Africa and the Middle East* 30 (3): 547–62. https://doi.org/10.1215/1089201X-2010-033.

Scott, James C. 1985. *Weapons of the Weak: Everyday Forms of Peasant Resistance*. New Haven, CT: Yale University Press.

Seikaly, Sherene. 2018. "How I Met My Great-Grandfather: Archives and the Writing of History." *Comparative Studies of South Asia, Africa, and the Middle East* 38 (1): 6–20.

Selim, Gamal M. 2013. "The United States and the Arab Spring: The Dynamics of Political Engineering," *Arab Studies Quarterly* 35 (3): 255–72.

Shabout, Nada. 2007. *Modern Arab Art: Formation of Arab Aesthetics*. Gainesville: University of Florida Press.

Shannon, Brettany. 2012. "The 'Dubai Effect': The Gulf, the Art World & Globalization." In *The Emerging Asian City: Concomitant Urbanities and Urbanisms*, edited by Vinayak Bharne. London: Routledge.

Sharp, Jeremy M. 2019. "Jordan: Background and U.S. Relations." Congressional Research Service. Last modified April 9, 2019. https://fas.org/sgp/crs/mideast/RL33546.pdf.

Sheikh, Simon. 2008. "In the Place of the Public Sphere? Or, the World in Fragments?" *Republicart*. http://www.republicart.net/disc/publicum/sheikh03_en.htm.

Shepp, Jonha. 2011. "Six Artists Test Power of Pubic Art in Amman. *Jordan Times*. January 24, 2011

Shohat, Ellah. 1993. "Notes on the 'Post-Colonial.'" *Social Text* 31–32: 99–113.

Shurayḥ, Maḥmūd, ed. 2011. *Mudhakkirāt Tawfīq Sạ̄yigh bi-khatṭ yadihi wa-huwa yastaʿiddl-isḍār majallat* Ḥiwār: *7 Nīsān- 31 Tamūz 1962, Bayrūt—London—Bārīs—Bayrūt* [*Memoirs of Tawfīq Sạ̄yigh in His Own Hand Writing as He Was Preparing to Publish the Journal Ḥiwār*]. Beirut: DārNelson.

Shweiki, Omar. 2014. "Before and Beyond Neoliberalism: The Political Economy of National Liberation, the PLO, and 'Amal Ijtima'i." In *Decolonizing Palestinian Political Economy: De-development and Beyond*, edited by Mandy Turner and Omar Shewiki. London: Palgrave Macmillan.

"Side Effects of a Post-Oslo Spatial Regime." 2009. *Ramallah Syndrome* (blog). http://ramallahsyndrome.blogspot.com/2009/06/it-has-become-small-nucleus-of.html.

Siegelbaum, Sami. 2013. "Business Casual: Flexibility in Contemporary Performance Art." *Art Journal* 72 (3): 48–63. http://doi.org/10.1080/00043249.2013.10792853.

Silvestri, Sara. 2014. "Religion and Societal Cohesion at the Heart of the Intercultural Debate." *The Anna Lindh Report 2014. Intercultural Trends and Social Change in the Euro-Mediterranean Region.* https://www.annalindhfoundation.org/report/religion-and-social-cohesion-heart-intercultural-debate.

Simpson, Colin. 2011a. "Sharjah Biennial Chief Sacked Over One Work." *National*, April 7, 2011. http://www.thenational.ae/arts-culture/art/sharjah-biennial-chief-sacked-over-one-work.

———. 2011b. "Biennial Exhibit Led to Director's Dismissal: Organisers." *National*, April 10, 2011. https://www.thenational.ae/uae/biennial-exhibit-ledto-director-s-dismissal-organisers-1.576434.

Sklair, Leslie. 2000. *The Transnational Capitalist Class*. Malden: Blackwell.

Slim, Lokman Mohsen. 2007. "Al-Tamwil al- gharbi li al-thaqafa fi Lubnan: ma al-badil al-thaqafi muqabil al-'umla al-sa'ba?" *Al-Quds Al-Arabi*, November 11, 2007.

Snider, Erin A., and David M. Faris. 2011. "The Arab Spring: U.S. Democracy Promotion in Egypt." *Middle East Policy* 18 (3): 49–62.

Spivak, Gayatri Chakravorty. 1985. "Three Women's Texts and a Critique of Imperialism." *Critical Inquiry* 12 (1): 243–61. http://www.jstor.org/stable/1343469.

Stallabras, Julian. 2004. *Art Incorporated: The Story of Contemporary Art*. Oxford: Oxford University Press.

Stefan Weiner, Andrew. 2015. "Insurgency and Circumspection: The Legacies of Pan-Arabism." *Afterall: A Journal of Art, Context, and Enquiry* 40:90–101.

Steyerl, Hito. 2010. "Politics of Art: Contemporary Art and the Transition to Post-Democracy." *e-flux* 21. https://www.e-flux.com/journal/21/67696/politics-of-art-contemporary-art-and-the-transition-to-post-democracy/.

Stonor Saunders, Frances. 2013. *The Cultural Cold War: The CIA and the World of Arts and Letters*. New York: New Press.

Strategic Communications Division, European Union. 2016. "A Partnership for Democracy and Shared Prosperity with the Southern Mediterranean." Last updated February 5, 2016. http://eeas.europa.eu/euromed/docs/com2011_200_en.pdf.

Sukarieh, Mayssoun. 2012. "From Terrorists to Revolutionaries: The Emergence of 'Youth' in the Arab World and the Discourse of Globalization." *Interface: A Journal for and about Social Movements* 4 (2): 424–37.

———. 2015. "The First Lady Phenomenon: Elites, States, and the Contradictory Politics of Women's Empowerment in the Neoliberal Arab World." *Comparative Studies of South Asia, Africa and the Middle East* 35 (3): 575–87.

———.2016. "On Class, Culture and the Creation of the Neoliberal Subject: The Case of Jordan." *Anthropological Quarterly* 89 (4): 1201–25.

Sylvester, Christine. 2009. *Art/Museums: International Relations Where We Least Expect It*. Boulder, CO: Paradigm.

Tabar, Linda, and Alaa Al Azzah. 2014. "Al- Muqawamah Al-Shaabiyah taht il ihtilal: Qiraa Naqdiyah wa Tahliliyeh" [Popular Resistance in Palestine: A Critical Reading]. Beirut: Institute for Palestine Studies, Special Monograph Series.

Tamari, Salim. 2009. *Mountain against the Sea: Essays on Palestinian Society and Culture*. Berkeley: University of California Press. http://www.jstor.org/stable/10.1525/j.ctt1pp131.

Tamari, Vera, and Yazid Anani, cur. 2010. *Ramallah—The Fairest of Them All?* Birzeit: Ethnographic and Arab Museum, Birzeit University.

Tanner, Jeremy. 2003. *The Sociology of Art: A Reader*. New York: Routledge

Tao-Wu, Chin. 2009. "Biennials without Borders?" *New Left Review*, May–June 2009. http://www.newleftreview.org/?view=2783#_edn3.

Taraki, Lisa. 2008. "Urban Modernity on the Periphery: A New Middle Class Reinvents the Palestinian City." *Social Text* 26 (2): 61–81.

Taraki, Lisa, and Rita Giacaman. 2006. "Modernity Aborted and Reborn: Ways of Being Urban in Palestine." In *Living Palestine: Family, Survival, Resistance, and Mobility Under Occupation*, edited by Lisa Taraki. Syracuse: Syracuse University Press.

Tawil-Souri, Helga. 2011a. "The Necessary Politics of Palestinian Cultural Studies." In *Arab Cultural Studies: Mapping the Field*, edited by Tarik Sabry. London: I. B. Tauris.

———. 2011b. "Where Is the Political in Cultural Studies? In Palestine." *International Journal of Cultural Studies* 14 (5) (September): 467–82. http://doi.org/10.1177/1367877911408656.

Taylor, Charles. 2007. *A Secular Age*. Cambridge, MA: Harvard University Press.

Tolan, Sandy. 2011. "Picasso Comes to Palestine." *Al Jazeera*, July 16, 2011. https://www.aljazeera.com/indepth/features/2011/07/2011715131351407810.html

Toufic, Jalal. 2000. *Forthcoming*. Berkeley, CA: Atelos.

Toukan, Hanan. 2011. "Boat Rocking in the Art Islands: Politics, Plots and Dismissals in Sharjah's Tenth Biennial." *Jadaliyya*, May 2, 2011. https://www.jadaliyya.com/Details/23938/Boat-Rocking-in-the-Art-Islands-Politics,-Plots-and-Dismissals-in-Sharjah%60s-Tenth-Biennial.

———.2012. "Art, Aid, Affect: Locating the Political in Post-Civil War Lebanon's Contemporary Cultural Practices." PhD diss. School of Oriental and African Studies, University of London.

———.2014. "On Delusion, Art, and Urban Desires in Palestine Today: An Interview with Yazid Anani." *Arab Studies Journal* 22 (1): 208–30.

———.2015. "Whatever Happened to Iltizam? Words in Arab Art after the Cold War." In *Commitment and Beyond: Reflections on/of the Political in Arabic Literature since the 1940s*, edited by Friederike Pannewick, Georges Khalil, and Yvonne Albers. Wiesbaden: Reichert Verlag.

———. 2019. "Liberation or Emancipation: Counter-hegemony, Performance and Public Space in Lebanon." *International Journal of Cultural Studies* 23 (2): 264–81.

Toukan, Oraib. 2011. 2011. "Transcript from the International Academy of Art Palestine: Events Called Schools." *Red Hook Journal*, November 28, 2011. https://ccs.bard.edu/redhook/events-called-schools/index.html.

———. 2014. "'We, the Intellectuals': Re-routing Institutional Critique." *Ibraaz* 007 (July 29). https://www.ibraaz.org/essays/98.

Touq, Toleen. 2016. "A Sense of Scale: Art and Cultural Practices Beyond Institutions in Amman." In *Future Imperfect: Contemporary Art Practices and Cultural Institutions in the Middle East*, edited by Anthony Downey. Berlin: Sternberg Press.

Touraine, Alain. 2001. *Beyond Neoliberalism*. Cambridge: Polity.

Traboulsi, Fawwaz. 2007. *A Modern History of Lebanon*. London: Pluto Press.

Tripp, Charles. 2013. *The Power and the People: Paths of Resistance in the Middle East*. Cambridge: Cambridge University Press.

Turner, Mandy. 2007. "Creating 'Partners for Peace': The Palestinian Authority and the International Statebuilding Agenda." *Journal for Intervention and State* 5 (1): 1–21.

———.2014. "The Political Economy of Western Aid in the Occupied Palestinian Territory Since 1993." In *Decolonizing Palestinian Political Economy: De-development and Beyond*, edited by Mandy Turner and Omar Shweiki. London: Palgrave Macmillan.

———. 2019. "No 'Plan B' Because 'Plan A' Cannot Fail: The Oslo Framework and Western Donors in the OPT, 1993–2017." In *From the River to the Sea: Palestine and Israel in the Shadow of "Peace,"* edited by Mandy Turner, 271–302. Lanham, MD: Lexington Books.

Tvedt, Terje. 1998. *Angels of Mercy or Development Diplomats: NGOs and Foreign Aid.* Oxford: James Curry.

United Nations Development Program. 2002. *Arab Human Development Report*. Vol. 1, *Creating Opportunities for Future Generations*. New York: UNDP.

———.2003. *Arab Human Development Report 2003*. New York: UNDP.

Van Abbemuseum. 2011. "Picasso in Palestine: A Modern Icon to be Exhibited in Ramallah." https://vanabbemuseum.nl/en/programme/programme/picasso-in-palestine/.

van der Vlist, Eline, ed. 2017. *Hiwar: Conversations in Amman*. Amman: Khalid Shoman Foundation.

Vazquez, Michael. 2012. "The Bequest of Quest." *Bidoun: Art and Culture from the Middle East* 26. https://www.bidoun.org/articles/the-bequest-of-quest.

———.2016. "A Civilized Revolution: Aesthetics and Political Action in Egypt." *American Ethnologist* 43 (4): 609–22.

Von Eschen, Penny M. 2004. *Satchmo Blows Up the World: Jazz Ambassadors Play the Cold War*. Cambridge, MA: Harvard University Press.

von Maltzahn, Nadia. 2018. "Ministry of Culture or No Ministry of Culture? Lebanese Cultural Players and Authority." *Comparative Studies of South Asia, Africa and the Middle East* 38 (2): 330–43.

Wade, Jean-Philippe. 1991. "'The Humanity of the Senses': Terry Eagleton's Political Journey to 'The Ideology of the Aesthetic.'" *Theoria: A Journal of Social and Political Theory*, no. 77, 39–57.

Wang, Dan S. 2003. "Practice in Critical Times: A Conversation with Gregory Sholette, Stephanie Smith, Temporary Services, and Jacqueline Terrassa." *Art Journal* 62 (2): 68–81.

Wedeen, Lisa. 1999. *Ambiguities of Domination: Politics, Rhetoric and Symbols in Contemporary Syria*. Chicago: University of Chicago Press.

Werbner, Pnina, Martin Webb, and Kathryn Spellman-Poots. 2014. *The Political Aesthetics of Global Protest: The Arab Spring and Beyond*. Edinburgh: Edinburgh University Press.

West, Cornel. 1990. "The New Cultural Politics of Difference." *October* 53:93–109. http://doi.org/10.2307/778917.

Westcott, James. 2011. "Art Dubai and the Sharjah Biennial: Talking about a Revolution." *Guardian*. March 23, 2011. https://www.theguardian.com/artanddesign/2011/mar/23/art-dubai-sharjah-biennial.

Westmoreland, Mark R. 2009. "Post-Orientalist Aesthetics: Experimental Film and Video in Lebanon." *Invisible Culture: An Electronic Journal for Visual Culture* 13.

https://ivc.lib.rochester.edu/post-orientalist-aesthetics%E2%80%A8experimental-film-and-video-in-lebanon/.

Wiktorowicz, Quintan. 1999. "The Limits of Democracy in the Middle East: The Case of Jordan." *Middle East Journal* 53 (4): 606–20.

Wilford, Hugh. 2008. *The Mighty Wurlitzer: How the CIA Played America*. Cambridge, MA: Harvard University Press.

———. 2013. *America's Great Game: The CIA's Secret Arabists and the Shaping of the Modern Middle East*. New York: Basic Books.

Williams, Raymond. 1961. *The Long Revolution*. London: Chatto & Windus.

———. 1977. *Marxism and Literature*. New York: Oxford University Press.

Wilson-Goldie, Kaelen. 2005. "On Matters of Size and Scale." *Daily Star*, November 17, 2005. https://www.dailystar.com.lb/Culture/Art/2005/Nov-17/96247-on-matters-of-size-and-scale.ashx.

———. 2006. "Contemporary Art Practices in Post-War Lebanon: An Introduction." In *Out of Beirut*, edited by Suzanne Cotter. Oxford: Modern Art Oxford.

———. 2009a. "Object Lessons." *National*, October 2, 2009. https://www.thenational.ae/uae/object-lessons-1.591289.

———. 2009b. "On the Politics of Art and Space in Beirut." Tate Papers. https://www.tate.org.uk/research/publications/tate-papers/12/on-politics-art-and-space-beirut.

———. 2010a. "Home Discomforts at Beirut's Premier Arts Event." *National*, May 6, 2010.

———. 2010b. "Home Works 5." *Bidoun* 21. https://www.bidoun.org/articles/home-works-5.

http://www.tate.org.uk/research/tateresearch/tatepapers/09autumn/wilson_goldie.shtm.

———. 2011. "On Bandwagons: The Problem of Funding Art During the Time of Revolution." *Frieze*, October 1, 2011. frieze.com/article/bandwagons.

Winegar, Jessica. 2006. *Creative Reckonings: The Politics of Art and Culture in Contemporary Egypt*. Stanford, CA: Stanford University Press.

———. 2008. "The Humanity Game: Art, Islam and the War on Terror." *Anthropology Quarterly* 81 (3): 651–81.

———. 2012. "The Privilege of Revolution: Gender, Class, Space, and Affect in Egypt." *American Ethnologist* 39 (1): 67–70.

Witoszek, Nina. 2013. *Origins of the Regime of Goodness: Remapping the Cultural History of Norway*. Oslo: Universitetsforlaget.

Wolff, Janet. 1981. *The Social Production of Art*. London: Macmillan.

Wright, Stephen. 2002. "Like a Spy in a Nascent Era: On the Situation of the Artist in Beirut Today." *Parachute* 108:13–31.

———. 2006. "Territories of Difference: Excerpts from an Email Exchange between Tony Chakar, Bilal Khbeiz and Walid Sadeq." In *Out of Beirut*, edited by Suzanne Cotter. Oxford: Modern Art Oxford.

———. 2008. "Behind Police Lines: Art Invisible and Invisible." *Art & Research: A Journal of Ideas, Contexts and Methods* 2 (1). http://www.artandresearch.org.uk/v2n1/wright.html.

Wu, Chin-Tao. 2009. "Biennials without Borders?" *New Left Review* 57. http://www.newleftreview.org/?view=2783#_edn3.

Yahya, Abbad. 2012. *Ramallah al-shaqra* [*Blonde Ramallah*]. Jerusalem: Dar el Fil.

———. 2017. *Jarima fi Ramallah* [A Crime in Ramallah]. Milan: Al-Mutawassit.

Yom, Sean L. 2005. "Civil Society and Democratization in the Arab World." *Middle East Review of International Affairs* 9:19–20.

Yom, Sean L., and F. Gregory Gause. 2012. "Resilient Royals: How Arab Monarchies Hang On." *Journal of Democracy*, no. 4, 74–88.

Youngs, Richard. 2015. "20 Years of the Euro-Mediterranean Partnership." *Mediterranean Politics*, May 18, 2015. http://carnegieeurope.eu/2015/05/18/20-years-of-euro-mediterranean-partnership-pub-60337.

Younis, Ala. 2016. "Individuals as Institutions: A Partial Cartography." In *Future Imperfect: Contemporary Art Practices and Cultural Institutions in the Middle East*, edited by Anthony Downey. Berlin: Sternberg Press.

Zangwill, Nick. 2002. "Against the Sociology of Art." *Philosophy of the Social Sciences* 32 (2): 206–18.

Zellman, Gail L., Jeffrey Martini, and Michal Perlman. 2011. Identifying Arabic-Language Materials for Children That Promote Tolerance and Critical Thinking. TR-856-OSD. Santa Monica, CA: RAND.

Žižek, Slavoj. 1999. *The Ticklish Subject: The Absent Centre of Political Ontology*. London: Verso.

Zogby, James J. 2002. *What Arabs Think: Values, Beliefs and Concerns*. Washington, DC: Zogby International/Arab Thought Foundation.

Zolghadr, Tirdad. 2005. "The Forward Thrust of Christine Tohme." *Bidoun* 3. https://bidoun.org/articles/the-forward-thrust-of-christine-tohme.

Zubaida, Sami. 1992. "Islam, the State and Democracy: Contrasting Conceptions of Society in Egypt." *Middle East Report* 179:2–10.

———. 2001. *Islam, the People and the State: Political Ideas and Movements in the Middle East*. London: I. B. Tauris.

———. 2010. "Community and Democracy in the Middle East." In *Civil Society: History and Possibilities*, edited by Sudipta Kaviraj and Sunil Khilnani. Cambridge: Cambridge University Press.

Index

Stanford Studies in Middle Eastern and Islamic Societies and Cultures

Joel Beinin and Laleh Khalili, editors

The Paranoid Style in American Diplomacy: Oil and Arab Nationalism in Iraq 2021
BRANDON WOLFE-HUNNICUTT

Dear Palestine: A Social History of the 1948 War 2021
SHAY HAZKANI

A Critical Political Economy of the Middle East and North Africa 2021
JOEL BEININ, BASSAM HADDAD, and SHERENE SEIKALY, editors

Between Muslims: Religious Difference in Iraqi Kurdistan 2020
J. ANDREW BUSH

Showpiece City: How Architecture Made Dubai 2020
TODD REISZ

Archive Wars: The Politics of History in Saudi Arabia 2020
ROSIE BSHEER

The Optimist: A Social Biography of Tawfiq Zayyad 2020
TAMIR SOREK

Graveyard of Clerics: Everyday Activism in Saudi Arabia 2020
PASCAL MENORET

Cleft Capitalism: The Social Origins of Failed Market Making in Egypt 2020
AMR ADLY

The Universal Enemy: Jihad, Empire, and the Challenge of Solidarity 2019
DARRYL LI

Waste Siege: The Life of Infrastructure in Palestine 2019
SOPHIA STAMATOPOULOU-ROBBINS

Heritage and the Cultural Struggle for Palestine 2019
CHIARA DE CESARI

Banking on the State: The Financial Foundations of Lebanon 2019
HICHAM SAFIEDDINE

Familiar Futures: Time, Selfhood, and Sovereignty in Iraq 2019
SARA PURSLEY

Hamas Contained: The Rise and Pacification of Palestinian Resistance 2018
TAREQ BACONI

Hotels and Highways: The Construction of Modernization Theory in Cold War Turkey 2018
BEGÜM ADALET

Bureaucratic Intimacies: Human Rights in Turkey 2017
ELIF M. BABÜL

Impossible Exodus: Iraqi Jews in Israel 2017
ORIT BASHKIN

Brothers Apart: Palestinian Citizens of Israel and the Arab World 2017
MAHA NASSAR

Revolution without Revolutionaries: Making Sense of the Arab Spring 2017
ASEF BAYAT

Soundtrack of the Revolution: The Politics of Music in Iran 2017
NAHID SIAMDOUST

Copts and the Security State: Violence, Coercion, and Sectarianism in Contemporary Egypt 2016
LAURE GUIRGUIS

Circuits of Faith: Migration, Education, and the Wahhabi Mission 2016
MICHAEL FARQUHAR

Morbid Symptoms: Relapse in the Arab Uprising 2016
GILBERT ACHCAR

Imaginative Geographies of Algerian Violence: Conflict Science, Conflict Management, Antipolitics 2015
JACOB MUNDY

The authorized representative in the EU for product safety and compliance is:
Mare Nostrum Group
B.V Doelen 72
4831 GR Breda
The Netherlands

www.ingramcontent.com/pod-product-compliance
Lightning Source LLC
LaVergne TN
LVHW041111080826
845145LV00007B/1761

* 9 7 8 1 5 0 3 6 2 7 7 5 8 *